Interpreting
Educational
Research

Interpreting Educational Research

Armand J. Galfo
College of William and Mary

Earl Miller
San Francisco State College

SECOND EDITION

WM. C. BROWN COMPANY PUBLISHERS
Dubuque, Iowa

Copyright © 1965, 1970 by
Wm. C. Brown Company Publishers

ISBN 0—697—06116—7

Library of Congress Catalog Card Number 76-106944

Second Printing, 1970

Printed in the United States of America

Preface

What do professional educators need to know about educational research? It would seem logical that the answer to the question should be found in some of the required undergraduate and graduate studies for students who become teachers, school administrators, guidance counselors, supervisors, and curriculum specialists. The truth is, however, that programs offered by universities and colleges range from practically no work in educational research to a heavy emphasis in some schools on research techniques.

Originally, almost all graduate students in education studied research methods in order to prepare themselves to carry out a study for a master's thesis or doctoral dissertation, but strong objections to research-oriented graduate programs were raised from time to time. President Truman's 1946 commission of distinguished educators and civic leaders, for example, said: "Too frequently advanced degrees are granted in a narrow field of research, thus producing technicians in a very special field . . ." It was suggested by the commission that ". . . interpretive ability as well as research ability, skill in synthesis as well as analysis, and achievement in teaching as well as in investigation . . ."[1] should be included in a broader concept of scholarship.

Similarly, a group of educators assembled in 1954 by the Fund for the Advancement of Education concluded:

(a) Graduate schools are not providing effective training for college and high school teachers.

---

[1]President's Commission on Higher Education, *Higher Education For American Democracy* (New York, N. Y., Harper, 1947) Vol. I p. 103.

(b) The training in research is not producing men and women capable of providing the moral, intellectual, and political leadership needed . . .

(c) Graduate schools must produce more people who are neither mere scholars nor unscholarly teachers, but scholar-teachers . . .[2]

By the mid 1950's many schools of education had dropped the requirement for graduate students to do original research. In place of the thesis some schools merely substituted more course work or a project. Interest in educational research waned.

There have been indications recently of a renewed interest in educational research. Innovations in methods, materials and curriculum have made educators acutely aware of the need for careful investigations to evaluate the new procedures and inventions. As a result, the question posed in the opening paragraph of this preface is still with us.

It is the contention of the authors of this text that the answer lies not in a return to a preparation of teachers and other professional educators as researchers, but rather in their preparation as *consumers* of research. The Truman commission report of 1946 stated the point in another way when it emphasized that educators need to be versed in interpretive ability and skilled in synthesis. Teachers, as professionals like medical doctors and engineers, need to acquire the ability to read, interpret and apply the results of research carried out by researchers; this text has been prepared primarily to help the educator gain these skills. The text can also serve, however, as a primer for students who plan to carry out original research.

A. J. Galfo

---

[2]Harris, Chester W., *Encyclopedia of Educational Research* (New York, N. Y.: The Macmillan Co., Third Edition, 1960) p. 599.

Acknowledgments

The authors are indebted to many people who have contributed to the preparation of this volume. Several contributed directly by permitting use of material they had published elsewhere; the following authors allowed us to use such material: Barbara Wilbur; George E. North and O. Lee Buchanan; Richard J. Gordon; Virginia F. Brown; Tracy H. Logan and Kenneth H. Wodtke; Wilbur B. Brookover, Ann Paterson, and Shirley Thomas; Stanley Krippner; Marlin Baxter; H. I. Willet, Jr.; Joseph F. Callahan; Jesse M. Hart; Mrs. C. Corty; Jacqueline Benento; John P. Deason; and Robert Schild.

The tables that appear in the appendix of this text have been reproduced from several sources. We are indebted to: Sir Ronald A. Fisher, F. R. S., Cambridge, Dr. Frank Yates, F. R. S., Rothamsted, and Messrs. Oliver and Boyd Ltd., Edinburgh, for permission to reprint an abridged version of Table IV from their book *Statistical Tables for Biological, Agricultural, and Medical Research;* Dr. George W. Snedecor and the Iowa State University Press for permission to reprint a portion of a table of significant r values; Professor E. S. Pearson and the editors of *Biometrika* for permission to reprint a table of inverted beta (F) distribution; Dr. Edwin G. Olds and the editors of *Annals of Mathematical Statistics* for permission to reprint a table of 5% significance levels for sums and squares of rank difference; the Wadsworth Publishing Company, Inc. for permission to reprint a table of normal curve areas; Houghton Mifflin Company to reprint a table of squares and square roots from *A First Course in Statistics;* and Appleton-Century-Crofts for permission to reprint several tables from *Elementary Statistics.*

Finally, we wish to express our gratitude to Mr. J. R. Dawson and Mr. Peter Hoyle, of the College of William and Mary, Computer Center, and to the International Business Machines Company for their contributions to the development of the statistical test package which appears in the appendix. Mr. Dawson programed the material with Mr. Hoyle's assistance. The IBM Company allowed us to adapt portions of their scientific subroutine programs for the package.

Contents

PART I

An Introduction
to Research
Methology

Chapter 1

The Basis and Nature of Educational Research

The conventional way to read a book is to start with Chapter 1 and proceed through the remaining chapters in order. This book, however, may be an exception. Although it has been written to answer questions often voiced by beginning researchers, many topics extend to some depth and will be of interest to more professional investigators. Chapter 1 has been written primarily for orientation purposes. The more experienced reader should proceed to Chapter 2.

The Development of Science

A student of science very quickly becomes aware of the impact that research has had upon human thought and endeavor. A consideration of the history of science, however, is necessary to appreciate the gradual development of the method of attacking problems which is called research.

Deductive Reasoning

The ancient Greeks must be given credit for devising an important element of scientific methodology — deductive reasoning. The method involves a thinking process in which one proceeds from general to specific statements using the prescribed rules of logic. The process can be initiated, for example, by the major premise, *"All men are mortal,"* followed by the definition or minor premise, *"John is a man,"* and the conclusion, *"Therefore John is mortal."* Although the deductive method is a powerful tool which has contributed to the development of abstract mathematical analysis and to scientific fields, it has been found to have a number of serious limitations.

Aristotle stated that the major premise must be universally true. The statement *"All men are mortal"* can be accepted as true without difficulty, but if the premise *"All men have ten fingers"* were followed by the conclusion *"Therefore, John has ten fingers,"* serious objections could be raised by most rational people who would ask for verification of the major premise. The need to follow Aristotle's edict to establish the universal truth of the major premise points out two basic flaws in the deductive method. First, and most obviously, it is difficult to establish the universal truth of many statements that deal with scientific phenomena. As a result, scientific philosophers, including Aristotle, neglected the verification process and substituted *a priori* statements for the major premise which "should be universally true," or were accepted as true without proof. The second limitation is less obvious than the first but equally as damning. Verification of the *a priori* *"All men are mortal"* would require inspection of all men including John, making the minor premise and conclusion unnecessary. In addition, deduction from a single premise involves other technical problems which will not be discussed here.

As a consequence of its very nature, the classical deductive technique stifled creative thinking, an ingredient necessary to scientific inquiry. Since the method involved selection of an *a priori* statement as a "universal truth," it limited the scope of scientific inquiry by establishing a study of words in place of the study of things.

Some scholars have attributed the lack of progress in science following the decline of the Greek civilization to the easy transition from the deductive method to the erroneous dogmas accepted as scientific truths during the Dark Ages. Until the time of Galileo, no one thought to question Aristotle's *a priori* proposition that the motion of falling bodies was dependent upon their mass; no one doubted the Ptolemian system of the universe — with its earth-centered description — even when observation of the motion of the planets led to a direct contradiction of Ptolemy's conclusions.

Although the process of deductive reasoning has aided as well as retarded progress in science, it remains today a valuable method for relating educational experimentation to educational theory. Once a generalization in the form of a theory or law has been established through scientific inquiry, the deductive process can help establish new relationships that may not have been apparent otherwise.

Inductive Reasoning

As the flaws in the classic deductive method became evident to men of science, new approaches to gain knowledge were sought. Since one misuse of the deductive technique lay in the failure to establish the truth of the initial or major premise, the obvious solution was to develop means of verification. Within a relatively short span of history men such as Copernius, Kepler, Galileo, Bacon, Harvey and many others helped establish a new method of gaining knowledge — the inductive method based upon empirical observation and experimentation. The inductive method involved reversing the processes employed in the deductive method. Each successive step resulted in a more general statement of the fact contained in the preceding step. A careful collection of elements or facts was made, these were painstakingly fitted together — like pieces in a puzzle — and resulted in a generalization. The exclusive use of inductive reasoning, however, created a series of unrelated, isolated bits of information which lacked unity and did little to advance the frontiers of knowledge.

Inductive-Deductive Methods

It was natural that scientists should very soon learn to integrate the most valuable aspects of the inductive and deductive methods into a new technique, namely the inductive-deductive or scientific method. Charles Darwin's theory of evolution is an outstanding product of the application of the modern scientific method. During a long sea voyage, Darwin made careful observations of flora and fauna in various parts of the world. His data indicated that species of plants and animals were in a constant state of change, in most cases, a change so gradual that man had failed to observe it was taking place. These observations led Darwin to hypothesize the idea of universal evolution. Using the hypothesis, Darwin, and others following his lead, predicted specie changes which have been verified by means of the study of fossil remains. Darwin's theory has carried science to such diversified fields as agriculture — in livestock selective breeding and foodstuff improvement; medicine — in the search for a cure for man's diseases; biology — in the study of changes which have taken place in plants and animals; and in anthropology and archaeology — in a search for the origin of man.

The Science of Education?

The essential ingredient of the natural sciences has been described, but what is the status of education as a science? Does the systematic study of education constitute a true science? The second question has been debated by scholars since Rice studied the teaching of spelling in the 1890's. Critics maintain that the formulation of laws concerning fields of human behavior including education is impossible. Many events studied cannot be duplicated and even if duplication were accomplished, the number of variables makes control impossible. Critics deride not only the quality of studies in the field of education but the choice of topics as well. In reply to such criticisms, several statements concerning the status of education as a science can be made.[1]

Inability to Duplicate Phenomena

Many educational studies deal with events which can occur only once. Historical and many descriptive studies, described later in this chapter, deal with events which cannot be reproduced. Critics assert that this characteristic makes duplication and verification of the findings impossible; therefore, educational studies are unscientific. Few would deny that astronomy is a science, yet many events in the greater universe occur only once and cannot be manipulated to reoccur. The study of education therefore cannot be called unscientific merely because John Smith, the subject of study, moves from age 6 to age 11 and cannot be made to repeat this developmental process.

Inability to Control Variables

Education as well as the other branches of social science is considered unscientific by many because of the impossibility of controlling the factors being studied. Without control the formulation of laws is impossible. A typical classroom presents the investigator with a number of conditions, some of which can be identified and controlled (such as sex and age), others which can be identified but not controlled (for example, after school activities), and probably many significant factors which can be neither identified nor controlled. Does this lack of control over phenomena justify labeling educational investigations as unscientific? No! Physical scientists are confronted with exactly the same kinds of problems; for example, much is known about the effects of gravitational force on falling bodies. Aerodynamics and meteorology are acknowledged as scientific fields, but ask a physical scientist to determine the exact spot to which a gum wrapper will fall when thrown from an airliner, and he will be confronted by the same dilemma facing the educator who attempts to study a sixth grade classroom. He will be unable to predict the exact effect of multiple variables even though many individual factors affecting the wrapper are known. The inability to identify and control conditions in educational investigation does not divorce these studies from the realm of science.

---

[1]For an informative and enlightened analysis of the social sciences as science see Ernest Nagel, *The Structure of Science*. New York: Harcourt, Brace & World, Inc., 1961, Chapter 13.

Quality of Investigations

As indicated in Chapter 9, some educational studies have been more carefully conducted than others. The quality of any investigation, however, has no bearing on the question, "Is the investigation of the type which can be classified as a science?" If a college chemistry student blows up the laboratory because he misuses experimental procedures, the conclusion cannot be reached that chemistry is unscientific. The study of education will be more readily accepted as a science when the number of studies employing questionable procedures is reduced.

Trivial Topic?

Some educational topics chosen for study appear trivial and may not contribute to the advancement of knowledge. The importance of the contribution made by a study, however, cannot be ascertained by reading the title of the work; the significance of the study can be determined only by authorities in the same area of knowledge. The topic "The Incidence of Pimples Among Post Adolescents" may appear trivial to the general public but may be of extreme importance to the authority who deals with personality problems of young adults. The usefulness of the study depends on how accurately and carefully it was conducted, not on the title. Education is not unscientific merely because the significance of the topic being investigated is not clearly understood by the layman.

The study of education is a science. Its stature among other sciences will increase when the quality of scientific investigation employed becomes more systematic and rigorous. Methods for improving the product of educational inquiries are discussed in the remainder of this volume.

The Nature of Research

At this point, it may be well to ask the question that serves as the title of this section of the chapter, "What is Research?" Surely it is not the deductive method of the early Greeks alone; much of man's knowledge has been gleaned by other means. Neither the inductive nor the inductive-deductive method accounts for all progress in our understanding of nature and mankind. Does research activity include all of these ways of gaining knowledge to which the various labels have been applied?

Definition of Research

Semanticists state that the definition of words is not in the words but in ourselves.[2] The word research does not mean the same thing to everyone within the field of education. While reading studies related to education or critical reviews of these studies, one becomes aware of the division of opinion regarding the meaning of research. Many authorities would describe only the experimental design discussed on page 16 as research. What distinguishes research from other activities?

There is one element that is common to all research studies; this element is contained in what has been described by the term *systematic study.* In the deductive method the factor of system and consistency was crucial; system was evident in the other methods. If research implies system, however, then it is necessary to establish what is meant by systematic study.

First, for a study to be systematic, the nature of the problem must be clearly understood. Unless the area of knowledge to be researched is identified at the outset, no proper basis — or framework — can be established. A lack of foundation upon which to begin can be labeled only as an *un*systematic approach.

Second, whatever method is used to approach a problem, the researcher must postulate any assumptions which have a bearing on the problem and collect all possible relevant data in a way which insures completeness and rules out useless repetition or duplication. This process requires carefully controlled methods of data compilation which relate directly to, or converge upon, possible solutions to the problem under attack. It is this requirement of convergence that has dictated devices that are familiar to the student of science: the control factor in experimentation; the careful recording of observations; the use of specially designed apparatus and instruments for data gathering; and the structured procedures which reduce the area being investigated for answers.

The third way to insure system in the search for knowledge involves the method used in analyzing data which are collected. Early in the development of research, men learned the value of reducing data to quantitative terms. As has been observed, the deductive nature of mathematics makes it a powerful tool for analysis; therefore, the expression and analysis of data in quantitative terms has become a hallmark of most research studies. One should realize, however, that meaningful investigations dealing with data that cannot be expressed quan-

---

[2]S. I. Hayakawa, *Language in Thought and Action.* New York: Harcourt, Brace & World, Inc., 1949. p. 292.

titatively are often conducted and are recognized as outstanding research studies; the criteria of systematic study are satisfied even though numerical values are not employed.

The final element of system in research is found in the method of drawing conclusions or making generalizations. In research, conclusions never extend beyond the perimeter established by the identification of the problem, the search for the data, and the analysis of the data. It is possible at times to anticipate new avenues and possible outcomes, but such conjectures are never properly presented as conclusions.

In summary, research implies a systematic study. The methods developed in connection with man's quest for knowledge, especially in the natural sciences and mathematics, gave great impetus to the development of research in all fields of human endeavor.

How Is Research in Education Conducted?

No formula or recipe can be offered to serve as a guide to research activities. To offer one would unduly limit the effectiveness of the individual in seeking solutions to problems yet to be defined. To insure system and provide a framework to be used to execute and evaluate studies, four general guidelines are listed in the following paragraphs.

Establishing the Purpose

Anyone who engages in serious research soon learns the values that accrue from a clear, concise statement of the problem to be solved. It is almost impossible to make progress if the purpose of the research has not been clearly indicated. Without purpose systematic study becomes unattainable, for system implies a basis — a frame of reference. The identification and statement of the problem provide the most essential element in constructing a frame of reference that gives direction to the study.

What is a good statement of the problem? It is easier to consider just what a good problem statement is *not*. A clear definition of the problem does not confuse the purpose of study with hypotheses used to predict possible solutions. When a researcher says that his research was carried out ". . . to show . . ." or ". . . to prove . . .," his objectivity is immediately suspect. The term research implies that something unknown needs to be discovered or that some fact must be verified or explained.[3] If the researcher has ideas concerning how a problem may

---

[3]The fact to be explained may be "the average reading achievement of second grade boys is lower than for girls of the same grade." The researcher must determine why, if possible. The fact to be explained is also called the explicandum.

be solved, these ideas should be stated as hypotheses and tested by appropriate procedures. Confusing hypotheses with the problem to be solved, however, indicates inferior research methodology.

A good statement of the problem:

1. Clarifies what is to be determined, discovered, solved.
2. Reduces the scope of the investigation to a specific area.

Making Preliminary Analysis

When a problem has been identified and delimited, a new phase of research, the analytical phase, begins. Analysis involves the search for, and careful study of, data that may help bring about a solution to the problem. In the chapters that follow, the methods used to collect, organize, and extract meaning from data will be discussed in detail, but at this point it is well to consider what is meant by systematic analysis.

Systematic analysis begins with an exhaustive study of previous research that has a bearing on the problem selected for study. Often this step alone may turn up the solution sought, but a review of research will often raise many more questions and problems. The study of related research and literature, however, is not merely — as some prospective researchers seem to believe — a way to insure that the problem has not been previously researched; rather, the primary purpose of the step is to save much lost motion in data gathering. Further, important insight may be gained by studying the work of other researchers who have explored a field.

Finally, a review of related literature enables the research worker to start at a point where competent scholars have stopped in the past. Einstein probably could not have developed the general field theory if he had not relied on the foundation established by Aristotle, Newton, Descartes and others. The review of the literature may result in modification of the original statement of the problem. It also determines the form and nature of the hypothesis.

Formulating the Hypothesis

The technique of science has prompted study of phenomena within a frame of reference. A clear understanding of the problem gives research purpose; the hypothesis, or educated guess, can provide direction, another important element in constructing a frame of reference.

Although hypotheses are not essential to research, their use may prevent a study from becoming too broad in scope or loose in construction. The researcher cannot be concerned with a mere collection of facts connected with a problem; sooner or later it becomes necessary to look for relationships, trends, and generalization. He may be able to reduce time and effort by proposing possible solutions to a problem. Orientation of research toward testing specific hypotheses helps the investigator arrive at valid conclusions.

What is the basis for proposing hypotheses? Obviously, wild guesses can be worse than no guesses at all. The key to hypothesizing is careful preparation and analysis of available evidence (see Chapter 2). The hypothesis may connect known facts with the solution of a problem by providing: (1) missing links in the chain of evidence; (2) organization and system where none seems to exist; (3) an interpretation of unknown causes of phenomena. Criteria for evaluating the hypothesis will be presented in Chapter 9.

Gathering and Processing Data

Systematic analysis continues with data gathering and processing. The collection and analysis of data requires a working knowledge of the proper tools and procedures; ability for systematic analysis implies possession of this knowledge. The researcher who attempts to determine human behavior in specific cultural settings by means of a questionnaire survey, for example, may have chosen the wrong means for collecting data; observation techniques may be more appropriate. The need to understand analysis procedures, however, is important to any educator whether he is engaged in original research or is a professional person attempting to review and apply the findings of research. The ability to read, understand, and evaluate research literature stems from knowledge of proper techniques.

In the previous section of this chapter one characteristic of systematic analysis, the reduction to quantitative terms, was identified. Scientists have demonstrated the analytical power of mathematics. In educational research, as in other branches of science, the presence of many variables usually requires that data be analyzed by a relatively new mathematical process — statistics. A knowledge of statistics is essential for the consumer as well as for those who conduct research studies.

Developing Conclusions

Although it would appear that formulating conclusions should be a relatively simple task once data are analyzed, this phase of research is often the most troublesome. The major difficulty that some researchers appear to have in drawing conclusions is a tendency to make incorrect generalizations; this results from a failure to appreciate the complexity of factors such as:

1. *A plethora of uncontrollable variables.* The researcher is often forced to make "common-sense" decisions that many of the important variables are not significant to his study because he cannot control them.
2. *Emotion provoking factors.* The ability to be objective is partially a function of emotional factors. As a result, investigations in the social studies place the researcher in a position where his objectivity may be colored by the traits and characteristics that constitute his personality.
3. *Interaction of the researcher and the phenomena being studied.* The social scientist often cannot disassociate himself and his research from the phenomena he wishes to investigate; the very act of investigating may produce changes which might not have occurred otherwise. The effect of the observer may be such that he cannot reproduce a given situation in its entirety; inability to repeat an event with precision dictates caution when conclusions are to be drawn.

Faulty generalizations may also stem from any of the errors previously discussed in connection with the construction of studies in education. A lack of understanding of the limitations of statistical sampling, for example, may cause the researcher to apply conclusions to populations not represented in his study — to overgeneralize. If a study is poorly defined and delimited, conclusions cannot be clear-cut.

Any list of criteria to evaluate conclusions in educational research should include consideration of the following points:

1. Conclusions should be kept within the boundaries established by the statement of purposes, the problem, and the limitations of the study.
2. Conclusions should never be extended to incorporate findings or facts that have not been subjected to analysis. (In addition, it is considered poor form to include the analysis of findings with the conclusions of a study.)
3. Since research in the social sciences is complicated by many factors, educational researchers must exercise extreme caution in making generalizations from studies. Often broad generaliza-

tions can develop only after many studies in an area have consistently confirmed initial findings.

Classification of Educational Research

Although educational research studies may not always lend themselves to a rigid system of classification, it is usually possible and desirable to put them into one of three general categories. The reason for using some means of classification stems from the fact that criteria for evaluating research studies become clearer when they are related to specific methodological characteristics of each category. For example, a study whose purposes indicate how and why conditions in a certain period of time came about as a result of previous factors is considered to be historical. Classification as history will dictate appropriate criteria that should be used by the researcher to collect and analyze data as well as the way to state conclusions.

The three broad categories of research generally recognized by educators are as follows:

1. Historical studies
2. Descriptive studies
3. Experimental studies

The Historical Study

The historian usually is concerned with the determination of past factors which have led to a set of conditions during a later period. In using the broader definition of research stated on page 8, there is danger of accepting as research meaningless relating or retelling of past events. Conversely, it must be recognized that some scholars do not consider the identification of trends as the legitimate role of the historian. To them, history should be an accurate description and critical analysis of past events. Irrespective of the historian's purpose, the methods employed should be systematic and rigorous. The evaluator of historical research has the responsibility of determining the researcher's degree of skill in collecting and analyzing his data.

In evaluating evidence which is collected for a historical study, awareness of the kinds of material available to the researcher is essential. Data are classified as derived from primary and secondary sources. As the term implies, primary sources are firsthand materials related to events which have taken place: documents such as diaries of eyewitnesses, court records, and vital statistics; artifacts such as tools and art objects of past civilizations; and on-the-spot records such as files and photographs. Secondary sources are those which are not firsthand. Evidence such as textbooks, newspaper accounts of an event not written by eyewitnesses, biographies, and other secondhand descriptions, are usually termed secondary sources. The distinction between primary and secondary sources, however, is not always too helpful. The important consideration is this: Did the historian secure the most accurate data available? Secondary sources may be more credible than primary sources because of the greater perspective and objectivity found in the former.

Furthermore, the same source, depending on the particular research problem, may be either primary or secondary. For example, if a research were conducted to determine the policies of a board of education in a locality during a given period of time, newspaper editorials on the subject written during the time would very likely be secondary sources. On the other hand, if the purpose of the research were to study editorial policy toward the school board, the editorials would certainly be primary sources.

The analysis of historical data should include two ways of determining the usefulness of evidence; namely external criticism and internal criticism. By external criticism the genuineness of data is determined. External criticism implies that evidence is carefully checked by every means available to establish that it is not a forgery or a fabrication; but merely proving that evidence is genuine does not mean it is useful. A diary allegedly kept by General Grant during the Civil War may be the genuine article; however, before its contents are accepted as true, it must be demonstrated that there is no reason to doubt that Grant's entries are accurate. Determining the validity of actual historical data is what is meant by subjecting the evidence to internal criticism.

The historian may use many ways to determine the genuineness and validity of a source; external and internal criticism require the use of the methods employed by detectives. Some such methods include:

CROSS CHECKING PIECES OF EVIDENCE AGAINST EACH OTHER. If a diary of one of General Grant's associates indicates that Grant also kept a diary, this is one bit of evidence that the Grant diary is genuine. If the entries in the associate's diary show similar observations and entries, this helps establish the validity of Grant's entries and observations, *but one such cross reference does not necessarily establish the accuracy of either document.*

ESTABLISHING AUTHORSHIP OF A DOCUMENT BY COMPARATIVE STUDY. When the author of a document is unknown, or if the genuineness of the material is questioned, authorship can be established by comparing the document with another whose author is known. Comparison can be made in terms of language usage, style, handwriting, and even style of type used to prepare rough drafts of the original manuscript.

INVESTIGATIONS OF CHRONOLOGICAL EVENTS. Whether events described in a document correspond chronologically with the happenings of the times can be a useful method to determine genuineness and validity.

WORD AND LANGUAGE INTERPRETATION. The historical researcher often must interpret the meaning of a document in order to reach conclusions. The process is not a simple one; word meanings and usage tend to change over the years.

Descriptive Studies

While historical studies describe past conditions, descriptive research is concerned with depicting the present. For the sake of convenience, descriptive studies in education can be placed in several subcategories as follows:

1. Surveys
2. Case studies
3. Comparative studies

SURVEYS. The most frequently employed and probably the most misused method of determining conditions as they currently exist is labeled survey research. Surveys include studies in which a large quantity of data related to the subject under investigation are collected; therefore, surveys, of necessity, are studies of wide magnitude rather than studies in depth. The broad aspects of surveys provide the advantage of "rough sifting" in an area of investigations; from this, factors may emerge that require closer study. When the survey is used as a screening device, or when the purpose is to gain an accurate description of present status, it has been properly employed.

There are many examples of survey research in the field of education. The self-evaluation studies required by the various regional accrediting associations of colleges and secondary schools are developed largely around surveys and based upon criteria established by the associations. Educators also continually engage in surveys that include topics such as population trends and movements; pupil drop-out rate, personnel, buildings and equipment needs; pupil, public, and teacher opinions on various matters; curriculum trends; and pupil follow-up studies.

CASE STUDIES. Unlike the survey, the case study is essentially research in depth rather than breadth. Whereas the purpose of the survey is to map the surface, the case study probes beneath the surface, sometimes exposing the causes of factors discovered by surveys.

The longitudinal characteristic of case studies would explain why they are generally limited in scope; cases are usually confined to studies of individuals or small groups. Researches involving the case method may require combining many cases that have been studied by various case workers. At times, however, comprehensive studies have been initiated to encompass entire communities. Some of these research efforts have been so thorough that they are regarded by authorities as case studies. In the field of education, case studies often deal with a variety of topics with emphasis on depth rather than scope.

COMPARATIVE STUDIES. Comparative studies form a link between the descriptive studies previously discussed and experimental research. It often is possible to make comparisons of existing situations which provide much of the same kind of information that experiments might yield; cause-effect relationships may be determined. Such studies may be called causal-comparative or *ex post facto* studies. Teachers in a school system, for example, may have taught a subject for years using a "traditional" approach. Then, for some reason or other, a "new" approach is installed. By comparing the past progress of similar groups of pupils who have been taught by the two methods, it may be possible to evaluate their relative merits.

Comparison can also be made by determining relationships, which may or may not have a cause-effect basis. Studies of this type often employ statistical correlation to determine relationship. Although some writers refer to correlation studies, it is best to consider correlation as but one way of making comparisons.

Experiments in Education

While the historical study describes conditions as they were and descriptive research conditions as they are, experimental studies can give us a clue as to what will occur in the future under a given set of conditions.

EXPERIMENTAL AND CONTROLLED CONDITIONS. The essential element of the experimental design is the development of experimental and control situations prior to the actual experiments. What is meant by control?

Experimental educational research has been derived from the laboratory method often used in the natural sciences. In its most elementary form, the experimental method of science is based upon two assumptions regarding variables which may be identified with the phenomenon under investigation:

1. If two situations are equal in every respect except for a factor present in one of the situations, any difference which appears between the two situations can be attributed to the factor. This statement is referred to as the "law of the single variable."

2. If two situations are not equal but it can be demonstrated that none of the variables are significant in producing the phenomenon under investigation; or if significant variables are made equal, any difference occurring between the two situations after the introduction of a new variable to one of the systems can be attributed to the new variable. This statement is referred to as the "law of the only significant variable."

The purpose of establishing experimental-control condition, thus, is to create a situation in which the effect of a single variable can be studied.

APPLICATIONS OF THE LAWS OF VARIABLES. The law of the single variable is more easily applied by the physical scientist than by the educator. Since educational researchers are usually concerned with human beings, many variables will always be present; therefore, experiments in education require study in terms of those significant variables which can be identified and measured.

The application of the law of the only significant variable in experimental and causal-comparative studies in education requires comparing groups on the basis of significant variables. A number of methods have been devised for making comparisons. These include:

1. Using a single group under both control and experimental conditions.
2. Selecting two or more groups on the basis of a random sampling method.
3. Equating two or more groups on the basis of statistical analysis of group means in test results, which tend to indicate that in terms of significant variables the groups are similar.
4. Equating two or more groups on the basis of matched pairs.
5. Rotating equated groups in experimental and control conditions.

The use of a single group to serve in both experimental and control capacity is predicated upon the assumption that all variables are held constant by the process. It is reasoned that the same individuals, under each condition, will not differ in any factors which might be significant. If, for example, a new method of teaching a group of pupils is to be tried, the pupils are pretested by conventional methods at the beginning of a unit of work: this is the control situation. When the unit is completed, the group is tested again and a mean gain is determined. A pretest is again applied before the beginning of the experimental unit and a post-test is given at the conclusion. A statistical comparison of mean gain under control and experimental conditions is made to determine if there is a significant difference between the two methods.

Difficulties in using a single group for an experiment of the type described include the following:

1. It is necessary to equate the quality and quantity of material to be learned under the two conditions.
2. Pupil learning ability will vary from one time to another.
3. Teacher competence and enthusiasm may tend to vary.
4. There may be carry-over effect of learning from one unit to the next.
5. A halo effect may result from the novelty of an experiment and distort results in favor of the "new" or experimental method.

Selection of groups on the basis of random sampling from a population is an excellent method of insuring that the groups will be equated, but making random selections from a large population can pose an insurmountable problem. (Sampling theory will be explored in some detail in Chapter 6.)

Probably the most useful method of equating groups for experimental and causal-comparative studies is carried out through the use of tests applied to determine comparability of groups on significant factors. If valid tests which measure the factor(s) which has (have) been identified as significant are available, groups may be formed arbitrarily by insuring that their average scores are approximately equal. At times it is determined that a single test can be used for both the process of selection and the determination of changes to be measured; this would be true when the only significant factor is the one measured by the test. A researcher might be interested in determining the effect of using various methods for teaching arithmetic. Because many valid tests of arithmetic are available, a prior measurement of achievement in arithmetic with the test can be used to form or insure the selection of groups of equal achievement. The experimental and control factors may then be applied and a post-test with the same or an equivalent instrument can be used to measure and compare results.

The matched pairs method involves the selection of individuals who are as alike as possible in respect to significant factors, i.e., sex, age, intelligence, and/or many other variables. The members of each matched pair are placed in separate groups; one of the groups is then exposed to the experimental conditions while the other, the control, is not. Frequently, to insure that the various groups are equated on the basis of critical factors, tests are administered and analyzed to determine whether the groups are significantly different in any respect.

Rotation of groups which have been equated by a method previously described has the advantage of equating external factors such as the competence of teachers and the novelty of the experimental situation. In the rotation method, groups serving in the experiment and control periodically reverse roles. If the variable applied in the experimental situation consistently produces results different from those found in the control group, the evidence indicates that the experimental factor is causing the difference.

Hierarchy of Studies

The nature of historical, descriptive and experimental studies has been discussed. What relation, if any, exists among them? Certainly all should be based upon a systematic framework or rationale, otherwise they cannot be designated as research. Other factors, however, distinguish one from the other.

Is it true, as some authorities contend, that one type of investigation is superior to another? No! The differences are due to methods employed and the order in which one type may logically follow from another. Assume, for example, a beginning researcher wishes to devote his professional career to the study of educational programs for emotionally disturbed children. He may start with a historical study of teaching methods used in the past. The second step may involve a detailed, descriptive survey study to determine the number and general nature of existing programs in the state or in the nation. Third, a descriptive case study could be made of school programs judged as being especially effective in dealing with the emotionally handicapped. The fourth stage would bring the researcher in contact with a number of emotionally disturbed children — another descriptive case study. Finally, the researcher is ready to utilize the *experimental* method to test the effect of variables identified by *historical* and *descriptive* studies. He may use any or all of the experimental techniques described on pages 16–19 to study the effect of these variables. All three methods of inquiry can make important contributions to knowledge; none should be judged inferior to others.

Selected Exercises

1. Indicate whether each of the following studies demonstrates the use of the (1) deductive, (2) inductive, or (3) scientific method. Explain.

   a. Kepler studied the astronomical observations which Tycho Brahe compiled during a lifetime, and proposed a series of equations which predicted the orbits of planets in the solar system.
   b. Mendel studied many generations of plants growing in his monastery garden and developed a theory of inherited characteristics.
   c. Accepting Pasteur's germ theory, Lister developed antiseptic surgery.
   d. Archimedes observed that his own body displaced a volume of water equal to the volume of his body. After duly insuring his place in history by shouting "Eureka" (and running down the street naked), he concluded that bodies displace their own volume of water when immersed. He then determined the density of an alleged gold crown and concluded that all that glitters is not gold.
   e. A public school researcher experiments with teaching machines in his school using all the ninth grade classes in algebra. He finds that students using the teaching machines do significantly better than those who are taught by conventional means. The researcher hypothesizes that teaching machines may be a better method of teaching other courses in his school. He devises another experiment in which all ninth grade general science classes are involved.

2. A historian studying the Civil War finds that the diary of a general in the Union Army states that on May 12, 1863, his forces took the town of Raymond, Mississippi. The diary of a Confederate general indicates that his forces were still in Raymond on May 12. What procedures should the researcher use to determine what actually happened on May 12?

3. A researcher plans to carry out a study of pupils who drop out of school. What factors should he take into consideration in determining whether to use the survey or a case study method?

4. The teachers of Algebra I in a large school system would like to determine the value of programed learning for the course. What factors should be taken into consideration in determining whether to use the experimental or a comparative study?

5. An elementary school supervisor wishes to determine the effectiveness of the sixth grade teachers in his school system as compared to the fifth grade teachers. He carries out a two year project in which he:

   a. Pretests all entering fifth grade pupils in various subjects.
   b. Post-tests the fifth grade pupils at the end of the year in the same subjects.
   c. Pretests the same pupils in the various subjects as they are entering the sixth grade (pupils are kept in the same groups as they were in during the fifth grade).
   d. Post-tests the pupils at the end of the sixth grade on the same subjects.
   e. Carries out a statistical analysis which compares the growth of the pupils in the subjects during the fifth grade and the sixth grade

   Write a critical analysis of the study.

6. Discuss the possible flaw or flaws in each of the following researches:

   a. A historian states that the purpose of his study was "To show that John Dewey's philosophy had an adverse effect on American education."
   b. A researcher states that it was the purpose of his study to learn about conditions which affect the school curriculum.

7. Why is the historical method generally employed as a part of all researches? How can you determine a classification for a given study (historical, descriptive, experimental)?

8. Why is it that most of the recognized philosophers of recorded history have also been natural scientists and mathematicians?

Suggested Activities

1. Plan a classroom discussion on the topic:
   "Can the study of problems in education be objective enough to be classified as scientific?" (Assign participants to select readings from the bibliography at the end of the chapter that may help provide a basis for the discussion.)

2. From the bibliography at the end of the chapter, select and read a piece, written by a scientist, that is concerned with scientific methodology. Select and read another book or article by an author who writes about research in education. Compare and contrast the view of research that each author appears to hold.

3. Make a list of problems you have heard discussed in faculty meetings that you believe might be solved by reviewing research studies already carried out elsewhere.

4. By consulting an encyclopedia of educational research, several volumes of the *Review of Educational Research*, and the *Education Index*, compile a short bibliography of studies that, from their titles, would appear to fall into the various categories of educational research: historical, descriptive, and experimental.

5. Select and read a study that appears to be based upon the historical method. Make a list of the primary and secondary data sources.

6. Select and read a study that appears to be descriptive. Describe the kind of data used by the researcher. How did he obtain his data?

7. Select and read a study that appears to employ the experimental technique. Describe how the researcher established controls over significant variables.

Selected Readings

1. ACKOFF, RUSSELL L., *Scientific Method.* New York: John Wiley & Sons, 1962.
2. American Educational Research Association and the Department of Classroom Teachers, *The Implications of Research for the Classroom Teacher*, Joint Yearbook, Washington, National Educational Association, 1939.
3. ANGELL, ROBERT C., AND RONALD FREEDMAN, "Use of Documents, Records, Census Materials, and Indices," *Research Methods in the Behavioral Sciences.* Dryden Press, 1953 (Chapter 7).
4. AUSUBEL, DAVID P., "The Nature of Educational Research," *Educational Theory.* (October 1953) 3:314-20.
5. BERGMANN, GUSTOV, *Philosophy of Science.* Madison: University of Wisconsin Press, 1957.
6. BEST, JOHN W., *Research in Education.* Englewood Cliffs, New Jersey: Prentice-Hall, Inc., 1959. (Chapters 1, 4, 5, and 6.)
7. BLOCH, M. L. B., *The Historian's Craft*, New York: Alfred A. Knopf, 1953.
8. BRICKMAN, WILLIAM W., *Guide to Research in Educational History.* New York: New York University Bookstore, 1949.
9. BURTT, EDWIN A., *The Metaphysical Foundations of Modern Physical Science.* New York: Doubleday Anchor Books, 1955.

10. BUSWELL, GUY T. "Structure of Educational Research," *The Phi Delta Kappan.* (December 1941), 24:167-169.
11. CAJORI, FLORIAN. "Baconian Methods of Scientific Research." *Scientific Monthly.* (January 1925), 20:85-91.
12. CHURCH, HAROLD H. and others, *The Local School Facilities Survey.* Bulletin of the School of Education, Indiana University, Vol. 29, Nos. 1 and 2. Bloomington. Division of Research and Field Services, Indiana University. 1953.
13. COLLIER, RAYMOND O., JR. AND DONALD L. MEYER, "Research Methods: Experimental Design and Analysis," in "The Methodology of Educational Research." *Review of Educational Research*, 30:430-39; December 1960.
14. CONANT, JAMES B., *Modern Science and Modern Man.* New York: Columbia University Press, 1952.
15. COX, D. R., *Planning of Experiments.* New York: John Wiley and Sons, 1958.
16. EDWARDS, NEWTON, *The Courts and the Public Schools.* Revised Edition. Chicago: The University of Chicago Press, 1955.
17. EINSTEIN, ALBERT, *Essays in Science.* New York: Philosophical Library, 1934. (Chapters 1, 3 and 4.)
18. FESTINGER, LEON, AND DANIEL KATZ, Editors, *Research Methods in the Behavioral Sciences.* New York: Dryden Press, 1953, (pp. 15-97, 243-299, 327-535).
19. FONDEL, ISAAC L., "Educational Research," *School and Society,* (October 7, 1950) 72:232.
20. FREEMAN, FRANK N., "The Contributions of Science to Education," *School and Society,* (July 27, 1929) 30:107-12.
21. GARRAGHAN, GILBERT J., *A Guide to Historical Method.* New York: Fordham University Press, 1946.
22. GOOD, CARTER V., and DOUGLAS E. SCATES, *Methods of Research.* New York: Appleton-Century-Crofts, 1954. (Chapter 1)
23. GOOD, CARTER V., *Introduction to Educational Research.* New York: Appleton-Century-Crofts, 1963. (Chapters 1, 2, 4, 5, 6, 7 and 8)
24. HOCKETT, HOMER C., *The Critical Method in Historical Research and Writing.* New York: The Macmillan Co., 1955.
25. KAUFMAN, FELIX, "The Nature of Scientific Method." *Social Research* (May, 1954), 12:464-480.
26. KERLINGER, FRED N., *Foundations of Behavioral Research.* New York: Holt, Rinehart & Winston, Inc., 1965. (Chapters 1 & 2)
27. LECHATELIER, HENRY M., "The Methodology of Scientific Research," *Journal of Chemical Education.* (November, 1930), 7:2584-2589.
28. MARTZ, VELORUS, "Philosophy and Science." *Encyclopedia of Educational Research.* New York: The Macmillan Co., 1941.
29. MONROE, WALTER S. (ed.), "Science of Education," *Encyclopedia of Educational Research.* New York: The Macmillan Co., 1950.
30. MOULY, GEORGE J., *The Science of Educational Research.* New York: American Book Co., 1963. (Chapter 1)
31. NORTHROP, F. S. C., *The Logic of the Sciences and the Humanities.* New York: The Macmillan Co., 1949. (Chapter 2)
32. PERDEW, PHILIP W., "Criteria of Research in Educational History." *Journal of Educational Research.* (November, 1950) 44:217-223.

33. RUMMEL, J. FRANCIS, *An Introduction to Research Procedures in Education.* New York: Harper & Row, Publishers, 1958. (Chapter 1)

34. SAX, GILBERT, *Empirical Foundations of Educational Research.* Englewood Cliffs, New Jersey: Prentice-Hall, Inc., 1968. (Chapters 1 and 2)

35. SEARLES, HERBERT L., *Logic and Scientific Method.* New York: The Ronald Press Company, 1948. (Chapters 10 and 11)

36. SEARS, JESSE B., "School Surveys," *Encyclopedia of Educational Research.* Second Edition. Edited by Walter S. Monroe. New York: The Macmillan Co., 1950. (p. 1126-33)

37. State of Michigan, "What Does Research Say?" Lansing, Mich., Dept. of Public Instruction, 1937.

38. STRAYER, JOSEPH R., Editor, *The Interpretation of History.* Princeton: Princeton University Press, 1943.

39. VAN DALEN, DEOBOLD B., AND WILLIAM J. MEYER, *Understanding Educational Research: An Introduction.* New York: McGraw-Hill Book Co., 1962. (Chapters 2, 3, 4, 9, 10 and 11)

40. WHITEHEAD, ALFRED NORTH, *Science and the Modern World.* New York: The American Library, 1956. (Chapters 1-4)

Chapter 2

Methods for
Data Collection

In Chapter 4, the rationale for data collection will be explained. Certain rules and conventions will be described which develop the nexus between empirical verification and the development of theories and other aspects of what is considered the known body of educational knowledge. The whole inductive-deductive process utilized in gaining knowledge is, however, dependent on the quality of the data collecting process which may constitute the weakest link in present research in the social sciences.

A number of specific research methodologies have been singled out for discussion in this volume. The student of research should realize, however, that most investigators utilize a number of methods in completing an investigation. Further, social scientists are constantly striving to find new methods which will more accurately portray the exact nature of phenomena under study.

Four methods of data collection most commonly employed are described here. They include questionnaires, interviews, content and document analysis, and observation. The list is not complete and the treatment is far from exhaustive because a thorough understanding depends on a background in mathematical statistics. Beginning researchers are encouraged to seek additional information in texts dealing with advanced data collecting techniques.

Questionnaires

Questionnaires are said to be the most used and misused methods in educational research. Objections are both practical and philosophical.

The practical objections to this instrument result from its apparent ease of construction and use. Beginning researchers tend to utilize this method of data collection without fully understanding its nature or correct purpose. A second practical limitation is the tendency for respondents to give inaccurate information about themselves. For example, subjects have been found to report voting in national and local elections inaccurately. More careful questioning on a face-to-face basis may eliminate some of these discrepancies.

Although questionnaires have certain advantages other methods lack, such as low cost per subject surveyed, constructing reliable and valid questionnaires and insuring nonbiased response are challenging and time consuming tasks; the collection of data with a questionnaire should not be considered an "easy" method if used properly.

Philosophically based objections center on the use or misuse of information gathered. First is the fallacious belief that widespread practice makes "good." Consider the school district in which the new program of non-English language instruction is developed on the basis of what the majority of other school districts which had on-going language programs reported doing on a questionnaire survey. If the district officials wished to develop a program similar to other programs, they succeeded. If, however, the intent was to establish a program which was most effective for the pupils in the district, they may or may not have succeeded. Good educational practices cannot be determined solely on the basis of popular vote.

A second misplaced philosophic orientation, which critics have asserted is promulgated through the use of questionnaires, is the notion that the truth of a fact is directly proportional to the number of people who accept its accuracy. A school board member, for example, may instruct the district administrators to carry on an evaluation of the school program. Part of the evaluation process might include circulation of a questionnaire in which parents of children in the district schools are asked to evaluate various areas of the instructional program including reading, social studies, and mathematics. Suppose the results indicate that the reading and social studies programs are rated inferior and the mathematics program average. When the results are reported to the board, it may direct the administrators to initiate steps to improve the reading and social studies curriculum. Obviously such an evaluative process would be wasted: it is not proper to ask parents to make judgments concerning programs for which the majority have neither the facts nor skill required to make an accurate evaluation.

Surveys of parental opinion can provide useful information for teachers and administrators in improving the image of the school;

they have only limited use as a basis for making curriculum changes. Following are guidelines to questionnaire construction that will reduce the dangers of misuse previously described.

Purpose

Questionnaires are used to obtain factual data, opinions and attitudes in a structural framework from respondents not contacted on a face-to-face basis. Schedules are similar in content to questionnaires but an individual responds in the presence of the investigator. The absence of direct communication, which is the essential feature of the questionnaire, imposes a responsibility on the person developing the instrument to make the intent and mode of response clear, because there is little possibility that the respondent will attempt to obtain clarification of ambiguous points from the person circulating the instrument.

Use

Due to the many practical and technical limitations, questionnaires should be used only when other data gathering techniques have been considered and rejected. The inability to communicate purpose to the respondent, the unreliability of responses and the difficulty of inducing respondents to complete and return the questionnaires detract from the effectiveness of this instrument as a data collecting device.

Structured interviews or schedules may produce more satisfactory results than questionnaires but the cost of personally contacting several hundred or a thousand subjects is prohibitory. The ease of contacting a great many subjects at a low unit cost adds to the attractiveness of the questionnaire.

When data are readily available in compiled form, it is unwise to request the same information in a questionnaire. A questionnaire to superintendents of schools, for example, should exclude items such as tax rate or assessed valuation which are available from state or local agency reports. The content of questionnaires generally should deal with biographical data about the respondent, requests for the respondent's evaluation of certain conditions, and statements of attitudes or opinions which can be obtained from only the respondent.

Item Construction

A number of statistical and mathematical techniques are available for the purpose of refining questionnaires. Some of these have been described in the section dealing with precision. In addition to mathematical analysis, a number of rather simple steps can be taken to improve the quality of questionnaires prior to use in a research study. The process of initial development includes careful attention to item construction and mode of response with continual refinement during successive administrations to pilot groups.

Item construction is a time-consuming process in which the investigator serves as his own devil's advocate by carefully criticizing each word, phrase, and mode of response. The investigator should examine each item and apply the following evaluative criteria:

1. Can the item convey to the respondent a meaning different from the intended meaning? The inexperienced investigator, in seeking biographical information, may include the item "Where do you live?" The expected response is an address, for example 146 Maple Street. However, can the respondent develop other extensional meanings for the word live? The respondent may reason that the type of housing unit is wanted and respond apartment, single family dwelling, trailer house or a geographic location with a response, "in Kansas," "in the Bay Area," "in the South." The item could be improved by rephrasing the question, "What is the address of your present residence?" or "List your home address."

2. Can the item or mode of response limit or distort the response? A member of the Prohibition Party asked to check political affiliation, when the two choices given are Republican or Democrat, would be unable to give the correct information. In this instance, a blank with the instructions: "indicate other affiliation ...." would improve the item. Another example of the problem would arise if a college professor, in seeking student evaluations of his class, were to include an item as follows:

   The teaching observed in this class is ....
   a. Stimulating
   b. Rewarding
   c. Fine
   d. Excellent

   Some class members might wish to choose adjectives other than the ones stipulated to describe the teacher's performance. Items thus can be constructed to deliberately elicit only certain types of information. More frequently, however, such technical deficiencies are unintentional but the results are nevertheless biased because the population of all possible responses which the individual could make to the item is greatly reduced. The reduction in sampling range may be due to the wording of the item or to the way in which the subject is asked to respond.

3. Will the mode of response enable the investigator to tally the results readily? To facilitate a rapid compilation of returns, the mode of response should be objective. A question, "What is the total number of years you have taught at each grade level" can be structured so that the respondent need check only certain blanks or insert numbers, for example, "In each blank space below, list the number of years teaching experience at the given grade level."

Grade Span	Number of Years Teaching Experience
K-3	....
4-6	....
7-8	....
9-12	....
Other indicate	....

The response "other indicate" is to accommodate special cases. Without it a teacher with 35 years' experience in a one-room, eight-grade school could report 35 years' experience in each of the first three categories for a total of 105 years' teaching experience. Organization of responses as illustrated in the preceding example somewhat reduces the range of accuracy but greatly decreases the amount of time required to compile questionnaire results.

4. If sorting or computer processes are to be used, is the mode of response organized so that it can be coded for mechanical electronic data analysis? The increased use of sorters and computors enables many investigators to avail themselves of this service. To convert data to punched cards, it usually is necessary to develop an objective mode of response. If so-called free response or completion items are to be included, they must be analyzed and grouped into similar types so that a coding system can be developed. (See page 39 for a description of content analysis.)

5. Is the format arranged for ease of response? The mode of response should be arranged to reduce the time required to complete a questionnaire. Vertical rather than horizontal organization should

be used whenever possible. For example, the following question concerning marital status, "Check marital status .... single, ... married, ... divorced, ... separated, ... spouse deceased," will increase the probability that the incorrect response will be made because the person may check the blank following rather than preceding the appropriate adjective. The uncertainty can be eliminated by utilizing vertical rather than horizontal organization. Thus:

Check marital status:

.... Single

.... Married

.... Divorced

.... Separated

.... Spouse Deceased

One disadvantage of vertical organization, however, is that questionnaires require many more pages and may appear long to the potential respondent; increased length can result in a reduction in the number of instruments completed and returned.

PILOT ADMINISTRATION. A questionnaire usually improves with use. After a preliminary list of items has been developed, the questionnaire should be administered to a number of individuals for criticism. The instrument should be first submitted to individuals familiar with the area of knowledge being studied. For example, a survey to ascertain the scope of kindergarten programs should be reviewed by authorities in kindergarten education, school principals, curriculum coordinators and school superintendents. They will be able to judge the effectiveness of the instrument for obtaining the desired information and whether the questions are realistically stated with reference to operating kindergarten programs. Unsatisfactory items should be eliminated or revised.

Following this initial inspection, the questionnaire should be administered to a group similar to the intended respondents. If kindergarten teachers are to be surveyed, the instrument should be given to a pilot group of kindergarten teachers who will not be part of the final sample in the study. One way to avoid mixing the pilot group with the final group is to select the sample first and then choose a pilot group from members of the population not included in the sample.

Administration to a pilot group similar to the sample group may unearth a number of inadequacies in the questionnaire which lead to further revision and perhaps a second pilot administration. By utilizing the administration-refinement cycle, the reliability of the instrument can be increased.

SAMPLE SELECTION AND BIAS. The sample may include all or a small fraction of the total population. Surveys relating to conditions in small school districts or even entire states may well include each member of the population. When the total population cannot be sampled because of time and money limitations, the sample should be randomly selected and efforts expended to insure as large a return of questionnaires as possible.

One salient weakness of questionnaires is the bias introduced by the characteristics of the individuals responding in comparison to the individuals not responding. Even though the random sample is carefully selected and represents nearly a perfect miniature of the population, the nature of the response can introduce bias which will invalidate the results. Suppose a questionnaire was circulated to 1,000 kindergarten teachers to determine how many had characteristic X and how many had characteristic Y. X and Y could represent, for example, the possession or nonpossession of a master's degree, a teaching certificate or some other pair of mutually exclusive qualities. Further, suppose that most persons with quality X had a third quality, Z, which was possessed by only a few with quality Y. If quality Z involves a strong reticence to submit reports on time, prepare lesson plans, and complete and return questionnaires, the results might indicate a larger proportion of quality Y in the population than actually existed. The bias would result from a lower proportion of responses from individuals possessing qualities X and Z.

Maximizing Returns

A number of steps must be taken to maximize the number of questionnaires returned and to check the bias of the nonresponding portion of the sample. One of the most effective methods for insuring return is to make the respondent aware that he has an important contribution to make to a field that will affect him personally. The kindergarten teacher is more apt to complete and return a questionnaire if the results of the study will bring about changes in kindergarten education such as the elimination of the practice of assigning one kindergarten teacher to two kindergarten sessions, the first in the morning and the second in the afternoon.

A cover letter accompanying the questionnaire can supply the information to induce the respondent to complete the instrument and return it to the investigator. The cover letter should be short and contain the following information: (1) Purpose and significance of the study, (2) The importance of the information to be furnished by the respondent, (3) Whether the responses are anonymous and how anonymity is to be guaranteed, (4) A deadline date for return of the instrument. A second short letter of inducement by a well-known and respected individual or an officer of a recognized state or local professional organization may increase the individual's desire to respond. A stamped, self-addressed envelope should be included if the response is to be returned through the mails.

The process of circulating questionnaires, receiving and tabulating responses, and issuing appeals for a greater return is carried on in three cycles. The first consists of the initial circulation, usually through the mail. After the stated deadline date, the results are tabulated from questionnaires returned and the per cent computed.

The second cycle is initiated by circulating a plea for return of the remaining questionnaires. The plea, listing a second deadline date, may be a form letter addressed to each nonrespondent. If the identity of the respondent is to be kept anonymous, the request for returns must be addressed to all subjects in the sample with the instructions "if you have not returned the questionnaire . . . ." Few questionnaires are circulated, however, without some means of tracing nonrespondents. The results from the second appeal are tabulated after the revised deadline date and kept separate from the first response.

The next cycle involves a third appeal in the form of a personal letter including a second copy of the questionnaire or a telephone call to solicit a response. A third deadline date is set after which time the final responses are tabulated.

Adequate Returns

How large should the return be? What per cent return from a questionnaire survey is large enough to safely generalize from the sample to the population? These are difficult questions with no ready answers. Some general principles, however, can be stated. The return is sufficiently large when the nonrespondents represent a random sample from the same population as the respondents, that is, when the answers made by the respondents are the same as the responses which would be made by the nonrespondents.

If the three-cycle plan described in the preceding section is used, bias of response or nonresponse can be detected. The process is illustrated by considering the response pattern to one sample question addressed to parents: "Have any children in your custody appeared in juvenile court? "Yes," "No." Assuming that this question and others relating to delinquency were circulated among a random sample of 1,000 parents, the results might be as follows:

Cycle	Per Cent Response		Total Number
	Yes	No	
1	10	90	600
2	30	70	100
3	60	40	50
			750

Six hundred of the responses were returned prior to the first deadline date. Of this number, 10 per cent reported dependent children who had appeared in juvenile court. The second cycle of 100 responses resulted in 30 per cent reporting court appearances and the final cycle, 60 per cent. Are the remaining 250 nonrespondents a representative sample of the population from which the initial 1,000 subjects were chosen? Probably not. The nature of the questions discouraged some from answering. In this instance, a 75 per cent return is not adequate. If, however, the pattern of response had been unchanged throughout the three cycles with approximately 16 per cent responding yes in each case, evidence of bias would not be present; a 75 per cent return would be considered adequate.

TREATING BIAS. What can be done if the three-cycle analysis indicates bias? One of two steps can be taken by the investigator. First, an effort can be made to increase the per cent return to include a very high proportion of the total sample. This involves using every possible means to elicit returns from nonrespondents. Obviously substitution cannot be made in a sub-sample where bias is known to exist. The methods employed in increasing the response depend on the situation. The researcher must do his best.

The second step is less difficult than the first. The investigator merely calculates the effect on the statistics if all individuals respond in a manner to introduce the greatest change in results. Using the previous example, assume the 250 nonrespondents (1) would all respond yes, and (2) would all respond no. Then compute the effect of each on the total pattern of responses.

		Number Responding		
Cycle		Yes	No	Total
1		60	540	600
2		30	70	100
3		30	20	50
Non Respondents		(250)	(250)	(250)
Total		(120)	(880)	1,000
or				
Total		(370)	(630)	

The researcher would conclude that as many as 37 per cent in the total of 1,000 would answer yes and as many as 88 per cent would answer no. Yes responses could vary from 12 to 37 per cent and no responses from 63 to 88 per cent. Clearly a biased response such as the one described would greatly reduce the accuracy of the results of this questionnaire study.

Overview

The questionnaire is probably the method most frequently used for collecting data. Its principal advantage is economy because many subjects can be surveyed for the cost of postage. The investigator can solicit the donation of thousands of hours of work from others to complete his study. Properly used, however, the questionnaire is not an easy method to employ. There must be a great deal of refinement before the questions can be considered reliable and valid data gathering instruments. Utilization of a carelessly prepared questionnaire wastes countless hours of respondents' and investigators' time because the results are of little value in adding to the known body of knowledge and may actually cause educators to make decisions based on fallacious information.

Interviews

While the questionnaire is employed to secure information from individuals who are not contacted on a face-to-face basis, interviewing is a process of obtaining information directly from the respondents. Interviews are especially useful in obtaining data from children or from other subjects who cannot read with sufficient facility to complete a questionnaire. Most of the principles that have been discussed in questionnaire development also apply to interviewing techniques, namely sample selection, scaling, establishing precision and validity, and the importance of a nonbiased pattern of response. A few additional points should be discussed, however.

Training

The success of interview techniques depends on the skill of the person conducting the interview. The person must know how to enlist cooperation from the respondent, how to ask questions tactfully that relate to subjects of concern to the respondent, how to obtain the desired information, and how to avoid projecting his bias or permitting the respondent to give only partial answers to questions. Graduate students choosing interviewing as a method for data collection should be prepared to spend hours in training practice sessions before going into the field to gather data.

Bias

Do individuals tend to hear what they want to hear and reject what is unacceptable to them? Psychologists would say yes. Perception, the process an individual uses to organize sensory stimuli into a meaningful whole, is governed by previous experience. The nature of his previous experience can cause an individual to organize certain stimuli in a way quite different from the average. Unique perception patterns prevent certain individuals from reporting facts because, as indicated earlier, facts must be shareable and verifiable. If an individual always distorts certain types of stimuli through the perception process, his account of an event is not a fact because it is not the same interpretation that most individuals would make. Undue distortion of facts through the perceptive process has important implications for interviewing as a data collection method.

PERSONAL INVOLVEMENT. Should the person conducting and reporting the study do the interviewing? An investigator is vitally interested in the results of a study he has designed. He is personally involved. Although he may be completely honest, the subconscious influence of his personal involvement may cause him inadvertently to distort interview data. Serious consideration should be given to assigning interview and observation duties to others. Because of inadequate financing, the graduate student unfortunately may be forced personally to conduct interviews needed to complete his study. He should recognize and guard against bias introduced by distorted perception.

INTERACTION WITH RESPONDENT. Interviewer Jones may contact several hundred people in a period of two weeks. Because the experience background of Jones differs from that of each respondent, he will be more effective in obtaining reliable data from one individual than from another. What effect will the interaction between interviewer and respondent have on the results of the study? Very possibly the effect will be random and not distort the findings; however, bias may be introduced. One method for ascertaining the effect of interviewer-respondent interaction is to have a second investigator contact some or all of the sample group for a second interview; a comparison of the reports of the two investigators will indicate the nature and degree of distortion caused by interaction.

Types of Interviews

There are a number of labels to indicate the type of interview to be used in data collection. Generally, a knowledge of the names applied to each type is not as helpful as an understanding of the relation between form and reliability. The more highly structured interviews are most reliable, and those with least structure are least reliable. Structured interviews limit the amount of information which can be obtained, however, and present few advantages not available through the use of questionnaires. Two additional factors exist which can reverse the general trend between structure and reliability. First, the skill of the interviewer influences reliability. A skillful group of interviewers can use unstructured interviews and demonstrate reasonable reliability. The second factor is time. Data obtained from longer or more frequent interviews are usually more reliable than those obtained during shorter or less frequent sessions. After reviewing some of the difficulties encountered in conducting interviews, the following types will be described briefly: (1) interviews with schedule; (2) structured interviews; and (3) unstructured interviews.

INTERVIEWS WITH SCHEDULE. The most highly structured type of interview involves the administration of a printed list of questions, or schedule, in the presence of the investigator who gives directions and answers questions. The respondent reads the questions and responds in writing. Utilization of a schedule reduces the possibility of introducing bias to a minimum. One well known example of the use of a schedule is an achievement examination administered to a group of children in the classroom.

STRUCTURED INTERVIEW. The best example of a structured interview is the type conducted by census takers. Questions are direct and responses consist of single words such as yes or no, numerical values including age, short statements which describe the occupation of the head of the household, and other items which require a limited response. Structured interviews are quite reliable but the range of information obtained tends to be narrow.

UNSTRUCTURED INTERVIEWS. The unstructured interview is characterized by an apparent lack of rigid organization in the manner in which questions are asked and responses made. The interviewer informally leads the respondent through the area to be covered. Certain areas are explored more fully than others, and new areas not previously identified add to or change the scope of the study. The unstructured interview is used to obtain information concerning attitudes and opinions which is difficult to elicit through structured interviews, schedules, or questionnaires. The success of this method is determined by the skill and experience of the interviewer. Because of the lack of structure, there is opportunity for the interviewer to introduce bias and consciously or subconsciously distort the results obtained.

Procedures

Although a great deal of skill is required to conduct an interview for the purpose of assessing attitudes, feelings, and opinions accurately, the novice can obtain certain kinds of information successfully. The steps used in developing an interview study usually include sample selection, initial contact, establishing rapport, recording data, and analyzing results.

SAMPLE SELECTION. As in questionnaire studies, the sample selected should be representative of the group about which generalizations are to be made. Once the sample is selected, an attempt should be made to contact each subject included. Substitutions should be made only when the investigator can clearly demonstrate that the substitution process does not change the characteristics of the original sample.

INITIAL CONTACT. The initial contact with prospective respondents is apt to be successful if the investigator prepares himself in much the same way a salesman would prior to an important selling venture. Some authorities recommend that for interviews of short duration the initial contact should be made personally and the interview follow immediately. Busy people can say no rather easily over the telephone or through the mail but will be more apt to grant time to the investigator who appears in person. Regardless of the kind of initial contact, the interviewer should state his purpose clearly and indicate the amount of time involved in the interview process.

If the initial contact results in rejection, it is absolutely necessary if at all possible to determine the reason for refusal to participate in the interview. The interviewer must determine if any bias is operating that will differentiate between respondents and nonrespondents. The nonrespondent should be persuaded to answer at least two questions.

First, he should be asked to explain why he does not wish to grant the interview. A frequent response is "I don't have time." The investigator should attempt to find if there are other reasons for rejection. Second, the subject should be encouraged to answer one question which reflects the central purpose of the study. For example, in analyzing voting behavior relating to schools, the nonrespondent might be asked whether he favored passage of a pending school bond election, if he usually votes in school bond elections, or if he feels that school costs should be reduced. Answers to these questions will enable the investigator to estimate the degree of bias resulting from the elimination of the nonrespondent from the sample.

The interviewer should not give up easily. A second contact at a more favorable time may result in success. The importance of interviewing all or nearly all of the subjects included in the original sample cannot be overemphasized.

ESTABLISHING RAPPORT. After securing permission to conduct the interview, the investigator should lay the groundwork so that the subject will respond freely. Usually a freer response will be obtained if the person is interviewed privately. The subject should not be told that his response will be confidential because data from the interview will eventually become part of the published results; assurance can be given, however, that the anonymity of the respondent will be maintained if at all possible.

RECORDING DATA. The note-taking process usually will affect the respondent and govern the amount of information he will elicit. The influence is not, however, always negative or restricting. Many individuals will become more communicative if they know their comments are sufficiently important to be recorded by the investigator. Others, however, may hesitate to divulge certain kinds of information because they know the content of their statements is being noted. The interviewer must use his own judgment on the matter of note-taking. It can be eliminated if interviews are short and the number of items relatively small. To eliminate note-taking during the interview, the investigator listens attentively and records the observations immediately afterwards. Elimination of note-taking during the interview can result in added distortion because of the interval between the interview and the time the results are described.

The most accurate and reliable but perhaps the least valid method of recording data from interviews involves the use of a tape recorder. Interviewers are cautioned to record the exact responses made to questions and to avoid paraphrasing. Unless a person is skilled in shorthand, however, a verbatim written account is very difficult to obtain. The portable battery-operated tape recorder provides a means for obtaining the entire context of the interview for future analysis. The use of the tape recorder may invalidate the results, however, because of its effect on the person responding. A request for permission to use the recorder and an explanation why it is to be used may alleviate the apprehension of the interviewee.

If a recorder is used, the investigator should prepare a written commentary in which the nonverbal aspects of the respondent's behavior are noted.

ANALYZING RESULTS. As mentioned previously, the reliability and validity of data secured by interview can be increased if one person conducts the interview and records the observations and a second interprets the data.

Data from structured interviews can be analyzed in the same way as questionnaire results. Gaps in information can be obtained by a second contact or a follow-up phone call.

Information from nonstructured interviews is difficult to quantify. The technique of content and document analysis to be described next can be utilized in classifying data obtained from unstructured interviews.

Content and Document Analysis

Content analysis as used in this volume refers to the process of analyzing, classifying, and quantifying data presented in written form. Materials used can be either historical or contemporary. Sources for analysis may consist of published materials such as newspaper accounts, textbooks, novels, almanacs, or speeches recorded in the congressional record. Other written materials include court testimony, responses to questionnaires or the content of interviews and observations, pupils' cumulative records, deeds to property, health records and school board minutes. This list is illustrative but not exhaustive. Following a brief explanation of basic considerations, some of the methods of content analysis will be described.

Basic Considerations

Content analysis presents serious problems to the competent investigator who utilizes this useful method and attempts to generalize findings to a larger group or population. The difficulty stems from a realization that a difference exists between the occurrence of an event and the written report of the event. More specifically, the limitation of content analysis proceeds from the nature of the sample, the need for quantification, and the lack of opportunity to duplicate the events described or to obtain further clarification from data which essentially represents a process of one-way communication.

A SELECTIVE SAMPLE. Any written material must be considered a sample of all possible material the author or recorder could have written. What is written is only a sample of what actually occurred to stimulate the writing. Certain comments concerning phenomena might not be recorded, for example, because no word or combination of words exist in any given language such as English which permit complete descriptions of states, events, or objects. A transcription which includes the total essence of any situation probably cannot be made.

One example of the inadequacy of written accounts can be illustrated by considering the minutes of school board meetings. Meetings of school boards may continue for hours and a great many factors impinge on board members and influence their decisions. Oral reports, comments from the audience, members' comments to the group and to each other in confidence, variations in affective tone used to make statements all may have an influence, but few of these types of behavior are described in the minutes. The official record may consist merely of motions and resolutions passed and a brief summary of comments made. Further, school board minutes may be audited by the administrator, the chairman and individual board members before final presentation in written form. Minutes are also corrected by action of the governing board during the next succeeding meeting. In short, the official records of proceedings represent a very inadequate and perhaps biased account of events which actually occurred during the time the board was in session.

Perhaps historians utilize content analysis to a greater extent than any other group of scholars. They recognize the fallibility of written accounts and have developed special techniques of internal criticism to make the results of document analysis more valid.

PROBLEMS OF QUANTIFICATION. When data secured from content analysis is to be treated statistically, some method of quantification must be used. The difficulties can be illustrated by considering a content analysis of the action of a certain board of education during a two year period. The purpose was to determine the amount of consideration given curricular issues in comparison to matters of finance, school construction, personnel, intergovernmental affairs, public relations and miscellaneous actions. The results of the study are presented as follows:

Topic	Per cent of Total
Instruction	10
Finance	50
School Construction	15
Personnel	10
Intergovernmental Affairs	5
Miscellaneous	10
Total	100

Several questions immediately arise. Does the investigator mean that 10 per cent of the time at school board meetings was spent discussing instruction or that 1/10 of the recorded motions dealt principally with instructional matters. There is a difference. When school boards act, their policy formulations may have a very great influence on the organization for instruction in the district. The 10 per cent devoted to instruction may represent a much more potent influence than the 50 per cent devoted to finance. In short, the relative contribution of each type of school board action to practice in the school district cannot be ascertained by the data listed even if an exact understanding of the meaning of the data is conveyed to the reader. The quantification of data which represents a sample of a sample forms a flimsy basis for making conclusions in absence of other supporting data. Quantification of data obtained from content analysis must be interpreted with caution.

LACK OF INTERACTION WITH DATA SOURCE. Written materials are the raw materials which serve as the basis for content analysis. The essential characteristic of these materials is the one-way channel of communication. In contrast, when conducting an interview the investigator can reverse the chain of communication from the subject and work for clarification of statements which are not clear. The questionnaire exercises some control over the response patterns of the respondent by the manner in which items are worded or by the mode of response which has been adopted. In most instances, persons utilizing content analysis must accept the information at hand; they have infrequent opportunities to modify the data. Newspaper editors cannot be asked to reprint editorial comment because the meaning is not clear. The investigator must distill meaning from sources over which he has little or no control.

Procedures

Content analysis, whether used to organize historical materials or quantify the written account obtained from observing kindergarten children, can be described as a four-step process: (1) collection of written material, (2) development of categories, (3) classification and assignment to categories, and (4) quantification.

COLLECTION. The nature of content analysis dictates the need to examine all, or at least a representative sample of, the materials which are to be classified. If rare documents or other restricted materials are to be analyzed, copies should be obtained so that the investigator has all of the sources for review during the preliminary stages of classification. Unless an example of each kind of content which will eventually be placed in individual categories is noted at the beginning, the classification system may be incomplete or unsystematic. When written materials cannot be reproduced reasonably, the analysis should be made where the materials are housed.

DEVELOPMENT OF CATEGORIES. One of the most difficult steps in completing a content analysis is the development of categories. Classification systems or more formal taxonomies involve the collection of items (content in this case) into a rational system. The division of flora and fauna into genus and species represents one of the better known taxonomies. Four principles guide the researcher.

First, content with meaningful similarities are grouped together. Units of content in a given category should have greater similarity with other units of the same group than with units of other groups in one important aspect. For example, to analyze school board minutes the investigator might place in one group all motions initiated by member X and in a second group all motions initiated by member Y, continuing until each motion had been assigned to one of the members of the board. Using the functional system of classification, however, the actions could be divided according to the educational activity affected: administration, instruction, transportation, or capital outlays. A third approach would utilize categories previously listed on page 41: instruction, finance, school construction, personnel, intergovernmental affairs and miscellaneous actions.

Second, all content should be included in one of the selected categories. If the investigator encounters a great many examples which do not "fit" in any established category, the classification system is probably unsuited to the data. The categories should be defined so that few items must be placed in a miscellaneous, catch-all category.

Third, the number of categories should not be too large to make the management of data difficult nor too small for identification of meaningful differences. In analyzing school board actions, for example, the investigator might list each of 1,600 motions adopted during the course of a year, utilizing 1,600 categories without attempting to combine similar units. The account would be complete but not very helpful. Conversely, the investigator might lump all 1,600 motions into the single category "school board actions." Between these two extremes are a number of categories ranging from 8 to 12 which would accommodate all content, minimize assignment to miscellaneous categories, and serve to identify meaningful relationships.

Fourth, the categories adopted should be related by some unifying principle. A case in point is the system for classifying content previously discussed which was based on the identity of the board member initiating the specific action. The system of classification has unity because it is based on a common element, school board membership.

The investigator reviews all of the material to be analyzed, keeping the four principles in mind. After careful study, a tentative array of categories can be chosen which he hopes will include most items listed on the written materials.

ASSIGNMENT TO CATEGORIES. Criteria must be developed to determine (1) what constitutes a unit of content and (2) in which category the unit of content should be placed.

The process of the identification of units of content can be illustrated by considering the analysis of school board minutes. Criteria could be developed to limit content to formal motions or could be expanded to include consideration of comments of board members, the superintendent, and the audience participants.

The decision concerning placement of content within categories should be made by utilizing objective criteria. In the analysis of school board minutes using the categories listed on page 41, a motion in which both personnel and curriculum were included would present difficulties of classification. It could be placed in either category. Further rules governing placement must be made. Even with precise category definition, certain content items will not be discrete units but will overlap into adjacent categories.

QUANTIFICATION. The quantification of content is accomplished by assigning weights to the content in each category for purposes of comparison. Weighting can be in terms of the per cent of total content or by indicating the number of content items in each category. Whatever plan is used should be clearly described so the reader can evaluate the researcher's conclusions. Some fallacious interpretations which can result from quantification include a statement that one category is more important or has greater influence than another category simply because it contains a greater number of content items. Weights should be interpreted in the way they are made: "Using the system described, category X contained a greater number of items than category Y."

Observation

Observation is one of the most fruitful but least utilized methods for data collection. It involves direct study of objects or subjects. Observation can be described in terms of use, basic considerations, and methodology.

Uses

Observation can be employed as a data gathering technique when other methods are unsuitable. Classic examples of its use include studies of the behavior of infants who lack the facility of verbal communication, examination of primitive cultures, work with mentally ill persons, and systematic studies of the behavior of animals.

In addition to these present uses of observational studies, researchers are recognizing observation as a valuable method to employ in place of the more conventional interviews, questionnaires, and schedules. In addition, observation can be used as a supplement to other methods to verify the existence of differences which are purported to exist between experimental and control groups.

AS A PRINCIPAL METHOD. Several examples of studies can be described in which observation is the primary means of data collection.

First, observation techniques frequently are used to record the perceived behavior of individuals over an extended period of time. Detailed observational studies of children are made in which the investigators attempt to record every aspect of the subjects' behavior. Even though the accounts of these observations are very detailed they can represent only a small fraction of what actually transpired during the period of study.

Second, observation is employed as a method for studying groups of individuals functioning in natural or controlled situations. In one instance, the observer may study the actions of a board of education with or without their knowledge. A great many studies also have been based on the observations of teachers and pupils in the classroom. Control can be achieved by giving groups various predetermined tasks to perform during the observation period.

SUPPLEMENTS TO OTHER METHODS. Observation provides a means for establishing the validity of other research methods. For instance, suppose an investigator circulated a questionnaire to teachers asking the extent of grouping done in teaching reading. After receiving all replies the investigator could check on the accuracy of the responses by selecting a sample from those responding and observing their classroom performance. If the teachers reported practices actually used in grouping children accurately, the validity of the questionnaire would be supported. If not, the need for revision in the questionnaire instrument would be indicated.

Later in this volume, the experimental method will be described. Observation techniques can be used to confirm differences which are said to exist between experimental and control groups. Two not unequal groups of first graders, for example, could be instructed in reading; a phonic approach could be used with one and the sight method with the other. After a period of time, each could be given a reading test to determine which demonstrated the greater gain in reading skill. The two groups could be observed during the course of the experiment to verify the fact that one teacher was adhering to instructions to use the phonic method and the second teacher was using the sight method.

Basic Considerations

Before describing the more commonly accepted methods for conducting observational studies, certain basic considerations underlying the use of this technique must be weighed. These include perception, intervention and scope.

PERCEPTION. Sensation refers to the action of sound waves, light waves, and tactile stimuli on the sensory receptors of the organism. Perception is the organization of these sensory stimuli into meaningful units and constitutes our understanding of what is occurring around us. The perception of a given situation for a deaf or a blind person will differ from that of an individual who does not suffer from these handicaps for he has a greater range of sensations which can be used to interpret the situation. Even among "normal" individuals, however, perceptions of a specific situation will display great differences.

An individual's pattern of perception is dependent on his past experiences. Because no two individuals share identical life experiences, their perception will differ. Variations in patterns of perception constitute a serious problem in conducting observational studies. If two observers are in disagreement about what occurred in a school board meeting, the researcher must decide which, if either, has given the correct interpretation of events.

Differences in perception tend to increase with the extent of interpretation which must be made by the observers. In studying a school board in action, the observers may be instructed to describe the emotional states of various board members. When Chairman Jones pounds on the table during the course of a heated discussion, one observer may interpret this action as a manifestation of anger while a second observer may record it as frustration. They would disagree on the interpretation of the act. If the observers had been instructed to record behavior rather than emotional states, however, they would probably both record the comment that at a specific time during the meeting, Chairman Jones pounded on the table. They would show greater agreement about what happened than about why it happened.

INTERVENTION. Observational studies often are said to be invalid because the presence of observers changes the pattern of actions of those being observed. For example, the beginning teacher's performance is affected when the school principal drops in to observe her class. No doubt the observation interferes with the phenomena being observed. The interference of data collection, however, is common to nearly all research procedures in the behavioral sciences as well as in the physical and biological sciences. One example recognized by classroom teachers occurs when arithmetic achievement tests are used to sample all possible responses a child could make in arithmetic problem situations. The knowledge that he is being evaluated, that the test is important, will produce a certain amount of stress which may retard or enhance his performance. The data gathering instrument has affected the nature of the data being collected.

Beginning research workers must recognize that the presence of the observer will influence the behavior of subjects studied. Efforts must be made to reduce or compensate for the effect of the observer on the phenomena under study.

SCOPE. What aspects of behavior should be observed? The reader can spend 15 minutes in the average classroom and appreciate the difficulty of recording even a fraction of all behavior which occurs. Somewhat less difficulty would be encountered if the observer concentrated on certain aspects of teacher behavior or on the behavior of one pupil. If less than the total situation is considered, however, can the researcher be certain that significant aspects of behavior are not neglected? Because all behavior cannot be observed and recorded the researcher must decide which aspects are important.

The use of mechanical devices such as tape recorders, motion picture cameras and TV kinescopes are serving to broaden the scope of observation and will no doubt enable researchers to improve the reliability and validity of this important data gathering method.

Methodology

The reader is referred to the previous section dealing with content analysis. Many of the principles for developing a framework for observation are derived as a result of content analysis. Generally, the observation process can be described as development of a framework, data collection, and quantification.

DEVELOPMENT OF A FRAMEWORK. As previously stated, the investigator must establish the limits within which the observation is to be made. Two general approaches can be used. In conducting exploratory studies in which no attempt is being made to relate the phenomena being observed to an existing theoretical orientation, the structure is usually developed as a result of analysis of the content of the observation. To cite a specific instance, assume that an investigator wished to study the power structure of administrative councils composed of the superintendent of schools, assistant superintendent and representative principals, teachers, and curriculum consultants. In the absence of any specific theoretical rationale which might be used to explain how decisions were made by these groups, the investigator would of necessity have to develop one specifically for groups of this type.

A most productive first step in the process would bring the researcher in contact with the group at work. After a number of observations of administrative councils in action in several school districts, the investigator may be able to identify factors which indicate the most influential members of the group. He may tentatively decide that there is some relationship between the quantity and nature of participation and influence on group decisions. An observation schedule incorporating these features would be developed, a number of observations made and a statistical analysis of results completed. The technique of factor analysis would indicate if there was a specific *constellation* of behavior exhibited by group members which made them especially effective (powerful) or ineffective in influencing the decisions made by administrative councils. These constellations could serve as the basis of categories which could be used for further observation with other groups. By this process theoretical foundation would evolve as a result of preliminary observations.

The second method for establishing categories is to develop them prior to observation ordinarily using an established theoretical framework as the underlying rationale. In the example mentioned previously, the researcher might proceed as follows: Because of his status, the superintendent of schools will usually be the most influential member of the group. Using similar reasoning, the assistant superintendent will have the second highest degree of power over decisions, principals and consultants will rank third in influence and the teacher representative least. The measure of an individual's power could then be gauged in terms of how his effectiveness represented a departure from status hierarchical relations. The framework for observation would involve classifying behavior as to source — teacher, superintendent or principal and the relation of the behavior to the final resolution of the issue. The person with the greatest power could be a teacher whose wishes prevailed against the initial opposition of other more influential members of the group. In this instance, the framework for observation would be determined prior to observation on theoretical grounds.

DATA COLLECTION. Once the method for establishing a framework has been decided upon, attention should be directed to problems encountered in data collection. Several questions present themselves. Should data be recorded on the basis of units of behavior or units of time or both? How will the data be recorded? Are the categories too numerous to promote accurate recording or too few to accommodate required variations in behavior? Can all behavior be readily included in one of the meaningful categories or will a great many be relegated to a miscellaneous category?

Because total behavior cannot possibly be observed in any situation and only a small part of what is observed can be recorded, observation data must represent a sample. To avoid undesirable bias in the compiling process, some system for obtaining data must be devised. Common approaches include taking observations at given time intervals. The observer may record what is occurring at each five second interval, for example, or he may summarize what has occurred during the preceding five second interval. Another approach would involve the identification of certain behavioral acts and a notation of the duration of each. The sampling process will depend on the nature of phenomena being observed.

Many ingenious methods have been devised for recording data. An important consideration is that the method of recording is as simple as possible consistent with the purposes of the study. Short-cut notations can be used to code and record aspects of behavior. Grids combining descriptions of behavior on the left margin and time intervals in columns extending across the page prove quite helpful. Because sequence of acts may be as significant as the acts themselves, methods must be devised to determine which behavior preceded and followed other behavior.

The use of a great many categories tends to reduce the ease with which records of observations can be made. The observer could spend a great deal of time identifying the proper category in a long list of behaviors especially if the observed behaviors change in character rather rapidly. About 10 to 12 categories can be used most easily. With this number, the observer can memorize each and its location on the recording sheet. Usually there must be one section for observations which do not logically belong in any of the established categories. Interruptions, silence, and the occurrence of a number of behaviors simultaneously necessitate the need for the observational catch-all. If preliminary trial of the observation schedule indicates that a large per cent of observed behavior is placed in the miscellaneous category, the entire schedule should be revised to accommodate more of the ambiguous items within the established framework.

QUANTIFICATION. Quantification involves assignment of numerical weights to various observation specimens for the purpose of making quantitative comparisons such as equal to, greater than or less than, more similar or less similar. The beginning researcher should develop an arbitrary system of weighting which seems logically consistent with the data being treated. Advanced statistical techniques have been developed and are being formulated to deal with the problem of quantifying observation data which are beyond the scope of this volume.

Selected Exercises

1. List the advantages and disadvantages resulting from the use of questionnaires.
2. Give four examples of investigations in which the interview method would be more acceptable than the questionnaire method. Explain why.
3. Explain how observation could be used to establish the validity of an interview technique.
4. Describe a study in which all four data collecting methods described in the chapter could be used.
5. Indicate which of the four data gathering techniques would be most effective in studying the following:
   a. A city council in action.
   b. The previous school record of selected 16-year-old school dropouts.
   c. Attitudes of a small high school faculty concerning team teaching.

d. The behavior of infants during periods of play.

e. The influence of faculty advisers on editorial policy expressed in school or college newspapers.

Suggested Activities

1. Develop a questionnaire which will yield the required information with the fewest number of questions. Circulate the questionnaire among ten individuals selected as a representative sample of a larger group. The questionnaire must stand alone. You may not answer questions for clarification raised by the respondents. Insure complete response and analyze the relationship which exists among the items of required information. Determine the following:

   a. age in years and months
   b. sources of income
   c. years experience in various occupations
   d. number of years education
   e. political affiliation
   f. attitude toward kindergarten programs

2. Using the required information described in question 1, conduct five interviews with subjects who constitute a random sample of a given population. In addition to securing the required information, identify added variables which relate to attitudes toward kindergarten programs.

3. Obtain one copy of the local newspaper. Analyze the content in terms of articles which:

   a. relate directly to education
   b. relate indirectly to education
   c. have no relationship to education

   Develop criteria for (a) identification of units of content, and (b) assignment of content to one of the three categories. Develop conclusions supported by the data.

4. Secure the permission of a classroom teacher for a fifteen-minute visitation. During each ten-second interval describe the type of behavior occurring during that time period. Describe procedures, analyze the data and develop conclusions supported by the data. Make suggestions for changes in the list of categories. Use the following categories:

Communication:

a. from teacher to total group
b. from teacher to part of group
c. from teacher to individual class members
d. from class member to teacher
e. from one class member to another
f. which cannot be classified in foregoing categories

Selected Readings

1. Good, Carter V., and Douglas E. Scates, *Methods of Research*. New York: Appleton-Century-Crofts, 1954. (Chapters 5 and 6)
2. Medley, Donald M., and Harold E. Mitzel, "Measuring Classroom Behavior by Systematic Observation," Gage, N. L. (Ed.) *Handbook of Research on Teaching*. American Educational Research Association, Chicago: Rand McNally & Company, 1963.
3. Sax, Gilbert, *Empirical Foundations of Educational Research*. Englewood Cliffs, New Jersey: Prentice-Hall, Inc., 1968. (Chapters 6, 7, and 8)
4. Travers, Robert, M. W., *An Introduction to Educational Research*, New York: The Macmillan Co., 1958 (Chapters VIII, IX and X)

Chapter 3

Library Research

One of the key factors which is the hallmark of the professions of medicine, engineering, and law is the ability of the members to use research findings from their own and related fields.

The professional educator must assimilate an increasing amount of knowledge to keep abreast of recent developments. Literally thousands of books, periodicals, documents, and pamphlets are placed on library shelves each year. Skill is required in making a comprehensive search for educational materials about a specific topic. A failure to develop these skills will lead to much wasted effort and frustration.

Although a knowledge of library methods is desirable for the consumer of research, it is essential for the research worker. Too often graduate students and other beginning research workers try to solve a problem without attempting to determine if others have conducted investigations in the same area.

This chapter, designed to help the consumer and research worker gain knowledge of library skills, is presented in three parts to emphasize that library study is not a meaningless activity but an essential ingredient of the systematic approach to problem solving. The sections include: (1) a statement of the purpose of library study, (2) a description of the sources utilized, and (3) suggestions of methods which will aid in the collection of data from printed sources.

Purpose

The purpose of library study is dictated by the activity involved. The educational practitioner uses the library to determine new developments which have a bearing on his speciality whatever it might be:[1] reading, the teaching of social studies, or the conduct of school business management. Although the research worker uses the library for somewhat different purposes, a knowledge of his use of the literature is essential to evaluate the quality and interpret the findings of studies.[2]

Determining Current Status

Before an educational researcher initiates a study he must first determine what has previously been done in the area. An investigation of the nature of learning among kindergarten children would require a knowledge of the works of Froebel, Thorndike, Montessori, Hull, Guthrie, Skinner, and others. In addition to these classic studies, a thorough knowledge of contemporary research in learning would be necessary. Current status in a specific area of education cannot be determined by skimming and by reading summaries of studies; intensive analysis is required. Determination of current status in a field of knowledge requires access to the most accurate sources available in education and related fields.

KNOW THE ORIGINAL SOURCE. Like rumor, the restating of conclusions presumably reached by a pioneer in a field of knowledge can result in gross distortion of the original findings. If Thorndike's law of effect is related to the problem selected for study, the original account of the investigation should be read. Descriptions of his work written by contemporary psychologists should not be considered a substitute for the original. When a study published in an unfamiliar language is to be used, a comparison of more than one translation of the original work should be made if at all possible. Although examination of original articles sometimes requires much time, the practice eliminates second-hand scholarship.

BE MORE INFORMED ABOUT OTHER DISCIPLINES. In researching a specific topic in education, the library search may extend to directly related fields such as psychology, social psychology, and sociology; however, books are catalogued and journals are classified on the basis of broad subject areas. As a result, the educational researcher may fail to encounter references to relevant studies in other areas such as medicine and the life sciences unless he takes special steps in addition to prescribed library search methods. Useful findings from other fields may not be

---

[1]See Chapter 11 for descriptions of research applications in the school.
[2]See Chapter 9 for a list of criteria to be used in evaluating published research.

utilized by educators because of a lack of communication among researchers in the various fields of study.

CRITICALLY ANALYZE AND COMPARE FINDINGS. More than a single study usually has been conducted relating to a problem area selected. The report of related studies must be analyzed line by line; even the meaning of each word must be determined, if possible. The purpose of this critical analysis is threefold. First, the quality of individual studies must be ascertained (see Chapter 9). Second, the findings of two or more studies should be analyzed to determine if investigators concurred in their findings and should be contrasted to identify differences in their conclusions. Disagreements of two or more competent investigators about the exact nature of facts leads to the third consideration, namely, a determination of the gaps in the existing body of knowledge. Library scholarship is essential for constructing a foundation upon which quality research can be built.

Before moving ahead, the research worker must be aware of what is known with some degree of certainty, what is accepted as truth by some but not by others, and must have some inkling of the nature of unexplored areas where additional research should be conducted.

Identification of Validated Procedures

Studies in education, especially the survey and the experimental design, necessitate the use of instruments such as questionnaires, schedules, attitude scales, rating scales and achievement tests, and apparatus such as mazes soundproofed booths, one-way mirrors and other devices. Development of valid and reliable instruments with which to conduct an investigation may require a great amount of time and effort. If appropriate, the use of instruments developed and validated by others will save time and serve also to relate the problem under study to other better known "facts." A survey of the literature can be initiated for the primary purpose of identifying valid instruments, proven methods, or appropriate apparatus.

To Establish Statistical Procedures

To formulate the null and alternate hypothesis for statistical analysis in an experimental design (see Chapter 6) an investigator may be justified in guessing tentatively the outcome of the research. This guess, or estimate, of the outcome should be based on research findings from similar investigations and related to a theoretical rationale. In comparing the relative merits of the phonic and sight method for teaching partially sighted children to read, for example, the investigator should examine previous research studies in which these methods were compared. He could make one of four decisions: (1) If no previous studies were conducted comparing the two methods, the probable outcome could not be ascertained; (2) If a number of competent researchers had compared the methods using various types of subjects (normal children, mentally retarded children, illiterate adults and adults learning English as a second language, for example) and some investigators had found the phonic method superior and others indicated that the sight method produced greater learning, then no probability would be established because of conflicting conclusions; (3) If a majority of previous studies indicated the superiority of the phonic method, probability would be established. The investigator would formulate his hypothesis with the "guess" that the phonic method would result in greater learning among partially sighted children; (4) If nearly all previous studies indicated that the sight method was superior; the hypothesis could be formulated to indicate greater gain from this method.

A review of related studies serves as a guide to what is acceptable and what is not acceptable verification of the hypothesis in question. The exact nature of the application of the principle of probability and the uses of statistical tests will be described in Chapter 6. Library research is used to establish the appropriateness of certain statistical tools and analytical methods in educational experiments.

To Improve Educational Practice

The most important purpose for conducting library research is to improve the effectiveness of educational practice. The aims previously described for library research were directed toward improving the quality of planned research investigations. All investigations in education, however, are aimed at improving the effectiveness of the classroom teacher. Quite clearly, if the teacher and school administrator do not familiarize themselves with results of studies, most of the effort expended by research workers will be wasted.

A thorough review of the literature should be made before school district personnel embark on an experimental educational program or make changes in existing programs which have proven satisfactory in the past. In addition to other considerations including acceptance by teachers, parents and members of the general public, change must follow a careful examination of related research findings. By utilizing the library, practicing educators can profit from the successes of others and eliminate or circumvent causes of failure.

Sources

Many excellent libraries are available to graduate students throughout the world. Because of the differences in organization of materials, detailed instructions about the use of a library may not be helpful; therefore, attention has to be focused on general sources and on methods which can serve in any library setting.

A useful method for learning about library sources is to visit the library where the research is to be carried out. First, contact the head librarian and arrange for a description of the sources and their location. A guided tour of the various sections of the library should follow. The initial orientation time can be spent browsing to become familiar with the location of various sections and departments. To aid in the process of learning about the library, major sources of use to educational researchers are described in the following seven sections: (1) standard references, (2) books, (3) legal sources, (4) periodicals or journals, (5) documents, (6) pamphlets and directories, and (7) unpublished materials.

Standard References

Certain references are consulted first whenever there is a systematic library search for educational topics. The librarian can provide information about the availability of these sources although the best way to become familiar with the basic educational references is to study the organization of their contents carefully. A selected list and brief description of basic references in education follows:

How to Locate Educational Information and Data.[3] The title suggests the logic of beginning with this volume.

Encyclopedia of Educational Research.[4] The volume contains summaries of research studies arranged by topics. The content of each topic has been prepared by a specialist who volunteered to summarize research findings for his specific area of interest. These summaries cannot be considered as substitutes for the original research reports but can be used for screening purposes to limit the scope of the library search. If a study appears relevant, a reference to the original source is provided at the end of each section. Because of the time required

---

[3]Carter Alexander, *How to Locate Educational Information and Data.* Fourth Edition, New York: Bureau of Publications, Teachers College, Columbia University, 1958.
[4]Chester W. Harris and Marie Liba, *Encyclopedia of Educational Research.* Association NEA, New York: The Macmillan Company, 1960.

to prepare such a comprehensive volume, studies in print less than one year before the publication date of the *Encyclopedia* will probably not be described in this source. Reference to more recently published articles can be found by consulting the *Education Index*.

REVIEW OF EDUCATIONAL RESEARCH.[5] This periodical, published five times each year, presents a comprehensive review of research in selected areas of educational interest and serves as a useful supplement to *The Encyclopedia of Educational Research*. A separate topic is reviewed in each issue and repeated during a three year cycle. Following is a list of subjects given recent coverage:

Adult Education
Curriculum Planning and Development
Educational and Psychological Testing
Educational Organization, Administration, and Finance
Educational Programs: Adolescence
Educational Programs: Early and Middle Childhood
Educational Programs: Later Adolescence
Educational Research in Countries Other than the United States
Exceptional Children
Growth, Development, and Learning
Guidance, Counseling, and Personnel Services
Higher Education
Human Relations in Education
Instructional Materials
Language Arts and Fine Arts
Mental and Physical Health
Methodology of Educational Research
Natural Sciences and Mathematics
Philosophical and Social Framework of Education
Teacher Personnel
Twenty-Five Years of Educational Research
Vocational, Technical, and Practical Arts Education

THE EDUCATION INDEX. The *Index* contains the most comprehensive available listing of topics relating to education. Reference is made not only to periodicals, bulletins, and documents but also to books. Completion of the specially selected exercises at the end of this chapter will introduce the reader to the comprehensiveness of this document.

THE DICTIONARY OF EDUCATION.[6] This volume contains a technical definition of most terms used in educational research investigations.

[5]American Research Association NEA, *Review of Educational Research*.
[6]Carter V. Goode (Ed), *Dictionary of Education*, Second Edition, New York: McGraw-Hill Book Company, 1959.

The volume is not only a valuable guide in ascertaining the meaning of unfamiliar words but also serves as a standard for preparing definitions used in research studies.

GUIDE TO REFERENCE BOOKS.[7] This source contains reference to a variety of reference books; included are listings of authors or organizations, titles, publishers and brief accounts of contents and scope. Specific sections include listings for bibliographies, libraries, societies, encyclopedias, periodicals or newspapers, government documents, dissertations and various subject categories including topics such as applied science and religion. This standard reference contains a reference to nearly all reference materials needed for library study. Supplements are issued periodically to update the listings.

OTHER SOURCES. Many other basic sources are available to aid in systematic search. Only the most important have been enumerated here. The utilization of these sources will be illustrated in the section describing methods (see page 67).

Books

Material included in textbooks and other expository works may contain authoritative information that is very helpful to the research worker. Unfortunately, the contents of books are seldom classified in external sources in sufficient detail to insure complete access by conventional search methods. A list of sources is presented following and special methods for identification are described on page 71.

AUTHOR SUBJECT CARD INDEX. All libraries contain card catalogues. Many provide an author-title index and a subject index. The author-title index is an alphabetical listing of all the titles and a separate listing for authors; for example, three cards would be found in the author-title index for a book titled *Recreation* by Jones and Smith, one under recreation and one for each author. A card entry would also be found under "recreation" in the subject catalogue and also, depending on the contents of the book, references may be found under "camping," "fishing," "wild life," "golf" or "bird watching."

Each card in the author-subject card index will usually contain either a cross reference to another card or information regarding the

---

[7]Constance M. Winchell, *Guide to Reference Books*, Seventh Edition. Chicago: American Library Association, 1951.

(1) author or authors, (2) title, (3) date of publication, (4) description of contents, and (5) Library of Congress card number.

INTERLIBRARY LOAN. In the event a book, unpublished master's thesis or doctoral dissertation is not to be found in the library, the interlibrary loan service may make it available. The interlibrary department can secure volumes from cooperating libraries at nominal cost. Users of the interlibrary loan service should expect an extended delay of several weeks to secure certain volumes. Although the Library of Congress contains one of the most comprehensive selections of volumes in the world, graduate students do not usually have access to this excellent source except under special circumstances.

SUBJECT HEADINGS.[8] This source published by the Library of Congress is a valuable adjunct to the card catalogue system developed by the college library. As an example, if the researcher is unable to find a desired topic in the regular card catalogue, use of *Subject Headings* will indicate other categories where the topic might be found. Because many libraries use *Subject Headings* as a guide for establishing subject card catalogues, this volume is usually conveniently located near the main card catalogue. The library staff can assist in its use.

BOOKS IN PRINT.[9] This source is an author and title series index to the *Publishers Trade List Annual*. It contains a listing of most books printed by 1,400 American publishers and includes more than 163,000 entries. Included is a reference to author, title, publisher and cost; however, books published in English in foreign countries, government documents, certain law volumes and many paperback editions are not listed. Listings are divided into two sections; in the first, publications are arranged alphabetically by author. The second section contains an alphabetical listing of titles. Often, when only the author or title of a work is known, *Books In Print* will enable the researcher to obtain sufficient additional information to provide a complete bibliographic reference.

CUMULATIVE BOOK INDEX.[10] Issued since 1938, this source contains a listing of all books published in the English language; therefore, its coverage is somewhat broader than *Books In Print*. The source, however, does not list government documents.

---

[8]Marguerite V. Quattlebaum (Ed.), *Subject Headings*. Washington, D. C.: The Library of Congress.
[9]Sarah L. Prahhen (Ed.), *Books in Print*. New York: R. R. Bowker Company.
[10]Nina R. Thompson (Ed.), *Cumulative Books Index*. New York: H. W. Wilson Company.

BOOKS OUT OF PRINT. Frequently the researcher is unable to obtain a published volume in the library or through an interlibrary loan. Several methods for acquiring such a source can be used. First, the librarian can be requested to place the bibliographic reference on an out-of-print list which is circulated among librarians and book readers. Second, he can examine listings in the *Antiquarian Bookman* available from Box 1100, Newark, New Jersey. This periodical contains commercial listings of rare and out-of-print volumes. Third, the researcher can contact University Microfilms, Ann Arbor, Michigan, to determine whether facsimiles of the volume are available on microfilm or xerographic enlargements.

Legal Sources

Legal references are an important source of information for the researcher interested in analyzing the development of social thought in our society. Records of past legislative acts and court decisions have long been recognized as a reflection of basic changes occurring in the fabric of society. In addition to a scholarly interest in legal proceedings, the practicing educator should possess sufficient skill in legal research to meet the day-to-day requirements for information arising out of the practice of his profession. Legal sources[11] can be divided into four categories, namely, dictionaries, codes, administrative regulations, and court decisions.

LAW DICTIONARY. Before attempting to read laws and particularly legal decisions, the researcher should have access to a law dictionary. The *Law Dictionary*, edited by A. C. Black, is a standard legal reference. In addition, the educational researcher may need assistance in interpreting certain legal material. The aid of a law professor or practising attorney should be solicited when required.

CODES. Legal codes contain a list of laws enacted by the federal and state legislative bodies. Federal codes are listed in official sources in two ways: (1) serially by data and (2) by topic. The *Statutes At Large* contain a listing of each law arranged according to the date it was approved by the President; however, the *Statutes At Large* does not reflect subsequent amendments in laws. A more useful source for the current status of federal law is the *United States Code* in which federal laws are classified into more than fifty subject titles. Commercially

---

[11]For a detailed description of the use of legal sources for research in the social sciences see E. E. Schattschneider, Victor Jones and Stephen K. Bailey, *A Guide to the Study of Public Affairs*, New York: William P. Sloane Associates, 1952, Chapters 8 and 9.

prepared equivalents of the *United States Code* are the *United States Code Annotated* and *Federal Code Annotated.* These sources are superior because they contain numerous references to administrative regulations, judicial decisions and other federal statutes relating to a specific law; the reference notes enable the researcher to identify other developments which may change the interpretation of the statutes.

Each state has a system of codification of laws enacted by the legislatures. An accessible and usable source of the laws of individual states can be found in the West or Deerings series of *Annotated State Codes.* In these volumes, the laws of each state are classified into sections such as education, welfare, highways, and other topics. A supplement in the back of each volume reflects changes in the law which have occurred since the publication of the volumes. The commercial editions of state codes contain references to related judicial opinions and statutes. Both federal codes and the code of the local state laws can be found in most university libraries. Only large law libraries contain complete sets of codes for all of the states.

ADMINISTRATIVE REGULATIONS. Statutes frequently outline policy and delegate the responsibility for its administration to administrative agencies. Federal laws relating to allocation of funds for education, for example, frequently list the Department of Health Education and Welfare, Office of Education, as the agency responsible for administering provisions of the act. Regulations enacted by the Office of Education and by other federal agencies are listed in two sources. The *Federal Register* is a daily publication of administrative regulations of the President and governmental agencies. These regulations are codified in the *Code of Federal Regulations.* Topics used to classify administrative regulations are arranged in a manner similar to the classification of statutes in the *United States Code.* Administrative enactments which are not law in the sense they are enacted by legislative bodies nevertheless have the force of law in many instances. They have been called administrative laws.

Most states publish administrative codes listing the rules and regulations of agencies and boards at the order of state legislatures. Proceedings of state educational bodies such as state boards of education are incorporated in administrative codes. These regulations govern the actions of local school districts as well as other educational institutions.

COURT DECISIONS. While much of organized law has been established through legislative action, the courts are also guided by previous judicial decisions. These decisions may interpret, modify, and negate legislation, Courts may also render decisions relating to matters which have no reference in the federal or state statutes. The judicial decisions provide a rich resource for the educational historian or for authorities dealing with school law.

One of the most important groups of judicial decisions are those of the United State Supreme Court. The record of proceedings can be found in the series *United States Reports*. The cases are arranged according to the date the decisions were made. In addition to the principal decision, the volume contains concurring opinions of justices who agree with decisions of the court but disagree with some of the reasons cited by the majority. Dissenting opinions listing arguments of justices who disagreed with the majority opinion are also listed. References to specific cases are made according to the volume and page number of the *Reports*; for example, *Maryland v. Baltimore Radio Show*, 338 U.S. 912, refers to volume 338, page 912 of the *Reports*. Prior to 1875, the name of the court reporter is listed in place of the citation U.S.[12]

References to cases brought before lesser state and federal courts can be found in the *National Reporter System*. Coverage includes the *Federal Reporter* citing appellate and other federal court decisions. The regional reports deal with state court cases in various sections of the country. The *Northeastern Reporter*, for example, includes cases from the states of Illinois, Indiana, Massachusetts, New York, and Ohio.[13]

Periodicals or Journals

Periodicals and journals usually contain more recent accounts of current research than standard references or books. Utilization of periodical references will enable the researcher to examine the results of studies soon after they are completed. Further, original sources of classic studies are frequently found in periodicals. The principal reference to studies in education is described following, together with a number of important guides to other sources. The most important source of educational information, the *Education Index*, has already been described.

Other Indexes and Abstracts

A list of other indexes which may be available in the library follows:

Agricultural Index
Applied Science & Technology Index

---

[12]Schattschneider et al., op. cit., p. 112.
[13]Ibid, p. 121.

Art Index
Bibliographic Index
Biography Index
Biological Abstracts
Book Review Digest
Business Education Index
Business Periodicals Index
Chemical Abstracts
Child Development Abstracts
Engineering Index
Essay and General Literature Index
Index Medicus
International Index to Periodicals
Music Index
Psychological Abstracts
Public Affairs Information Service
Readers' Guide to Periodical Literature
Science Abstracts
Sociological Abstracts

A number of these indexes such as the *Art Index, Biological Index, Business Education Index, Music Index,* and *Science Abstracts* have direct interest for educators conducting research in these areas. The *Child Development Abstracts, Psychological Abstracts and Sociological Abstracts* contain many references relating directly to educational matters as well as research studies relating to theories of anxiety, role analysis, and organizational behavior which complement research conducted by educational researchers. Knowledge of other disciplines frequently enriches and adds a new dimension to educational knowledge.

Newspapers

Newspapers often constitute an excellent record of past events. Public officials and attorneys utilize newspaper accounts to determine the legality of certain action taken by boards of education. The educational historian or chronicler will find newspapers a rich reference source. The most authoritative index to newspaper articles reflecting a national interest is the *New York Times Index* issued since 1913. Although many libraries do not have original editions of the *Times,* many possess microflim copies. The *Index* is published monthly with yearly summaries. Topics are arranged alphabetically. Each entry briefly describes the contents, lists the date the article appeared in the *Times* and its page and column number.

In addition to the *New York Times,* back copies of regional and local papers are available in many libraries on microfilm. Even many small public libraries have copies of local dailies or weeklies. Files of actual copies of old newspapers are maintained by some libraries and publishers although storage presents a serious problem. Local and state historical societies should be contacted concerning the location of extant newspaper collections.

Documents

Documents are publications issued by the federal and state governments. They provide excellent sources of information but because of the number of publications, diversity of topics, and variety of agencies involved, ready access to specific sources is difficult.

FEDERAL DOCUMENTS. Government documents provide a rich reference source frequently bypassed in routine library searches. Of particular interest is the record of testimony delivered before investigating committees. Because of the wide range of federal government activity, expert testimony and supporting data relating to topics of interest to many education researchers can be found in government documents. In addition, regular publications of the Department of Health, Education and Welfare constitute an authoritative source describing educational statistics for the fifty states.

Documents published by the federal government are listed in the *Guide To United States Government Publications,* published monthly, annually and decennially. Publications are listed in two ways. First, each agency is listed alphabetically and any publications issued from this body during the time period covered by the guide are subsumed under this heading; for example, most educational publications would be listed under the heading "Department of Health, Education and Welfare of the Office of Education." Second, all publications issued during a given period are listed by titles in the second section of the *Guide.*

Coverage of certain governmental functions is not complete. Instructions in the Guide indicate that some records of testimony heard by congressional committees are available in published form. Specific congressional bills are seldom published and the reader is referred to his congressman for copies. Information is also listed in the Guide as to whether the publication can be obtained from the Government Printing Office or from the issuing agency.

College libraries have devised various methods for cataloguing government documents. Some are designated as depositories for these documents; others are not. Inquiries made of library staff personnel will indicate the method of cataloguing government documents and their accessibility.

STATE DOCUMENTS. Documents issued by state governments often can be found in indexes of state publications. A few of the more circulated state documents relating to education are listed in the *Education Index*. Information concerning publication for which bibliographic data are available can be secured by contacting the state agency which issued the publication.

Pamphlets and Directories

Pamphlets include publications of local governmental and private agencies which do not exceed a certain number of pages. Examples would include public relations releases issued by private organizations, information bulletins, conference notices, manuals and handbooks issued by local governmental and educational agencies. Some libraries catalogue these publications in the regular cataloguing system, thus references to pamphlets can be found in the card catalogue. The location and method used for cataloguing pamphlets can be found by consulting the library staff.

Directories are an essential tool in drawing a sample from a known population for the purpose of circulating a questionnaire. If the investigator wishes to ascertain the opinions of city managers concerning the role of schools in city government, for example, he will need a list of all city managers in the area of the study. From this "population" of names, a sample could be chosen. All names of city managers can be found in *The Municipal Year Book* issued by the International City Managers Association. Similarly, a survey of a sample of curriculum consultants, school principals or teachers would make necessary a list of these individuals. The local college librarian can be of assistance in finding specific directories.

Unpublished Materials

Results of most recently conducted research studies quite frequently are first available in unpublished form. Many worthwhile studies in addition to masters' theses and doctoral dissertations do not appear in published form. These include papers presented at conferences, intern research reports, studies conducted for associations and groups and the product of the efforts of school district personnel. The assumption should not be made that the highest quality research is always published in journals. On the contrary, because of the limited interest in certain topics, valuable studies may not be included in the conventional educational research journals. A number of sources which list unpublished material are described following.

MASTERS' THESES. Two useful listings of masters' theses include *Masters' Theses In Education*[14] and *Masters' Abstracts*.[15] The former source has been published for a number of years and includes a title and short description of masters' theses completed by degree candidates at major colleges and universities. The second source, *Masters' Abstracts*, is relatively new. It contains a short summary of studies completed by masters' candidates of contributing institutions. Copies of masters' theses listed in the *Abstracts* can be obtained in microfilm or xerographic enlargements from the publisher.

DOCTORAL DISSERTATION. In comparison with masters' theses, a more complete listing of doctoral dissertations is available. Most dissertations submitted to colleges and universities in the United States can be found listed in a number of sources.

Doctoral Dissertations Accepted By American Universities includes most dissertations accepted by higher institutions since 1933. This listing service has been replaced by *Dissertation Abstracts*[16] which contains a short summary of each study including a brief statement of findings. The beginning researcher is cautioned, however, to obtain a copy of the original investigation through the interlibrary loan service or from the publishers of the *Abstracts* before citing the results in a research study. Proper evaluation of the research findings can be made only by examining the entire document.

The *Phi Delta Kappan* publishes listings of "Doctors' Dissertations Under Way in Education" and "Doctoral Studies Completed In Education." Further information concerning investigations under way can be obtained by contacting the institution or graduate candidate directly. Copies of completed investigations can be obtained from *Dissertation Abstracts* or through interlibrary loans.

OTHER UNPUBLISHED SOURCES. Other unpublished sources can be found in the pamphlets section of the library in the card catalogue or in special field service collections. Direct contact can be made with associations and school districts where certain types of research are known to be under way.

Unpublished research studies provide a rich source of information for the investigator who desires to give an accurate portrayal of the

---

[14]Iowa State Teachers College, *Masters' Theses in Education.* Cedar Falls, Iowa: Bureau of Research.

[15]*Masters' Abstracts.* Ann Arbor, Michigan: University Microfilm, Inc.

[16]*Dissertation Abstracts.* Ann Arbor, Michigan: University Microfilm, Inc.

present status of knowledge in a specific educational area. The sources, however, are less systematically organized and catalogued than other published sources.

Methods

The most effective methods for utilizing library resources depend to a certain extent on the facilities and organization of the library which is available. As mentioned previously, consultation with library staff members will prove a valuable aid in obtaining the most effective use of this source. Methods for library use can be described as note-keeping, standard search procedures and other search methods.

Note-Keeping

A systematic method for collecting information will help the investigator utilize the results of library research more fully. In conducting a historical study, an extensive content analysis, or a comprehensive survey to determine the current status of knowledge in a special field, the researcher may collect material from a great many sources for future use. He must develop a method for recording and filing notes that maximizes accuracy and minimizes time spent in nonproductive clerical work.

NOTE CARDS. Note cards are most convenient for recording notes from printed sources. Most commonly used sizes are 4 x 6 or 5 x 8 inches. Entries on the card can be made in handwriting; however, if a typewriter can be used in the library, note-taking is faster, especially when quantities of material are to be recorded verbatim.

Entries on note cards should be arranged to facilitate ease of access when the materials are being analyzed for writing the research report. The cards can be filed in small recipe boxes, steel files or fibre folders.

Cards should be indexed in two ways — by author and subject. The card should be arranged with the author's surname listed in the upper left-hand corner, using the standard bibliographic reference form. Cards can then be filed alphabetically by author. If more than a single topic is covered in the survey and if large numbers of cards are collected, a system of coding by topic is desirable. One method involves placing colored marks or metal tabs in various positions on top of the card. The colors and the positions utilized on the cards provide a different combination to indicate a number of separate topics.

MECHANICAL SYSTEMS. Key sort systems can be used to classify extensive notes obtained from surveys of the literature. The key sort system consists of cards with a number of holes in all four margins, a filing cabinet and thin steel rod. When the cards are filed, designated holes are punched out of them indicating specific topics; later when notes relating to a specific topic are needed, the steel rod is pushed through the designated hole of the entire file of cards. Those cards which have the designated hole opened will fall from the stack of cards and the others will be retained. The use of key sort cards eliminates the need to alphabetize or otherwise organize the cards in the file to assure ready access.

COMPUTER STORAGE. With the development of computer storage systems, a means is available to store many items of information for almost instant future access. The system has been used for accounting and inventory control purposes. It can provide a means for storing information gathered from very extensive surveys of the literature. Items of information gathered from library research can be coded, fed into a computer and the magnetic impulses stored in discs or magnetic tape. When the information is needed at a later date, certain instructions can be fed into the machine and the desired information can be made available in printed form almost immediately.

CONTENT. What information should be recorded on note cards? The following items of information are absolutely essential:

1. A complete bibliographic listing including the library call number, placed at the top of the card.
2. The page number from which specific items of information have been taken.
3. The exact wording of passages which are to be listed later as direct quotations.
4. A note indicating how the source can be located.

These items enable the investigator to make accurate references to the sources at a later date when the report is written.

SCOPE. Should the investigator paraphrase or record statements verbatim as they are listed in the library sources? Paraphrasing saves time and provides the beginning researcher with practice in analyzing passages, obtaining facts and determining the ideas and attitudes expressed by the author. The process also increases the possibility of error. The person preparing the notes can project his own attitudes and bias and perhaps distort the meaning intended by the author whose work is being reviewed. Frequently, information recorded on note cards is not immediately utilized by the investigator and may be placed in storage for a long period of time. Paraphrased passages thus may lose much of their original meaning.

Limitations imposed by paraphrasing can be overcome if items from the original source are recorded word for word. Although this takes more time, the possibility for distortion is reduced. The use of a typewriter to record notes from sources enables the investigator to record a great deal of information in a short time. Care must be taken, however, to include sufficient information from the printed source to avoid quoting out of context.

For purposes of critically analyzing the results of research studies, reproduction of the entire study should be obtained. Most libraries have book copiers for photo reproduction of material from bound volumes. To avoid its high cost, the publishers of journals can be contacted to determine if reprints of studies are available.

The researcher must exercise judgment in selecting and accurately recording the essential parts of printed materials.

Standard Search Procedures

Following is a description of two phases in library search procedures which can be utilized in nearly all college and university libraries:

1. DETERMINATION OF TOPICS. The key to a successful library search is proper selection of key topic words, signposts which will guide the researcher through the labyrinth of library sources. The list of topics should be developed with the aid of the *Education Index*. After determining the area for which the survey is developed, a list of words should be made which describes the topic. For instance, assume the researcher wishes to study the literature dealing with methods for teaching arithmetic to underachievers. The topic employed in the *Education Index* should be examined to determine those which deal with arithmetic methods and underachievers or slow learners. The list of topics selected will appear in most of the editions of the *Education Index* extending back to 1929 and will serve as a guide to articles concerning education appearing in the *International Index* dating to 1907. The selected topics will also serve as a guide to the subject index of the library card catalogue. The final list of search topics should be recorded for the researcher's use and can be listed in the written report to indicate the scope of the library search.

2. FINDING SOURCES. Once the list of topics has been developed, the investigator can begin the process of methodically examining each listing of books and periodicals. The *Education Index* should be used first. Begin with the most recent edition of the *Index*. Consult each of the key topics and work back through older

editions. For certain topics such as developments relating to the National Defense Education Act, the search need not be continued prior to when the date reference to the Act could first be expected to appear in the literature. For studies dealing with learning, the investigator may find a need to continue the search into the earlier literature dealing with education or educational psychology.

Many of the journal articles listed under the appropriate topics in the Index can be eliminated from consideration by examining the titles. Experienced investigators recognize the need to develop titles which to the greatest extent possible accurately describe the contents of articles and research reports. Certain references can be rejected as inappropriate merely by examining the title. A list should be made of journal articles and books with titles which indicate a relationship to the selected topics. Sufficient bibliographic information should be recorded to insure location of the sources.

Usually the researcher should collect topics from the most recent yearly edition of the *Education Index,* review the sources and then continue the search to the preceding edition. In this way topic headings which result in the identification of unusable sources can be discarded from the topic list before the entire search is completed.

An examination of the most recent sources will provide bibliographies to earlier works which may be useful. A list of these should be compiled and checked off when the search is continued in earlier editions of the *Index.*

After the search of the *Education Index* has been completed, additional sources should be obtained from other basic sources described on page 56. Reference to the detailed index in the *Encyclopedia of Educational Research* will produce commentaries which give a general overview of the topics. At the end of each section, bibliographies are listed. These can be checked against titles selected and reviewed and new references noted. Issues of the *Review of Educational Research* can be examined for additional references; however, articles from the Review are listed in the *Education Index* under the subheading "Research."

An important source of information concerning current research not in published form can be obtained by examining copies of the *Dissertation Abstracts* or the *Masters' Abstracts* which contain a short summary of doctoral dissertations and masters' theses completed by graduate students in subscribing institutions. If the description of the study indicates it contains needed information, the complete work should be obtained through the interlibrary loan service or from the publishers of *Dissertation Abstracts.*

The description of standard search procedures presented in the preceding paragraphs emphasizes one principle. It is absolutely necessary to refer to original sources; use commentaries on and summaries of research only as a means of identifying original sources.

Other Search Methods

In addition to standard search procedures outlined, these further steps are recommended to broaden the investigator's scope of inquiry beyond the traditional boundaries.

1. COURSE WORK IN OTHER DISCIPLINES. A graduate survey course can provide a means for the investigator to become familiar with other areas which may have a bearing on the subject of the investigation. Doctoral candidates with dissertation topics relating to other disciplines such as psychology, political science, economics, history or sociology are counseled into appropriate courses at this level. The assigned readings and lectures offer an opportunity to select pertinent areas of these disciplines to add to the body of educational knowledge.

2. READERS. Reader is a name commonly used to designate selections of works which have been collected into one volume with editorial comments and explanation by the editors. The readers present an excellent source for the educational researcher who wishes to gain knowledge about other academic areas. One example of a reader is the two volume series *Theories of Society.*[17] It contains a rather complete listing of the classic works of sociology together with copious comments and explanations. Other readers are available which deal with nearly every major field of knowledge.

3. THE INTERDISCIPLINARY TEAM. The interdisciplinary team is increasingly utilized in a number of large scale educational research endeavors. The sociologist, psychologist, historian, social psychologist, political scientist, anthropologist and philosopher can add new perspective to a problem which may be considered essentially educational in nature. Some debate exists concerning the

---

[17]Talcott Parsons, Edward Shils, Kaspar D. Naegele, and Jesse R. Pitts, *Theories of Society,* Vol. I and II. Glencoe, Illinois: The Free Press of Glencoe, Inc., 1961.

point during study development when talent from other areas should be utilized. Some feel that personnel from related disciplines should be involved during the planning stages while others assert that the outside expert is most helpful after the preliminary plan for the study has been made. In any event, individuals with training in noneducational discipline, professionals, professors or graduate students, can be of assistance to the researcher.

4. Browsing. Many graduate students have encountered a study with important implications for their investigation while browsing through books and periodicals. The ease of browsing depends on the physical organization of library facilities. When books and periodicals are catalogued in open stacks without restrictions, browsing can be more easily accomplished than when each book or periodical must be checked out prior to examination.

Selected Exercises

1. Which of the following is not a purpose of library study? Why?
   ....determine current status
   ....predict future events
   ....improve educational practice in the field
   ....relate findings from other disciplines
   ....perfect instruments and apparatus
2. Would one consult the *Encyclopedia of Educational Research* to find descriptions of the most recent research dealing with team teaching? Why?
3. What difficulties are encountered in attempting to find references to government documents dealing with educational opportunities in government service?
4. Explain why summaries of doctoral studies presented in *Dissertation Abstracts* should not be used for purposes of analyzing related literature.
5. List the advantages and disadvantages gained from paraphrasing.

Suggested Activities

1. Using the title "Seasonal Variations in School Tax Election Results," consult the topics included in the *Education Index* and list those which would serve as a guide to related studies.
2. Find the exact date of the following events, and include a brief quotation from a newspaper in which each event was described.
   a. Lindberg's Atlantic flight

      b. The elimination of intercollegiate football at the University of Chicago

      c. General Eisenhower's appointment as president of Columbia University

      d. Passage of the National Defense Education Act

      e. The establishment of the Civilian Conservation Corps

3. Find the following references in the library. Describe the exact process used to locate each source.

      a. Reisner, Edward H., "Philosophy and Science in the Western World; A Historical Overview." NSSE, *The Forty-First Yearbook*: Part I Philosophies of Education.

      b. Educational Facilities Laboratory, *The Cost of a Schoolhouse*. New York: EFL, 1960.

      c. Rockefeller, Nelson A. "Our Public Schools and an Expanding Economy." *Your AASA in Nineteen Fifty-Nine-Sixty,* official report of the American Association of School Administrators for the year 1959.

      d. Griffiths, Daniel E. *Research in Educational Administration.* New York: Bureau of Publications Teachers College, Columbia University, 1959.

      e. Board of Governors, *The Federal Reserve System, Washington,* D. C., 1954.

      f. NEA "Small-Sample Techniques," *Research Bulletin,* Vol. 38, No. 4.

      g. Coleman, W., "Susceptibility of the Minnesota Teacher Attitude Inventory to 'Faking' with Experienced Teachers." *Educ. Admin. Superv.,* 1954, 40, 234-237.

      h. Jospen, N., "Contribution of Especially Designed Sound Motion Pictures to the Learning of Skills." Unpublished Doctoral dissertation, Pennsylvania State University, 1949.

Selected Readings

GOOD, CARTER V. AND DOUGLAS E. SCATES, *Methods of Research*. New York: Appleton-Century-Crofts, 1954, Chapter III.

VAN DALEN, DEOBOLD B. AND WILLIAM J. MEYER, *Understanding Educational Research*. New York: McGraw-Hill Book Company, 1962. Chapter 6 and pp. 340-364.

Chapter 4

Rationale for Collecting Data

The number of facts which presently exist, have existed in the past, and will exist in the future is beyond comprehension. The researcher with access to these innumerable facts has the option of choosing among them at will. He can select only those bits of information which support his position and consciously or unconsciously reject contradictory evidence. As a result, with slight exaggeration, the statement can be made that the truth or falsity of any proposition can be established provided sufficient data are studied from a biased viewpoint. Because the results of educational research are frequently used to make decisions about curricula that affect a large number of children, those conducting and using research studies have a responsibility to establish facts which are as accurate as possible. The methods used to collect data often establish the confidence with which the results of the study can be used to improve educational practice.

Some of the methods which give a study direction and increase the veracity of the findings are described in the sections which follow. One word of caution is appropriate, however; the form and style of research studies differ depending on the type of training and the research purpose of the investigator. A study should not be negatively evaluated solely on the basis that it does not conform to the style described in this volume. A rather precise form will be presented to enable beginning researchers to structure creditable investigations and to permit consumers of research to make analyses of existing works. Competently conducted studies may not, however, appear to contain all of the elements described as desirable in the following pages. Diversity of thinking should be encouraged in educational research as well as all fields of endeavor.

In this chapter important basic principles which provide the orientation and understructure for the data-gathering process will be described. The importance of developing a clear, concise statement of the problem is given additional emphasis. The nature of proof and the contribution of theory to the advancement of knowledge is followed by a description of operational definitions and methods used to establish the precision and validity of data-gathering instruments. In Chapter 2, specific research methods are described.

Form Used in Stating Purposes

Several initial remarks can be listed about the statement which sets forth the purpose of the investigator. First, it should be explicitly stated. Some investigators describe in general what they have done while conducting the study but fail to make an exact, concise statement of the central purpose of the research effort. In other instances, the purpose is buried in a paragraph describing background or hidden among speculations about the contribution the study will make to the field of knowledge. To aid in identifying the statement of purpose as well as other important sections of the report, appropriate headings can be used as signposts to guide the reader through the research report.

A second concern involves the use of the word "problem"; educational research is replete with references to problems. The extensive reliance on this word is unfortunate, since it indicates a negative rather than a positive assertion which phrases such as "fact to be explained" or "area to be investigated" convey to the reader. Further, the use of "problem" indicates a slavishness to practical concerns with less attention to the theoretical, nonapplied aspects of educational phenomena. No doubt because of tradition, the term "problem" will continue in use; however, a full realization of the implications of using the term should be clearly understood.

Third, the proper scope of the statement of purpose is the subject of some debate. Should the statement be long, detailed, and specific or short and general, leaving a more detailed listing of specifics to a later section? A good rule to observe in writing a statement of purpose is to match the scope with the area to which generalizations are to be made. The study of school district voting behavior in which the generalizations were restricted to the district investigated, for example, might have as a statement of purpose "Voting Behavior During Tax Increase Elections in Wilson School District." If, however, valid generalization to the entire nation could be made, the statement of purpose might be stated as follows: "Voting Behavior During Tax Increase Elections."

Irrespective of other factors, the purpose of the investigator should be clearly stated and located in the written report so that it can be easily identified. In addition to location, generality, and length of the statement, logic, grammar and content should be given special attention while formulating the purposes of the study.

Logic

Logical words give language its form. Their use indicates the connection between ideas and concepts which are to be communicated. The following two statements of purpose are identical except for the logical words *or* and *and*. (1) "Is a child's performance in the early grades affected most by maturation *and* the psychodynamic structure of his environment?" (2) "Is a child's performance in early school grades affected most by maturation *or* the psychodynamic structure of his environment?" The first question indicates a dual contribution to school performance while the second indicates a mutually exclusive relation between physical growth and development and social development. Each question conveys an idea which is somewhat contradictory to the other. Attention to logical form is essential in structuring statements of purpose or problem to be investigated.

Problems or purposes of an investigation can be stated in many logical forms. They can, for example, be stated as a question, "Is the sight method superior to the phonic method for teaching physically handicapped children to read?" or as a proposition. The purpose of the study is to determine if the sight method is superior to the phonic method for teaching physically handicapped children to read."

Hypotheses, on the other hand, may be stated in the form of the universal conditional: if x, then y, or more simply, if this occurs and these conditions are present, then this will happen. Let us take the example cited previously: If physically handicapped are taught to read and the sight method and phonic method are employed, *then* the growth in reading achievement of children who are physically handicapped and taught by the sight method will be greater than that of the children who are physically handicapped and are taught to read by the phonic method. By reducing the statement of purpose to the hypothesis in universal conditional form, the methods required to demonstrate or refute the truth of the proposition become more evident to the researcher.

Grammar

Currently a controversy exists between grammarians and semanticists about the importance of adhering to the strict rules of grammar in literary works and expository writing. Grammarians tend to disapprove of deviations from the formal rules of sentence structure, punctuation, and syntax while the semanticists place priority on clarity rather than form. Social scientists and educational researchers tend to take the middle-of-the-road position. Generally, their writing endorses the principles of clarity; however, few employ words not well established in dictionary vocabularies or sentence form which may offend grammarians.

Content

Grammar indicates the correct relations among words in a sentence; logicians are concerned as to how assertions stated in sentences are related. Grammar and logic, however, can be studied without reference to the meaning of the words in the sentence; more specifically, sentences can have correct grammatical and logical structure without the use of words which convey a specific meaning. Consider "if x and y, then z." Until the meanings of x, y and z are known, the statement lacks sufficient specificity to be informative.

The words which give specific meaning to sentences are called descriptive words. Unfortunately, some researchers use terms such as attitude, motivation, interest and learning which are as vague as the x, y and z cited in the previous example. To communicate the purpose of an investigation, the research worker must clearly state what is indicated by the descriptive words he uses. Consider the statement, "Motivation increases learning." As stated, the descriptive terms motivation and learning lack specificity. Learning what? Learning by whom? Rats, children, sophomore college psychology students? What is meant by motivation? Willingness to learn? How is the degree of learning determined? What tests are given? When? Numerous questions present themselves to the discerning reader. To make a meaningful contribution to the field of knowledge, the significance of descriptive terms which indicate the content of the statement of purpose must be clearly understood by the reader as well as by the writer. Operational definitions, described later in the chapter, aid in giving specific meanings to descriptive words.

What Constitutes Proof?

What kind of evidence offers proof that a statement is true or false? What is a fact? An understanding of the relation among evidence, proof, and the initial statement of purpose is essential to developing or evaluating research studies. Some general principles are described in the following paragraphs.

Nature of Facts

Facts are occurrences or states, the existence of which can be verified. A statement by a member of the board of education during a meeting concerning the need for additional classrooms can be verified by consulting the school board minutes. If this source of verification proves unsatisfactory because the member's remarks were not recorded, then testimony of eye witnesses and newspaper accounts can be used in verification. The statement is a fact. In contrast, George Wilson's dream described in a diary is not a fact because no means are available for verification.

The results of a study which indicate that rats learn to make their way through a maze more rapidly when food is encountered at the end can be considered fact if the experiment is described in sufficient detail to permit replication and similar results are observed.

Verifiability presents a serious obstacle when the researcher deals with states of being such as motivation, ego, test anxiety, anger or frustration. Should all research efforts directed at determining the nature of unverifiable states be discarded as useless? No, not if a distinction is made between facts and theories. The latter refer to events or states of being that are invented to explain certain observable or verifiable phenomena. Theories will be described later in this chapter.

The researcher should not confuse facts with the interpretation of facts. To convince the reader, the research worker must present his facts in a manner which makes verification possible. The interpretation of facts, which presumably follows from the nature of the data, is separated from it. All therefore can agree on what happened even though the reader's opinion as to why it happened may differ from the writer's interpretation.

From Known to Unknown

The researcher usually attempts to relate an unknown concept to one which is better known. Consider the following example: In stating problems or purposes, if the universal conditional, "if x then y," is not employed directly, the statement can nevertheless be reduced to this general form. Consider: "If high I.Q. pupils and average I.Q. pupils hear classical music, then appreciation will be greater for high I.Q. pupils." I.Q. is the independent variable — a component of the if part or premise of the statement. Music is a treatment variable and appreciation is the dependent variable or the content of the consequent portion of the "if x then y" statement.

The intelligence quotient is considered a well established concept of mental alertness, and many valid measures of intelligence have been developed. The researcher would have a number of acceptable methods (tests) which could be used to establish the intelligence quotient of subjects of an investigation. Music appreciation, however, is not a well established concept; at least in terms of quantification. Perhaps the investigator would, of necessity, be compelled to develop a measure specifically for the study.

Because more is known and accepted about intelligence measurement than about music appreciation, the investigator is using a well established concept to "explain" a less well accepted concept. His work will perhaps be more acceptable to critics than if he tried to relate two relatively unestablished concepts such as those of the following problem: Do pupils with an appreciation of intellectual activities also appreciate classical music?" In this second example neither the independent variable, appreciation of intellectual activities (the x in if x, then y), nor the dependent variable, music appreciation (y) are as well accepted as the concept of intelligence.

To build on present knowledge, propositions concerning undefined or unmeasured qualities usually should be related to better known concepts.

Avoiding ad hoc Explanations

An ad hoc explanation is a statement explaining a special case as opposed to explanations which are more inclusive in nature. Because scientists generally seek statements of laws that are as general as possible, ad hoc explanation should be avoided in research. Further, the need for ad hoc explanations indicates weakness in the basic structure of the study. As an illustration, consider the researcher who studied voting behavior during school bond elections and the editorial sentiments expressed in the local small town weekly newspaper. The statement of purpose was described as follows: "Has the editorial policy of the *Johnson Courier* influenced the results of bond elections for the Johnson School District?" A careful investigation of the 1964 school bond campaign indicated that even though opposition sentiment was expressed in the *Courier*, the measure passed 700 to 300. Further, it was noted that many of the long-standing residents opposed the election and that newcomers to the community of Johnson did not read the

Courier. The ad hoc explanation given by the researcher was that the *Courier's* editorial policy would have had an influence if the majority of voters in the district had read the weekly. The necessity for an ad hoc explanation could have been avoided if the purpose of the study had been stated as follows: "Will a person who resides in Johnson, participates in school bond elections, and reads the *Courier* be influenced in his voting by the editorial policy of the paper?"

The conditions required to avoid reliance on ad hoc explanations need not be listed in the initial statement of purpose. The delimitation section of the study may provide ground rules for the collection of data which obviate the use of these special explanations.

The Use of Theory

Many aspects of behavior which are the concern of the social scientist and educator cannot be directly observed. Examples include forces which are said to direct human activities. These include motives and drives, intellectual processes such as creativity and intelligence, and affective predispositions which are labeled attitudes, interests, and opinions. Theoretical terms or constructs and the meanings affixed to them have been developed by social scientists to explain why certain types of behavior occur. Why does Sally receive straight *A* grades and Billy only *C*'s and *D*'s? A combination of the constructs intelligence, creativity, and motivation can be used to account for the differences between the two children.

Theory is indispensable in stimulating the development of knowledge. Without the theory of atomic structure, atomic members and weights, valence, light rays, the means of chemical combination, radioactivity and atomic energy would be without a satisfactory explanation. Lacking the "whole is greater than the sum of its parts" concept which is the core of Gestalt psychology, concepts of closure, insight, and many other higher order mental processes possibly would not exist.

Need for Theory

Critics have frequently censured educational researchers as being too concerned with *what* the relations among various types of behavior are and too little concerned with the reasons *why*. An explanation of why usually precipitates the use of theoretical constructs. Conversely, some state that the literature abounds with theories, some of dubious value. More attention, they say, should be directed toward perfecting methods of collecting and analyzing data to raise existing theories to a higher level of predictive value. Although there is disagreement about the methods for theory development, most authorities acknowledge the worth of theory in adding to the known body of knowledge. Some caution about the use of theory and constructs should, however, be stated.

LAW OF PARSIMONY. The law of parsimony places emphasis on the need to make explanations of behavior as simple as possible and consistent with observations. If a child is observed falling from a ladder, for example, one might conclude that the child was driven by Thanatos, Freud's death wish. A more parsimonious explanation would be that the child's foot slipped because the rungs of the ladder were wet. Further investigation, which could be used to confirm the second explanation, might confirm the presence of water, oil, or some other slippery substance on the rungs of the ladder. Or some psychological problem could be identified through careful analysis of the child's background that would lead us to partially reject at least the rational aspects of behavior. The explanation or theory nevertheless should be as uncomplicated as possible to be consistent with the observed behavior. Violations of the law of parsimony often lead to a vast superstructure of theoretical speculation that contributes little, if any, to the science of education.

REIFICATION. Treating theoretical constructs as if they actually existed is called reification. Consider the construct inferiority complex, now abandoned by most psychologists. Initially the term was used to explain a certain syndrome of behavior which included apparent feelings of worthlessness and compensatory acting-out behavior. Reification of the construct inferiority complex led to such statements as "George has an inferiority complex; William does not. Sally's inferiority complex is greater than George's, but Roger's is greater than the sum of both Sally's and George's." Although somewhat exaggerated, the example cites the misuse of theoretical fictions which serve the purpose of clarifying and unifying the meaning of behavior but do not actually exist.

Theory Construction

After considering some of the possible misinterpretations of theoretical constructs, an examination of theory development will now be made. A knowledge of theory development is essential to understand the purpose of studies which are said to be theory oriented and contribute to the general development of theories.

The ground rules for theory development in the physical sciences have been carefully defined. Less agreement about the relation of experimentation exists in education. Generally, however, theory modification involves a combination of inductive and deductive reasoning described in Chapter 1. Most theories consist of three parts: (a) the postulates and constructs, (b) the model or paradigm, and (c) the hypothesized relation of the theory to observable, measurable elements so that verification or refutation is possible. The following description of a sample theory is made for the purpose of illustrating form using concepts familiar to most educators; it is not presented as a serious attempt to add to the present body of knowledge.

A. *Postulates and Constructs*
   Attitudes are the predispositions of individuals to act and can be positive or negative.
   Direct experience refers to the amount of information an individual is able to gain concerning objects, individuals, organized collections of individuals or (*attitude objects*).

B. *Paradigm or model*
   The intensity of attitudes from a point of zero attitude is directly related to the direct experience with attitude objects.

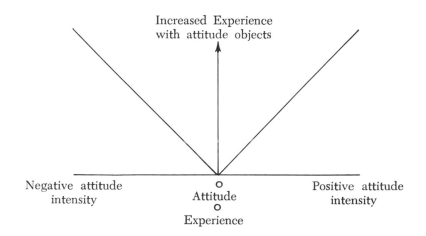

C. *Empirical relations*
   The intensity of attitudes concerning various aspects of the school program will be greater for individuals who have frequent direct experience with these attitude objects than for those individuals with less direct experience.

D. *Specific Hypotheses*

This "theory" could serve as the basis for many hypotheses drawn not only from education but also other areas of social science. One specific example follows because of the emphasis on the deductive process.

1. An educator's attitude, whether positively or negatively oriented, will be greatest toward those attitude objects with which he has greatest contact, and conversely.
2. The intensity of attitudes can be assessed by means of a method described by Guttman.[1]
3. School superintendents have greater "direct experience" with problems of school finance than with problems of teaching reading.
4. First grade teachers have greater contact with problems of teaching reading than with problems of school finance.
5. The intensity of school superintendents' attitudes will be greater toward issues of school finance than toward issues of reading and the intensity of first grade teachers' attitudes will be greater toward reading issues than toward issues of school finance.

Two Guttman type scales, one involving an opinionnaire toward a specific school foundation program concept of state school support and a second dealing with the merits of using phonics as the first method of teaching reading would provide the means for testing the hypothesis.

EMPIRICAL VALIDATION. Confirmation of the hyphothesis indicating a greater intensity of attitude about objects most familiar to educators would support but not confirm the theory. Many other hypotheses derived from the theory must be tested before confidence can be placed in the predictive relation between attitude intensity and direct experience.

Possibly some hypotheses derived from the theory would lead to negative results. If, for example, the intensity of parents' attitudes toward the treatment of subject matter in the classroom were contrasted with teachers' attitudes, the former might manifest a stronger intensity about the topic even though they may have less direct experience.

---

[1]Louis Guttman, "The Principal Components of Scalable Attitudes," cf Paul F. Lazarsfeld *Mathematical Thinking in the Social Sciences*. Glencoe, Ill.: The Free Press, 1954.

Failure to confirm hypotheses would lead to a complete rejection of the theory or the introduction of additional elements in the model or paradigm section to explain inconsistency uncovered as a result of experimentation. As an example, the addition of the term "significant experience" with "attitude objects" might be used to explain the parents' greater concern with subject matter.

Operational Definitions

A clear statement of purpose should lead directly to the development of procedures required to satisfy the purpose. The investigation "What is the number of children aged 5 to 7 residing in single family housing units in Jonesville?" is somewhat self-defining. Criteria for "single family housing units" and for "residing" will rather clearly indicate the purpose of the study. Consider, however, the following topic: "Is a teacher's authoritarian behavior directly related to his attitudes concerning punishment received from his parents?" Although this statement of purpose is quite detailed, it conveys little information unless the meanings of "authoritarian behavior," "attitudes concerning," "punishment" and "received" are clearly defined. Even though these terms have meanings known to most individuals, they lack sufficient precision for use in scientific investigations.

The investigator can define the terms more specifically by using other terms, that is, by substituting words about words. He may, for example, define authoritarianism by using phrases which include "respect for order," "stereotyped thinking," "need for authority" and "dependence." The meaning is no clearer, however, unless each of these terms is further broken down into a description of states which can be directly observed. To avoid this dilemma of indefiniteness, the investigator can relate how authoritarianism will be measured. He can employ an operational definition in which a process is substituted for the conventional definitional description.

Bi-conditional Tautologies

Statements in the form "if and only if," which are called bi-conditional tautologies, can provide a valuable tool in developing definitions. Using the previous example, a teacher is said to be authoritarian *if and only if* his score on the Adorno F Scale is in the highest quarter when compared with the scores of the other 100 teachers involved in the study. The term authoritarianism has now been operationally defined so that everyone understands what the author means. Other testing instruments can be used to define operationally "attitudes toward the parental punishment." To cite another example, "gifted" can be operationally defined as follows: "If and only if a child scores at or above a point two standard deviations above the mean on the Stanford Binet (132 I.Q.)."

Assessment of Operational Definitions

The use of operational definitions enables the researcher to indicate the exact means used to determine unobservable states referred to in the statement of purpose. Even though the meaning is clear, the acceptability of the measure used to determine such conditions as "attitude toward punishment" and "authoritarianism" may be questioned by the discerning reader. By indicating the exact nature of measurements made or things studied, however, the researcher has achieved clarity if not acceptance. Greater progress can be made toward the establishment of a solid foundation of knowledge if both researcher and critic are aware of the extensional meanings associated with terms used in stating hypotheses. Without operational definitions, scholarly disputations are reduced to words about words.

Insuring Accuracy in Data Collecting

As indicated at the beginning of the chapter, an almost infinite supply of data concerning most fields of knowledge are available for collection. The problem confronting the investigator is how to choose information which will correctly serve the purpose of the investigation without introducing bias. Stated in a different way, how can one select data that represent a true picture of the workings of the total universe from which the data are chosen? The following account illustrates the difficulty encountered in studying large populations. If a researcher wished to study the dietary patterns of nursery school pupils in the United States, how would he proceed? Could he study children in Illinois or Texas and expect the observed pattern to represent conditions in the remaining 48 states? Probably not, and a survey of nursery schools in the fifty states would probaly cost more than the information would be worth to society. Could one state be selected as a model of the United States on the basis of ethnic composition, median wages, occupational patterns, divorce rates and incidence of working mothers? Following the selection of the state, what method would be used to collect data? Would all parents of nursery school pupils be interviewed? The result would be excessive cost. Would a questionnaire be sent to all parents? To all teachers? To administrators? Could a representative group within the representative state be chosen? These questions are of significance to beginning and experienced research workers. Some of the possible approaches will be examined in the following sections.

Representativeness

When the results of a study are to apply to a group of subjects or objects, the total group is called the population. In the nursery school study, the population would include all nursery school pupils in the fifty states. In certain instances, such as maintaining daily attendance accounts in public schools, all individuals in the population are measured or counted. This is called perfect induction. The conclusion that, on Tuesday, 98 per cent of the 500 pupils in Jefferson School were present is not an estimate but an actual count and represents a process of perfect induction. If, however, the principal relied on the per cent in attendance by counting the number present in two of the twenty classrooms, the results would be an estimate of attendance — the process would be labeled sampling or partial induction. The accuracy of the estimate of attendance of the whole school population would depend on how representative the two classrooms were of the total of twenty classrooms.

SAMPLING. Because of the limitations of time and funding, perfect induction or complete enumeration of the total population being studied is not always possible. The investigator must work with only a sample of the population.

Studying a sample and making inferences about the population from which it was drawn is called generalization or statistical inference. A person is guilty of overgeneralization when he generalizes from a nonrepresentative sample or from a sample to a population not represented in the sample.

Measurements of samples are called statistics; measurements of corresponding populations are labeled parameters, and the process of generalizing from statistical measurements to parameters is called statistical inference. If a researcher wished to estimate the political affiliation of teachers in a large urban school district, for example, he would select a sample which represented the total group and check the political party by circulating a questionnaire or checking voter registration rolls. If he chose a sample of fifty and found thirty Democrats and twenty Republicans, the statistics would indicate 60 per cent and 40 per cent party affiliation, respectively. The generalization could then be made concerning the parameter of the total population of teachers in the district. He could conclude that 60 per cent of the total population were

Democrats and 40 per cent Republicans; this conclusion would be tempered with an estimate of error based on the number sampled.

RANDOMIZATION. The accuracy of the survey of political affiliation described in the preceding paragraph would be dependent on how accurately the proportion of Republicans and Democrats in the sample reflected the proportion in the total population. The investigator has no assurance that the 60-40 division actually reflects the population parameter. In designing the study, however, he can take all possible precautions to guard against a biased or unrepresentative sample. The process of attaining the greatest degree of representativeness is called randomization. Stated simply, it is a process in which each element of the population is equally likely to be included in the sample. A number of methods can be employed to achieve randomization. The lottery system would require listing the name of each teacher on a card of uniform size, placing the cards in a container, mixing them and drawing out fifty names. A less time-consuming method could be employed by numbering the teachers' names in the school directory sequentially and referring to a table of random numbers which would produce fifty numbers that would correspond to fifty names on the list. Generally, the practice of using fixed intervals such as every fifth or tenth name on the list is not a satisfactory method because of the possibility of introducing bias.

STRATIFICATION. In surveying the political affiliation of teachers, the researcher may wish to insure proportional representation from all levels — elementary school, junior high school, high school and junior college. To insure proportional representation he would establish a stratified random sample. If forty per cent of the teachers taught in elementary grades, the investigator would randomly select forty per cent of the sample of fifty (or twenty teachers) from this population. If junior college teachers represented 10 per cent of the total teacher population, he would randomly select 10 per cent of fifty or five teachers at this level. The total sample would be stratified as follows:

Level	Per cent of Total Teachers	Number in Sample
Elementary	40%	20
Junior high	30%	15
Senior high	20%	10
Junior college	10%	5
		50

SAMPLING VARIABILITY. Although the mathematical properties of sampling will be described in Chapter 6, a brief discussion of the concept will be presented at this time. Suppose the investigator who inferred that forty per cent of the teachers were Republicans and sixty per cent were Democrats were to draw a second random sample. Would he find the same proportional division of party affiliation? Probably not. A third sample would probably differ slightly from the first two even though the parameters of the total population had not changed; (the assumption must be made that the teachers did not change their party affiliation during the period the samples were taken). If 10,000 samples were taken the investigator might find his results would vary from ten per cent Democrat to ninety five per cent Democrat with corresponding variations in assessments of Republican affiliation. The average value of all of the statistics observed would provide a rather accurate estimate of the parameter even though there was a great deal of variation among individual samples. The variation in the statistical nature of samples from the same population during successive samplings is termed sampling variability.

Measurement

In addition to representativeness, the researcher must be concerned with the problem of measurement. Measurement presents one of the most difficult methodological problems the researcher faces. Faulty measurement frequently weakens the fabric of a study which is otherwise satisfactorily designed. The problem arises when the investigator wishes to quantify constructs such as intelligence, motivation or anxiety. They are more easily discussed than measured, for none of them can be directly observed; they may not "exist" in the truly substantive sense. Measurements are made of observable behavior which indicate the presence of the condition being studied. The use of indirect measurement is not restricted to the areas of social science and education. Pluto, the planet most remote from the sun, was detected in the twentieth century not by direct observation but as a result of its effect on adjacent planets.

Although measurement difficulties are not unique to the study of education, they nevertheless present a perplexing problem to the reseacher. The process of measurement can be described in terms of scaling, precision, and validity.

SCALING. Three types of scales are employed to provide differential values for measurable quantities namely interval, ordinal, and nominal. The interval scale, including temperature, I.Q. scores and grade level assessments of achievement, has equal intervals between successive values. That is, the difference in temperature between fifty and fifty-five degrees is of the same magnitude as the difference between 100 and 105 degrees. A range of five I.Q. points presumably indicates an identical difference in mental alertness whether the range is ninety to ninety-five or one hundred forty to one hundred forty-five.

The ordinal scale gives an indication of rank or order. Examples are percentile ranks; ratings such as above average, average or below average; and rankings, first, second, third as well as other measures denoting order. The use of ordinal scales does not imply equal intervals between successive values.

The characteristics of interval and ordinal scores become apparent by contrasting assessments of I.Q. and rank order of three pupils.

Pupil	I.Q. (Interval Scale)	d	Rank (Ordinal Scale)	d
Sally	148		1	
Jim	130	18	2	1
George	90	40	3	1

The difference in rank between Sally and Jim and between Jim and George is one in both instances. The difference between Sally and Jim's I.Q. score, however, is 18, and between Jim and George the difference in I.Q. score is 40. Clearly, order or rank does not provide an assessment of the magnitude of existing differences.

The third example is the nominal or classificatory scale which signifies neither quantity nor order but type. Nominal scales are used to make such designations as boy or girl; upper class, middle-class or lower class; Protestant or Catholic; or whether a person answered yes, no, or undecided to a question asked by an interviewer. Interval, ordinal and nominal scales are all utilized by researchers, but distinction must be made when statistical analyses are employed.

In addition to the type of scale used, the researcher must be concerned with the method of scale construction or with scaling techniques. A nonmathematical explanation of some of the more commonly used scaling techniques is described in the following paragraphs.

Raw score scales are frequently used to interpret teacher-made achievement tests and other instruments employed by researchers. In the simplest form, the raw-score scale is the number of responses correctly answered in an achievement test. Certain questions may be arbitrarily given greater weight than others. In addition, a correction for guessing may be used in which the final score represents the number correct minus a certain proportion of the number incorrect.

The meaning of raw scores can be increased if the scores are standardized. Standardization involves comparison with a larger group with known characteristics. Suppose an investigator wished to standardize a test of mathematical reasoning he had developed to assess the ability of seventh grade pupils. The test would be administered to all seventh graders in a certain school and the mean and standard deviation computed. Subsequently, any individual or group taking the test could be compared with the seventh grade standard group on the basis of whether the score or scores were above or below the mean. The magnitude of difference from the mean of the standard group could also be determined by using the standard deviation as a measuring unit. Following is an example:

Math. Reasoning 100 Seventh Graders (Standard Group)		Bill, a subject subsequently taking the same test.	
Mean	32		
Standard Deviation	6	Bill's Score	41

The conclusion could be made that Bill's score was 1.5 standard deviation units above the mean of the standard group. The standard group provides a known basis for determining the magnitude of scores obtained from other subjects.

Attitude scaling presents greater problems than achievement test scaling because responses cannot be considered correct or incorrect. A method of scaling attitudes described by Thurstone utilizes a series of statements that reflect varying degrees of attitude concerning objects or issues. To assess attitudes about homogeneous grouping in the elementary grades, for example, statements could be developed ranging from a positive (1) "Homogeneous grouping permits each child to progress at a rate best for him" to a negative (2) "Homogeneous grouping attaches a stigma of superiority or inferiority to the child," with a number of less judgmental statements supplying a continuum of attitudes between the extreme positions reflected in the two statements. A number of these statements would be submitted to a large number of judges, persons familiar with semantics, education, and attitude testing. They would be instructed to place each statement in one of eleven categories ranging from most favorable to least favorable. Statements about which judges tended to agree would be retained and placed in descending order of attitude expressed. Average weights assigned by all judges would be compiled. The respondent would be asked to check those statements with which he agreed. His score would be the median value of the items checked. If he checked, for example, one item, the weighting assigned to this item would represent his score. If three items were checked, then the value of the middle statement would represent the respondent's score.

The Likert scale developed later is designed to enable subjects to give differential responses to a number of statements. The following is an example:

	Strongly Agree	Agree	Disagree	Strongly Disagree
1. Homogeneous grouping permits each child to progress at a rate best for him.				

The respondent would place a check mark in the column which best expresses his attitude. Arbitrary weights can be assigned as follows: strongly agree 6, agree 5, disagree 2, strongly disagree 1. For a ten item attitude scale, a maximum favorable attitude would be represented by a score of 60 and a maximum unfavorable attitude by a score of 10. Rather than assign arbitrary weights, the score could be determined by computing the mean value of all individuals' responses to each individual statement, computing the standard deviation, and determining the sum of each deviation in standard deviation units or z-scores above or below the mean score of all individuals responding to the statement.

More recently, Guttman has described a scaling method which is gaining wide acceptance among social scientists and educators because it offers a means of determining the intensity of attitudes. Although complete understanding of Guttman's method requires a knowledge of differential equations, a simple illustration of the workings of the scale can be presented. Consider the two statements listed earlier in describing Likert-type scales. Assume that the mode of response is now yes or no. After administration of the scale to 100 teachers, 70 answered yes and 30 answered no to item 1. The second item received 40 affirmative and 60 negative answers. The relationship can be demonstrated in the following contingency table provided those responding negatively to question 1 responded positively to question 2.

1. Homogeneous grouping permits each child to progress at a rate best for him.

2. Homogeneous grouping attaches a stigma of superiority or inferiority to the child.

	Yes	No	Total
Yes	10	30	40
No	60	0	60
	70	30	100

From the information in the table a simple continuum of attitude from positive to negative can now be developed as follows:

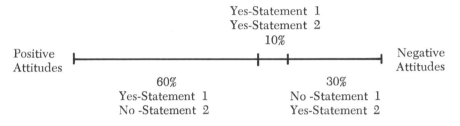

From an analysis of responses to only two questions, the investigator is able to identify three degrees of attitude: (1) those responding yes to statement 1 and no to statement 2, (60 per cent), (2) those responding yes to both statements (10 per cent), (3) those responding no to question 1 and yes to question 2 (30 per cent). The absence of no-no responses is the characteristic which identifies this response pattern as a perfect scale. Although most response patterns do not assume the form of a perfect scale, the mathematical model for perfect scales can be used to analyze attitude responses. The dichotomous yes or no can be replaced by a multiple response pattern and more than two questions can be analyzed; however, the foregoing principle operates in the same way.

By further mathematical analysis, the identification of a number of principal components enables the investigator to (1) assign weights which make the scale differences greatest between individuals with the strongest positive and negative attitudes; (2) identify the point between positive and negative attitudes as a point of zero attitude; (3) divide the attitudes into four segments including strongly positive, positive, negative and strongly negative.[2]

---

[2]Guttman, loc cit.

Recent developments in the mathematics of scaling indicate the need for researchers to consult library references before developing scaling techniques when designing instruments.

Precision

The reliability or precision of an instrument refers to its dependability as a measuring device. In surveying land, for example, measurements should be exact; one would object if the surveyor substituted a rubber tape for the steel measuring device usually used so that distances reported as 100 feet might be as long as 110 feet or as short as 90 feet depending on how much the rubber tape stretched. The rubber tape would be an unreliable measure. The cubit, the distance from the elbow to the end of the extended middle finger, was not a reliable measure because of the variations among individuals. The educational researcher faces an overwhelming problem when he attempts to develop instruments which provide uniformity of measurement, do not stretch or contract, are consistent from one observed situation to another, and measure similar quantities.

DETERMINING RELIABILITY. Instrument precision can be established by a number of techniques. First, the investigator can make successive measurements of qualities known to be constant. If the instrument yields consistent identical measures of these qualities, he has established the precision of the questionnaire, attitude scale, observation blank or other instruments. Unfortunately, many of the qualities studied in education, such as maturation, anxiety, attitudes toward homogeneous grouping and intelligence, are not stable for a given group of individuals from one period of time to another. Changes in attitude scores of thirty elementary school teachers between Easter and the Fourth of July may reflect not only the lack of reliability of the instrument used but also changes in the willingness of teachers to complete the instrument. Nevertheless, the test-retest procedure in which the same group responds to the instrument on two separate occasions does provide an estimate of the reliability or stability of the instrument.

REFINING UNITS OF MEASUREMENT. Units of measurement can be made more uniform to establish precision. Consider the architect specifying dimensions of a schoolroom. He will state measurements in feet and inches. We know that all feet and inches used in the statement of dimensions conventionally will be of equal length. Similarly, the educational researcher who lists an individual's attitude score toward homogeneous grouping will wish to provide some assurance that the units used are somewhat uniform.

Lack of uniformity of measurement in instruments such as questionnaires and tests results from ambiguity and divergent content. An attitude scale item, such as "Government officials have a propensity for overspecialization of function," might prove to be ambiguous and unreliable if administered to members of the general public, many of whom lack knowledge of the terms used. Without a specific meaning "anchor," an individual is apt to respond differently to the item from one testing situation to another. The same item may not be ambiguous, however, if administered to persons with more than seventeen years of formal education. Ambiguity may result from the use of unfamiliar content, wordy, faulty grammar and syntax or statements so complex that few can ascertain the logical connections between the ideas expressed. The statement "The schools should not pursue a policy of not placing children in situations in which some sort of homogeneous grouping is not absent" would probably prove to be quite ambiguous to most respondents. To avoid ambiguity, the statement used should as far as possible convey the same meaning to the investigator and all respondents.

Lack of precision resulting from divergent content would occur if a spelling test item were included in an arithmetic achievement test. The item measures a skill unrelated to arithmetic reasoning or computation. Similarly, divergent items should be identified and eliminated from attitude scales and other instruments to improve precision. Divergent items can be identified by comparing the pattern of response to the item with patterns of response to other convergent items. Preliminary administration of instruments to trial groups will enable the investigator to eliminate ambiguous and divergent items. To determine homogeneity and reduce ambiguity and divergent content, the researcher can use item analysis and statistical techniques.

ITEM ANALYSIS. Item analysis refers to the process of comparing all responses to a single item with all responses to all items. One method used to refine achievement test items consists of the following steps: (1) arranging test papers from highest to lowest score; (2) identification of 27 per cent of the papers which have the highest scores and the 27 per cent which represent the lowest scores; (3) determination of the number in the top 27 per cent answering the item correctly and in the bottom 27 per cent answering correctly; (4) computation of the per cent of respondents answering the item correctly. If a greater number in the low group than in the high group answers a question correctly, the item obviously does not discriminate between the persons with greatest knowledge and those with least knowledge and should be discarded. Item analysis is based on the assumption that those with greater knowledge or skill will receive the highest scores and those with lesser ability

will score low. An item which nearly everyone answers correctly or
an item which few answer correctly is of little value in differentiating
among individuals. Very easy or very difficult items should be eliminated.

STATISTICAL ANALYSIS. Mathematical formulas can be used to determine the homogeneity of items. The items of an instrument can be
analyzed with regard to the relationship of single items to responses
on the total instrument through the use of the biserial correlation,
Kuder-Richardson formulas, or other statistical techniques described in
texts dealing with test construction.

A method frequently used for determining internal consistency is the
split halves technique. The total instrument is divided into two equal
parts by random assignment of items to one of two groups or by including all evenly-numbered items in one group and all odd-numbered items
in the other group. If the standard deviations of the scores of the two
subtests are not significantly different, the scores of all individuals on
one half of the test are correlated with their scores on the other half.
The correlation coefficient is then corrected by using the Spearman-
Brown proficiency formula to estimate the reliability of the total instrument. The beginning researcher is encouraged to consult testing authorities and recent literature to determine the best methods to use in refining instruments.

Validity

Validity refers to the accuracy of an instrument relative to the question, "Does the instrument really measure what the researcher says it
measures?" In forming an operational definition of favorable attitudes
to homogeneous grouping of elementary school children, the researcher
states the following: "A teacher is said to have a favorable attitude
toward homogeneous grouping if and only if he scores with the upper
quarter of all respondents who completed the attitude scale constructed
by the author." Although the researcher has honestly stated what he
means by favorable attitude so that no question about his meaning
plagues the reader, one might continue to question the adequacy, truth-
fulness, or reliability of the measure used to determine attitudes. How
can the researcher prove to the discerning reader that the instrument
he has constructed actually measures an unobserved state such as attitude
toward homogeneous grouping? The American Psychological Association
has developed four standards for determining validity which are useful
to the researcher in his attempts to establish true measures. These include content validity, status validity, construct validity, and predictive
validity.

CONTENT VALIDITY. Content validity is appropriate when achievement instruments are designed. If the items in a final examination for a research course are a representative sample of the course content, then the test has content validity. Content validity is demonstrated by a systematic comparison of course content with each area represented by a test item.

STATUS VALIDITY. Status validity is established by indicating that different response patterns in the instrument reflect real differences in subjects. If a principal were asked to identify carefully five of the teachers in the school who were quite favorable to the practice of homogeneous grouping and five teachers who were most unfavorable, the status validity of the attitude scale concerning grouping would be substantiated if the mean score of the favorable group of teachers was significantly greater than the mean score of the previously identified unfavorable group. The process would depend on the principal's ability to identify correctly teachers with favorable and unfavorable attitudes. The status validity of the arithmetic reasoning test designed by elementary school pupils could be established by determining if the average score of sixth graders was significantly greater than the average score of fifth graders. Once differences are established independent of the instrument with some degree of certainty, the status validity of an instrument can be determined. Unfortunately, many states of being which are the concern of the educational scientist cannot be ascertained by independent means; thus, status validity methods cannot be employed.

CONSTRUCT VALIDITY. Construct validity is established by demonstrating that the scores obtained by an instrument form a pattern consistent with what is known about the construct being studied. Suppose an investigator attempted to develop an instrument to measure the verbal intelligence factor among elementary school pupils. Verbal intelligence is a construct which is used to describe that part of the mental capacity which enables a person to use language effectively. The verbal subscale of the Wechsler Intelligence Scale for Children is an accepted measure of this capacity. The instrument being developed will have construct validity if measurements obtained from its use are comparable to measurements obtained by using the W.I.S.C. with the same group of students. The degree of comparability can be determined by utilizing the Pearson product-moment correlation technique described in Chapter 7.

Another example of establishing construct validity can be cited by using the construct anxiety. In simple terms, anxiety can be said to be highest in stressful situations and lowest in relaxed, nonstress situations. Although these relationships are somewhat circular because of the interdependence of the definition of anxiety and stress, they conform generally to what is known about anxiety. To ascertain the construct validity of an instrument designed to measure test anxiety among high school pupils, the scale could be given to a group on the following occasions: (1) during a relaxation period in physical education class, (2) prior to a weekly civics examination, and (3) just prior to the time the group was to take a battery of college entrance examinations for admission to an Ivy League college. Assuming that all the respondents wished to pass civics and enter college, the theory of anxiety would indicate a successively greater state of anxiety ranging from a low in situation (1) to a high in situation (3). If the instrument reflected the expectations established by the theory, that is, if average anxiety scores were lowest in the relaxed situation and highest during the period prior to the administration of the college entrance examinations, the construct validity of the instrument would be supported.

PREDICTIVE VALIDITY. Predictive validity can be established by comparing an individual's performance on an instrument with his performance on a related activity as explained in Chapter 7. The predictive validity of a college aptitude test can be determined by comparing the scores of a number of college-bound high school graduates with subsequent grade-point averages earned during the freshman college year. In such cases, the Pearson product-moment correlation is most frequently used for the purpose of comparison. At the other end of the educational continuum, the predictive validity of a check list to identify potential dropouts during early elementary school grades can be established in two ways: (1) by selecting persons who have currently dropped out of school and using the check list to evaluate records of their early elementary school experiences and making comparisons with the records of non-dropouts; (2) by using the check list to evaluate a large number of early elementary school children and following their progress through the grades to determine the accuracy of predictions made using the check list.

Relation of Validity and Reliability

Reliability is not dependent upon validity. An instrument can meet the criteria previously discussed as an indication of reliability and fail

to meet the criteria of validity. Validity, however, is limited by reliability. A case in point would be a five-item essay question, an ad-
mittedly small but nevertheless representative sample of the content of
a one-semester course in American History. The examination could have
reasonable content validity, but, because of the nonobjective mode of
response, it may not meet the standards for reliability satisfactorily.
Testing experts would probably judge the test an invalid measure of
achievement in history, but their decision would be based on the lack
of reliability; they could not make a direct assault on the validity of the
test.

Conclusion

Topics have been introduced in this chapter to prepare the reader
for a treatment of the better known methods for gathering data. Before
moving forward, however, several points need re-emphasis. First, the
purpose of an investigation should be stated so that its meaning is
understood by other investigators and by consumers of educational
research. The burden of clarity rests with the writer. Second, those
conducting research studies and publishing the results have a burden-
some responsibility to administrators, teachers, parents, and, most of all,
to children to conduct studies carefully and interpret the results with
caution. Third, educational practitioners must critically evaluate research
findings before using the results as the basis for making decisions which
affect children. Fourth, all educators should recognize the limitations
which presently exist in the field of educational research and strive
continuously for improvement.

Selected Exercises

1. Develop a statement of purpose. Express it as a question; as a
   proposition; and place it in the universal conditional form "If x
   then y."
2. Refer to the theory concerning the intensity of attitudes described
   in this chapter. Use deductive reasoning to develop a specific
   hypothesis and describe a study to test the hypothesis. Explain
   the effect on the theory (a) if the hypothesis (positively stated)
   is confirmed and (b) if it is disproved.
3. You have been asked to determine whether teachers in the
   Wilson School District favor merit pay. Because the district is
   large you are asked to contact only 250 teachers. Determine the

number you would choose from each of the following levels in developing a stratified random sample:

Level	Total Number
elementary	4,000
high school	1,500
junior college	320
Total	5,820

4. Does the accuracy of a sample in representing the characteristics of the population from which it was drawn always increase with the size of the sample? Explain.

5. Given the following, indicate which are examples of nominal, ordinal, or interval scales:

   a. The dimensions of a room expressed in feet and inches.

   b. Homogeneously grouped classes designated as high, middle and low.

   c. Political affiliation (assuming one is not superior to the other).

   d. Time required for each of seven pupils to run 100 yards.

   e. The sequence in which seven competing pupils completed the 100 yard dash.

Suggested Activities

1. Secure a reference book containing a table of random numbers. Assume that you have a list of pupils numbered from 1 to 1,132. Use the table of random numbers and select a sample of 37 from the hypothetical list. List the sample numbers selected and explain why you were unable to use certain numbers which appeared in the table.

2. Secure the records of a class of upper grade school children (25 to 40 pupils). Use the following table to make an approximate determination of the validity of achievement tests as determined by teacher assigned grades. Choose a year when achievement tests were given. Use arithmetic grades and scores. Discard cases for which data are missing. Divide the achievement test scores so that the number of average scores equals the number of average grades. Write conclusions.

ACHIEVEMENT TEST SCORES

		Above Average	Average	Below Average
GRADES	High			
	Average			
	Low			

3. You have been asked to prepare an instrument to determine parental attitudes toward corporal punishment administered by school personnel. Explain in detail several methods which you would use in establishing the validity of the instrument.

4. Develop two questions to assess your colleagues' attitudes toward foreign language instruction in the primary grades. Arrange the responses in a form similar to the Guttman format described in this chapter. If the responses do not conform to a perfect scale, redesign the questions and try again. Report your results.

Selected Readings

1. CRONBACH, LEE J., *Essentials of Psychological Testing*. Second Edition. New York: Harper & Row, Publishers, 1960, p. 103-123.

2. BRODBECK, MAY, "Logic and Scientific Method in Research on Teaching" cf. Gage, N. L. (ed.) *Handbook of Research on Teaching*. The American Educational Research Association, Chicago: Rand McNally & Co., 1963.

3. TRAVERS, ROBERT M. W., *An Introduction to Educational Research*. New York: The Macmillan Company, 1959. Chapters 1 and 2.

4. VAN DALEN, DEOBOLD B. AND WILLIAM J. MEYER, *Understanding Educational Research*, New York: McGraw-Hill Book Company, 1962. pp. 392-419.

5. WEBB, EUGENE J. *et al, Unobtrusive Measures: Nonreactive Research In The Social Sciences*. Chicago: Rand McNally & Co., 1966.

PART II

An Introduction to the Statistical Method

Chapter 5

Concepts that Serve as a Basis for Statistical Data Analysis

Research dealing with human traits often leads to data that require the special analytical tools of the statistician. Beginning students of research may be confused and bewildered by the necessity to deal with the abstract concepts of statistics. As a result, there may be a tendency for students to memorize formulae religiously without understanding the rationale upon which they are based.

Whether an individual will become a researcher or a consumer of research, he must command an understanding of the concepts that serve as a basis for the analysis of research data. The researcher cannot design his studies properly if he does not have a thorough knowledge of the analytical tools he will use. In addition, the research consumer cannot hope to evaluate and apply research findings in his professional work if he does not understand the technical methods and data handling used in reporting investigations.

Chapters 5, 6, 7, and 8 of this text are designed to help the student of research develop an understanding of statistical tools and method. Primary emphasis has been placed upon the more fundamental ideas of statistics. To accomplish the task: (1) the basic mathematical concepts are explored through a liberal use of graphs; and (2) elementary problems are presented for consideration. (Answers to the problems are given on page 397.) Both approaches are aimed to provide students who have little or no training in mathematics with concrete illustrations of some of the abstract ideas involved in statistics.

To ease the student's work in doing the problems at the end of each chapter in Part II of this text, Appendix B contains a "statistical package" for problem solving. The package consists of a computer program which may be used to make sixteen common statistics tests. Once the program has been placed on IBM cards or stored in a computer, students may make many of the statistical tests described in the following chapters by preparing IBM control and data cards according to the simple directions given with the "package" in Appendix B. The computer will then do the tedious arithmetic often involved in solving statistics problems.

The Organization of Research Data

When research data have been collected, and before they can be analyzed, they must be assembled and organized. The purpose of organizing data is to expedite the process of analysis. Data that are collected can be expressed in two ways, qualitatively and quantitatively. The qualitative form is usually associated with historical studies; however, some descriptive studies may also express data wholly or partially in words rather than numerically.

There are no rigid rules that apply to the way data in qualitative form should be organized. Organization of nonnumerical material is a matter of accomplishing the objective of research — solving a problem. If there is any generalization that can be made, it is that data should be examined for patterns of order in the data itself or for similarities to other situations in which order has been perceived previously: patterns, relationship, order, this is the "stuff" of which research is composed.

In conducting historical studies, researchers are usually concerned with describing accurately events of the past, determining possible cause-effect relationship in past events, and with discerning trends which led to conditions that followed the era studied. As a result, the organization of historical data requires that:

1. Facts be placed correctly in the continuum of time.
2. Evidence be recorded in proper perspective so as not to give undue emphasis merely to prove hypotheses.
3. All aspects be matched point by point and fact by fact, if a comparison is made to a seemingly similar event or era.

Descriptive research is concerned with the determination of factors such as present status, prevailing conditions, group attitudes, activities or practices of individuals or groups, relationships that exist between phenomena and trends or possible trends. It must be noted that in any descriptive study it is necessary to identify properly what data are to be collected and also the population from which they are to be obtained; therefore, proper organization of qualitative description data includes:

1. Limiting data to the population or sample of the population, of people or things identified in the purposes of the study.
2. Placing events in proper time sequence and perspective.

Whereas the organization of data in qualitative form may be described only in generalities, numerical data are subject to the processes of mathematical analysis; therefore, organization of material expressed quantitatively is a matter of preparing the data in ways that are known to expose mathematical patterns and order whenever they exist.

Organizing Quantitative Data

Quantitative data lend themselves to mathematical analysis. Before analytical tools can be applied, however, it is necessary to organize quantitative data. Organization of data (1) helps insure that patterns stand out, and (2) gives the researcher a basis for the selection of proper analytical tools. Nothing can be more confusing and meaningless than quantitative data that are not organized.

The Frequency Distribution

Suppose that a test which measures some kind of mathematical ability were administered to 92 students and in scoring the papers in random fashion the following marks were found: 87, 62, 79, 52, 66, 76, 97, 83, 69, 57, 72, 85, 93, 75, 65, 84, 47, 87, 70, 89, 71, 60, 80, 91, 75, 55, 73, 79, 80, 96, 69, 90, 58, 68, 92, 61, 75, 85, 60, 80, 54, 51, 82, 95, 70, 91, 62, 69, 76, 64, 86, 60 67, 74, 83, 70, 57, 77, 90, 66, 72, 60, 77, 80, 64, 84, 77, 84, 72, 75, 78, 80, 62, 87, 78, 73, 76, 87, 73, 85, 81, 76, 78, 71, 81, 72, 75, 61, 83, 80, 90, 81.

If the data are left in this helter-skelter way, little of value can be discerned; however, as a first step in organization, the scores might be rearranged in numerical order, either from the lowest to the highest or vice versa. It is the conventional practice to arrange measurements of this kind from the highest to the lowest. Now we have a *distribution* of the scores as follows: 97, 96, 95, 93, 92, 91, 91, 90, 90, 90, 89, 87, 87, 87, 87, 86, 85, 85, 85, 84, 84, 84, 83, 83, 83, 82, 81, 81, 81, 80, 80, 80, 80, 80, 80, 79, 79, 78, 78, 78, 77, 77, 77, 76, 76, 76, 76, 75, 75, 75, 75, 75, 74, 73, 73, 73, 72, 72, 72, 72, 71, 71, 70, 70, 70, 69, 69, 69, 68, 67, 66, 66, 65, 64, 64, 62, 62, 62, 61, 61, 60, 60, 60, 60, 58, 57, 57, 55, 54, 52, 51, 47.

The distribution provides a clearer picture of the scores; for example, it can be seen that there is a tendency for them to cluster toward

TABLE 5.1 A Frequency Distribution of Scores

	f		f		f
97	1	80	6	63	0
96	1	79	2	62	3
95	1	78	3	61	2
94	0	77	3	60	4
93	1	76	4	59	0
92	1	75	5	58	1
91	2	74	1	57	2
90	3	73	3	56	0
89	1	72	4	55	1
88	0	71	2	54	1
87	4	70	3	53	0
86	1	69	3	52	1
85	3	68	1	51	1
84	3	67	1	50	0
83	3	66	2	49	0
82	1	65	1	48	0
81	3	64	2	47	1

the middle of the distribution and trail off at the two extremes, but there is still a lack of precision. Questions arise such as: How much clustering has occurred? What is the central point of the distribution? What score best characterizes the group as a whole? How does one particular score compare to other scores in the distribution?

Some answers to these questions can be determined by preparing a *frequency distribution*: i.e., all possible measures from the highest to the lowest can be placed in a table, but instead of repeating scores, the frequency with which each occurs is noted as in Table 5.1.

The frequency distribution as depicted in Table 5.1 is not entirely satisfactory; with so many scores and such a wide range, it is still difficult to see clustering that has occurred. Furthermore, since scores are not precise measurements, it would be just as well to group scores that are nearly alike. The *grouped frequency distribution* provides another step in bringing order and organization to numerical data based upon measurements, but problems arise in connection with the grouped frequency distribution such as: How should the scores be grouped? How many scores should be included in each group or *interval*?

It has been determined that the use of ten to twenty intervals or groups of scores generally will yield the best results. Groupings which fall within that range seem to provide the best picture of how the scores are distributed. Since the scores in the mathematics test that has been used as an example begin from a low of 47 and end at a high of 97

TABLE 5.2   Grouped Frequency Distributions With i of 5 and i of 3.

Scores ($i = 5$)	f	Scores ($i = 3$)	f
96-100	2	97-99	1
91-95	5	94-96	2
86-90	9	91-93	4
81-85	13	88-90	4
76-80	18	85-87	8
71-75	15	82-84	7
66-70	10	79-81	11
61-65	8	76-78	10
56-60	7	73-75	9
51-55	4	70-72	9
46-50	1	67-69	5
N = 92		64-66	5
		61-63	5
		58-60	5
		55-57	3
		52-54	2
		49-51	1
		46-48	1
		N = 92	

the range, "R," is 97-47 = 50. If the scores are grouped in about 10 intervals, each interval of scores will need to be five score units in width (50/5 = 10). On the other hand, should an interval size of three score units be used, there will be approximately 17 intervals (50/3 = 16.67). Table 5.2 shows the two grouped frequency distributions that result by selecting either 3 or 5 as the i, or interval size, to organize scores of the mathematics test previously used as an example.

Which interval size yields the "best" results? Actually there is no absolute answer to the question, but since an i of 3 combined with the relatively wide R of 50 and an N, or number of scores, of 92 still produces quite a bit of scattering, it would appear that the i of 5 is more satisfactory.

Graphic Representation of Data

Since abstract relationships can be more readily understood when represented in pictorial form rather than as tables and formulas, graphs are often used to present research data. Two dimensional graphs are based upon the principle that the relationship between two variables can be shown by placing the dimensions of one variable along a horizontal axis — usually called the "X" axis — and the other variable along a vertical axis — usually called the "Y" axis. When, as with a frequency distribution of data, there are two factors that vary in relation to one another, a graph can be employed to show the relationship visually.

The Histogram

The histogram is a graph which uses bars to depict the way two variables are related. When the histogram is applied to the frequency distribution, it is customary to place the measurements that have been made on the X, or horizontal axis, and the corresponding frequencies on the Y, or vertical axis. Measurements on the X axis start from lowest at the left to the highest at the right; frequencies on the Y axis start with the lowest at the bottom to the highest at the top.

The center of each bar corresponds to the midpoint of the intervals of measurements; the width of each bar is in terms of the width of the intervals. Since frequencies are placed along the Y axis, the height of each bar will represent the frequency of the measurements within the particular interval. Figure 5.1 illustrates a histogram of the data on a test in mathematics previously presented in tabular form.

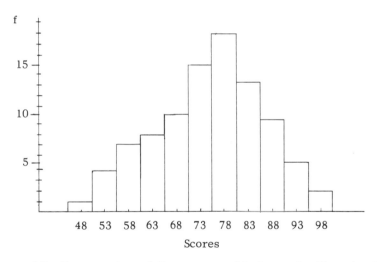

Figure 5.1 Frequencies of Scores on a Mathematics Examination

In reading the graph, the following information is seen at a glance.

1. The interval 46-50 — actually 45.5 to 50.5 — with a mid-point of 48 contains the fewest scores — only one.

2. The mode, or most frequently occurring score, is taken to be 78 since the interval 76-80 contains the most scores: 18.

3. The distribution is slightly out of balance or unsymmetrical since there is a slightly greater concentration of high scores than low scores. (Since the distribution is not symmetrical, it is said to be *skewed*.)

The Frequency Polygon

The frequency polygon is very similar in construction to the histogram; however, instead of bars to represent the scores or measurements in a given interval a series of points are used to show the number of scores that have occurred in a particular interval. Points are placed on the graph paper so that for any interval a point will appear immediately above the place along the X axis which marks the middle of the interval. The height at which the point appears corresponds to the frequency, or number, of scores that occurred in the interval. Adjacent points are connected by means of straight lines. Figure 5.2 demonstrates the use of a frequency polygon based upon the same data used to construct the histogram in Figure 5.1.

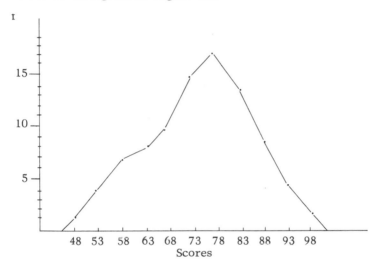

Figure 5.2 Frequency of Scores on a Mathematics Examination

It is to be noted that the same information obtained by means of the histogram can also be quickly read from the frequency polygon graph.

The Preparation of Graphs

Graphic representation of data can create a distorted impression if graphs are not prepared carefully. The reason for this difficulty can be readily seen from the following example. Given the following data, Figures 5.3, 5.4, and 5.5 show various kinds of frequency polygons that may result from the same numerical data: (See page 110).

Figure 5.3 shows what happens when the measurements along the Y (vertical) axis are spaced so that the greatest vertical length is very small compared to the greatest horizontal (X axis) length. The graph

Interval	f
80-84	8
75-79	12
70-74	26
65-69	30
60-64	34
55-59	46
50-54	50
45-49	48
40-44	40
35-39	26
30-34	18
25-29	12
20-24	3
	N = 353

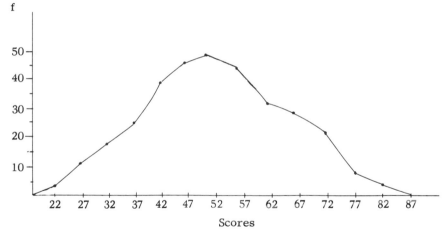

Figure 5.3 Frequency Polygon Graph with Small Y axis to X axis Ratio

takes on a squashed down appearance which gives an impression that the measurements were widely dispersed. On the other hand, using the same data in Figure 5.4, the graph gives an impression that there is little dispersion in the measurements; this has resulted from selecting units along the Y and X axis such that the vertical length is large when compared to the horizontal length.

In Figure 5.5, a better balance has been achieved by the selection of units that cause the greatest vertical length to be about three-fourths of the greatest horizontal length. Generally, it is best to draw graphs in such a manner that the ratio of the length of highest point along the

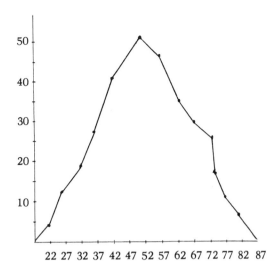

Figure 5.4 Frequency Polygon Graph with Large Y axis to X axis Ratio

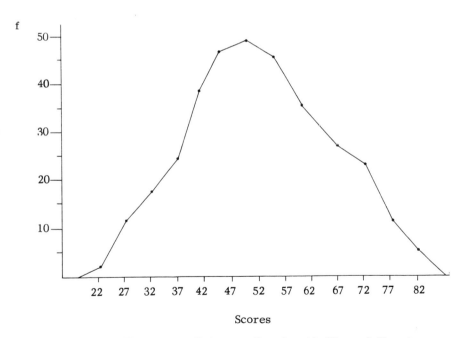

Scores

Figure 5.5 Frequency Polygon Graph with Normal Y axis
to X axis Ratio

Y axis to the longest point along the X axis should be anywhere from about 2/3 to 3/4.

What Is Average?

The layman tends to use the word average in so many ways that it has become a very vague and imprecise term. There is one element of consistency in what people mean by average, however; to most people "average" means typical. This general definition also holds in statistics for various measures which are encompassed by the term "average."

Statisticians usually refer to single measures which are meant to typify a group of measurements as "measures of central tendency." Three measures of central tendency which are found in literature dealing with tests and measurements and research are: the median (abbreviated Mdn), the mean (abbreviated M), and the mode (abbreviated Mo).

The Median and the Mode

The median is nothing more than a special percentile — the fiftieth percentile. It is the point in a distribution of scores (ranked from the highest to the lowest) at which half the scores will fall above and half below.

Since the median — which may also be called the second quartile, or Q_2 — is determined by placing scores or measurements in rank order, it is not affected by the size of measurements in determining the order. The largest measurement in a distribution, therefore, is counted merely as the largest measurement; the fact that it is one unit larger, twice as large, or a thousand times larger than the next measurement does not enter into the calculation of the median. This is true of every measurement; its size comes into play in determining the position of the measurement in the distribution, but once the placement is fixed, size is no longer a factor in computing the median.

The mode will not be discussed in any detail since it is merely the score or measurement which occurs the most often in a distribution. Sometimes more than one mode may appear in a distribution.

Figure 5.6 illustrates (a) a frequency distribution in which the mode is 78 (the midpoint of the interval containing the largest number of scores); (b) the graphic representation of the score distribution; (c) a frequency distribution which has two modes; (d) the graphic representation of the distribution that is bimodal.

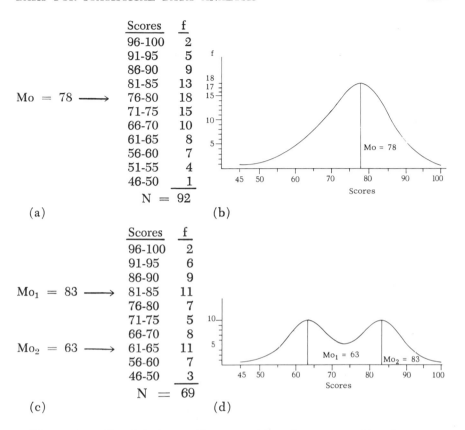

Scores	f
96-100	2
91-95	5
86-90	9
81-85	13
76-80	18
71-75	15
66-70	10
61-65	8
56-60	7
51-55	4
46-50	1
N = 92	

Mo = 78 ⟶

(a)

(b)

Scores	f
96-100	2
91-95	6
86-90	9
81-85	11
76-80	7
71-75	5
66-70	8
61-65	11
56-60	7
46-50	3
N = 69	

Mo_1 = 83 ⟶

Mo_2 = 63 ⟶

(c)

(d)

Figure 5.6 The Mode as Shown in Two Frequency Distributions and Accompanying Graphs

The Mean

Very often the *arithmetic mean,* or more simply the mean, is the "average" that people think about when they are referring to an average computed from groups of measurements. If one were to ask, "What is the average salary of bus drivers in a certain city?", most people would add up the salary of each bus driver and divide the total figure by the number of drivers. In this way a typical salary for the group would be determined.

In the language of mathematics, the formula for the mean can be written as:

$$M = \frac{\Sigma X}{N}$$

where

M is the arithmetic mean
Σ is the Greek letter sigma and indicates "the sum of" or "sum up"
X stands for each measurement or score
N is the number of measurements which have been made

In words, the formula reads: In order to find the mean (M), sum up the measurement and divide this sum total by the number of measurements.

The following measurements (scores) are the result of an examination in Algebra: 94; 92; 88; 86; 83; 82; 82; 80; 79; 78; 77; 77; 77; 76; 75; 75; 74; 73; 73; 73; 72; 72; 68; 68; 67; 67; 67; 67; 66; 66; 65; 65; 65; 64; 64; 64; 64; 62; 62; 62; 62; 60; 59; 58; 58; 57; 57; 56; 56; 54; 52; 52; 52; 51; 42; 41.

ΣX (found by summing the scores) = 3778
N = 56

therefore, since $M = \dfrac{\Sigma X}{N}$

$$M = \frac{3778}{56}$$

$$= 67.46$$

$$= 67 \text{ (to the nearest whole number)}$$

If the scores had been placed in a distribution, a slightly different formula could have been used to determine M. Using a five point score interval, the distribution would look like this:

	f	X (mid-point)	fX
90-94	2	92	184
85-89	2	87	174
80-84	4	82	328
75-79	8	77	616
70-74	6	72	432
65-69	11	67	737
60-64	9	62	558
55-59	7	57	399
50-54	5	52	260
45-49	0	47	0
40-44	2	42	84
N = Σ f = 56			Σ fX = 3772

From the distribution it can be seen that the scores are no longer considered as they actually existed, but individual scores within an interval are represented by the midpoint of the interval. The first two scores in the original distribution (94 and 92) are now both represented by the number 92; the second two scores (88 and 86) are represented by the mid-point of the interval in which they occur, 87. When the first two scores are added together individually, the sum is 186; 94 + 92 = 186; but by letting 92 represent these two scores and adding the two 92's (actually 2 x 92), the sum is 184 — which is slightly less than 94 + 92. It is obvious that although some errors in doing this will produce subtotals that are too small, other errors will give subtotals in the intervals that are too large. The net result is that the sum of the subtotals will be close to the sum obtained by actually adding the individual scores; and in our example $\Sigma fX = 3772$, while ΣX in the original problem $= 3778$.

A formula for the M which uses ΣfX should give a fairly good estimate of M, even when all scores within intervals are *represented* by midpoints of the intervals. Then, $M = \dfrac{\Sigma fX}{N} = \dfrac{3772}{56} = 67.4$ or 67 in whole numbers.

THE MEAN FURTHER DEFINED. Like many concepts in mathematics, the mean may be considered in several ways. An important way to conceive of the mean is as a balance point. In order to do this, the idea of *deviations* from the mean must be developed. (Consider, for example, the following measurements: 20; 17; 16; 12; and 10. The $\Sigma X = 75$, and $M = \dfrac{75}{5} = 15$. The deviation of each measurement will be defined as the number of score units each measurement (or score) is from the M. Representing each deviation by the letter x, then $x = X - M$; i.e., the deviation, or distance, of each score from the mean can be found by subtracting the mean from each score.

Placing these data in a table, the following results are obtained:

X	x
20	+5
17	+2
16	+1
12	−3
10	−5

Note that the $\Sigma\,x = 0$ (when the x's are summed algebraically). If the measurements are placed along a line with the mean at a point, the reason for the result obtained in summing deviations becomes clear.

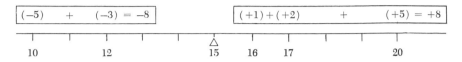

The mean, then, is the balance point at which the sum of deviations in measurement from this point equals zero. In the next section you will find that this balance point concept of the mean becomes important in determining variability, or typical deviations, from the typical score.

A Short Method to Determine M from a Distribution. By using the concept of the mean as the point at which total positive deviations are equal to the total negative deviation — that is, where positive and negative deviations add up to zero — a short method of computing the mean from grouped data can be developed.

Referring back to the illustration of scores on an algebra test, a guess can be made concerning the point at which the mean will occur. This *assumed mean*, AM, may be taken at any point in the distribution, but it is an obvious advantage to make the best guess possible. In this case the best guess is probably an M of 67. Then the deviation, x', of each *interval*[1] from the interval in which AM is found will be as shown:

	X	f	x'	fx'	
	90-94	2	+5	+10	
	85-89	2	+4	+ 8	
	80-84	4	+3	+12	
	75-79	8	+2	+16	
	70-74	6	+1	+ 6	
AM = 67→	65-69	11	0	0	($\Sigma + fx' = 52$)
	60-64	9	−1	− 9	
	55-59	7	−2	−14	
	50-54	5	−3	−15	
	45-49	0	−4	0	
	40-44	2	−5	−10	
		N = 56			($\Sigma - fx' = -48$)
					$\Sigma\,fx' = +4$

[1]The amount that each f deviates from the AM could have been used; however, if this were done, in each deviation the factor of five would be present due to the interval size. By using the interval deviations instead of exact amounts, five units have been factored out to simplify our figures. The factor is then reintroduced later.

The Σ fx' of +4 indicates that the AM of 67 is too low; if the guess, or AM, had been the correct M, Σ fx' would have been equal to zero. The number +4 can help us to find the true M. Note that +4 was derived by finding the number of interval units above and below the interval of the assumed M. Now in terms of score units, the factor 5 must be introduced, since each interval is five score units in size. Then, (5) (+4) = +20 is the total number of score units which we have guessed too low, but obviously, adding 20 to 67 will not give us the true mean. Recalling that the mean was found by dividing total numbers of score units by N, then the total number of score units that we have guessed too low must be divided by N also; $\frac{20}{56}$ = .4. Therefore,

$$M = 67 + .4 = 67.4.$$

In summary,

M = AM + or − ic where i = size of the interval in score units and

$$c = \frac{\Sigma \, fx'}{N}$$

Note that:

1. In the formula M = AM plus or minus ic. (Conceivably the guess might have been too high in which case Σ fx' would give a negative number that would "pull" the guess down to the true M.)
2. The formula calls for finding c by dividing Σ fx' by N then multiplying by i. (In our illustration, the order of operations was (i · Σ fx') ÷ N, but the result will be the same.)

The Normal Probability Curve and Variability

One of the most interesting and astonishing discoveries man has ever made was the determination of a relationship between measurements of many kinds of natural phenomena and the mathematical laws of chance. The discovery was made by the mathematician Gauss. In noting the distribution of errors made in astronomical observations, Gauss found that the distribution was approximated by DeMoivre's probability curve. The probability curve graphically described the mathematical distribution of chance happenings such as the flip of coins, the rolling of dice, etc.

The Probability Curve

To illustrate the DeMoivre curve, suppose five coins are flipped all at one time. The probability of getting a certain number of heads appearing on a given flip can be determined in one of two ways: the five coins could be tossed many thousands of times and the number of times a given number of heads appeared divided by the number of tosses would give some idea of the chance, or probability, of the event occurring; or, the probability of the event(s) happening could be determined by applying mathematical laws of chance. In our example, a histogram which describes the probability of getting a certain number of heads on any given toss will turn out as shown at the left in Figure 5.7. Shown in Figure 5.7 also are the histograms which describe the probability of a given number of heads appearing if one were to flip 7 or 14 coins.

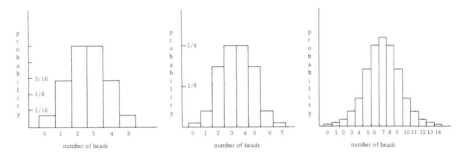

Figure 5.7   Probability of the Number of Heads Appearing When 5, 7, and 14 Coins Are Tossed

If the number of coins flipped is increased to a very large number and the ends of the bars of the histogram are connected, it can be seen that a curve will be formed such as shown in Figure 5.8.

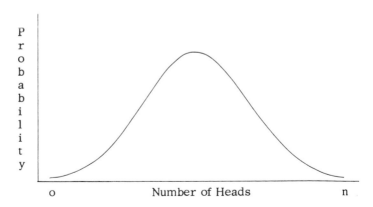

Figure 5.8   Curve which Describes the Probability of a Given Number of Heads Appearing on a Given Toss when n Is Large.

The Normal Curve

Consider now what happens when measurements are made of many phenomena associated with our study of human beings. If a researcher were to keep a tally of the height of men who reported over a period of a month in response to a draft for the armed services, the results might look something like this:

Height (inches)	f
82-84″	1
79-81″	3
76-78″	6
73-75″	8
70-72″	11
67-69″	9
64-66″	6
61-63″	2
58-60″	1

In Figure 5.9 the data presented above are plotted as a frequency polygon.

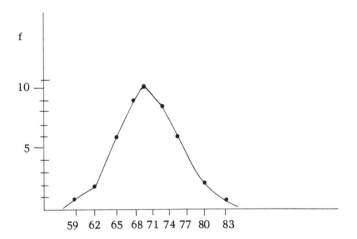

Figure 5.9 Frequency Polygon

From the Figures 5.8 and 5.9 it would appear that the frequency polygon of the "normal" distribution of measurements — such as men's heights — is similar to the probability curve obtained with chance factors

— such as the flipping of a coin. Actually this apparent coincidence is not a coincidence at all; it is now known that the factors in nature which determine height, weight, I.Q.'s, etc., are governed by laws of chance also. Geneticists have found that genes — chemicals that seem to be responsible for the heredity of characteristics — are distributed according to the laws of chance. In addition, environmental factors and random selection of people or things to be measured will tend to cause measurements to follow the laws of chance.

Variability and Normal Distributions

At the beginning of this chapter it was stated that the measures of central tendency — the mean, the mode, and the median — represent the "typical" measurement within a group of measurements; however, the use of a particular point in a distribution of measurements to typify the distribution leaves much to be desired. There is no way of telling how widely dispersed from the point other measurements might be; nor is it known within what range of measurements the typical group of measurements might be found. Figure 5.10 illustrates the problem that develops in using the mean as the typical score on an I.Q. test given to two groups of pupils.

The graphs show that Groups I and II have the same mean of 100 score units, but it is obvious that the score of 100, which represents the average in both groups, is not adequate in describing the two groups. What is required is a measure which shows how much variation there is from a central point within a group of measurements.

The range (denoted by the letter R) — found by subtracting the lowest measurement from the highest in a distribution — gives some indication of dispersal, but it has several drawbacks:

1. It is possible that the highest and lowest score in a distribution are not at all representative of the extreme scores.
2. R does not give any indication of where the greatest concentration of scores occurs.

Average Deviation

One way to approach the problem is to find the "average" amount which scores deviate from the mean. The average deviation, or AD, can be determined by finding the sum, or total, of the deviations from M and dividing this total by the number of deviations. A difficulty arises, however, if deviations from the mean are summed up algebraically. In discussing the mean it was pointed out that the mean is a balance point

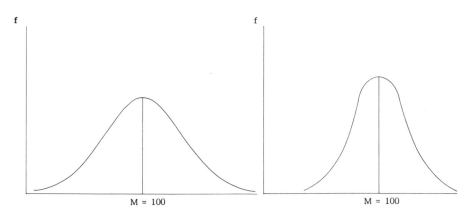

GROUP I   GROUP II

Figure 5.10 Distribution of I.Q. Scores Given to Two Different Groups

where positive and negative deviations are equal; thus, if deviations are summed as signed numbers, the sum will equal zero ($\Sigma x = 0$, where $x = X - M$). By ignoring the signs of the deviations and instead summing x's in terms of absolute values, the average deviation can be determined. Then, $AD = \Sigma|x|/N$ where AD is the average deviation, $\Sigma|x|$ is the sum of absolute values of the deviations from M, and N is the number of measurements (therefore, also the number of deviations).

Standard Deviation

The most useful measure of variability in terms of describing concentration of scores in a distribution is called the standard deviation. It is computed in a manner which is similar to the way of finding the average deviation. The standard deviation of a representative sample from a large population of scores can be given the symbol SD; the standard deviation of the entire population of scores or measurements possible is given the symbol σ (the Greek letter sigma). The formula for finding σ (or SD) is given as follows:

*1.

$$\sigma = \sqrt{\frac{\Sigma x^2}{N}}$$

---

[1]Actually in dealing with SD, the formula $SD = \sqrt{\frac{\Sigma x^2}{N-1}}$ applies since the selection of a *sample* to compute SD introduces an error which is compensated for by subtracting one unit from N; however, unless the sample is small — N is less than 30 — the error is not large enough to cause concern.

Note that the formula indicates that σ is the square root of the average of squared deviations. From this it is obvious that the standard deviation is similar to — but not the same as — the average deviation.

The formula also shows that the difficulty encountered with signs of deviations in computing the average deviation is eliminated in the determination of σ; squaring x's produces nothing but positive values. This advantage is but a minor one compared to the information that σ produces concerning a normal (or somewhat normal) distribution of measurements.

In order to understand the importance of σ as a measure of variability, reference must be made to the normal probability curve. Mathematicians have found that the probability curve — and hence the normal curve — is determined by the following mathematical equation

$y = \dfrac{N}{\sigma \sqrt{2\pi}}\ e^{\frac{-x^2}{2\sigma^2}}$. It is not necessary to understand all the mathe-

matical why's and wherefores involved in the formula to see that σ plays an important part in the equation and that σ thus helps to determine the shape of the probability curve which can be graphed from the equation. What specific part does it play?

A diagram of the normal probability curve illustrates the concept. Figure 5.11 shows that in a normal distribution the scores which are one standard deviation below, and one standard deviation above the mean occur at precisely the points of inflection on the curve: i.e., the points where the normal probability curve changes direction of curvature in moving away from the mean. The importance of the inflection point lies in what happens in terms of the value of y (or the frequency of scores). The sudden change in the shape of the curve indicates that there is a rapid drop in the frequency of scores to the left of $-1\ \sigma$ and to the right of $+1\ \sigma$; therefore, it can be concluded that the area between $-1\ \sigma$ and $+1\ \sigma$ is the locale of the greatest concentration of scores; it is the area within which the most typical scores occur. The area beyond the two points is the area of *atypical* scores.

The formula SD (or σ) $= \sqrt{\dfrac{\Sigma x^2}{N}}$ defines the computation neces-

sary to find the standard deviation mathematically. At times, though, depending on the data, it may be desirable to determine SD in other ways. If the data have been arranged in a frequency distribution, for example, the standard deviation can be obtained more easily by using the following formula:

$$SD = \sqrt{\frac{\Sigma fx^2}{N}}$$

Obviously this formula will give the same result as the original formula for SD, but it will save some computations where there are duplicate scores since each deviation that reoccurs is multiplied by the number of duplications (f).

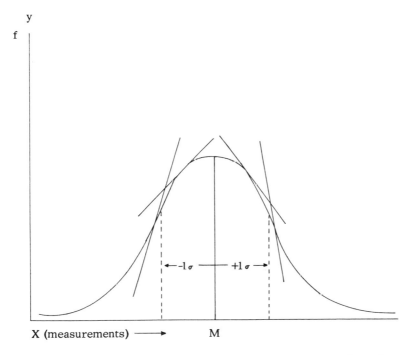

Figure 5.11 The Normal Probability Curve as Related to the Standard Deviation

When scores are placed in a frequency distribution, a short method can be applied using the assumed mean idea. The method is illustrated using the same problem presented in the section of this chapter concerned with the mean.

	f	x′	fx′	fx′²
90-94	2	+5	+10	50
85-89	2	+4	+ 8	32
80-84	4	+3	+12	36
75-79	8	+2	+16	32
70-74	6	+1	+ 6	6
AM⟶ 65-69	11	0	0	0
60-64	9	−1	− 9	9
55-59	7	−2	−14	28
50-54	5	−3	−15	45
45-49	0	−4	0	0
40-44	2	−5	−10	50
	N = 56		$\Sigma fx' = +4$	$\Sigma fx'^2 = 288$

$$SD = i \sqrt{\frac{\Sigma fx'^2}{N} - c^2}$$

where i = the size of the interval

$$= 5$$

and $c = \dfrac{\Sigma fx'}{N}$

$$= \frac{4}{56}$$

$$SD = 5 \sqrt{\frac{288}{56} - \left(\frac{4}{56}\right)^2}$$

As with the assumed mean method of finding M, the short method of finding SD saves much computation by factoring out "i" and allowing us to work with small figures.

The standard deviation may also be determined directly from raw scores without having to find deviations from the mean. The formula for finding SD in this manner can be derived from the original equation for SD as follows:

Since $SD = \sqrt{\dfrac{\Sigma x^2}{N}}$ then $(SD)^2 = \dfrac{\Sigma x^2}{N}$

but $x = X - M$

then $SD^2 = \dfrac{\Sigma (X-M)^2}{N}$

$$= \frac{\Sigma (X^2 - 2MX + M^2)}{N}$$

$$= \frac{\Sigma X^2 - \Sigma 2MX + \Sigma M^2}{N}$$

$$= \frac{\Sigma X^2}{N} - \frac{\Sigma 2MX}{N} + \frac{\Sigma M^2}{N}$$

$$\text{but } \frac{\Sigma\, 2MX}{N} = \frac{2M\,\Sigma\, X}{N}$$

since 2M is a constant factor which would sum up each time

$$\text{also, } 2M \frac{\Sigma\, X}{N} = 2M^2$$

$$\text{since } \frac{\Sigma\, X}{N} = M$$

$$\text{also, } \frac{\Sigma\, M^2}{N} = \frac{NM^2}{N} \text{ since}$$

$$M^2 \text{ sums N times}$$

$$\text{and } \frac{NM^2}{N} = M^2$$

$$\therefore\ (SD)^2 = \frac{\Sigma\, X^2}{N} - 2M^2 + M^2$$

$$\therefore\ (SD)^2 = \frac{\Sigma\, X^2}{N} - M^2$$

$$\boxed{\therefore\ SD = \sqrt{\frac{\Sigma X^2}{N} - M^2}}$$

Thus, the standard deviation can be found directly from scores or measurements by the following steps:

1. Square each measurement (X^2 represents this step).
2. Sum the X^2's and divide this sum by N.
3. Subtract M^2 from the figure obtained in step 2.
4. Extract the square root of the figure obtained in step 3.

As a final note, it must be observed that although several formulas for finding SD have been presented, all of the formulas have reference to, or are derived from, the original definition.

$$SD = \sqrt{\frac{\Sigma x^2}{N}}$$

Often research investigators will use many variations of the same formula. The choice of formula will depend on the form in which the data have been organized as well as the kind of equipment available to carry out computations.

The Semi-interquartile Range

Variability may also be expressed in terms of rank order of measurements. For this purpose the semi-interquartile range, represented by the letter Q, is determined. Q is calculated by finding the score distance between the 1st quartile or 25th percentile (Q_1), and the third quartile (Q_3) or 75th percentile. This distance is divided in half to produce the semi-interquartile range. The semi-interquartile range, Q, is laid off on each side of the median — rather than the mean — by adding it to and subtracting it from the median. In terms of this description of Q,

$$Q = \frac{Q_3 - Q_1}{2} \qquad \text{where} \qquad Q_3 = \text{75th percentile}$$

$$Q_1 = \text{25th percentile}$$

If the distribution is normal, adding Q to and subtracting Q from the Mdn will produce a range from Q_1 to Q_3. As Figure 5.12 shows, however, if the distribution is skewed, the limits of Q will not coincide with Q_1 and Q_3.

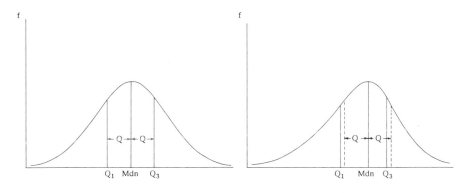

Figure 5.12 Q in a Normal and a Skewed Distribution

More About the Normal Probability Curve

At the beginning of this chapter there was a discussion of the close relationship between the probability curve, obtained by plotting the distribution of chance happenings, and the normal curve, obtained by plotting measurements of various kinds. The section of the chapter concerning variability demonstrates how the relationship provides an excellent way to measure variability in terms of the standard deviation; but the remarkable relationship between the normal and the probability curves pays further dividends which will be described in this section of the chapter.

Figure 5.13 represents the normal distribution curve which might be obtained by plotting data obtained by measuring the I.Q. of 1 million randomly selected individuals.

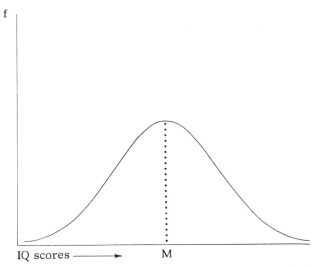

Figure 5.13 The Normal Distribution of 1 Million I.Q. Scores

Note that the line which extends from the point called the mean to the curve can be thought of as a series of points that represent the number of individuals who attained an I.Q. score equal to the mean. The total of all the points is the total f denoted by the corresponding f found along the y axis.

If we now move to the right along the X axis a very short distance (that distance will be designated as Δ), another ordinate line (vertical from the X axis to the curve) will provide information regarding the number or frequency of I.Q. measurements at the point we have selected. In moving a short distance, Δ, to the right, we now have a long narrow figure which is very close to being a rectangle. Figure 5.14 shows that the rectangle-like area will enclose the number of scores that fall between M and M + Δ. Also, the scores within the area will represent a certain percentage of all 1 million scores that would fall within the total area under the curve.

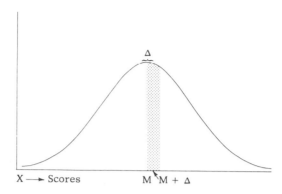

Figure 5.14 The Number of Scores That Occur Between M and M + Δ

Another short move to the right generates another small rectangle-like area that will enclose a certain number, and hence a certain percentage of the 1 million measurements. It is to be noted that as moves are made to the right or the left from the mean, the narrow rectangle-like figures will grow shorter and shorter and thus enclose less and less of the total area (or percentage of the total area) under the curve.

Obviously, the method described for finding the percentage of area (or percentage of the total 1 million scores) would be long and tedious. Fortunately, the calculus provides us with a mathematical method of summing up ordinates as they move from one point to another under a curve. This summing of ordinates — by the process called integration — gives an accurate figure representing the area under the curve from any point selected to any other point.

In our example of 1 million I.Q. scores, we would find that the integration of the equation for the normal probability curve $\left(y = \dfrac{N}{\sigma \sqrt{2\pi}}\ e^{\frac{-x^2}{2\sigma^2}} \right)$ from the mean to $+ 1\ \sigma$ would include about 341,300 out of the 1 million scores; i.e., the area under the curve from M to $+ 1\ \sigma$ is about 34.13% of the total area.

Table A.2 in Appendix A has been compiled for the express purpose of facilitating the determination of areas under the normal probability curve from the mean to various numbers or fractions of σ's. The table was computed by the method of integration described. It is to be noted that the figures are only from the mean toward the positive direction; in other words, only the area under the curve to the right of the mean is given. Since the normal probability curve is symmetrical, negative σ values will give the same percentages of area under the curve that are obtained by the corresponding positive values.

Problems Involving the Normal Probability Curve

Table A.2 in Appendix A has been computed in terms of the equation for the probability curve. If the number of measurements, or scores, made in a normal distribution is known, the percentage of area under the curve, between the mean and any point, multiplied by the total number of scores will produce the number of scores that fall within the area. This occurs because the normal distribution can be regarded as the same as the probability distribution.

Since the figures in Table A.2 are in terms of a general concept which describes any normal probability distribution, areas are determined in terms of standard deviation units from the mean; i.e., $+ 1 \sigma$ unit, or 1.2σ unit, etc. It is required, therefore, that X scores, which ordinarily are plotted along the base (X) axis, should be converted to σ units.

Converting X scores to σ units is a relatively simple matter. The converted unit is called a z score. The formula for changing a raw score (measurement) to its corresponding z score (in standard deviation units measured from the mean) is as follows:

$$z = \frac{x}{\sigma} \quad \text{or in other words} \quad z = \frac{X-M}{\sigma}$$

If the standard deviation is taken from a sample of the total population of scores, $z = \frac{X-M}{SD}$.

From the formula it can be seen that the score distance that the score deviates from the mean is found first, $(X-M)$; then, by dividing by the standard deviation the distance is changed to the number of σ units the score distance represents.

Illustrative problems:

An I.Q. test given to a large group of people results in a normal distribution of scores with mean of 100 and a standard deviation of 16 I.Q. score units.

1. Find the z score which corresponds to the I.Q. score of 120.

Answer: $z = \frac{120-100}{16} = 1.25$

2. Find the number of deviation units that a score of 90 is below the mean.

Answer: $z = \dfrac{90-100}{16} = -.625$

3. What X score corresponds to a z score of +1.8?

Answer: $X = z \ (SD) + M$
$X = (+1.8)(16) + 100$
$X = 128.8$

Generally, a normal distribution will range from approximately -3σ units below M to about $+3 \ \sigma$ units above M. Theoretically the probability distribution from which the mathematical properties of the normal probability curve are derived extends infinitely in both directions from the mean, never quite reaching the X axis. Table A.2 illustrates, however, that 99.74 per cent of the area under the curve is to be found between $\pm 3 \ \sigma$ units measured from the mean; therefore, most of the cases fall within this area. If the number of cases measured, in terms of a factor that produces a normal distribution, were 1 million then 1 million times $.9974 = 997,400$ cases would fall between $-3 \ \sigma$ below M to $+3 \ \sigma$ above M.

Illustrative problems:

If the foregoing hypothical I.Q. measurement had been made on 1 million people:

1. How many scores would fall between $-2 \ \sigma$ units (below M) and $+1.3 \ \sigma$ units (above M)? The problem can be pictured graphically as shown in Figure 5.15.
2. How many scores (or measurements) would fall between $1.0 \ \sigma$ and $1.5 \ \sigma$ units above M? The graphic representation of the problem is shown in Figure 5.16.

The properties of the normal probability curve can provide additional useful information. To illustrate more of the kinds of questions that can be answered, the following hypothetical situation involving scores on the College Board Examination will be discussed in the remainder of the chapter.

DATA:

Many high school students throughout the United States have taken the College Board Examination. The General Aptitude portion of the examination consists of a section concerned with students' ability in

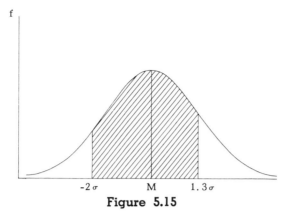

Figure 5.15

Answer: a. 0 to −2 σ units includes 47.72% of total area (Table A.2)
         b. 0 to + 1.3 σ units includes 40.32% of total area (Table A.2)
         c. 47.72% + 40.32% = 88.04 % of area
         d. 1,000,000 x .8804 = 880,400 cases (approximately)

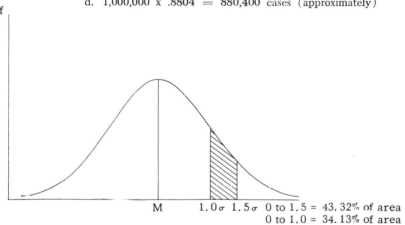

1.0σ 1.5σ 0 to 1.5 = 43.32% of area
                         0 to 1.0 = 34.13% of area

Figure 5.16

Answer: a. Between 0 and 1.0 σ there are 34.13% of all the cases
             (Table A.2)
         b. Between 0 and 1.5 σ there are 43.32% of all the cases
         c. Therefore between 1.0 and 1.5 SD units 43.32% − 34.13%
             = 9.19% of the cases would occur
         d. 1 million X .0919 = 91,900 cases(approximately)

handling mathematics. Over the years it has been found that there is
a normal distribution of scores on the mathematics section of the examination with a mean score of 500 and a standard deviation of 100.
Let us suppose that 1 million students have taken the examination.

PROBLEMS:

1. How many of the 1 million students scored 650 or more on the examination? The answers to this question can be found by a determination of the percentage of cases which are to be found beyond the score 650. In order to solve the problem, the score 650 must first be converted to standard deviation units (a z score).

$$z = \frac{650\text{-}500}{100} = \frac{150}{100} = +1.5 \ \sigma \text{ units}$$

Table A.2 shows that between M (0 σ) and +1.5 σ units there are 43.32% of the cases (area under the curve). Then beyond +1.5 σ units there are 50% − 43.32 = 6.68% of the cases; therefore, 1 X 10^6 X .0668 = 66,800 or almost 67,000 of the 1 million students received scores of 650 or better on the mathematics section of the examination. The problem is pictured graphically in Figure 5.17.

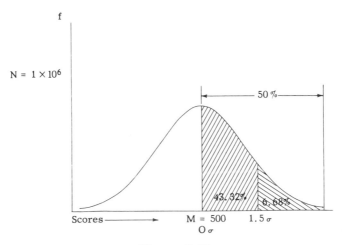

Figure 5.17

2. What proportion of the students scored less than 380? Converting the score 380 to standard deviation units (380-500) the answer is −1.2 σ units. Table A.2 shows that between M and −1.2 σ units, 38.49% of the cases will be found; therefore, 50% − 38.49% = 11.51% of the cases scored below the −1.2 σ point. In terms of

proportion, 11.51 can be expressed as .1151 (approximately 12 out of 100).

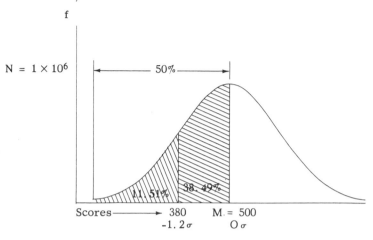

Figure 5.18

3. How high would a student need to score on this examination in order to be among the top 5%? The problem requires that we work in a direction opposite to that which was taken to solve questions 1 and 2. The first step to be taken is to determine the σ score that corresponds to the top 5%. Since Table A.2 scores are laid out from the M or 0 σ point rather than from the top, the top 5% must be expressed as 50% — 5% or the point which forms the outer boundary for the 45% of the area under the curve measured from the mean. From Table A.2 it is found that the point is approximately 1.64 σ units from the mean. Converting 1.64 σ units to raw score, X = (1.64) (100) + 500; X = 664. The graphic solution to the problem is shown in Figure 5.19.

4. What scores are so extreme that they were made by only 1% of all the students who took the examination? Since there are two extremes to the distribution, the extreme 1% of all the students means the top ½% and the bottom ½%. Again it is necessary to convert extreme percentages to percentages measured from M. Then 50% — ½% are the extreme boundaries which are of interest: 50% — ½% = 49.50% measured from the M. Entering Table A.2 we find that the two sections of 49.50% areas under the curve are found between —2.58 σ units (below M) and +2.58 σ units

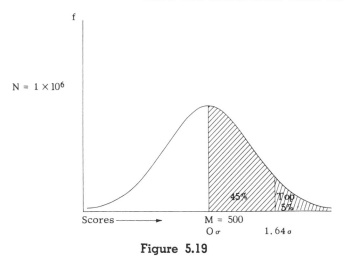

Figure 5.19

(above M). Converting to raw score units, $X = \pm 2.58\,(100) + 500$; $X = 242$ and $X = 758$ are the points which mark the boundaries of scores which are so extreme that they were made by only 1% of all the students. See Figure 5.20.

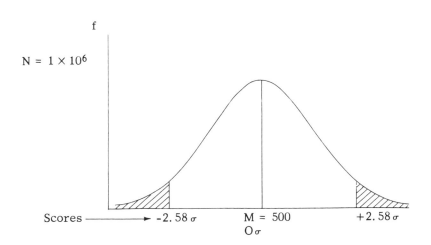

Figure 5.20

5. How many of the 1 million students scored between 340 and 620 on the examination? The scores 340 and 620 correspond to

−1.6 σ and +1.2 σ units respectively $\left(z = \dfrac{340\text{-}500}{100} \text{ and } z = \dfrac{620\text{-}500}{100} \right)$. Between the mean and −1.6 σ units and +1.2 σ units there are 44.52% + 38.49% = 83.01% of all the cases. Since 1 million students took the test, $1 \times 10^6 \times .8301$ or about 830,100 pupils scored between 340 and 620.

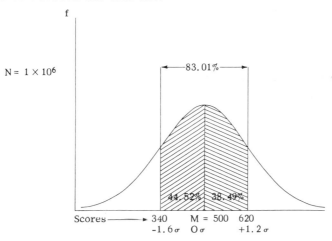

Figure 5.21

6. How many of the students scored between 620 and 700 on the test? It has been determined that the score 620 corresponds to +1.2 σ units. The score 700 is +2.0 σ units from the mean. From the mean to 2.0 σ units 47.72% of the cases are to be found: and from the mean to 1.2 σ units there are 38.49% of the cases. Since the 47.72% area contains part of the 38.49% of the cases which are of interest, then 47.72% − 38.49% = 9.23% of the total students between 620 and 700. This would be $1 \times 10^6 \times .0923 = 92.300$ students. (See Figure 5.22.)

7. What is the percentile rank of a student who scored 600 on the test? The score 600 corresponds to +1.0 σ units above the mean. From Table A.2 it is found that between the mean and + 1.0 σ units there are 34.13% of the cases. There are also another 50% of the cases below M; therefore, below the score 600 there are 50% + 34.13% = (about) 84% of the cases. Since the definition of percentile rank is precisely this, a student who scores 600 is at the 84th percentile.

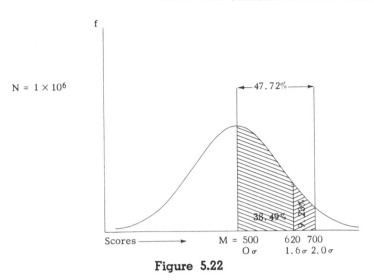

Figure 5.22

8. What score would a student make who placed at the 30th percentile? The 30th percentile must be measured in terms of its distance from the mean in order to use Table A.2. Since the 30th percentile indicates the percentage of cases below the point in question, there are still 50% − 30% = 20% of the cases between the point and the mean. Table A.2 indicates that −.53 σ corresponds to the lower boundary of the area immediately below the mean which contains 20% of the cases. Then X = (−.53)(100) +500 = 447 is the score which is at the 30th percentile. (See Figure 5.23.)

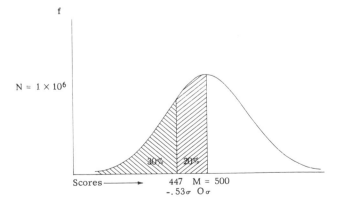

Figure 5.23

9. What is the probability that someone picked at random from the students who took the examination scored 700 or more? The score 700 is 2 σ units above the mean. From M to 700 there are 47.72% cases. Another 50% of the cases are below M; therefore, up to the score 700 there are 50% + 47.72% = 97.72% of the cases. Above 700 only 2.28% of the cases are found; thus the chances (or probability) of picking someone at random who scored 700 or better would be 2.28/100 or p = .0228.

10. What are the odds against picking someone at random who scored 700 or more? Odds against are determined from the probability by the following method:

   a. The probability for picking someone at random who scored 700 or more (from question 9) was found to be about 2/100 or 1/50.
   b. Since there is 1 chance in 50 of picking correctly, then there are 49 chances in 50 of picking incorrectly.
   c. The odds against picking correctly are 49 (wrong) to 1 (right).

Selected Exercises

1. State a problem that would require research in which data collected can be expressed either qualitatively or quantitatively. Discuss the advantages and disadvantages of both methods in the case you have cited.

2. a. Use the "raw score" methods to find the mean and standard deviation for the following scores:
      5, 3, 2, 4, 7, 8, 3, 10, 5, 4, 5, 4, 4, 5, 4, 6, 6, 6,
      6, 7, 1, 8, 2, 3, 5, 6, 4, 4, 6, 5, 6, 3, 2, 3, 3, 8,
      7, 7, 5, 6, 7, 4, 4, 6, 5, 4, 4, 6, 6, 6, 5, 5, 5, 5.
   b. Suppose the data listed above were from a teacher rating scale with the rating one (1) being the lowest and ten (10) the highest. Using the ranges −3 to −2 SD's (z-scores as very poor, −2 to −1 as poor, −1 to 0 as low average, 0 to +1 as high average, +1 to +2 as above average and +2 to +3 as superior), what terms may be applied to describe teachers who were rated on the scale as follows: 6? 3? 8?
   c. With no other information than that which has been given above, how should the terms used in b. be qualified?
   d. Compute the mean of the distribution.

3. Explain the difference among a simple distribution of measurements, a frequency distribution, and a grouped frequency distri-

bution. Explain when it would be most advantageous to use: (1) the simple distribution; (2) the frequency distribution; (3) the grouped frequency distribution.

4. Why is the selection of interval size for a grouped frequency distribution more or less arbitrary? What factors should guide the selection of interval size?

5. The following set of measurements (scores) was obtained by testing a group of 100 pupils with a list of 150 most frequently misspelled words: 109, 101, 116, 98, 106, 97, 70, 100, 101, 93, 83, 103, 100, 92, 80, 107, 103, 113, 92, 110, 95, 85, 112, 102, 104, 117, 92, 97, 107, 103, 82, 107, 100, 98, 104, 73, 105, 100, 76, 101, 111, 125, 113, 99, 100, 122, 86, 87, 93, 105, 94, 100, 99, 89, 84, 104, 102, 120, 89, 114, 100, 115, 101, 90, 81, 118, 119, 88, 130, 100, 101, 100, 87, 111, 111, 98, 102, 101, 100, 90, 88, 96, 97, 99, 106, 103, 91, 102, 91, 96, 100, 101, 105, 99, 102, 99, 99, 98, 91, 94.

   a. Arrange the scores in a frequency distribution (interval of one).
   b. What is the range of the scores? R = ...
   c. Arrange the scores in a grouped frequency distribution (use i = 5).

6. Using the table prepared in question 5c:
   a. Draw a histogram that represents the data.
   b. Draw a frequency polygon to represent the data.
   (for best results use graph paper)

7. Given the following frequency distributions of I.Q. scores administered to two groups of children:

I.Q.	Group I	Group II
120-124	2	
115-119	4	2
110-114	8	5
105-109	12	13
100-104	17	19
95-99	24	28
90-94	16	17
85-89	13	12
80-84	7	6
75-79	5	2
70-74	1	
	N = 109	N = 104

   a. Find the particular measurement (score) that typifies the scores in each group generally (to the nearest whole number). Use any method convenient to make the computations.

b. Does the "typical" score provide a good picture of the I.Q. that the typical child in each group is likely to have? Explain.

c. Using the data and data analysis you have at hand up to this point — that is without doing any further computations — draw a comparison between the two groups. What part of your comparison is precise? What part lacks precision? Why?

8. In a study of pupil ability to run the 100 yard dash a researcher compiled the following data:

Seconds	f
15	1
14.5	5
14	14
13.5	2
13	2
12.5	0
12	0
11.5	0
11	0
10.5	6

The investigator reported that the average pupil in the group could run 100 yards in 13 seconds. How did he arrive at the figure? What other figure could be given to represent the ability of the typical pupil in the group? Which figure better represents the typical pupil's ability?

9. Using the data provided in question 7:

a. Determine a range of scores (measurements) that mark off the most typical scores attained by children in each group. (Use any method convenient to make computations.)

b. Draw a comparison between the two groups.

c. What part of your comparison is precise? What part lacks precision? Why?

10. For the remaining questions, assume that both distributions of scores given for question 7 are distributed normally.

a. About how many scores in Group I fall between .5 σ and 1.5 σ?

b. How many scores in Group II fall between .5 σ and 1.5 σ?

c. About how many scores in Group I fall between -1 σ and 1.5σ?

11. a. How many pupils in each group scored 100 or better? (The answer can be determined directly from the distributions or by computation. Find the answer both ways and check one against the other.)

    b. How many pupils in Group II scored between 77 and 97 on the test?

    c. What percentile rank corresponds to the score 107 in Group I? In Group II?

12. a. What is the probability that someone picked at random from Group I scored 110 or more? From Group II?

    b. What are the odds *against* picking someone at random from Group I who scored less than 80?

Suggested Activities

1. Obtain a set of at least fifty measurements of one of the following types: scores on a test in your class; the weather bureau report of low temperatures recorded for the previous day in various cities throughout the country; the I.Q. scores of pupils in your classes; stock market quotations of the closing price of fifty stocks picked at random from the daily paper; the altitude of the capitol cities of the fifty states. (Write the measurements down in whatever order they happen to be obtained.)

    a. Make a guess regarding the median score of measurement also as to what measurement marks the beginning of the top twenty-five percent.

    b. Select a score at random and make a guess as to the percentile rank of the score.

    c. Arrange the scores in a grouped frequency distribution and make another guess as to the percentile rank of the score you selected for question b.

    d. Compute the median and 75th percentile. Compare the computed score with the guesses you made.

    e. Compute the percentile rank of the score selected for question b and compare the computation to your guesses.

2. Using the measurements obtained for question one, prepare a histogram and a frequency polygon to represent the data.

3. Prepare a cumulative frequency graph of the data obtained for question 1 (transform the cumulative frequency figures to percentiles).

4. List as many as you can of the traits and human characteristics that can be measured (for example, speed reading ability and the length of index fingers).

For the following questions refer back to the data collected for activity No. 1 above.

5. Determine which measurement or score typifies the measurements collected for activity #1. (Hint: remember that three different measures can be referred to as "typical.") Which measure is the best one for the data you have? Why?

6. What *range* of measurements includes the most typical measurements in the distribution?

7. Compute the average deviation for the data. (Hint: remember that AD = sum of the deviations from M and that sum is found by ignoring the signs of the deviation.) How does AD compare to SD found for question three? Refer to a normal distribution curve and tell why SD is a better indication of "typical" range of scores.

Selected Readings

1. BEST, JOHN W., *Research in Education*. Englewood Cliffs, N. J.: Prentice-Hall, Inc., 1959 (p. 211-225).

2. GARRETT, HENRY E., *Statistics in Psychology and Education* (fourth edition), New York: Longmans, Green and Co., 1954 (Chapters 2, 3, and 5).

3. GARRETT, HENRY E., *Elementary Statistics* (second edition). New York: David McKay Co., Inc., 1962 (Chapters 3, 4, and 6).

4. HAMMOND, KENNETH R., AND JAMES E. HOUSEHOLDER, *Introduction to the Statistical Method*. New York: Alfred A. Knopf, 1962(Chapters 3, 4, and 5).

5. JOHNSON, PALMER O., AND ROBERT W. B. JACKSON, *Modern Statistical Methods: Descriptive and Inductive*. Chicago: Rand McNally & Co., 1959 (Chapter 2).

6. KERLINGER, FRED N., *Foundations of Behavioral Research*. New York: Holt, Rinehart & Winston, Inc., 1965. (Chapters 8 and 9)

7. KOENKER, ROBERT H., *Simplified Statistics*. Bloomington, Ill.: McKnight & McKnight Publishing Co., 1961 (Chapters 1, 2, 4 and 5).

8. PETERS, CHARLES C., AND WALTER R. VAN VOORHIS, *Statistical Procedures and Their Mathematical Bases*. New York: McGraw-Hill Book Co., 1940 (Chapters 2, 3, and 10).

9. RUGG, HAROLD O., *Statistical Methods Applied to Education*. Boston: Houghton Mifflin Co., 1917 (Chapters 5, 6, 7, and 8)

10. RUMMEL, J. FRANCIS, *An Introduction to Research Procedures in Education*. New York: Harper & Row, Publishers, 1958 (p. 149-176).

11. SENDERS, VIRGINIA L., *Measurement and Statistics*. New York: Oxford University Press, 1958 (Chapters 5 and 6).

12. UNDERWOOD, BENTON J. and others, *Elementary Statistics*. New York: Appleton-Century-Crofts, 1954 (Chapters 5, 6, and 7).

13. VAN DALEN, DEOBOLD B., AND WILLIAM J. MEYER, *Understanding Educational Research*. New York: McGraw-Hill Book Co., 1962 (Chapter 13).

14. YONDER, W. J., *Experimentation and Measurement*. Washington: National Science Teachers Association, 1962 (Chapters 4 and 5).

Chapter 6

Statistical Design
of Experiments
in Education

The nature of experiments in education was discussed in Chapter 1; however, since experimental research in education is generally geared to produce quantitative data, the statistical methods used to analyze such data will largely determine the design of experiments. Statistical design is an integral part of experiments in education.

The sections which follow in this chapter present the basic ideas that underlie experiments in education and a few of the simple statistical methods used. The advanced researcher may use more sophisticated statistical tools, but the rationale which undergirds more complicated methods is the same as that which pertains to the methods to be discussed in this chapter.

Theory of Sampling

Educational research is often carried out to determine how various factors influence pupil learning. It is usually impossible, however, to experiment with all pupils who may fall into a particular category the researcher wishes to study. A statistical method, based on sampling populations, offers a way out of the dilemma.

Before the theory of sampling is described, it is necessary to define some terms. As you would probably guess, the term *population* means any set or group of things (including people) that are alike in respect to some particular characteristics; for example, all third grade pupils in the United States at a given time could be considered to be the "population" of the U. S. third graders. The "third graderness" of the pupils is the characteristic that all members of the group have in common. Similarly, all left-handed graduate students who have attended the

College of William and Mary between the years 1900 to 1960 can be grouped as a population: here the members of the group have several common characteristics.

A *sample* is any group drawn from a population. A sample may contain *any* number of cases less than the total number of cases which constitutes the population. Usually, however, samples of a population consist of a small proportion of the total population. It is possible that a sample may not be similar enough to the whole population to base conclusions about the entire population on data from the sample; for example, if a researcher were interested in determining the subject best liked by third graders in the United States, it would not do to use the opinions of third graders in the schools in New York City as the basis for formulating an answer. Obviously, a sample of third graders, even when selected from a relatively large proportion of the entire population, may not be representative of the population; therefore, in using samples — rather than the whole population — for purposes of research, it is necessary to select *representative samples*. A representative sample is one that reflect *all* the characteristics of the total population both qualitatively and quantitatively; i.e., a representative sample may be thought of as one that provides a miniature picture of the population in regard to the characteristics that are present in the entire or *parent* population.

One way to select a representative sample is to pick the individuals that are to make up the sample at random. Random selection is carried out in a manner which insures that every member of a population has an equal chance to be picked during each selection made to produce the sample. Various procedures may be employed in obtaining a random sample, but the basic idea is that chance factors in random selection will generally tend to produce a sample that is representative of the whole population.

Variability of Means of Random Samples

Suppose that a given population of 1 million individuals could be measured in regard to some characteristic — for example, I. Q. We know that — as was pointed out in Chapter 5 — measurements of human characteristics made in large populations generally display a normal distribution. The distribution will have a typical measurement, the mean. It will also have a group of typical scores (or measurements) clustered around the mean with a range of about 1 σ unit above and below M. For the sake of discussion let us suppose that in our example M= 100 I.Q. test units and 1 σ = 15 I.Q. test units.

If 200 random samples of 300 individuals each were drawn from the parent population, what would the mean of each sample be? Certainly it cannot be expected that the mean of each of the 200 samples would be an I.Q. of 100; chance should produce many samples with M's different from the M of the parent population. How would the M's of the 200 random samples distribute themselves?

Common sense would indicate that most of the means of random samples will tend to *approximate* the mean of the parent population. Some means of samples will deviate quite far from the true mean of the total population as a result of what might be called chance errors that come about from employing samples rather than the whole population; but since random samples tend to be representative samples, large deviations will be relatively few while small deviations will be many.

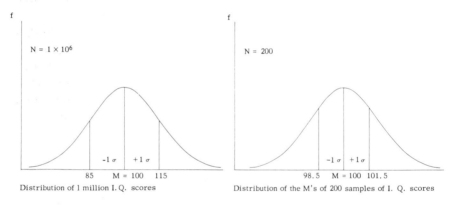

Figure 6.1   Distributions of a Total Population
and the M's of Random Samples

From the description of the distribution of random sample means it is apparent that a normal distribution of means will result. The mean of the distribution of means will be just about the same as the mean of the parent population; therefore, the *mean of means* of representative samples, for all intents and purposes, can be referred to as the true mean (symbolized at M_T). Figure 6.1 depicts the hypothetical distribution of 1 million I.Q.'s and also the distribution of means of 200 random samples.

It should be noted that although the M of the parent population and of the 200 random samples is about the same, the standard deviation of the distribution of means of samples is a much smaller number. This is to be expected since the means of samples will have a greater tendency to be the same as the total mean than will the individual scores that comprise the entire distribution.

Standard Error of the Mean

In the hypothetical situation described in the previous section, it is apparent that a large number of representative samples would be very useful in establishing the approximate location of the true mean of a population. In fact, from the discussion on the normal probability curve, it can be concluded that from a distribution of means of random samples the probable location of the true mean can be established with various degrees of certainty by computing the *standard deviation* of the distribution of means. It is obvious, however, that although it may be simpler to obtain such a distribution than it would be to measure a very large population, it still might be a very difficult — and sometimes impossible — chore to obtain a large number of representative samples.

Fortunately, an estimate of the standard deviation of a distribution of the means of representative samples can be made from just a *single* representative sample. The estimate is a statistic called the *standard error of the mean*: the symbol used to denote the statistic is σ_M. The formula for the standard error of the mean is based upon the standard deviation of the representative sample selected and the size of the sample:

$$\sigma_M = \frac{SD}{\sqrt{N-1}}$$

The derivation of the formula will not be discussed in detail; however, a few comments regarding the formula follow.[1]

The derivation of σ_M is carried out by a mathematical consideration of all possible different samples of a given size which could conceivably be drawn from the parent population. The mean of each sample is mathematically defined in terms of the deviations of scores within the sample from the mean of means that could be found by taking many representative samples. From the formula that results it can be seen that σ_M is directly proportional to the standard deviation of the sample and inversely proportional to the function $\sqrt{N-1}$.

---

[1]An excellent treatment of the mathematical manipulations involved can be found in the book *Statistical Procedures and Their Mathematical Bases* by Charles C. Peters and Walter R. VanVoorhis: McGraw-Hill Book Co., 1940; p. 126-133.

Let us examine the two functions independently. Consider first why $\sigma_M \propto SD$ (σ_M is proportional to SD of the sample). A small value for the SD of the representative sample would indicate that there is little variability within the parent population. If this is so, then there should be little variability in the M's of samples from the true mean of the parent population; that is, sample M's will tend to deviate but slightly from the true M. This small variability will be reflected in the fact that σ_M also tends to be small when SD is small; and since σ_M is used to predict the area within which we would expect to find M_{True}, a small SD of a sample produces a short range of σ_M units within which we expect to find M_{True}. Conversely, when SD is large, it signals a great variability in the parent population and a wider span of σ_M is produced — as needed — to predict the area where we would expect to find M_{True}.

On the other hand, since $\sigma_M \propto \dfrac{1}{\sqrt{N-1}}$ (σ_M is inversely proportional to $\sqrt{N-1}$), as the number of measurements that comprise the representative sample — or sample size — is made larger, σ_M becomes smaller. This result is to be expected since an increase in the size of the representative sample will insure that the sample mean will more closely resemble the true mean. Conversely, if the sample size is smaller, it is more likely that sampling error will occur and the standard error of the mean must be made larger in order to establish a satisfactory range within which the true mean is likely to fall.

Testing Hypotheses Regarding the True Mean

Since σ_M is an estimate of the standard deviation of many representative samples of means that might be drawn from a large population, it offers a way to make educated guesses regarding the location of the true mean. As an example, suppose the following data were compiled by measuring the height of each man in a representative sample of army draftees:

$$N = 101 \text{ men}$$
$$M = 69 \text{ inches}$$
$$SD = 3 \text{ inches}$$

With these figures it would be possible to test the hypothesis that the true mean height of all army draftees is 5'10".

The first step would be to determine the standard error of the mean.

$$\sigma_M = \frac{SD}{\sqrt{N-1}} = \frac{3 \text{ inches}}{\sqrt{100}} = .3 \text{ inch}$$

Figure 6.2 illustrates the graphic solution to the problem.

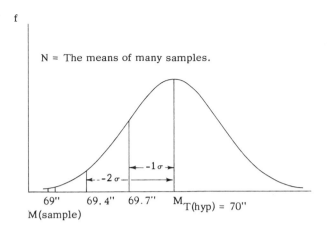

Figure 6.2 Testing a Hypothesis Regarding the True M of a Population

From the graph it is found that the mean of the sample — 69 inches — is more than 3 σ_M units away from the hypothetical true mean. How can we interpret the meaning of this 3 σ_M unit distance? In selecting a true mean of 70 inches the following two conditions are part of the hypothesis:

1. If many representative samples had been drawn from the total population of Army draftees, the mean of means ($M_{T(hyp)}$) would have been 70 inches.
2. The mean of the particular representative sample under observation — with its M of 69″ — would have deviated more than 3 σ_M units from the mean of means of many representative samples.

In a normal distribution of many sample means, however, less than 1% would have deviated as much as the one inch that our sample did from M_T (see Table A.2 in Appendix A); therefore, it must be concluded that it is *unlikely* that the true mean height of all Army draftees can be 5′10″ (70 inches).

The problem can be readily solved without resorting to a graph by the following method:

1. Find σ_M as previously described ($\sigma_M = \dfrac{SD}{\sqrt{100}} = .3$ in.)
2. Determine how far our sample M is from the hypothetical true M; i.e., $M_{Samp} - M_{True}$. (69″ − 70″ = −1″)

3. Calculate the number of σ_M units the two means are apart:

$$\frac{M_{Samp} - M_{True}}{\sigma_M} = \text{no. of } \sigma_M \text{ units apart } (\frac{-1''}{.3''} = -3.3 \sigma_M \text{ units}).$$

If we had hypothesized a true mean of 5'8-2/3", the result would be different as revealed by the following rationale:

1. $\sigma_M = \sqrt{\dfrac{SD}{100}} = 3/10 = .3$

2. $\dfrac{M_{Samp.} - M_{T(hyp)}}{\sigma_M} = \dfrac{69.'' - 68.67''}{.3} = \dfrac{.33}{.3} = 1.1\sigma_M \text{ unit}$

Since the sample mean and the hypothetical true mean are only about 1σ unit apart, it is apparent that it is quite possible the true mean height of army draftees could be 5'8-2/3"; the means of 32 per cent of a large number of representative samples can deviate $1\sigma_M$ unit, or more, from the M_T (see Table A.2 in Appendix A).

Confidence Intervals

The previous section may bring some questions to mind in regard to the number of σ_M units apart the sample mean and hypothesized true mean must be in order to reject the hypothetical true mean as being within the realm of the possible. It should be noted that when M_{Samp} and $M_{T(hyp)}$ were computed to be more than 3 σ_M units apart, it was stated that deviations of 3 σ_M magnitude between a true mean and sample mean are possible, although not probable. Since the normal probability curve theoretically never touches the base or X axis, in dealing with probability there is no point of complete rejection. What is needed, then, are points which will define "how unlikely" it would be that given M's would deviate a given number of σ_M units from a hypothesized M_T.

Actually, any number of σ_M units could be selected to set the limits for rejecting a given hypothesized true mean if the confidence with which the rejection is made is stated. For example, it was found that when M_S and M_T are 1 σ_M unit apart, the normal probability distribution table (Table A.2) shows that about 68% — that is 34% on the positive side of $M_{T(hyp)}$ and 34% on the negative side of $M_{T(hyp)}$ — of representative sample means would deviate as much as 1 σ_M from the M_T. Then 32% of representative sample means could deviate more than 1 σ_M from M_T. When M_S and M_T are 1 σ_M unit apart, therefore, the hypothesized M_T might be rejected at the 32% level of confidence; i.e., with a statement that deviations 1 σ_M in magnitude between M_S and

M_T can be expected, due to sampling error, in about 32 samples of every 100. But 32 chances out of 100 would indicate that it is quite possible to have a difference of 1 σ_M between M_S and $M_{T(hyp)}$ as a result of sampling error; thus a 1 σ_M difference is not a very good one to select for purposes of rejecting the hypothesized M_T.

Generally, researchers have selected the 5% level or the 1% level of confidence as the points at which to reject a hypothesized true mean. Table A.2 shows that a rejection of a hypothesized true mean at the 5% level of confidence requires that $M_S - M_{T(hyp)}$ must be of the size 1.96 σ_M units; and a rejection at the 1% level of confidence can be made when M_S and $M_{T(hyp)}$ are 2.58 σ_M units apart. In other words, less than 5% of sample means tend to deviate 1.96 σ_M units or more either on the positive or negative side of a mean of sample means. (Table A.2 shows that 95% of the sample means — of a distribution of sample means — would be found between the mean of means and ± 1.96σ_M units.) Similarly, less than 1% of sample means would deviate ± 2.58 σ_M units from a mean of the sample means.

How can confidence intervals for the location of the true mean be set from data derived from a given representative sample? In the problem concerning the height of army draftees it was found that M_S = 69" and σ_M = .3". The 5% confidence interval can be established by the following steps:

1. Convert ± 1.96 σ_M units to inches: ± 1.96 × .3" = ± .59"
2. Step 1 indicates that any hypothetical true mean which is .59" above or below the sample mean may be rejected at the 5% level of confidence.
3. 69" ± .59" = from 68.41" to 69.59" (this is the 5% confidence interval).
4. Any hypothetical true means above 69.59" or below 68.41" may be rejected at the 5% level of confidence since samples would deviate only by chance more than ± .59" from a true mean at the most in only about five representative samples out of 100 drawn.

The 1% confidence interval is more stringent since chance deviation of the magnitude 2.58 σ_M units occur in only 1% of the cases. In the problem, the 1% confidence interval would be found as follows:

1. Convert ± 2.58 σ_M units to inches: ± 2.58 × .3" = + .77"
2. 69" ± .77" = from 68.23" to 69.77" (this is the 1% confidence interval).

From the figures it is apparent that the 1% confidence interval is wider than the 5% interval. The reason for this is that greater deviations from a true M are less likely to happen than smaller deviations. In rejecting at the 1% level of confidence, a researcher is indicating that he is quite sure that the hypothetical M_T he has rejected is not actually the true mean since the M_S deviates quite far from it. How sure is the researcher? A 1% level of rejection shows that if the means of many random samples had been found, only one of the sample means out of 100 would have deviated from the mean of means — M_T — as much as the representative sample with which the researcher was working deviated.

Testing for Significant Difference of Pairs of Means

The previous section was concerned with a description of a way to determine the probable location of the true mean of a population by the method of sampling; however, the procedure has very limited application. Much more frequently, researchers are interested in finding whether certain experimental, or natural environmental conditions can bring about changes in members of a population to such an extent that they no longer will be regarded as members of that population.

Suppose, for example, that two representative samples from a population of school children which has a mean I.Q. of 100 (using a standardized test) are placed in vastly different teaching situations for a certain period of time and then retested. The two samples would probably diverge in I.Q. to some extent, but it is known that just sampling error may account for the difference between two samples taken from a parent population. What is needed is a way to determine if divergence between samples is "probably" or "not probably" a result of chance factors attributed to sampling error. In our example, if we were to find that the divergence of the two samples is probably *not* due to chance factors, it would indicate that it *is* probably due to the difference in teaching situations. The remainder of this chapter will be concerned with a description of the statistical procedures which can be used to test for a *significant* (not attributed to chance) difference in means of samples.

Variability of Mean Differences

Consider what would happen if the following procedure were to be carried out:

1. Many *pairs* of representative samples from a large population are drawn simultaneously and tested for some factor; for example, the height in inches that each individual in each sample can jump.

2. The mean height of jumps for each sample is determined.
3. The mean height of jumps for the *first* of each pair of samples is subtracted from the mean height of jumps for the second of each pair of samples. (This can be expressed as $M_2 - M_1 = M_{diff}$ for each pair of samples.)
4. The distribution of the difference of mean height of pairs is found.

Since the pairs of samples in each case are representative of the total population, it is to be expected that the mean of each pair will *approximate* the mean of the population. Then, the differences found by subtracting the mean of the first sample of each pair of samples from the second sample should be about zero. Sampling errors will, however, cause some numerical differences, i.e., in most of the cases the means of samples will deviate somewhat from the mean of the total population. Some of the differences will be in a positive direction from zero — when M_1 is smaller than M_2 — and some will be negative — when M_1 is larger than M_2. A very few differences of means will be relatively large. From this description it is obvious that the difference of means of pairs of representative samples will produce a normal distribution of positive and negative values; and since the pairs of samples will tend to have M's which are equal, or almost equal, to M_T for the whole population, the M of *differences* of means will *tend* to be zero. Figure 6.3 illustrates the distribution of differences of means that might be

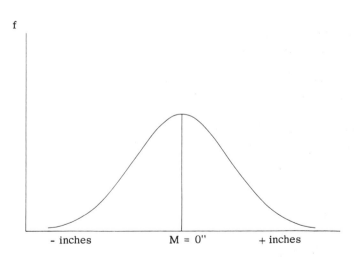

f

- inches   M = 0"   + inches

Figure 6.3 Distribution of Differences of Means of Many Pairs of Random Samples

obtained from measuring the mean jumps of many pairs of representative samples drawn from a large population.

Since the mean of the distribution of differences of means found in pairs of random samples drawn from the same population tends to be *null*, or zero, small differences between means of any samples would indicate that the samples are probably members of the same population. When the differences are large, inference can be drawn that the pairs of samples are *less likely* to be members of the same population. The principle is applicable to research in many ways. The example given in the beginning of the chapter can be used to illustrate the point.

You will recall that the hypothetical situation called for representative samples to be drawn from a population that has a mean I.Q. of 100. Suppose that two such samples were drawn and it were insured that the pair of samples were indeed representative of the population. (This can be insured either through random selection or by testing for a significant difference in the means using the method to be described later in this chapter.)

Prior to subjecting the two samples to different conditions of teaching, it is to be expected that the difference between means of two samples will be rather small. After the pairs of samples are exposed to the different situations, some numerical difference probably will still be found between the measured mean I.Q.'s of the pairs of samples. If the difference has become significantly large — i.e., large enough that it is unlikely that it can not be attributed to sampling error — then the difference is attributed to the variation in the conditions imposed (the experimental conditions).

Standard Error of the Difference

The previous discussion points to a need for a yardstick that can be used to judge the magnitude of differences in the mean of pairs of samples. Of course, merely subtracting the mean of one of a pair of samples from the other will provide information regarding the numerical difference which separates the means of the two samples, but it has been pointed out in the study of sampling theory that the means of samples may deviate from the true mean of a population by various amounts as a result of chance factors. What is needed is a way to test the mean difference in terms of probability that its magnitude is, or is not, due to sampling error (chance factors).

It has been shown that if many pairs of samples are drawn and the differences of means for each pair is determined, a normal distribution of differences will result that is grouped about a mean of null. The standard deviation of the distribution of mean differences will provide the yardstick needed to make statements concerning the probability that various differences between means will appear as a result of sampling.

Differences between means that are 1.96 standard deviation or more units in magnitude would tend to occur so seldom — as a result of sampling error (chance) — that the chance factor may be rejected at some level of confidence ranging from the 5% level downward.

The computation of the standard deviation of a distribution of differences of means from many pairs of random samples would be a difficult task. An estimate of the statistic — called the standard error of the difference — can be made by merely drawing one pair of samples. The estimate of the standard error of the difference is determined by the following formula:

$$\sigma_{\text{diff}} = \sqrt{\sigma_{M_1}{}^2 + \sigma_{M_2}{}^2}$$

where σ_{M_1} = standard error of the mean of sample #1

σ_{M_2} = standard error of the mean of sample #2

The mathematical derivation of the formula is beyond the scope of this book, but a consideration of the formula can demonstrate why it is reasonable. Note that σ_{diff} is computed from the standard error of the mean. In the previous section of this chapter it was pointed out that σ_M provides a range of measurements where the true mean of the population from which the sample has been drawn is most likely to be found. Then σ_{M_1} and σ_{M_2} will provide the range of measurements where the true mean of the population (to which sample #1 and sample #2 belong) is to be found. Also, since it is entirely possible that samples drawn in pairs may, by chance, be at opposite extremes away from M_T for the population from which they are drawn, the possible error range will be twice as great in a distribution of differences of means than it is in locating the true mean of the population. To compensate for the greater error inherent in finding σ_{diff}, the formula calls for adding the standard error of the means of the two samples.

The Null Hypothesis

When two samples are to be tested for significant difference of the means, the test is made on the basis of a determination as to whether the difference found is probably, or is not probably, a result of sampling error. If the samples can be regarded as one of many pairs that *could* have been drawn from the same population, the mean of the distribution of differences would be zero or null. The test made therefore is to determine if the difference of the means — found in the single pair of samples — is close enough to null that the pair of samples could have been part of the same population. For this reason it is hypothesized that the pair of samples to be tested for mean difference is indeed nothing more than one of many pairs of representative samples from the same population. Since the distribution of mean differences in such a case has a mean of null, the hypothesis is expressed as an assertion that the pair of samples is representative of such a distribution, i.e., that the sample pair is probably one of many whose mean of the distribution of differences is null. If a test of the hypothesis is applied and the mean difference proves quite large, the null hypothesis can be rejected at an appropriate level of confidence.

The t–Test

Testing for the significance of the difference between means actually is accomplished by measuring the distance between the means of two samples against the yardstick provided by σ_{diff}. The test is called the t-test and is a method of converting the $M_1 - M_2$ difference into standard deviation units.

$$t = \frac{M_1 - M_2}{\sigma_{diff}} \quad \text{or} \quad \frac{M_1 - M_2}{\sqrt{\sigma_{M_1}^2 + \sigma_{M_2}^2}}$$

From the formula it can be seen that t is a ratio which can be expressed in words in the following way:

$$t = \frac{\text{variability between groups}}{\text{variability within groups}}$$

How can the t-ratio help determine the question of whether two groups are (or are not) probably representative samples of the same population?

A study of some frequency distribution graphs of hypothetical samples can demonstrate pictorially what the t-ratio does numerically. Figure 6.4 illustrates three situations. It is obvious that only Graph A would indicate the probability of two distinct groups; Graphs B and C show a blending together of the groups. The t-ratio gives the same information, and, by quantifying the information, the ratio provides a precise basis for predicting how probable it is that the groups are not really drawn from the same population (tend not to blend together).

Note that in both Graphs A and B, Group I and Group II are equal in terms of shapes of the distribution curves. This means that the standard deviation and therefore the variability within the groups are the same. Graph A, however, indicates a greater variability between

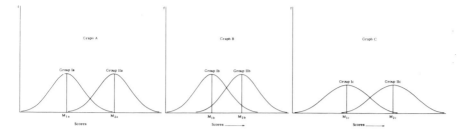

Figure 6.4 Distribution of Measurements of Pairs of Groups

groups than Graph B, i.e., $M_{2a} - M_{1a}$ is larger than $M_{2b} - M_{1b}$. The t-test would reflect the conditions as follows:

1. $t_a = \dfrac{M_{2a} - M_{1a}}{\sqrt{\sigma_{M1a}^2 + \sigma_{M2a}^2}}$ and $t_b = \dfrac{M_{2b} - M_{1b}}{\sqrt{\sigma_{M1b}^2 + \sigma_{M2b}^2}}$

2. Since the factors in both denominators, σ_{M1}^2 and σ_{M2}^2, are derived from the standard deviations of the samples and these are all equal, the denominator for the t_a will be equal to the denominator of the t_b.

3. However, since $M_{2a} - M_{1a} > M_{2b} - M_{1b}$, ($M_{2a} - M_{1a}$ *is greater than* $M_{2b} - M_{1b}$), $t_a > t_b$.

On the other hand, the graphs show that although $M_{2a} - M_{1a} = M_{2c} - M_{1c}$, Groups Ic and IIc — unlike Groups Ia and IIa — blend together as a result of the wide variability encountered in the measurements of Groups Ic and IIc. The t-test would show this as follows:

1. $t_a = \dfrac{M_{2a} - M_{1a}}{\sqrt{\sigma_{M1a}^2 + \sigma_{M2a}^2}}$ and $t_c = \dfrac{M_{2c} - M_{1c}}{\sqrt{\sigma_{M1c}^2 + \sigma_{M2c}^2}}$

2. Both numerators are equal.

3. However, the denominator of t_a would tend to be smaller than the denominator of t_c, since the lesser variability between Groups I_a and II_a, as compared to Groups I_c and II_c, will show up as smaller standard deviation figures. Since the standard error of means — σ_M — are derived from the standard deviation, the denominator of t_a will not be as large as that of t_c.

4. Then, $t_a > t_c$.

The formula for the t-test shows that it is nothing more than a special z score that measures how far apart two M's are in terms of an estimated σ_{diff}; therefore, t may be interpreted by use of Table A.2 in Appendix A or, if the size of the sample is small — i.e., less than

16 in each sample — Table A.3 is used. The tables indicate that as "t" becomes larger it becomes less likely that the two groups tested are representative of the same population. The null hypothesis thus can be rejected with more confidence in the case of Groups Ia and IIa than in either Groups Ib and IIb or Groups Ic and IIc.

Table A.3 is used with small samples since the selection of each sample tends to cut down the free chance choice of subsequent samples that could be drawn by the factor of one. With large samples the restriction of degrees of freedom by one in selection is not important. With small samples, however, the restriction of chance operating freely may be critical; therefore, Table A.3 is computed in terms of the degrees of freedom. The degree of freedom factor is found by the formula:

$$df = N_1 + N_2 - 2 \text{ where}$$
$$N_1 = \text{number of measurements in sample \#1}$$
$$N_2 = \text{number of measurements in sample \#2}$$

Note that Table A.3 indicates with small samples the rejection of the null hypothesis requires relatively larger values for t. This is so because smaller sized samples will be subject to more sampling errors. To compensate for this, the requirement is made for a greater range between the means being tested for significant differences.

Application of the t–Test

Several problems will be presented to illustrate the principles that have been discussed.

Suppose that in the hypothetical experiment which dealt with I.Q.'s, the following data were collected:

1. Two groups of 50 pupils each were determined to be essentially the same in terms of I.Q. and all other factors which may be significant. The distributions of I.Q. scores on a standard test were normal.

2. One group, labeled Group I, was placed in an ordinary classroom situation. The other group, called Group II, was given intensive training that the researcher believed would produce a significant change in the I.Q.

3. The two groups were again tested for I.Q. at the end of a given period of time. The results of the testing showed:

a. Group I   M = 100
              SD = 16
b. Group II   M = 110
              SD = 10

Has a significant change occurred?

Although the M of Group II seems to be quite a bit larger than that of Group I, it must be hypothesized that such a difference may be a result of chance or sampling error. The null hypothesis is therefore applied: it states that $M_1 - M_2$ in the pair of samples — Group I and Group II — is representative of a distribution difference of many pairs of M's from samples drawn from a single population, i.e., the M of the distribution in question would be null.

Then,

$$\sigma_{M_1} = \frac{SD_1}{\sqrt{N_1 - 1}} = \frac{16}{\sqrt{49}} = \frac{16}{7} = 2.3$$

$$\sigma_{M_2} = \frac{SD_2}{\sqrt{N_2 - 1}} = \frac{10}{\sqrt{49}} = \frac{10}{7} = 1.4$$

$$\sigma_{diff} = \sqrt{\sigma_{M_1}{}^2 + \sigma_{M_2}{}^2} = \sqrt{2.3^2 + 1.4^2} = \sqrt{5.29 + 1.96}$$
$$= \sqrt{7.25} = 2.7$$

$$t = \frac{M_1 - M_2}{\sigma_{diff}} = \frac{100 - 110}{2.7} = \frac{-10}{2.7} = -3.7$$

Table A.2 indicates that since M_1 and M_2 are more than 3.7 σ_{diff} units apart, we may reject the null hypothesis at more than the 1% level of confidence. In other words, it is very unlikely that Group I and Group II are representative samples of the same population. Since Groups I and II were demonstrated to be drawn from the same population at the start of the experiment, all other factors being equal it is very likely that whatever was done to the Groups brought about a significant divergence of I.Q. scores.

Let us now suppose some other data resulted from the same experiment as follows:

Group I $M_1 = 100$
            $SD_1 = 16$
Group II $M_2 = 104$
            $SD_2 = 10$

Then,

$$\sigma_{M_1} = \sqrt{\frac{16}{49}} = 2.3$$

$$\sigma_{M_2} = \sqrt{\frac{10}{49}} = 1.4$$

$$\sigma_{diff} = \sqrt{2.3^2 + 1.4^2} = 2.7$$

$$t = \frac{M_1 - M_2}{\sigma_{diff}} = \frac{-4}{2.7} = -1.5$$

We see here that $M_1 - M_2$ in this case is not large enough to reject the null hypothesis.

A more subtle variation of the problem can be examined using the following data:

Group I $M_1 = 100$ $N_1 = 50$
$\qquad\qquad$ $SD_1 = 35$

Group II $M_2 = 110$ $N_2 = 50$
$\qquad\qquad$ $SD_2 = 35$

Then,

$$\sigma_{M_1} = \frac{35}{\sqrt{49}} = \frac{35}{7} = 5$$

$$\sigma_{M_2} = \frac{35}{\sqrt{49}} = 5$$

$$\sigma_{diff} = \sqrt{5^2 + 5^2} = \sqrt{50} = 7.1$$

$$t = \frac{M_1 - M_2}{\sigma_{diff}} = \frac{-10}{7.1} = -1.4$$

The t value obtained here indicates that the null hypothesis should not be rejected, or if it is rejected, it may be rejected at no better than the 16% level of confidence. (From Table A.2 it is found that $\pm 1.4\,\sigma$ units account for about 84% of the cases; therefore, 16% of the cases can still occur beyond these limits as a result of chance.)

In the last version of the original problem it can be seen that although $M_1 - M_2$ was as large as in the original, an entirely different conclusion has been reached. What accounts for this?

Mathematically, it is obvious that since the denominator of t, σ_{diff}, is larger in the latter problem, t will become smaller than it was in the original problem. Why should this be so?

The answer to the question is that when the standard deviation of samples is large, a large variation within the group is indicated. This large variation in turn is reflected as greater uncertainty of where the true mean of the population is to be found; thus, the standard error of the mean is larger. Greater uncertainty of where the true mean of the population may be found is further reflected in the estimate of the area where the zero mean of difference of means for samples is to be found; as a result σ_{diff} is estimated as a larger range of measurements. Finally, the larger σ_{diff} demands that $M_1 - M_2$ must be a greater value before the null hypothesis is rejected.

The t-test for Small Samples

The following problem will serve to illustrate the t-test for small samples:

1. A research worker selected twenty high school physics teachers at random from a list of physics teachers in a state. For the purpose of the study, physics teachers were defined as any teacher who met state certification requirements and was currently teaching physics in a secondary school of the state.
2. The teachers were divided at random into two groups of ten teachers each and tested with a standard examination for ability to apply mathematical principles to physics problems. There was no significant difference between the groups.
3. Group I, designated the control group, was given a summer school refresher course in mathematics along with a refresher course in physics. Group II, the experimental group, was given a special course which integrated mathematics and physics.
4. Both groups were retested with an equivalent form of the same test which was administered at the beginning of the program. These results were obtained:

    a. Group 1 $M_1 = 75$
                    $SD_1 = 5$

    b. Group II $M_2 = 85$
                    $SD_2 = 5$

Analyzing the data,

$$\sigma_{M_1} = \frac{5}{\sqrt{10-1}} = \frac{5}{\sqrt{9}} = \frac{5}{3} = 1.7$$

$$\sigma_{M_2} = \frac{5}{\sqrt{10-1}} = 1.7$$

$$\sigma_{diff} = \sqrt{1.7^2 + 1.7^2} = \sqrt{5.78} = 2.4$$

$$t = \frac{M_2 - M_1}{\sigma_{diff}} = \frac{85-75}{2.4} = \frac{10}{2.4} = 4.2$$

In order to interpret t, Table A.3 must be used since the data is based upon small samples.

Finding the degrees of freedom in selecting the samples,

$$\begin{aligned} df &= N_1 + N_2 - 2 \\ &= 10 + 10 - 2 \\ &= 18 \end{aligned}$$

Then, from Table A.3, a t of 4.2 indicates that the null hypothesis can be rejected at better than the 1% level of confidence. Therefore, it can be concluded that in all probability the difference between Group I and

Group II cannot be attributed to chance and presumably resulted from the experimental procedure.

The Design of Experiments

Experiments which employ statistical tools for data analysis must be designed to do no violence to the rationale that underlies the tools. The t-test, for example, provides a powerful research tool; however, the researcher must be careful to abide by the rules of logic upon which the t-test is based or he may arrive at erroneous conclusions. Students of research must keep a sharp eye on the researcher's method of employing the t-test in order to evaluate the findings and conclusions drawn.

To summarize what has been said about the t-test:

1. When two samples are measured in regard to some particular characteristic, a difference of means very generally is found; however, it assumed that the difference results from sampling error and that the samples are actually representatives of the same population. The assumption is asserted through the null hypothesis.

2. The t-test is applied to determine if the difference of means is so large that such a difference occurs very infrequently as a result of sampling error.

3. If the t-ratio is indeed quite large, the null hypothesis is rejected — not outright — but at a particular level of confidence, and it is concluded that the two samples are *probably* not representative of the same population. This is interpreted to mean the samples probably have been drawn from populations whose true means differ in respect to the trait measured.

Implications of the t-Test

There are several implications which can be drawn regarding the t-test. First, the test has been derived from mathematical consideration of the distributions that result from measurements of traits in representative (random) samples of large populations. It therefore is assumed that the samples tested are representative of some—if not the same—large population(s) that would exhibit a normal, or near normal distribution in the trait measured. If there is any doubt concerning the assumption of normality, the use of the test is not valid.

Second, since random pairs of samples drawn from the same population can theoretically differ to *any* degree as a result of chance, or sampling error, no difference found between a pair of M's can allow a complete rejection of the null hypothesis. This means that the level of confidence at which the null hypothesis is rejected must be indicated.

Another problem which arises is that by establishing rigorous levels of confidence, the 5% or 1%, before rejecting the null hypothesis, a researcher may expose himself to the possibility of accepting null when he should be rejecting. For example, suppose the experimenter finds that a t-ratio of differences between experimental group and control group mean is 1.89. If he uses the 5% level of confidence, he must accept null and conclude that the group mean difference is so like a difference that can come about by chance that he is not willing to attribute it to the experimental conditions. But it is possible that the experiment did cause a difference, but that the difference is not very large; then he would have made an error in concluding that the experiment made no difference.

The experimenter in our hypothetical case was guarding against what researchers call a Type I error. Type I error occurs if a hypothesis, null in this case, is rejected when it should be accepted. By putting the level of confidence at the extreme 5% or 1% cases which can occur by chance, the researcher is reasonably sure that when he does reject, he is correct in doing so.

But in guarding against Type I error, the researcher has left himself open to committing a Type II error. Type II error occurs if a hypothesis is accepted when it should be rejected. Guarding against error of one type will allow a researcher to be open to making the other type error.

Generally, researchers prefer to guard against Type I error since this puts the burden of proof on the experiment; that is, the difference between experiment and control must be so large that there is little doubt that the difference came about as a result of the experiment and not chance.

Finally, since in an experiment groups are subjected to differing conditions, it must be determined beyond reasonable doubt that the groups were comparable — that is, drawn from the same population — in respect to any significant variables prior to the imposition of the experimental conditions.

Selection of Groups for Research

The last implication drawn is of particular importance in comparative studies as well as in experiments. What methods are available to the researcher to insure that groups are comparable? The most obvious method is one in which the population is *clearly defined* and groups to be studied are selected at *random* from the population. Various devices are used to insure random selection, but the basic principle of the random method is that each and every selectee has an equal chance to be chosen during each and every selection made. In actual practice, once a choice is made, the selectee is placed in a group and is not eligible to be selected on subsequent choices. Since groups are thus fixed and there is not complete freedom of choice, it is necessary for the mathematical formula used in computations to reflect the loss in freedom of selection through an expression of the degrees of freedom that were available in the random selection.

Although random selection is desirable, for various reasons it is not always possible to make such selections: the population may not be clearly defined; the task of random selection may be too difficult; or it may be necessary to work with groups that have already been formed,

If the over-all population is not clearly defined, it is still possible arbitrarily to define the population as the one that is at hand. If, for example, a teacher wishes to carry out research in the classroom teaching of secondary biology and is necessarily limited to do the study in his own school, he may define the population as being the students in the school's biology courses. Groups drawn at random from the limited population can be selected, but conclusions are applicable solely to the particular population.

When it is not possible to make random selections because of administrative considerations, groups can be pretested for comparability. In the foregoing hypothetical study of biology students for example, scheduling difficulties may make it impossible to assign arbitrarily pupils who have been randomly selected to specific classes. It may be necessary to use class groups just as they have been established as a result of administrative scheduling, but comparison of groups is still feasible. The existing biology classes can be tested with examinations that measure the groups in terms of significant factors such as ability to learn, current knowledge of biology, motivation, ability to read material from science texts, laboratory skills, etc. If one group of biology classes has been designated as experimental and another as control, the application of the t-test for significant difference of means on each pre-examination will show whether the groups are comparable (drawn from the same population). Even if it is found the groups are not comparable in regard to some significant factor or factors, there are two methods of producing similar groups:

1. If the groups are large enough, extreme scores can be disregarded to bring the means and standard deviations of the two groups closer together.
2. If the groups are small, members may be added in order to bring the groups closer together.

Again, it must be remembered that conclusions drawn from experiments and comparative studies utilizing limited populations may not be generalized to larger populations, but this does not disqualify these limited studies as important contributions to education. Much progress in research can be made through an accumulation of knowledge derived from restricted investigations.

Simple Analysis of Variance

The previous section was concerned chiefly with a description of the t-test of significant difference between a pair of means. At times, however, it is desirable to study the effect of more than two conditions at one time. In such a situation it is necessary to determine whether two or more groups are affected by the imposed conditions. The analysis of variance technique — as the name implies — provides a statistical method for determining if variations that appear among groups can be attributed to sampling error or to varying conditions. Analysis of variance, as with the t-test, is predicated upon the assumption that most factors within a population which can be measured will provide a normal distribution of measurements.

The following is an example of the kind of study in which a statistical method other than the t-test would be necessary. Suppose that a school system plans to institute a program of remedial reading for pupils who have need of such a program. It has been determined that five hours per week will be set aside for the program; however, there is a question regarding how the time should be allotted. Specifically, there is controversy on the matter of concentration of time: Should pupils spend all five hours in remedial reading in a single day, in a three day period, or in a one hour period each day? Experiments with pairs of the proposed concentrations of time would not be conclusive since various pairs selected conceivably could give various results. Before experiments with pairs of time blocks are undertaken, it would be advisable to determine if time concentration is a critical factor. Analysis of variance applied to the problem would give the information desired.

The Mathematical Basis for Analysis of Variance

Recall that in testing for a significant difference between a pair of means that $t = \dfrac{M_2 - M_1}{\sigma_{diff}}$. In words the equation can be expressed as the ratio $t = \dfrac{\text{variability between groups}}{\text{variability within groups.}}$. A similar rationale can be used to analyze the variance of several groups if measures of variability between and within several groups can be found.

Figure 6.5 illustrates what might happen if four groups were tested for progress in reading after the hypothetical experiment in teaching remedial reading in various time blocks.

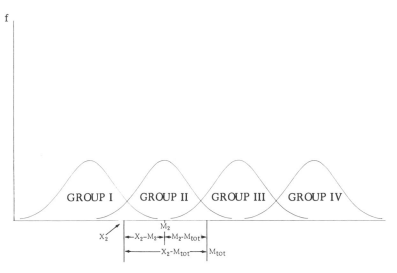

Figure 6.5 Scores of Four Groups Illustrating Variability Between and Within Groups

Note that using any particular score — in the illustration X_2 represents one such score for Group II — and the mean scores, the following information can be found:

1. The amount that a score deviates from the typical score *within* its own group — in the illustration it is $X_2 - M_2$.
2. The amount that a score deviates from the score which typifies all the scores (and all the groups). Since the score that typifies all the scores is M_{tot}, then the deviation of X_2 from M_{tot} is given as $X_2 - M_{tot}$.
3. The amount that the score which typifies a particular group deviates from the score which typifies all the groups. In the illustration the deviation is $M_2 - M_{tot}$.

From the description of the information that is available, it can be concluded that:

1. The deviations of individual scores from the mean of the group within which the scores are found give a measure of *variability within the group*. (Illustrated by $X_2 - M_2$)

2. The deviation of the means of the various groups from an over-all or total mean — obtained by lumping all scores together — provides a measure of the *variability among groups*. (Illustrated by $M_2 - M_{tot}$)

3. The deviations of individual scores from the total mean produce a new measure which can be called a *total deviation*. (Illustrated by $X_2 - M_{tot}$) The importance of this new measure is that it is really a composite of the other two, that is, the total variability = variability within groups + variability between groups. Figure 7.5 illustrates the idea mathematically. Note that:

$$X_2 - M_{tot} \quad = \quad (X_2 - M_2) \quad + \quad (M_2 - M_{tot})$$

tot. var. of X_2	var. of X_2 within Group II	var. of Group II from M_{tot}

Formulae

In order to make a mathematical comparison of the variability among groups to the variability within groups, it is necessary to sum the deviations that provide the basis for the determination of variability. Algebraic summation of deviations from means always results in the sum of zero, but the difficulty can be avoided through the use of the sums of squared deviations as is done in finding the standard deviation statistic.

Before presenting formulae for the measurement of variability through sums of squares, it would be well to present some of the symbols to be used:

X = any score or measurement from any of the groups.

M_{tot} = mean of all scores (found by dividing the sum of all scores by the number of scores)

M_g = mean of scores in any subgroups

M_1 = mean of Group I; M_2 = mean of Group II; . . . etc.

N_{tot} = the total number of all scores

N_g = number of scores in any particular subgroups

N_1 = number of scores in Group I; N_2 = number of scores in Group II; . . . etc.

k = number of subgroups

X_1 = a score from Group I; X_2 = a score from Group II; . . . etc.

SS_{tot} = sum of the squares total

SS_{wg} = sum of squares within groups

SS_{ag} = sum of squares among groups

Then from the previous discussion:

1. Total variability can be measured as $SS_{tot} = \Sigma(X - M_{tot})^2$. This means that the deviation of each individual score from each sub-group from the M_{tot} is found and squared. These squares are summed up to find SS_{tot}.

2. Variability within groups can be expressed as $SS_{wg} = \Sigma(X_1 - M_1)^2 + \Sigma(X_2 - M_2)^2 + \Sigma(X_3 - M_3)^2 \ldots$ up to k groups. This indicates that the deviation of each score of each subgroup from its own subgroup mean is found and squared. All these squared deviations are summed up to find SS_{wg}. (Actually, the equation calls for sub sums to be found first, but the result will be the same.)

3. Variability among groups can be shown as $SS_{ag} = N_1 (M_1 - M_{tot})^2 + N_2 (M_2 - M_{tot})^2 + N_3 (M_3 - M_{tot})^2 \ldots$ up to k groups. The equation indicates that SS_{ag} is determined by finding the sum of the squares of the deviation of each subgroup (as represented by M_1, M_2, M_3, etc.) from the measure that represents all the scores — M_{tot}. It is necessary, however, to multiply each subgroup squared deviation by the N for the group in order to weight the deviations according to the *number* of scores that contributed to producing the mean of each subgroup.

4. The relationship among the three measures of variability is $SS_{tot} = SS_{wg} + SS_{ag}$. Recall that in terms of individual deviations $(X_{any\ score} - M_{tot}) = (X_{any\ score} - M_g) + (M_g - M_{tot})$

The equations would indicate that a great many computations are necessary to find the sums of squares within groups — SS_{wg} — and between groups — SS_{ag}. Fortunately, through a manipulation of the last equation, $SS_{tot} = SS_{wg} + SS_{ag}$ and of the equation for SS_{ag} a short cut may be found to produce the necessary information.

Beginning with $SS_{tot} = \Sigma(X - M_{tot})^2$, then

$$SS_{tot} = \Sigma(X^2 - 2\ X\ M_{tot} + M^2_{tot})$$
$$= \Sigma X^2 - \Sigma 2\ X\ M_{tot} + \Sigma M^2_{tot}$$

but, $\Sigma M^2_{tot} = N_{tot}\ M^2_{tot}$ (since to find ΣM^2_{tot} it is necessary to add $M^2_{tot} + M^2_{tot} + M^2_{tot} \ldots$ up to N_{tot} times)

and $\Sigma 2\ X\ M_{tot} = 2\ M_{tot}\ \Sigma X$ (since $2M_{tot}$ is a common factor each time $2\ X\ M_{tot}$ is summed)

Therefore: $SS_{tot} = \Sigma X^2 - 2\ M_{tot}\ \Sigma X + N_{tot}\ M^2_{tot}$

but, $\Sigma X = N_{tot}\ M_{tot}$ since $M_{tot} = \dfrac{\Sigma X}{N_{tot}}$

therefore, $SS_{tot} = \Sigma X^2 - 2\ M_{tot}\ N_{tot}\ M_{tot} + N_{tot}\ M^2_{tot}$
$= \Sigma X^2 - 2\ N_{tot}\ M^2_{tot} + N_{tot}\ M^2_{tot}$

$$\boxed{\text{then } SS_{tot} = \Sigma X^2 - N_{tot}\ M^2_{tot}}$$

Also, it can be shown that:

$$\boxed{SS_{ag} = N_1\ M_1^2 + N_2\ M_2^2\ \ldots\ldots \text{ etc. } -N_{tot}\ M^2_{tot}}$$

SS_{wg} can now be found quickly as follows: $SS_{wg} = SS_{tot} - SS_{ag}$.

Once SS_{ag} and SS_{wg} have been computed, it is possible to estimate the variability of population from which the groups have been drawn. Recall that in dealing with a single over-all population variability is measured by finding the standard deviation, SD. Also, the statistic σ_M can be estimated from a single representative sample:

$$\sigma_M = \frac{SD \text{ sample}}{\sqrt{N-1}}$$

If the standard deviation of the population is squared, a new parameter is found which is labeled the variance: $\sigma^2_{variance} = \frac{\Sigma x^2}{N}$. Obviously variance is a sum of squares number and since it is derived directly from σ, the variance is also a measure of variability. Now if σ_M is an estimate of variability of the total population, then another new statistic can be determined that also provides an estimate of the variability of the total population in terms of sums of squares:

$$\sigma_M^2 = \frac{(SD)^2}{N-1}$$

Analyzing the statistic σ_M^2, it can be seen that it consists of (1) a numerator which estimates variability through sums of squares of deviations, and (2) a denominator that is determined by the size of N in terms of the degrees of freedom possible in selecting the sample.

Similar estimates of population variance using the sums of squares method can be obtained from data collected in terms of several groups. In the analysis of variance method, the two required estimates of population variance are:

1. The estimate of variance to be found *among groups* if many sample groups were to be measured from the entire population.
2. The estimate of variance to be found *within groups* if many sample groups were to be measured from the entire population.

Like the statistic $\sigma_M{}^2$, the estimates of variance are made from the limited sampling of just a few groups. The estimate of variance among groups is called the *mean square* among groups $-M_{Sag}$. The M_{Sag} is obtained through a procedure which is similar to one for producing $\sigma_M{}^2$.

$$M_{Sag} = \frac{SS_{ag},}{df_{bg}}$$ where SS_{ag} is the sum squares among groups, and df_{ag} is the degrees of freedom in selecting the groups. Since there are k groups, $df_{ag} = k - 1$.

The other estimate of variance required is called the mean square within groups (M_{Swg}); it can be obtained from SS_{wg} by using a similar procedure.

$$M_{Swg} = \frac{SS_{wg},}{df_{wg}}$$ where SS_{wg} is the sum of squares within groups and df_{wg} is the degrees of freedom in selecting the total number of measurements which were made. Since the total number of scores or measurements is N_{tot}, and one degree of freedom is lost with the fixing of each group, $df_{wg} = N_{tot}-k$.

Finally, like the t-test, a ratio is used to compare the variance between groups to the variance within groups.

$$\left(\text{Recall that } t = \frac{\text{variability between groups}}{\text{variability within groups}} = \frac{M_2-M_1}{\sigma_{diff}}\right)$$

In analysis of variance, the ratio is labeled F-ratio.

$$F = \frac{M_{Sag}}{M_{Swg}} \text{, or in words } F = \frac{\text{variance among groups}}{\text{variance within groups}}$$

The values of F can be interpreted through the use of Table A.4 in Appendix A. In drawing inferences from the F-ratio, as with the interpretation of the t-test, the null hypothesis is asserted. The null hypothesis, in analysis of variance, indicates that the groups tested with the F-ratio are representative of groups that might be drawn from the same population. If it is true that the groups are indeed representative of the same population, with a large number of samples the variance among groups as compared with the variance within groups will tend to be the same. F therefore provides a method of determining the likelihood that the groups tested are representative of a single population; if F is considerably larger than one, null may be rejected.

Figure 6.6 illustrates graphically what the F-ratio shows mathematically.

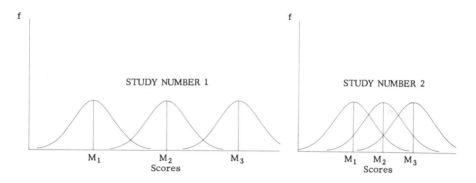

Figure 6.6 Two hypothetical studies in which F-ratio could be used as a Basis for Accepting or Rejecting the Null Hypothesis.

The graphs indicate that in Study Number 1 the three groups tested are probably *not* representative of the same population. They seem to be separate and distinct; therefore, the F-ratio will tend to be large, and the null hypothesis may be rejected with a relatively high confidence level. (Note that, as with the t-ratio, this means a *low* percentage number since rejection is in terms of the percentage of cases that may crop up in representative samples as a result of chance.)

On the other hand, the graph of data from Study Number 2 tends to demonstrate that the groups probably are drawn from the same population. The F-ratio will reflect this probability in that F will be a small number. In turn, Table A.4 will indicate that the null hypothesis may not be rejected at the 1% or even the 5% level of confidence.

Application

An application of the analysis of variance technique to the hypothetical study of a remedial reading program, previously discussed, may help clarify how the method is employed in research.

Suppose that in order to determine the effects of varying the concentration of time devoted to a program of remedial reading, an experiment has been conducted as follows:

1. All pupils in a large school system who were reading at a grade level below norm, as measured by a standardized test, were singled out for the study.
2. A random sample of thirty pupils was drawn.
3. The thirty pupils were separated into three groups through random selection.
4. Group I was given instruction in a remedial reading program five times a week; one hour per day for one year. Group II was given one and two-thirds hours of instruction on Monday, Wednesday and Friday of each week for one year. Group III was given the instruction in five hours on a single day each week for a year. (The day for the instruction was changed each week to eliminate the possible effect of a particular day.)
5. All instruction, given by a reading expert, was geared on an individual basis to help pupils raise their own reading level.
6. At the end of a year the pupils were tested to determine the improvement in reading. Table 6.1 shows how much each pupil improved in reading level (expressed in years).

TABLE 6.1 — Number of years in Reading Improvement

GROUP I	GROUP II	GROUP III
years	years	years
2.8	2.6	2.3
2.6	1.8	2.4
3.3	2.7	2.1
2.5	2.1	2.5
2.7	2.2	2.6
3.1	2.8	2.2
3.2	2.4	1.6
4.5	3.7	2.0
2.4	1.9	1.5
3.9	2.5	1.4

The analysis of variance technique can be used to determine whether the groups have diverged sufficiently to be considered as no longer representative of the same population. Table 6.2 shows the computations necessary to produce the F-ratio.

TABLE 6.2 Computations for the Analysis of Variance of Data in Study of Reading Improvement

GROUP I		GROUP II		GROUP III	
X_1	$X_1{}^2$	X_2	$X_2{}^2$	X_3	$X_3{}^2$
2.8	7.84	2.6	6.76	2.3	5.29
2.6	6.76	1.8	3.24	2.4	5.76
3.3	10.89	2.7	7.29	2.1	4.41
2.5	6.25	2.1	4.41	2.5	6.25
2.7	7.29	2.2	4.84	2.6	6.76
3.1	9.61	2.8	7.84	2.2	4.84
3.2	10.24	2.4	5.76	1.6	2.56
4.5	20.25	3.7	13.69	2.0	4.0
2.4	5.76	1.9	3.61	1.5	2.25
3.9	15.21	2.5	6.25	1.4	1.96

$\Sigma X_1 = 31.0$ $\qquad\qquad$ $\Sigma X_2 = 24.7$ $\qquad\qquad$ $\Sigma X_3 = 20.6$

$$M_1 = \frac{31.0}{10} = 3.1 \qquad M_2 = \frac{24.7}{10} = 2.47 \qquad M_3 = \frac{20.6}{10} = 2.06$$

$$\Sigma X^2{}_{tot} = 207.87 \qquad M_{tot} = \frac{76.3}{30} = 2.54$$

$$SS_{tot} = \Sigma X^2{}_{tot} - N_{tot}\, M^2{}_{tot} = 207.87 - 30(2.54)^2 = 14.37$$

$$SS_{ag} = N_1\, M_1^2 + N_2\, M_2^2 + N_3\, M_3^2 - N_{tot}\, M^2{}_{tot}$$
$$= 10(3.1^2 + 2.47^2 + 2.06^2) - 30(2.54)^2 = 199.5 - 193.5 = 6$$

$$SS_{wg} = SS_{tot} - SS_{ag}$$
$$= 14.37 - 6 = 8.37$$

$$M_{S_{ag}} = \frac{SS_{ag}}{df_{bg}} = \frac{6}{2} = 3 \qquad \text{where } df_{ag} = k - 1 = 3 - 1 = 2$$

$$M_{S_{wg}} = \frac{SS_{wg}}{df_{wg}} = \frac{8.37}{27} = .3 \qquad \text{where } df_{wg} = N_{tot} - k = 30 - 3 = 27$$

$$F = \frac{M_{S_{ag}}}{M_{S_{wg}}} = \frac{3}{.3} = 10$$

In order to interpret the F-ratio, reference must be made to Table A.4 in Appendix A. The figures in Table A.4 have been determined through a method similar to one used to prepare Table A.2; however, the F-ratio table is limited to values of F which lead to the rejection of the null hypothesis. Also, Table A.4 reflects the necessity to consider the degrees of freedom in sample selection.

In using Table A.4 to interpret the F of 10 computed in the sample problem, it is first necessary to determine the df's associated with the numerator and the denominator of F. The numerator of F is $M_{S_{ag}}$, and the df used to find $M_{S_{ag}}$ was two: i.e., $df_{ag} = k - 1 = 3 - 1 = 2$. The denominator of F is $M_{S_{wg}}$, and the df used to find $M_{S_{wg}}$ was 27. (The computations were: $df_{wg} = N_{tot} - k = 30 - 3 = 27$.)

Table A.4 shows that with an F of 3.35, null can be rejected at the 5% level of confidence, and with an F of 5.49 rejection at the 1% level is possible. Since the F-ratio obtained in the problem is 10, the hypothesis that the three groups are representative of the same population can be rejected at better than the 1% level of confidence. It can be concluded that variation in concentration of time in a remedial reading program is probably the factor which has caused the groups to diverge.

A look at the computations also reveals that the greatest gains appear among the pupils whose remedial reading instruction is spread throughout the week; however, more experiments would be necessary to determine the best arrangement.

Selected Exercises

1. A researcher selected a random sample of 37 eleventh grade pupils from a large city school system and administered a vocabulary test to the group. The following results were recorded:

$$M = 72$$
$$SD = 6$$

Upon seeing the results, an English teacher in the system expresses her belief that the average eleventh grade pupil in the system would more likely get about 65 on the test.

a. How probable is it that the English teacher is right?

b. Establish 5% and 1% confidence intervals for the data.

2. The researcher (referred to in question 1) hypothesized that if students were given intensive drill in vocabulary one school period a week for ten weeks their knowledge of words would increase appreciably. He arranged, therefore, for the group of 37 pupils to meet once a week for a drill period. At the end of ten weeks he gave the same vocabulary test with the following results:

$$M = 76$$
$$SD = 18$$

    a. Was the researcher correct in his hypothesis?

    b. What appeared to happen to the group as a result of the instruction? What might account for what happened?

    c. Why is it *probably* safe to use the same group for the control and experiment?

    d. Suggest a method of conducting the experiment that may be better. Explain your method.

3. A group of 145 senior boys — from the same city school system mentioned in question 1 — was selected at random and given a physical test to determine the number of push-ups each boy could do. The data provided the following results:

$$M = 8$$
$$SD = 1$$

It was hypothesized that if the students were given intensive practice in doing push-ups during one school period a week for ten weeks their ability to do push-ups would increase appreciably; arrangements were made for the practice sessions. At the end of the ten week period the group was tested again and the following results were recorded:

$$M = 9$$
$$SD = 2$$

    a. Upon seeing the results of the two tests, an administrator in the school system said it wouldn't be necessary to make further computations to see that the practice did not produce an appreciable gain. He based his conclusion on the fact that a gain of 4 points in the vocabulary experiment was not significant. Is he correct? What do your computations show? Why?

    b. Establish confidence intervals for the rejection of the null hypothesis at the 5% and 1% level of confidence.

    c. Why is it *probably* safe to use the same group as a control and experimental group in the experiment?

4. A researcher wishes to determine how dental school students who receive training in dental anatomy exclusively through a series of programed texts compare with students who are instructed in a regular classroom program. Seventy-four (74) students are randomly divided into two groups of thirty-seven (37) each. Group I learns dental anatomy by using the programed material,

and Group II in regular classroom presentations. Scores on a standard test in dental anatomy are shown below:

	N	M	SD
Group I	37	140	36
Group II	37	150	42

a. State the null hypothesis in terms of the data.

b. May we reject null at the 5% level of confidence? What does this mean?

c. What would have been the result if the same data had been obtained from a sample of 552 students? ($N_1 = 226$ and $N_2 = 226$) Why?

5. An experiment was performed to determine the effects of spelling similarity of words within a list upon ease with which pupils learn their meanings. Three groups, randomly assigned, of 16 individuals each were given lists of words to learn. Members of Group I learned a list in which there was little or no spelling similarities; Group II learned a list in which there were some similarities; and Group III was given a list in which words were very similar. The number of trials required for the members of each group to learn the given lists perfectly was recorded. These data were collected:

$$M_1 = 17.9 \quad M_2 = 16.9 \quad M_3 = 16.5 \quad M_{tot} = 17.1$$
$$\Sigma X^2 = 14,255$$

a. Why did the researcher design his experiment with three rather than two groups?

b. Analyze the data and draw conclusions.

6. A study is to be conducted to determine if years of teaching experience in a given school system affect teacher performance on a National Teachers Examination. Suppose that random samples of ten teachers with one year of teaching experience, ten teachers with five years' teaching experience, and ten teachers with ten years' teaching experience were selected and given the examination and the following data collected:

GROUP I (1 yr. exp.)	GROUP II (5 yrs. exp.)	GROUP III (10 yrs. exp.)
48	50	58
46	38	54
48	56	64
50	38	48
54	46	58
44	56	60
32	50	62
46	72	80
32	38	50
26	52	56

a. If a significant difference is found, can we conclude that teachers do a better job of teaching as a result of their professional experience?

b. Do the data indicate a significant difference among the groups?

7. In a study of the effects of alcohol on reaction time, subjects were randomly assigned to four groups. Group I received no alcohol; Group II subjects each received ½ oz. of alcohol; members of Group III were given 1 oz. of alcohol each; and Group IV people were given 1½ oz. each. After a 10 minute waiting period, all groups were tested simultaneously with a device designed to record right foot reaction time. The stimulus was a red light. The time, in tenths of a second, is given below:

Group I	Group II	Group III	Group IV
1	1	3	5
1	2	2	4
2	2	2	4
1	1	2	5
2	2	2	3
1	2	1	2
1	1	2	2
2	1	2	3
3	3	4	4
1	3	5	5

a. State the null hypothesis in terms of this experiment.

b. Is there a significant difference among the groups? (Use the 5% level of confidence for the critical ratio.)

c. Why was the experiment performed with four groups instead of two?

Suggested Activities

For each of the situations outlined following, write a brief critique of the methods used and conclusions formulated and suggest how improvements can be made in the studies.

1. An investigator wished to determine if homogeneous grouping improves pupil learning in a first course in algebra. The investigator designated one of two high schools in a small city to serve as the experimental school and the other as the control. Both schools had about the same number of pupils in each of five sections of Algebra I. In the experimental school pupils were grouped homogeneously on the basis of I.Q. and ability tests in mathematics; in the control they were placed in sections at random. At the end of the year all pupils were given a standardized test in Algebra I. The t-test for significant difference of means showed the experimental group to be superior and a computed F-ratio confirmed the conclusion.

2. An administrator decided to compare the progress of elementary pupils in his school system who were to be instructed in American history by a television instructor to another group which was to continue to be instructed by the normal classroom procedures. Both groups were given a standard I.Q. test with the results indicating no significant difference between the groups; however, a standard test in American history for the particular grade level showed that the pupils to be taught in the ordinary way scored significantly higher in knowledge of American history. Since no adjustments could be made in pupil assignments, the administrator decided to drop the project.

3. A researcher wished to determine if the size of high school biology classes in a given school would affect the performance of pupils on a standard biology examination. At the beginning of the school year, classes of twenty and twenty-five biology pupils were selected and through tests found to be similar in mental ability, knowledge of biology, socioeconomic backround, and interest in biology. The same teacher taught the two classes during the first two periods in the morning, but the time for each group to take biology (Period I or Period II) was rotated each quarter. A t-test of how the two groups performed on the biology test at the end of the year indicated no significant difference. The researcher concluded that class size was not important.

4. At the beginning of a school year an investigator selected two groups of seventh grade children, one group from an urban area

and another from a rural area, and compared their mental ability as measured by a standard test. He found the mean scores of the groups differed significantly (null was rejected at the 1% level of confidence). The groups continued regular schooling in their own area but the rural seventh graders were given extra training in vocabularly, spatial relationships, speed reading, arithmetic operations and estimating solutions. At the end of the year the pupils were retested with the same I.Q. examination. It was found that the mean scores of the two groups were no longer significantly different. Since the mean score of the urban group showed a slight gain and the rural scores were significantly higher than they were at the beginning of the year, it was concluded that children's I.Q.'s can be materially improved by giving them the kind of training given the rural children.

Briefly describe the research methods you would use to solve each of the following problems:

1. Problem: to determine if teaching the first year of a foreign language through an oral-aural approach rather than in the traditional classroom method will alter pupil performance on standard year-end tests in grammar, reading and vocabulary.
2. Problem: to determine if the time of day that mathematics is taught in the high schools of a large city affects pupil performance on final standard mathematics tests. (Assume that the teachers teach multiple sections of the same course throughout the day.)
3. Problem: to determine if a carefully planned pre-first grade reading readiness program is more effective in promoting reading progress of first grade children than normal kindergarten activities.
4. Problem: to determine if fourth grade pupils in a given school system who are taught science by means of a team teaching approach acquire more knowledge of science than pupils taught in the traditional manner by regular fourth grade teachers.

Selected Readings

1. Brunk, H. D., *An Introduction to Mathematical Statistics.* Boston: Ginn and Co. 1960 (Chapters 9, 10, 14, and 15)
2. Collier, Raymond O., and Slantery M. Elan (Editors), *Research Designs and Analysis.* Bloomington, Indiana: Phi Delta Kappa Incorporated, 1960.
3. Garrett, Henry E., *Elementary Statistics* (Second Edition). New York: David McKay Co., Inc., 1962 (Chapters 9, 10, and 11).
4. Garrett, Henry E., *Statistics in Psychology and Education* (Fourth

Edition) New York: Longmans, Green and Co., 1954 (Chapters 8 and 9).

5. HAMMOND, KENNETH R., AND JAMES E. HOUSEHOLDER, *Introduction to the Statistical Method*. New York: Alfred A. Knopf, 1962 (Chapters 7, 8 and 9).

6. LI, JEROME C. R., *Statistical Inference*, Volume I. Third Edition. Ann Arbor: Edwards Brothers, Inc., 1966.

7. JOHNSON, PALMER O., AND ROBERT W. B. JACKSON, *Modern Statistical Methods: Descriptive and Inductive*. Chicago: Rand McNally & Co., 1959 (Chapters 6, 7, 8, 9, 12 and 14).

8. KOENKER, ROBERT H., *Simplified Statistics*. Bloomington, Ill.: McKnight and McKnight Publishing Co., 1961 (Chapters 7 and 8).

9. PETERS, CHARLES C., AND WALTER R. VAN VOORHIS, *Statistical Procedures and Their Mathematical Bases*. New York: McGraw-Hill Book Co., 1940 (Chapters 6, 12 and 16).

10. RUMMEL, J. FRANCES, *An Introduction to Research Procedures in Education*. New York: Harper & Row, Publishers, 1958 (Chapters 6 and 8).

11. SENDERS, VIRGINIA L., *Measurement and Statistics*, New York: Oxford University Press, 1958 (Chapters 10, 11, 12, 13, 14 and 15).

12. UNDERWOOD, BENTON J., and others, *Elementary Statistics*. New York: Appleton-Century-Crofts, 1954 (Chapters 8, 9, 11 and 12).

13. VAN DALEN, DEOBOLD B., AND WILLIAM J. MEYER, *Understanding Educational Research*. New York: McGraw-Hill Book Co., 1962 (Chapter 14).

14. YONDER, W. J., *Experimentation and Measurement*. Washington: National Science Teachers Association, 1962 (Chapter 5).

Chapter 7

The Application of Statistical Analysis in Descriptive Research

Chapter 5 of this text was concerned with some elementary statistical methods which can be used in the analysis of data that result from descriptive studies. Such studies might analyze measurements of various factors and describe what is typical and atypical. Descriptive statistical methods are not confined to data studied in terms of central tendency and variability, however; nor is the study of phenomena confined to the experimental method.

It was pointed out in Chapter 1 that many phenomena cannot be manipulated through experimental conditions. Instead, a researcher may need to be content to collect quantitative data to determine if a relationship or correlation exists between various kinds of measurements. Meteorologists, for example, measure air pressure, temperature, and other weather factors but are unable to conduct comprehensive experiments with the factors; however, it is possible to subject weather data to statistical analysis to find relationships which may be useful in making predictions.

At other times descriptive studies are concerned with quantitative data that *do not* result from measurements but rather from counting how frequently an event occurs. A researcher may wish to determine the opinion of a given population without polling the entire population. His data might consist of yes and no answers, or categories of answers, to questions by a sample of the population. The data are quantitative but since they are not derived from measurements, they cannot be analyzed in terms of the t or F-ratio.

Statisticians have developed analytical tools that help the researcher to derive meaning from many kinds of data. This chapter is devoted to a consideration of the basis and application of a few of the elementary statistical tools used in descriptive educational research dealing with finding relationships and analyzing data expressed as frequencies. As in the discussion of statistical methods applied to experiments in Chapter 6, Chapter 7 will not present a comprehensive treatment of the methods but rather will consider the basic concepts involved. It must also be pointed out that some of the statistical tools that find primary use in experiments may, under some circumstances, be applied in the analysis of descriptive data. Similarly, the statistical tools that are usually associated with descriptive studies may at times be used in experiments.

Measuring Relatedness

Several methods can be used to test relatedness or correlation. One such test, developed by Karl Pearson, is known as the Pearson product-moment coefficient of correlation. The coefficient is denoted by the symbol r.

In order to understand the Pearson test, let us first examine several hypothetical sets of data. Table 7.1 represents scores that a group of high school seniors have received on achievement examinations in mathematics. Table 7.2 gives the scores received by our hypothetical senior group on achievement tests in physics. Table 7.3 shows the group's scores on tests in Latin, and Table 7.4 the scores in biology.

If the data are graphed (in terms of the z-scores) by plotting each student's mathematics score along the X axis with the corresponding score in the other subject along the Y axis, the graphs derived from Tables 7.1, 7.2, 7.3 and 7.4 will appear as shown in Figures 7.1, 7.2 and 7.3.

The graphs indicate the following:[1]

1. The scores in mathematics and physics are perfectly correlated in a direct ratio, i.e., pupils who obtained high scores in mathematics also had high scores in physics and vice versa. This is called *positive* correlation. The graph in Figure 7.1 shows the relationship as a straight line that runs through all the points at an angle of 45 degrees in an upward direction from left to right. (Actually, perfect or near perfect correlation of data is found only rarely — usually in measurements made on physical phenomena in nature. They are found seldom if ever in measurements involving people.)

---

[1]Keep in mind that these are hypothetical scores. In a real situation it would be extremely unlikely that the relationships would exist as shown.

TABLE 7.1. Scores Obtained By 26 Seniors In Mathematics; TABLE 7.2. Physics; TABLE 7.3. Latin; TABLE 7.4. Biology.

Student	MATH Test Score (X_M)	z_M Score	PHYSICS Test Score (Y_P)	z_P Score	LATIN Test Score (Y_L)	z_L Score	BIOLOGY Test Score (Y_B)	z_B Score
A	100	+2.22	100	+2.22	50	-2.22	81	+.57
B	95	+1.83	95	+1.83	54	-1.83	70	-.39
C	90	+1.35	90	+1.35	59	-1.35	75	+.04
D	86	+1.00	86	+1.00	63	-1.00	63	-1.00
E	83	+.74	83	+.74	66	-.74	59	-1.35
F	82	+.65	82	+.65	67	-.65	50	-2.22
G	81	+.57	81	+.57	68	-.57	86	+1.00
H	80	+.48	80	+.48	69	-.48	78	+.30
I	79	+.39	79	+.39	70	-.39	100	+2.22
J	78	+.30	78	+.30	71	-.30	73	-.13
K	77	+.22	77	+.22	72	-.22	54	-1.83
L	76	+.13	76	+.13	73	-.13	77	+.22
M	75	+.04	75	+.04	74	-.04	82	+.65
N	74	-.04	74	-.04	75	+.04	69	-.48
O	73	-.13	73	-.13	76	+.13	74	-.04
P	72	-.22	72	-.22	77	+.22	95	+1.83
Q	71	-.30	71	-.30	78	+.30	72	-.22
R	70	-.39	70	-.39	79	+.39	90	+1.35
S	69	-.48	69	-.48	80	+.48	80	+.48
T	68	-.57	68	-.57	81	+.57	66	-.74
U	67	-.65	67	-.65	82	+.65	71	-.30
V	66	-.74	66	-.74	83	+.74	79	+.39
W	63	-1.00	63	-1.00	86	+1.00	67	-.65
X	59	-1.35	59	-1.35	90	+1.35	76	+.13
Y	54	-1.83	54	-1.83	95	+1.83	83	+.74
Z	50	-2.22	50	-2.22	100	+2.22	68	-.57
	M = 74.5 SD = 11.5	(math test)	M = 74.5 SD = 11.5	(physics test)	M = 74.5 SD = 11.5	(Latin test)	M = 74.5 SD = 11.5	(Biology test)

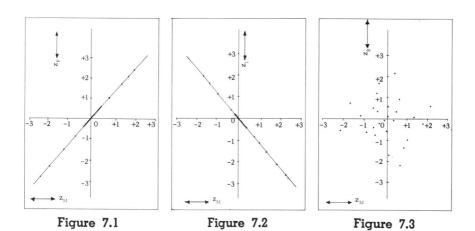

Figure 7.1   **Figure 7.2**   **Figure 7.3**

Figure 7.1. Perfect Positive Correlation. Hypothetical z-scores in Math. (X-axis) vs. Physics (Y-axis); **Figure 7.2.** Perfect Negative Correlation. Hypothetical z-scores in Math. (X-axis) vs. Latin (Y-axis); **Figure 7.3.** No Correlation. Hypothetical z-scores in Math. (X-axis) vs. Biology (Y-axis)

2. The scores in mathematics and Latin are also correlated, but in an inverse manner; pupils who had high scores in mathematics did poorly in Latin and vice versa. This is called *negative* correlation. The graph of data results in a line sloping down from left to right at an angle of 45 degrees to the horizontal.

3. The scores in mathematics and biology seem to have no relationship: some students who did well in mathematics also did well in biology, but others did not, etc. As a result, in Figure 7.3 no single straight line can be drawn through all the points, nor can a tendency toward correlation be discerned.

Suppose now that hypothetical data which might be more nearly representative of a real situation are examined. Tables 7.5, 7.6, 7.7, and 7.8 present another set of such data. Again we have hypothetical senior class scores in various subjects compared to scores in mathematics. Now, however, the scores are more representative of the kind that would be obtained in a real testing situation. (The relationships shown are not necessarily representative of what would be found, however, if the research were actually carried out.)

Graphs of the data are shown in Figures 7.4, 7.5 and 7.6 in terms of the deviations of the scores from the respective means.

TABLE 7.5		TABLE 7.6		TABLE 7.7		TABLE 7.8	
	MATH		PHYSICS		LATIN		BIOLOGY
Student	Test Score (X_M)	z_M Score	Test Score (Y_P)	z_P Score	Test Score (Y_L)	z_L Score	Test Score (Y_B)	z_B Score
A	100	+2.22	90	+1.35	95	+1.83	81	+ .57
B	95	+1.83	86	+1.00	66	- .74	82	+ .65
C	90	+1.35	100	+2.22	50	-2.22	78	+ .30
D	86	+1.00	83	+ .74	67	- .65	77	+ .22
E	83	+ .74	54	-1.83	63	-1.00	100	+2.22
F	82	+ .65	79	+ .39	59	-1.35	90	+1.35
G	81	+ .57	81	+ .57	69	- .48	70	- .39
H	80	+ .48	77	+ .22	71	- .30	75	+ .04
I	79	+ .39	82	+ .65	68	- .57	63	-1.00
J	78	+ .30	78	+ .30	74	- .04	83	+ .74
K	77	+ .22	75	+ .04	72	- .22	79	+ .39
L	76	+ .13	80	+ .48	73	- .13	59	-1.35
M	75	+ .04	76	+ .13	70	- .39	50	-2.22
N	74	- .04	70	- .39	76	+ .13	86	+1.00
O	73	- .13	73	- .13	80	+ .48	73	- .13
P	72	- .22	72	- .22	75	+ .04	54	-1.83
Q	71	- .30	74	- .04	78	+ .30	69	- .48
R	70	- .39	68	- .57	82	+ .65	74	- .04
S	69	- .48	71	- .30	77	+ .22	95	+1.83
T	68	- .57	69	- .48	81	+ .57	72	- .22
U	67	- .65	59	-1.35	79	+ .39	80	+ .48
V	66	- .74	63	-1.00	54	-1.83	66	- .74
W	63	-1.00	67	- .65	83	+ .74	71	- .30
X	59	-1.35	50	-2.22	100	+2.22	67	- .65
Y	54	-1.83	66	- .74	86	+1.00	76	+ .13
Z	50	-2.22	95	+1.83	90	+1.35	68	- .57

The graphs illustrate what happens in the more lifelike situation when measurements are made. In Figure 7.4 note that there seems to be a direct, or positive, correlation between mathematics and physics indicated, but the relationship is not perfect. No single line can be drawn through every point, but a line which approximates the general trend of the scores can be placed on the graph paper. The same is true of the graph in Figure 7.5; a negative correlation is indicated and a line of best fit — i.e., a line that is placed as close as possible to all points — can be drawn with a slope down from left to right. Figure 7.6 shows, however, that the scores are too unrelated to discern a general trend: correlation is just about nonexistent. A line of best fit would parallel the X axis.

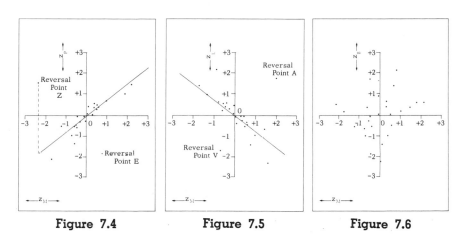

| Figure 7.4 | Figure 7.5 | Figure 7.6 |

Note: The dotted line represents the amount of distance by which the regression line misses point Z in terms of *vertical* distance.

Figure 7.4. High Positive Correlation. Hypothetical z-scores in Math. (X-axis) vs. Physics (Y-axis); **Figure 7.5.** High Negative Correlation. Hypothetical z-scores in Math. (X-axis) vs. Latin (Y-axis); **Figure 7.6.** Little or No Correlation. Hypothetical z-scores in Math. (X-axis) vs. Biology (Y-axis)

When the data are plotted on graph paper, the pattern, or scatter, of points is useful in providing a general idea of correlation; however, the scattergram — as the graphic representation is called — is not precise enough to furnish a basis for making predictions. What is needed is a mathematical expression that gives a quantitative indication of degree of correlation.

A glance at Figures 7.4 and 7.5 shows that the general trend of points, as revealed by the scattergram, is a function of the slope of the line of best fit.[2] The line that best fits the data is sometimes called a regression line. What determines where the line of best fit or regression line should be placed? Logic would indicate that a regression line will be one which lies as close as possible to each point. Figure 7.1 reveals that when there is perfect correlation the line passes through all points, and for every rise of one unit along the X axis, there is a corresponding rise of one unit along the Y axis. In Figure 7.4, however, the regression line is shown to be a compromise that is placed so it misses the group of points by the least total amount possible. Actually, two regression lines can be drawn: one which makes the smallest misses in terms of vertical distance, the other in terms of the least amount of misses measured along the horizontal axis. Generally, the regression line used is one which measures amount of misses for each point in a vertical direction (along the Y axis).

Figures 7.4 and 7.5 also reveal that points which are counter to the general trend — points Z and E in Figure 7.4 and A and V in Figure 7.5 — tend to require the regression line to be rotated in a direction that would bring it parallel to the X axis. The reason for this is that relatively large misses by points that are counter to the general trend will require the regression line to be rotated in a direction to bring it closer to the points. Since the line goes through the origin which represents the mean of both distributions plotted, the line rotates around the origin.

Figures 7.7, 7.8 and 7.9 demonstrate more clearly why regression lines will tend to rotate toward a horizontal position as data scatter away from perfect correlation. Figure 7.7 is a graph of hypothetical data that show a perfect correlation between two kinds of measurements having a normal distribution. Note that most of the scores fall close to the means of each kind of measurement (the 0 point of the graph). As points scatter away from perfect positive correlation (Figure 7.8), those near the mean will tend to be found not only in quadrants I and II of the graph but also in quadrants III and IV. (Mathematically, a data sheet would show that in the perfect positive correlation, positive z-scores are matched with positive z-scores and negatives with negatives,

---

[2]The slope of a line is labeled in mathematics as b, and is defined as the ratio of y, a distance along the Y axis, that corresponds to x, a distance along the X axis. From Figure 7.1, therefore, in a perfect direct correlation b = 1; i.e., $b = \frac{y}{x}$, and the number of y units along the Y axis will be the same as x, the corresponding number of units along the X axis. Also, from Figure 7.2 slope b = −1 since for every unit moved in the (+) direction to the right along the X axis, y drops or goes in the (−) direction 1 unit.

whereas imperfect correlation shows some matching of negative and positive scores. These run counter to the trend.) Since the regression line is the one which lies as close as possible to all the points, the counter-trend points will tend to rotate the line toward a horizontal position. It is true that points like Q and R, in order to be placed close to the regression line, require the line to be rotated toward a steeper slope, but points at the extremes are very few in a normal distribution, and the many scores that tend to scatter from around the mean into quadrants II and IV more than offset their effect. Finally, in Figure 7.9 it can be seen that the line of best fit in terms of vertical distances from the points is one with no slope at all; a line that is horizontal and parallel to the X axis. (A perpendicular line also fits the data, but in terms of *vertical* distance the points would be an infinite distance from the line.)

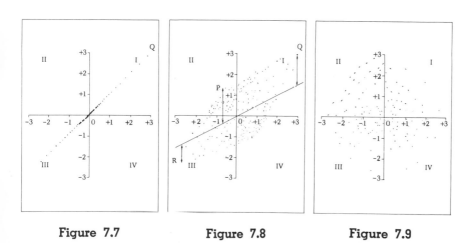

Figure 7.7   **Figure 7.8**   **Figure 7.9**

It is therefore apparent that the slope of regression lines will range from: +1 when correlation is perfect and direct, to 0 or no slope when there is no correlation, to −1 when correlation is perfect and inverse. The Pearson product-moment coefficient of correlation, r, is nothing more than the slope of a regression line which may range from the values of −1 to +1.

Deriving an Equation for Finding r

The problem of determining a mathematical expression for the slope of the regression line resolves itself into one of deriving an equation for the line of best fit; but what is "a line of best fit" *mathematically* speaking?

Remember that a regression line may be conceived as one that misses the points of a scattergram by the smallest possible amount — that is, it lies closer to each and every point than any other line would. Since each point on the scattergram is a certain number of units away from the X axis — as measured up or down along the Y axis — the amount that the point deviates away from the X axis may be labeled as y. Now, imagine that each point could be moved up or down to a position $\bar{y}$ exactly *on* the regression line. Since the distance of any point from the X-axis has been called y, then the distance by which a point misses the regression line can be expressed as $y - \bar{y}$. (See Figure 7.10)

Figure 7.10   An Expression for the Distance from Any Point to the Regression Line

Mathematicians have found that the line of best fit is one such that the sum of all $(y - \bar{y})^2$ distances is at a minimum, i.e., a regression line is one which has the smallest total of misses, and, therefore, $\Sigma(y - \bar{y})^2$ will be at a minimum.

The slope is defined as distance moved up as compared to distance moved along a base line or, in mathematical terms,

$$\text{slope } b = \frac{y}{x} \begin{array}{l} \leftarrow \text{distance along y axis} \\ \leftarrow \text{distance along x axis} \end{array}$$

Since any point on the regression line will have a distance of $\bar{y}$ up or down, $b = \dfrac{\bar{y}}{x}$ and $\bar{y} = bx$. Then $\Sigma (y - \bar{y})^2 = \Sigma (y - bx)^2$. The expanded expression $\Sigma y^2 - 2b \Sigma yx + b^2 \Sigma x^2$ therefore can be thought of as another way of stating $\Sigma(y - \bar{y})^2$. It was previously stated, however, that $\Sigma(y - \bar{y})^2$ must be at a minimum in order to have a line of best fit; therefore, when $\Sigma y^2 - 2b \Sigma xy + b^2 \Sigma x^2$ is at a minimum, we have a line of best fit.

Mathematicians use the calculus to determine an expression, from the one given, that will produce the minimum function. The method will not be described, but students versed in the calculus will remember that a minimum function can be found by taking the first derivation of an expression and setting it equal to zero. The equation, as determined from the derivation of $\Sigma y^2 - 2b \Sigma xy + b^2 \Sigma x^2$ with respect to b, turns out to be $-2 \Sigma xy + 2b \Sigma x^2 = 0$.

Then $2b \Sigma x^2 = 2 \Sigma xy$. Close examination of the latter expression shows that dividing both sides of the equation by 2N will change it into a form which can be used to take advantage of the standard deviation of scores in X:

1. $\dfrac{2b \Sigma x^2}{2N} = \dfrac{2 \Sigma xy}{2N}$

2. $\dfrac{b \Sigma x^2}{N} = \dfrac{\Sigma xy}{N}$, but $\dfrac{\Sigma x^2}{N} = \sigma_x^2$ (since $\sigma_x = \sqrt{\dfrac{\Sigma x^2}{N}}$)

3. therefore, $b \, \sigma_x^2 = \dfrac{\Sigma xy}{N}$ and $b = \dfrac{\Sigma xy}{N\sigma_x^2}$

The values of x and y, however, are not necessarily expressed in the same units, and the slope, b, lacks a standard meaning. Since slope b is in terms of $\dfrac{y \text{ units,}}{x \text{ units}}$ it can be placed into a single standard by dividing the y units and x units by the respective standard deviations for the Y measures and X measures: this procedure changes y and x deviations into standard deviation units, i.e. z scores.

But $\dfrac{y \div \sigma_y}{x \div \sigma_x} = \dfrac{y}{x} \cdot \dfrac{\sigma_x}{\sigma_y}$

Slope b therefore can be changed into a standard expression for slope by multiplying it by $\dfrac{\sigma_x}{\sigma_y}$. The symbol for the slope, when it is in terms of standard deviation units, is now labeled r, the coefficient of correlation. In other words $r = b \dfrac{\sigma_x}{\sigma_y}$.

But since $b = \dfrac{\Sigma xy}{N\sigma_x^2}$ then $b \dfrac{\sigma_x}{\sigma_y} = \dfrac{\Sigma xy}{N\sigma_x^2} \cdot \dfrac{\sigma_x}{\sigma_y}$

Therefore $r = \dfrac{\Sigma xy}{N \sigma_x \sigma_y}$

What does the equation for r direct us to do in finding the coefficient of correlation (slope of the regression line)? First, the deviation of each score in X from the mean of scores in X must be found — these deviations are what have been called x's. Then the deviation of each Y score from the mean of Y scores is found — the y's. Next each x and its corresponding y is multiplied; the results are expressed as xy's. A sum of xy's is found and labeled Σxy. Finally, Σxy is divided by $N \cdot \sigma_x \cdot \sigma_y$, where N is the number of pairs of scores.

Application

The use of the formula as it has been given can be illustrated by applying it to the hypothetical data previously given concerning tests in mathematics and another subject. One such set of scores was on tests in physics and mathematics. Table 7.9 illustrates the computations of r from the data that appeared in Table 7.4 (Note: the only data required from the table to compute r by the formula derived so far is Σxy, and also ΣX and ΣY used to compute σ_x and σ_y. The data in the last column XY will be used later with a different formula.)

How can we interpret an r of $+ .5$? The positive value of r indicates a slope up from left to right. The relationship between the mathematics and physics scores therefore is direct; i.e., as one set of scores increases, the other set also tends to increase and vice versa. But what about the value of r?

TABLE 7.9. Computing r from Measurements

Student	X Math	X²	x	z_m	Y Physics	Y²	y	z_P	xy	XY
A	100	10000	+ 25.5	+ 2.22	90	8100	+ 15.5	+ 1.35	395	9000
B	95	9025	+ 20.5	+ 1.83	86	7396	+ 11.5	+ 1.00	236	8170
C	90	8100	+ 15.5	+ 1.35	100	10000	+ 25.5	+ 2.22	395	9000
D	86	7396	+ 11.5	+ 1.00	83	6889	+ 8.5	+ .74	98	7138
E	83	6889	+ 8.5	+ .74	54	2916	- 20.5	- 1.83	-174	4482
F	82	6724	+ 7.5	+ .65	79	6241	+ 4.5	+ .39	34	6478
G	81	6561	+ 6.5	+ .57	81	6561	+ 6.5	+ .57	42	6561
H	80	6400	+ 5.5	+ .48	77	5929	+ 2.5	+ .22	14	6160
I	79	6241	+ 4.5	+ .39	82	6724	+ 7.5	+ .65	34	6478
J	78	6084	+ 3.5	+ .30	78	6084	+ 3.5	+ .30	12	6084
K	77	5929	+ 2.5	+ .22	75	5625	+ .5	+ .04	1	5775
L	76	5776	+ 1.5	+ .13	80	6400	+ 5.5	+ .48	8	6080
M	75	5625	+ .5	+ .04	76	5776	+ 1.5	+ .13	1	5700
N	74	5476	- .5	- .04	70	4900	- 4.5	- .39	2	5180
O	73	5329	- 1.5	- .13	73	5329	- 1.5	- .13	2	5329
P	72	5184	- 2.5	- .22	72	5184	- 2.5	- .22	6	5184
Q	71	5041	- 3.5	- .30	74	5476	- .5	- .04	2	5254
R	70	4900	- 4.5	- .39	68	4624	- 6.5	- .57	29	4760
S	69	4761	- 5.5	- .48	71	5041	- 3.5	- .30	19	4899
T	68	4624	- 6.5	- .57	69	4761	- 5.5	- .48	36	4692
U	67	4489	- 7.5	- .65	59	3481	- 15.5	- 1.35	116	3953
V	66	4356	- 8.5	- .74	63	3969	- 11.5	- 1.00	98	4158
W	63	3969	- 11.5	- 1.00	67	4489	- 7.5	- .65	86	4221
X	59	3481	- 15.5	- 1.35	50	2500	- 25.5	- 2.22	395	2950
Y	54	2916	- 20.5	- 1.83	66	4356	- 8.5	- .74	174	3564
Z	50	2500	- 25.5	- 2.22	95	9025	+ 20.5	+ 1.83	-523	4750

$\Sigma X^2 = 147776$ $\Sigma Y^2 = 147776$ $\Sigma xy = 1639$ $\Sigma XY = 146000$

$M_X = 74.5$ $M_Y = 74.5$

$$\sigma_x = \sqrt{\frac{\Sigma X^2}{N} - M^2} = \sqrt{\frac{147776}{26} - 5550}$$

$$= \sqrt{5684 - 5550} = \sqrt{134}$$

$$= 11.5$$

$$\sigma_y = \sqrt{\frac{\Sigma Y^2}{N} - M^2} = \sqrt{\frac{147776}{26} - 5550}$$

$$= \sqrt{5684 - 5550} = \sqrt{134}$$

$$= 11.5$$

$$r = \frac{\Sigma xy}{N \, \sigma_x \, \sigma_y} = \frac{+1639}{(26)(11.5)(11.5)} = \frac{+1639}{3439} = +.5$$

It has already been established that as the value of the correlation coefficient — the slope of the regression line — increases from 0 toward +1 or −1, the amount of relationship increases. Another factor, the size of the sample, must be taken into account. Obviously, a large representative sample is a much better indicator than a small sample that a coefficient of correlation is truly representative of the population from which it has been drawn. It is necessary, therefore, to include sample size in any evaluation of a coefficient of correlation unless conclusions are to be limited to the population tested.

Table A.5 of Appendix A has been prepared as a reference that can be consulted to test the significance of r. The value $+.5$ must be tested in terms of the df in selecting the sample. Since the sampling is in terms of *pairs* of measurements, df = N−2, where N is the number of pairs. For the example given, Table A.5 is entered at 24df. The table indicates than an r of .388 is required to reject the null hypothesis at the 5% level, and an r of .496 is necessary for a rejection at the 1% level. These figures may be interpreted as meaning that values for r lower than .388 could quite likely result from sampling error even when the r for the entire population from which the sample is drawn is zero. Then the possibility of a zero correlation for the parent population can be ruled out in the example at greater than the 1% level of confidence. The r obtained is $+.5$; therefore, if the group tested is a representative sample, it is a significant value in this case. On the other hand, if the sample size had been 12, an r of $+.5$ would not have been sufficient to reject the null hypothesis at the 5% level. Table A.5 shows that 10 df requires an r of .576 or greater to be considered significant. In addition, if we limit our conclusions to the group tested, it is obvious that a positive correlation between physics and mathematics scores exists for the particular group.

Other Formulae for Finding r

The researcher sometimes finds it more convenient to use formulae that are different from the basic one given. When a calculator is available, it is simpler to use the raw scores directly in determining r than to go to the trouble of obtaining deviations of the scores from the M's. The derivation of a raw score formula follows:

$$\text{Since } r = \frac{\Sigma xy}{N\sigma_x \ \sigma_y,} \text{ then}$$

$$r = \frac{\Sigma(X - M_x)(Y - M_y)}{N\sigma_x \ \sigma_y}$$

$$= \frac{\Sigma(XY - XM_y - YM_x + M_xM_y)}{N \ \sigma_x \ \sigma_y}$$

$$= \frac{\dfrac{\Sigma XY}{N} - \dfrac{\Sigma XM_y}{N} - \dfrac{\Sigma YM_x}{N} + \dfrac{\Sigma M_xM_y}{N}}{\sigma_x \ \sigma_y}$$

but $- \dfrac{\Sigma XM_y}{N} = - M_y \dfrac{\Sigma X}{N}$

and since $\dfrac{\Sigma X}{N} = M_x$ then $-M_y \dfrac{\Sigma X}{N} = -M_y \ M_x = -M_x \ M_y$

also $- \dfrac{\Sigma YM_x}{N} = -M_y M_x = -M_x M_y$

and $\dfrac{\Sigma M_x M_y}{N} = \dfrac{N M_x M_y}{N} = M_x M_y$

therefore, $r = \dfrac{\dfrac{\Sigma XY}{N} - M_x M_y - M_x M_y + M_x M_y}{\sigma_x \sigma_y} = \dfrac{\dfrac{\Sigma XY}{N} - M_x M_y}{\sigma_x \sigma_y}$

It can be seen that the new formula derived uses the raw scores, or measurements, directly rather than deviations from the mean. The new formula can be applied to compute r as follows:

(The ΣXY is obtained from Table 8.9 — last column.)

$$r = \dfrac{\dfrac{\Sigma XY}{N} - M_x M_y}{\sigma_x \sigma_y} = \dfrac{\dfrac{146000}{26} - (74.5)(74.5)}{(11.5)(11.5)} = \dfrac{5615 - 5550}{132} = .5$$

Finally, a consideration of the basic formula $r = \dfrac{\Sigma xy}{N\sigma_x \ \sigma_y}$ also leads to the development of a formula in terms of z-scores as follows:

$r = \dfrac{\Sigma}{N} \left(\dfrac{x}{\sigma_x}\right)\left(\dfrac{y}{\sigma_y}\right)$

but $\left(\dfrac{x}{\sigma_x}\right) = z_x$ and $\left(\dfrac{y}{\sigma_y}\right) = z_y$

then $r = \dfrac{\Sigma z_x z_y}{N}$

Rank Order Correlation

Sometimes data are reported in terms of rank order, rather than measurements; for example, the scores which pupils make on a test can be placed in descending order from the highest, ranked as number one, to the lowest, ranked as N.

The formula for correlation in terms of ranks was developed by Spearman. Beginning with an equation for r in terms of differences of paired measurements, derived from the Pearson equation, Spearman found an expression for correlation, labeled ρ (rho), which is computed from the differences in ranks of paired measurements. The formula for Spearman's rank order correlation is $\rho = 1 - \dfrac{6\Sigma d^2,}{N(N^2 - 1)}$ where d is the difference of ranks of paired measurements.

Application of Spearman's Formula

Table 7.10 illustrates the use of the Spearman formula in computing correlation from data that is given in rank order. The hypothetical scores on tests in mathematics and physics that appeared in Tables 7.3 and 7.4 to illustrate the computation of r have been converted to rank order in

TABLE 7.10   Rank Order of Test Scores and the Computation of ρ

Student	X Math Rank	Y Physics Rank	d=X-Y	d^2
A	1	3	- 2	4
B	2	4	- 2	4
C	3	1	2	4
D	4	5	- 1	1
E	5	25	- 20	400
F	6	9	- 3	9
G	7	7	0	0
H	8	11	- 3	9
I	9	6	+ 3	9
J	10	10	0	0
K	11	13	- 2	4
L	12	8	+ 4	16
M	13	12	+ 1	1
N	14	18	- 4	16
O	15	15	0	0
P	16	16	0	0
Q	17	14	+ 3	9
R	18	20	- 2	4
S	19	17	+ 2	4
T	20	19	+ 1	1
U	21	24	- 3	9
V	22	23	- 1	1
W	23	21	+ 2	4
X	24	26	- 2	4
Y	25	22	+ 3	9
Z	26	2	+24	576
			Σd^2 =	1098

$$\rho = 1 - \frac{6 \Sigma d^2}{N(N^2-1)} = 1 - \frac{6\,(1098)}{26\,(676-1)} = 1 - \frac{6588}{17550} = 1 - .4$$

$$\rho = + .6$$

Table 7.10. Note that in finding d, the difference in rank order, the rank on the physics test is always subtracted from the rank on the mathematics test. Actually, it makes no difference which column of ranks is used as the subtrahend as long as the rank from the same column is used each time.

Although ρ will tend to approximate r, the values will not always be equal. Sometimes tied ranks will occur requiring an interpretation in the computation of ρ which will cause the Spearman coefficient to differ from the Pearson r. Also, ρ is often considerably in error as compared with r as a result of a loss in accuracy in the translation of scores to ranks; therefore, Table A.6 in Appendix A is used as a basis for making decisions concerning the null hypothesis. Note that an N of 26 would require ρ to have a value close to .392 if the null hypothesis is to be rejected at the 5% level of confidence. In Table A.5 it was found that an N of 26 — i.e., 24df — requires an r of .388 for a rejection of null at the 5% level. The larger required value for ρ reflects what has been said about the lesser accuracy of ρ. Table A.6 also shows that, for the size of the sample, $\rho = .515$ is enough for a rejection of the null hypothesis at the 1% level of confidence; therefore, the ρ obtained in the example will allow a reject of null at better than the 1% level.

What Conclusions Can Be Drawn From Measures of Relatedness?

When two factors are found to be related, there may be an impulse to conclude that one of the factors has caused, or brought about, the other. If correlation between scores which students make in mathematics and physics is high, for example, it may seem correct to conclude that this is so because performance in one subject causes the result obtained in the other. In turn, it may also seem correct to conclude that the scores in physics can be improved by having students take more mathematics, or vice versa.

Actually, conclusions regarding cause and effect cannot be safely drawn from measures which show factors to be related *unless* the independent variable has been experimentally manipulated under controlled conditions. The reason for avoiding cause-effect conclusions concerning variables which are not studied under controlled conditions becomes apparent if one considers the following illustrations:

1. Studies of liquor consumption and church attendance from 1939 through 1943 show a positive correlation, but it would be ridiculous to suggest that one caused the other; it would be even more ridiculous to conclude that church attendance may be improved by dispensing free liquor to everyone. Possibly another factor was operative such as the fear and anxiety resulting from World War II.

2. There is a negative correlation between family size and income, but it is probably not true that having a large family causes income to drop. Again, other factors are most likely connected to the two factors.

3. Hat size and head size are correlated, but making larger hats will not produce larger heads.
4. Undoubtedly a correlation can be found between the number of motor accidents per year over the last 30 years and the average amount of schooling completed by Americans during the same period; both tend to go up each year, but is it safe to conclude that one caused the other?

If cause-effect conclusions cannot be drawn from descriptive correlation studies, of what use is such research? The answer to the question is that when two factors are found to be related, or correlated, it is possible to use the information in making predictions. If it is found that there is a direct relationship between grades or scores in mathematics and physics, it is possible to predict from one the outcome that will occur in the other with a degree of accuracy.

As a more useful example, colleges have found that there is a fairly high correlation between scores on the College Board examinations and grades in college. As a result, colleges have found it useful to use scores on these examinations as one of the factors in selecting students for higher education.

The Regression Line Equation

Prediction based upon correlation studies is made quantitative through the application of Pearson's coefficient to derive an equation for the regression line. The equation in turn can be applied to individual measurements in predicting one factor when the other of a pair is known. Referring again to College Board examinations, the regression line equation can be used to make a prediction of how well a particular student will do during his first year in a given college.

Recall that the slope of a straight line b is in terms of the ratio of how far up or down, symbolized as y, a point moves along the line to its lateral movement symbolized as X, or slope $b = \dfrac{y}{x}$; therefore, $y = bx$.

In plotting a scattergram, x and y are expressed as deviations of each given measurement, or score, from the respective mean; then, $x = (X - M_x)$ and $y = (Y - M_y)$. Remember that b is not a standard unit since X and Y are likely not measured in the same units, but b can be expressed in standard units by changing x and y to standard deviation units or z scores.

then, since $b = \dfrac{y}{x}$

and $r = \dfrac{y}{x} \dfrac{\sigma_x}{\sigma_y}$

therefore, $r = b \dfrac{\sigma_x}{\sigma_y}$

and $b = r \dfrac{\sigma_y}{\sigma_x}$

but $y = bx$

therefore $y = r \dfrac{\sigma_y}{\sigma_x} x$

Changing y and x to raw scores form ($Y - M_y$) and ($X - M_x$), we have:

$$Y - M_y = r \frac{\sigma_y}{\sigma_x} (X - M_x) \text{ and } Y = r \frac{\sigma_y}{\sigma_x} (X - M_x) + M_y$$

Application of the Regression Line Equation

Suppose that over several years a particular college has found that an r of $+.7$ resulted when the verbal portion of the College Board examination scores of entering freshmen was compared to the same students' grade point averages at the end of one year of study in the college. Can a prediction be made concerning a particular entering freshman's final grade point average at the end of his first year at the college?

Assume that the following information is also available:
1. X — the College Board examination score of the freshman = 400
2. M_x — the mean of College Board examination scores = 500
3. σ_x — standard deviation on the college board scores = 100
4. M_y — the mean grade point average for freshmen = 2.2 (based on a scale where 4.0 = A; 3.0 = B; 2.0 = C; 1.0 = D; 0 = F)
5. σ_y — the standard deviation in grade point averages = .4
6. Y — the grade point average predicted for the particular student

$$Y = (.7) \frac{(.4)}{100} (400 - 500) + 2.2$$
$$Y = .0028 (-100) + 2.2$$
$$= -.28 + 2.2$$
$$Y = 1.9$$

Thus, it is predicted that student X will complete his freshman year with a grade point average of 1.9, or C–. How accurate is the prediction? Obviously, if r were $+1.0$, one could predict the grade point average with complete accuracy; an r of $+1$ indicates a direct and complete correlation between two factors. As r deviates away from $+1$ or -1 toward 0, the prediction of one factor from the other becomes less accurate. In fact, it has been determined mathematically that when

r equals .10, only .5 per cent of predictions would be correct. When r is .80, predictions would be correct only 40 per cent of the time; an r of .95 still provides but 69 per cent correct predictions. It thus becomes obvious that in predicting individual measurements from correlation data, very high values of r are necessary.

The Chi Square Statistic

The chi square (χ^2) statistic provides the researcher with a way to analyze data that are expressed as frequencies rather than measurements. Very often, for example, research may be conducted to determine if, within a population, one particular opinion is more prevalent than another. Opinions are usually determined by either yes or no answers to questions or by the use of several more categories of answers such as "always agree" (to a given statement) "sometimes agree," or "never agree." In this way the number or frequency that a particular category is selected is found: nothing is measured in the sense that a test score or other scale is applied. Since it is usually necessary to use sampling in such studies, the researcher must judge whether deviations of sample frequencies from those he expected, or hypothesized, are likely to be due to sampling error, or if such deviations are significantly different from what was expected. Chi square may be used as a basis for making such a judgment.

Chi square also finds use in the analysis of contingency tables as a test for independence. The contingency table is one prepared by placing a given set of categories in a column and another set in a row. Groups or factors that belong to both a particular column and row category are recorded in the appropriate column-row space. Table 7.11 records hypothetical data regarding the amount of education completed by a group of air force men and their respective military ranks. Table 7.12 shows the computations for finding the expected frequencies.

TABLE 7.11

Education	Enlisted	Non-Commissioned Officers	Commissioned Officers	Totals
	O_f E_f	O_f E_f	O_f E_f	
Graduate	13(29. 7)	38(29. 7)	54(45. 6)	105
College	51(57. 9)	55(57. 9)	99(89. 1)	205
High School	60(43. 0)	41(43. 0)	51(66. 1)	152
Elementary School	21(14. 4)	11(14. 4)	19(22. 2)	51
	145	145	223	513

The numbers outside the parentheses were compiled by counting noses — in other words, these are observed frequencies. The numbers in the parentheses are the expected frequencies; these have been determined by disregarding how the numbers of people in a given education category have been divided up in terms of ranks. Thus the 105 men who have had graduate courses constitute the fraction 105/513 of all the men classified. Since 145 of all the men studied were in the enlisted ranks, 105/513 × 145 or 29.7 is the number we would have expected to be classified as enlisted graduates if their education and rank categories were not related to one another. It can be seen, however, that only 13 men fell into the two categories. What Chi square can help determine is whether the number of men observed as falling into various categories differ so much from what would be expected — if the categories were independent — that the differences should not be attributed to errors resulting from sampling. In other words, it may be possible that differences like the one we have in the first cell — 13 as compared with 29.7 — may arise just from sampling error. Chi square provides a basis for judging if differences are likely or unlikely to be a result of chance factors associated with sampling.

Table 7.12 provides the computations made to determine the expected frequencies in Table 7.11.

The Chi Square Formula

The formula for finding chi square from a given set of data is relatively simple, but the mathematical derivation of the formula stems from a consideration of a multinomial distribution and is beyond the scope of this book. An examination of the formula for X^2 demonstrates why it provides a reasonable solution to the problems discussed in the previous section.

$$X^2 = \Sigma \frac{(O_f - E_f)^2}{E_f}$$: where O_f represents each observed frequency

and E_f is the symbol for the expected frequencies that correspond with those observed. The formula indicates that these steps are to be carried out:

1. The difference between each observed frequency and its corresponding expected frequency is found by subtracting the latter from the former.
2. Each difference is squared and then divided by the expected frequency in each case.
3. The values found in step 2 are summed.

Note that for each observed frequency the amount by which it *deviates* from what was expected is found. (Squaring the deviations,

TABLE 7.12 Computation of Expected Frequencies
from a Contingency Table

Categories	Expected		
Grad. -enl.	$\dfrac{145 \text{ enl.}}{1}$	$\times \dfrac{105 \text{ grad.}}{513 \text{ total}}$	$= 29.7$
Grad. -non-com.	$\dfrac{145 \text{ non-com.}}{1}$	$\times \dfrac{105 \text{ grad.}}{513 \text{ total}}$	$= 29.7$
Grad. -com.	$\dfrac{223 \text{ com.}}{1}$	$\times \dfrac{105 \text{ grad.}}{513 \text{ total}}$	$= 45.6$
College-enl.	$\dfrac{145 \text{ enl.}}{1}$	$\times \dfrac{205 \text{ college}}{513 \text{ total}}$	$= 57.9$
College-non-com.	$\dfrac{145 \text{ non-com.}}{1}$	$\times \dfrac{205 \text{ college}}{513 \text{ total}}$	$= 57.9$
College-com.	$\dfrac{223 \text{ com.}}{1}$	$\times \dfrac{205 \text{ college}}{513 \text{ total}}$	$= 89.1$
High School-enl.	$\dfrac{145 \text{ enl.}}{1}$	$\times \dfrac{152 \text{ high sch.}}{513 \text{ total}}$	$= 43$
High School-non-com.	$\dfrac{145 \text{ non-com.}}{1}$	$\times \dfrac{152 \text{ high sch.}}{513 \text{ total}}$	$= 43$
High School-com.	$\dfrac{223 \text{ com.}}{1}$	$\times \dfrac{152 \text{ high sch.}}{513 \text{ total}}$	$= 66.1$
Elem. School-enl.	$\dfrac{145 \text{ enl.}}{1}$	$\times \dfrac{51 \text{ elem.}}{513 \text{ total}}$	$= 14.4$
Elem. School-non-com.	$\dfrac{145 \text{ non-com.}}{1}$	$\times \dfrac{51 \text{ elem.}}{513 \text{ total}}$	$= 14.4$
Elem. School-com.	$\dfrac{223 \text{ com.}}{1}$	$\times \dfrac{51 \text{ elem.}}{513 \text{ total}}$	$= 22.2$

which is dictated by the formula also avoids difficulties with negative numbers.) Next, the squared deviations of O_f from E_f are divided by E_f. This step is necessary since differences between observed and expected frequencies can take on meaning only when they are *compared* to the frequency expected. Finally χ^2 is the sum of $\dfrac{(E_f - O_f)^2}{E_f}$ ratios. If the E_f's are large numbers and $(O_f - E_f)$'s are small, χ^2 will be small and vice versa.

If χ^2 is large enough, the null hypothesis is rejected at some level of confidence. Null is hypothesized since if E_f's were the same as O_f's, χ^2 would equal zero. Sampling error can cause O_f's to differ from E_f's to some extent; but when differences between observed frequencies and expected frequencies are great — as measured by X^2 — in comparison to the expected frequency, a conclusion is drawn that the differences probably are not a result of sampling error: the null hypothesis is rejected. When $O_f - E_f$ differences are small as compared to E_f's, it is concluded that the differences are probably a result of sampling error. The decision of how large a figure for X^2 is large enough can be made on the basis of Table A.7 in Appendix A.

It thus is apparent that chi square does provide a way to make judgments as to whether frequencies found in categorized information are as expected, or if these frequencies deviate more from what was expected than can be accounted for on the basis of errors resulting from sampling.

Restrictions in the Application of Chi-Square

Before considering some problems to which chi-square can be applied, the limitations of the statistic will be discussed. Chi-square is applicable to the analysis of data that are classified in terms of frequencies of occurrences within categories; it *should not* be used to compare measurements. When data are the results of measurements, they are analyzed in terms of t-test, analysis of variance, coefficient of correlations, or other methods similar to those that have been studied in previous chapters of this book.

Because chi-square is mathematically derived from the multinomial distribution by substituting a series of approximations, several serious errors may result from its use. (In fact Lewis and Burke[3] have reported that a survey of fourteen researches which employed chi square showed that the application of the statistic was clearly unwarranted in nine of the studies.) Further, chi-square also suffers from the limitations inherent in the application of the assumptions of the multinomial distribution. The assumptions made are that:

1. Events categorized are randomly sampled.
2. Categories are mutually exclusive (not overlapping).
3. Outcomes are independent of one another.
4. $\Sigma\, O_f = \Sigma\, E_f$, or the sum of observed frequencies, must equal the sum of the expected frequencies.

The derivation of chi-square (from the multinomial distribution) requires the assumptions that the populations of observed frequencies

[3]Lewis, D. and Burke, C. J., "The Use and Misuse of the Chi Square Test," *Psychological Bulletin*, 1949, 46, pp. 433-489.

would be normally distributed around the expected frequency as a mean. Undetected departure from normal distribution of O_f's around E_f's within cells thus would tend to produce erroneous use of chi square.

Finally, since for values of E_f less than infinity chi square is an approximation, as E_f becomes small the reliability of chi square diminishes. Generally, statisticians have used a rule of thumb that E_f's smaller than 5 are unacceptable; however, even when applying this rule several shortcomings are overlooked, and some authors have urged that E_f should equal or exceed 10. The practice of combining categories to which some researchers resort when E_f is small is a direct violation of the assumption that sampling is random; when this is done, outcomes are being influenced by a non-chance factor. Actually, even the pre-selection of categories may be very crucial in that they must be established on some consistent and logical basis.

In summary, chi square should be applied with great care. When it is used, as described in this chapter, the following precautions should be observed:

1. The statistic should not be used with data that are in the form of measurements.
2. Categories should be established prior to sampling. The categories should be clearly understandable as possessing a unique quality. If there is any reason to doubt the validity of a category, it should not be used. If the reading habits of students were to be studied, for example, it would be very difficult to determine which literature books would or would not be classified in a category labeled "History Books."
3. The sum of observed frequencies must equal the sum of the expected frequencies.
4. Observed frequencies should be collected on the basis of random sampling.
5. Sampling should be carried out in such a way that the act of sampling does not cause one category or one event to influence another. If a group of people were asked to guess the color of a series of playing cards drawn from a deck, for example, it might be expected that half of the group would guess red and another half black. Were the cards to be drawn in succession with the entire group looking on, however, after a few draws there would be a tendency for previous selections to influence those that followed: this violates the assumption of independence.
6. Each expected frequency should equal or exceed ten.

Application of Chi Square

The chi square statistic finds application in many types of problems that produce frequency data. The various types of problems can be categorized as:

1. Tests of hypothesized expected frequencies. (The hypothesized frequencies may be educated guesses or based upon previous experiences or observations.)
2. Tests of independence.
3. Tests of tendency of data to assume a given distribution such as the normal distribution. (This kind of test is called "goodness of fit" since its purpose is essentially to determine if the data is close enough to the given type to draw an assumption that deviations can be attributed to sampling errors.)

Testing Hypotheses With X^2

Chi square has application as a test for hypothetical expected frequencies. Suppose, for example, that a particular election district has tended to vote 3:1 Democrat in presidential elections, but, in the latest election the district voted 800 Democrat to 200 Republican (4:1). Do the figures in the latest election indicate an unexpected departure from the previous elections? The chi square analysis of the data follows:

	Democrat	Republican	Total
O_f	800	200	1,000
E_f (from previous elections)	750	250	1,000
$O_f - E_f$ =	50	50	
$(O_f - E_f)^2$ =	2,500	2,500	
$\dfrac{(O_f - E_f)^2}{E_f}$ =	$\dfrac{2,500}{750}$	$\dfrac{2,500}{250}$	

$$x^2 = \sum \frac{(O_f - E_f)^2}{E_f} = 3.33 + 10 = 13.33$$

The chi square 13.33 must be interpreted in terms of Table A.7 in Appendix A; but before the table can be used it is necessary to establish the degrees of freedom which were possible in the sample. Unlike the t and F ratios, X^2 df is not dependent upon the number in the sample; rather, df is determined by the number of deviations between O_f and E_f that are free to vary. In the data cited, since the sum of O_f's and E_f's must be equal to each other, the total number of observed frequencies, 1,000, allows but one df in E_f. In other words, once the number 750 is placed in the first column, the second number, 250, is not free to vary: the total has been set as 1,000.

Table A.7 shows that with one df, a χ^2 of 13.33 would indicate a rejection of null at the 1% level of confidence; thus, the 4:1 split in voting in the recent election should be regarded as a significant shift from the expected 3:1 ratio that had prevailed in other elections.

Sometimes an even division in expected frequencies is hypothesized *a priori* on the basis of logic. For example, we would expect that, in prescribing aspirin to patients, doctors would not favor one brand over another. Suppose a random sample of 90 doctors polled regarding three leading brands of aspirin showed that doctors prescribed as follows: Brand A = 40, Brand B = 30, Brand C = 20. Do these figures indicate a deviation from the expected even split that can't be accounted for on the basis of sampling error? The computation in X^2 is given following:

		BRAND A	BRAND B	BRAND C	TOTAL
O_f		40	30	20	90
E_f		30	30	30	90
$(O_f - E_f)$	=	10	0	-10	
$(O_f - E_f)^2$	=	100	0	100	
$\dfrac{(O_f - E_f)^2}{E_f}$	=	$\dfrac{100}{30}$	$\dfrac{0}{30}$	$\dfrac{100}{30}$	—
$x^2 = \sum \dfrac{(O_f - E_f)^2}{E_f}$	= 3.333 + 3.333 = 6.67				

$$\chi^2 = \Sigma \frac{(O_f - E_f)^2}{E_f} = 3.333 + 3.333 = 6.67$$

In this problem there are three categories in which the sample total of 90 may be placed. The frequencies for any two of the categories are free to vary within the total of 90, but once two of the categories are fixed, the third category is not free to vary; thus df = 2.

With 2df we may reject the null hypothesis at the 5% level when X^2 exceeds 5.991. (See Table A.7.) It can be concluded, therefore, that the observed frequencies differ significantly from what was expected. It appears that doctors do favor certain brands of aspirin over others; the differences are not attributed to sampling error.

The X^2 Test for Independence

At the beginning of this chapter the use of χ^2 as a method to analyze contingency tables was discussed. A problem was given in which the military ranks of a group of men were matched with their respective levels of formal education. (Table 7.11) Expected frequencies were determined by treating the categories as if they were independent of one another. Table 7.13 shows the data given in Table 7.11 as well as the computations for finding chi square.

TABLE 7.13   Application of χ^2 as a test for independence

Education	Enlisted		Non-Commissioned Officers		Commissioned Officers		Total
	O_f	E_f	O_f	E_f	O_f	E_f	
Graduate	13	(29.7)	38	(29.7)	54	(45.6)	105
College	51	(57.9)	55	(57.9)	99	(89.1)	205
High School	60	(43.0)	41	(43.0)	51	(66.1)	152
Elementary School	21	(14.4)	11	(14.4)	19	(22.2)	51
Totals	145		145		223		513

Categories	O_f-E_f	$(O_f$-$E_f)^2$	E_f	$\dfrac{(O_f$-$E_f)^2}{E_f}$
Grad.-enl.	-16.7	279	29.7	9.4
Grad.-non-com.	8.3	69	29.7	2.3
Grad.-com.	8.4	71	45.6	1.6
College-enl.	-6.9	48	57.9	.8
College-non-com.	-2.9	8	57.9	.1
College-com.	9.9	98	89.1	1.1
High School-enl.	17.0	289	43.0	6.7
High School-non-com.	-2.0	4	43.0	.1
High School-com.	-15.1	228	66.1	3.4
Elementary School-enl.	6.6	44	14.4	3.1
Elementary School-non-com.	-3.4	12	14.4	.8
Elementary School-com.	-3.2	10	22.2	.5

$$\chi^2 = \Sigma \frac{(O_f\text{-}E_f)^2}{E_f} = 29.9$$

The χ^2 computed in Table 7.13, (29.9), must be compared with the values of χ^2 found in Table A.7 of Appendix A. If the df here is greater than one, how can df be determined from a contingency table?

Note that in preparing the contingency table the following conditions exist as a result of the fixed totals of frequencies that appear:

CATEGORY	X	Y	Z	(FIXED) TOTALS
A (Grad)	Free to vary	Free to vary	Fixed by total: not free to vary	→Fixed total
B (College)	Free to vary	Free to vary	Fixed by total: not free to vary	→Fixed total
C (H.S.)	Free to vary	Free to vary	Fixed by total: not free to vary	→Fixed total
D (E.S.)	Fixed by total: not free to vary ↓	Fixed by total: not free to vary ↓	Fixed by total: not free to vary ↓	→Fixed total
Fixed Totals	Fixed Total	Fixed Total	Fixed Total	Over-all Total

From the diagram, it can be seen that the number of cells, or squares, in the table is equal to the number of categories of one type (rows) times the number of categories of another kind (columns) — in this case (4 rows) (3 columns) = 12 cells. If they were all free to vary, the df would be 12; however, the diagram also shows that the fixed totals in effect prevent the numbers in one row and one column from being free to vary. The number of cells that are free to vary, or df, can therefore be found by the formula df = (rows−1) (columns−1). Since in the problem there are four categories of education level (rows) and three categories of service ranks (columns), df = (4-1)(3-1) = (3)(2) = 6.

Table A.7 in Appendix A indicates that with 6 df any value X^2 in excess of 16.81 calls for a rejection of null at the 1% level or better. It would appear that the disparity between O_f's and E_f's is too great to be accounted for on the basis of chance factors, but since E_f's were computed on the assumption that there is no relationship between the level of schooling and a man's service rank, it must be concluded that the assumption is probably not true. It seems likely, therefore, that ranks and schooling are related.

Test for "Goodness of Fit"

Chi square finds use in testing data for tendency toward normal distribution; in other words, sample data can be analyzed on the basis of a hypothesis that they have been drawn from a frequency distribution that is normally distributed. The idea of "goodness of fit" comes from the fact that the observed frequencies are measured against expected frequencies that would arise from a normal curve; a curve that would be derived from the hypothetical normal distribution. Chi square provides a method of determining how well the data fit the normal curve.

The following problem will serve to illustrate the chi square test for "goodness of fit." Suppose the 500 junior students from a large school system have taken the "verbal" portion of the College Board examinations and the distribution of scores were as follows:

Scores	O_f
750 and over	8
700 — 750	18
650 — 700	39
600 — 650	58
550 — 600	77
500 — 550	96
450 — 500	81
400 — 450	62
350 — 400	42
300 — 350	14
250 — 300	3
250 and less	2
	500

What would the frequencies have been if the scores assumed a normal distribution? Since the M for the given test is 500 and SD is 100, the percentages of scores to be expected in the given categories can be computed by consulting Table A.2 in Appendix A. (See Chapter 5.) The computations are as follows:

Scores	X-M	$Z = \frac{X-M}{SD}$	% of cases represented in a Normal Distribution
750 and over	250 and over	2.5	50-49.38 = .62
700 - 750	200 and 250	2.0 to 2.5	49.38-47.72 = 1.66
650 - 700	150 and 200	1.5 to 2.0	47.72-43.32 = 4.40
600 - 650	100 and 150	1.0 to 1.5	43.32-34.13 = 9.19
550 - 600	50 and 100	.5 to 1.0	34.13-19.15 = 14.98
500 - 550	0 and 50	0 to .5	19.15-0 = 19.15
450 - 500	- 50 and 0	0 to -.5	10.15-0 = 19.15
400 - 450	-100 and - 50	-.5 to -1.0	34.13-19.15 = 14.98
350 - 400	-150 and -100	-1.0 to -1.5	43.32-34.13 = 9.19
300 - 350	-200 and -150	-1.5 to -2.0	47.72-43.32 = 4.40
250 - 300	-250 and -200	-2.0 to -2.5	49.38-47.72 = 1.66
250 and less	-250 and less	-2.5 and less	50-49.38 = .62
		TOTAL =	100.00%

Since the percentage to be expected in the various categories has been computed from the normal distribution, chi square can now be determined:

Scores	% of Cases Represented in a Normal Distribution	O_f	E_f = % from Normal Distribution X500	O_f-E_f	$(O_f$-$E_f)^2$	$\frac{(O_f-E_f)^2}{E_f}$
750 and over	.62	8	3 = (.62%×500)	5	25	8.3
700 - 750	1.66	18	8 = (1.66%×500)	10	100	12.5
650 - 700	4.40	39	22 = (4.4 %×500)	17	289	13.1
600 - 650	9.19	58	46 = (9.19%×500)	12	144	3.1
550 - 600	14.98	77	75 = (14.98%×500)	2	4	0.1
500 - 550	19.15	96	96 = (19.15%×500)	0	0	0.0
450 - 500	19.15	81	96 = (19.15%×500)	-15	225	2.3
400 - 450	14.98	62	75 = (14.98%×500)	-13	169	2.3
350 - 400	9.19	42	46 = (9.19%×500)	-4	16	.3
300 - 350	4.40	14	22 = (4.4 %×500)	-8	64	2.9
250 - 300	1.66	3	8 = (1.66%×500)	-5	25	3.1
250 and less	.62	2	3 = (.62%×500)	-1	1	.3
TOTALS	100%	500	500		X^2 =	48.3

Before Table A.7 can be used, it is again necessary to determine the df. It would appear that if the degrees of freedom were associated with only the number of categories there would be twelve degrees of freedom, since the number of categories of scores is twelve. The degrees of freedom are reduced, however, by several factors; first, N, the number of scores, places one restriction on the df; second, M, the mean, as a measure that helps determine the values of E_f's, reduces df; and third, SD, the other measure that helps determine E_f's further reduces df. Therefore, in the application of X^2 to test "goodness of fit" with a hypothetical normal distribution, df = number of categories —3.

With 9 df a chi square value of 21.67 indicates that the null hypothesis may be rejected at the 1% level of confidence. It may be concluded, then, that the particular distribution of college board examination scores is not a sample drawn from scores that would be normally distributed.

Selected Exercises

1. Using the formula for r which employs z-scores:

$$r = \frac{\Sigma z_x z_y}{N}$$

   a. Compute r for math-physics from Tables 7.5 and 7.6.
   b. Compute r for physics-latin from Tables 7.6 and 7.7.
   c. Compute r for latin-biology from Tables 7.7 and 7.8.

2. An elementary school principal wished to determine if there was a relationship between the I.Q. scores of third grade pupils in her school — as measured by a standard test — and the final grades they received in arithmetic. She selected ten pupils at random and compiled the following data:

PUPIL	IQ	ARITHMETIC GRADE
A	97	95
B	89	70
C	115	90
D	121	90
E	100	85
F	105	80
G	95	75
H	130	95
I	125	90
J	85	75

a. Compute M_{IQ} and M_{AG} and make a scattergram of the deviations of the scores from their respective means. Draw a regression line through the scattergram.
b. Find the r for the data. How does this computed r correspond with what the scattergram indicated about the data?
c. Compute ρ for the data. How does ρ compare to r?
d. The principal concluded that since I.Q. cannot be improved, it would not be possible to improve the pupils' grades in arithmetic through better methods of teaching. Is her conclusion valid? Explain your answer.

3. In a study of the average temperature for a day in June in fifty cities of the United States selected at random, the weather bureau found the mean of the average temperature to be 60° F. with $\sigma = 10$. On the same day the average rainfall for the fifty cities was .2 in. with $\sigma = .05$ in. The bureau statistician decided to determine if a relationship between the two kinds of data might be established. He labeled the temperature T and the rainfall values R and produced the following table of values:

$$M_T = 60° \text{ F.}$$
$$M_R = .2 \text{ in.}$$
$$\sigma_T = 10°$$
$$\sigma_R = .05 \text{ in.}$$
$$\Sigma TR = 620$$

    a. Compute r from the data.

    b. Draw a conclusion from your analysis regarding the relationship between the average temperature and rainfall on the day in question.

    c. What conclusion can be drawn regarding the relationship of average temperature to rainfall for the days of the year?

    d. Will an increase in temperature produce more rainfall?

    e. Suppose ΣTR had been 605. What conclusion could be drawn regarding the relationship between the average temperature and rainfall for the day studied?

    f. Using the r from question a preceding, write the equation for the regression line. How much rainfall would you expect a city to have if its average temperature on the June day studied were 75° F?

    g. If the average temperature for the day studied were 75° F. in Richmond, Virginia, what would be the rainfall for the same day?

4. A researcher selected fifteen secondary teachers from a school system at random. He asked the two secondary supervisors from the same system to rank the teachers as to their ability to teach. (With the best teacher ranked # 1, etc.) The supervisors were allowed to consult their files on the teachers but were not allowed to consult each other. These data were compiled:

RATINGS

Teacher	Supervisor I	Supervisor II
A	5	15
B	3	7
C	12	9
D	7	4
E	11	10
F	15	13
G	1	5
H	8	12
I	9	6
J	14	8
K	6	1
L	2	3
M	4	2
N	10	14
O	13	11

    a. Is there a correlation between the supervisors' ratings?

    b. What conclusions can be drawn about the data?

    c. Suppose you were the researcher and the superintendent asked your advice concerning the use of the rating the supervisors might give teachers to determine if teachers are to get merit pay. What would you tell the superintendent?

5. A researcher selected 58 secondary school teachers and 63 elementary school teachers at random from a large school system. He asked them to check "yes" or "no" to the following question:

    "Should elementary pupils who do poorly at a given grade level be retained in the same grade for one year?"

These results were obtained:

	Yes	No
Elementary Teachers	27	36
Secondary Teachers	36	22

    a. State the null hypothesis in terms of the problem.

    b. Is there a significant difference in the way the elementary and secondary teachers in the school system tend to answer the question?

6. In the 1968 election Hubert Humphrey captured 55 per cent of the vote in a large city. Suppose that in the summer of 1970 a poll of 5,000 people — selected at random — in the same city showed that 2597 said they would vote again for Humphrey. Is there a significant difference between the 1968 election results and the poll?

7. A group of beginning secondary teachers in a state — selected at random — who had majored in English, social studies, mathematics, natural sciences, and foreign language were asked, at the end of their first year of teaching, to select their professional goal for ten years hence in terms of one of the following categories:

    a. High School Principal

    b. High School Supervisor of Instruction

    c. High School Guidance Counselor

    d. Classroom Teacher

The data collected in terms of selection are shown in the table following:

	English	Social Studies	Mathematics	Science	Foreign Language
Principal	12	20	4	15	2
Inst. Sup.	7	10	7	6	9
Guid. Coun.	18	12	7	2	4
Teacher	63	58	82	77	85

Do the various types of secondary teachers studied in the state appear to have similar professional goals?

8. A high school chemistry teacher gave a final examination to his 150 students with the following results:

GRADES	f
96-100	3
91- 95	8
86- 90	10
81- 85	16
76- 80	22
71- 75	31
66- 70	24
61- 65	15
56- 60	12
51- 55	7
46- 50	2
	N = 150

Can it be concluded that the scores are close enough to a normal distribution to represent a sample drawn from a normally distributed group of scores?

Suggested Activities

Write a critical analysis of the following studies and suggest how they might be improved.

1. An English teacher wished to determine if high school seniors, juniors and sophomores differed in their leisure reading habits. During the school year the English teacher assigned twenty book reports to each group. Students were free to choose the books they would read. The teachers were asked to keep track of books reported read by the pupils which fell into the following categories: biographies, autobiographies, historical novels, modern novels, classics. A contingency table was prepared and the χ^2 test for significant difference of preferences by the various groups was used to analyze the data.

2. A supervisor in a state department of education hypothesized that elementary children in larger schools are absent from school due to illness more often than children from smaller schools. He obtained representative samples of the absentee reports from schools of various sizes and tested for correlation between school size and number of absences for a month. He found a high positive correlation and concluded that children in larger schools are absent from school due to illness more often because there is a greater tendency for illnesses to spread in the larger schools.

3. A physical education instructor wished to determine if a series of exercises he had developed might help improve pupils' scores on a nationally accepted standard test of physical condition. He devised a scoring method for his exercises and tested pupils in his physical education classes with both the standard test and his own set of exercises. He found a high positive correlation between pupils' scores on the standard test and his test. He concluded that his exercises would bring about improvement in scores on the national test.

4. A researcher found that a national survey indicated that about 4% of all school administrators do not belong to any professional organizations. He took a poll of 100 randomly selected school administrators from the state and found that 12 did not belong to any professional organizations. Chi square was computed to determine if administrators in the given state differed significantly from those in the nation as a whole in their membership or nonmembership in professional organizations.

For the following problems, explain how you would carry out a study that might provide a solution.

1. Problem: to determine if a test in arithmetic for eighth graders, prepared by the mathematics department of a school, can be used to replace an expensive aptitude test in arithmetic currently in use.

2. Problem: to determine whether classroom teachers, school administrators and school board members differ in their views regarding the optimum number of pupils assigned per class.
3. Problem: to determine if boys and girls in a high school differ in their preference of male or female teachers.
4. Problem: to develop a college freshmen year success predictor scale based upon data from high school seniors' cumulative folders.
5. Problem: to determine what relationship — if any — exists between reading ability and visual acuity.

Selected Readings

1. BRADLEY, JAMES V., *Distribution — Free Statistical Tests*. Wright-Patterson Air Force Base, Ohio: Wright Air Development Division, 1960 (Chapter 3).
2. GARRETT, HENRY E., *Statistics in Psychology and Education* (Fourth Edition). New York: Longmans, Green and Co., 1954 (Chapters 6, 7 and 10).
3. GARRETT, HENRY E., *Elementary Statistics* (Second Edition). New York: David McKay Co., Inc. 1962 (Chapters 7 and 10).
4. HAMMOND, KENNETH R., AND JAMES E. HOUSEHOLDER, *Introduction to the Statistical Method*. New York: Alfred A. Knopf, 1962 (Chapters 6 and 8).
5. LI, JEROME C. R., *Statistical Inference*. Volume I. Third Edition. Ann Arbor: Edwards Brothers, Inc. 1966, (Chapter 21).
6. KOENKER, ROBERT H., *Simplified Statistics*. Bloomington, Ill.: McKnight and McKnight Publishing Co., 1961 (Chapters 6, 7 and 9).
7. PETERS, CHARLES C., AND WALTER R. VAN VOORHIS, *Statistical Procedures and Their Mathematical Bases*. New York: McGraw-Hill Book Co., 1940 (Chapters 11, 13 and 14).
8. RUMMEL, J. FRANCIS, *An Introduction to Research Procedures in Education*. New York: Harper & Row, Publishers, 1958 (Chapter 7).
9. SENDERS, VIRGINIA L., *Measurement and Statistics*. New York: Oxford University Press, 1958 (p. 516-520).
10. UNDERWOOD, BENTON J. and others, *Elementary Statistics*. New York: Appleton-Century-Crofts, 1954 (Chapters 10 and 13).
11. VAN DALEN, DEOBOLD B., AND WILLIAM J. MEYER, *Understanding Educational Research*. New York: McGraw-Hill Book Co., 1962 (Chapters 13 and 14).

Chapter 8

Parametric Versus Nonparametric Statistics

Although a few selected statistical tools discussed in previous chapters were classified in accord to the *kinds* of studies in which they are most often used, statisticians classify these tools as to the mathematical assumptions upon which they are based; i.e., parametric or nonparametric. Such assumptions may dictate the appropriateness of a particular statistical test in the analysis of research data. It is important, therefore, for the students of research to have some understanding of parametric and nonparametric statistics. The purpose of this chapter is to discuss the concepts concerning those two types of statistical tools and also to give examples of several nonparametric tests that have not been presented in previous chapters.

Definitions

Parameters and Statistics

The population value of a particular measure—such as the mean or standard deviation of all measurements of a given population—is called a *parameter*. In other words, if all scores or measurements of a defined population are available and the standard deviation is computed, the value found is a parameter of the population. If the mean were computed, that value would be another parameter.

On the other hand, when measures such as a mean and a standard deviation are computed from representative samples and serve as estimates of the population parameters, the values are called *statistics*. It may be said, therefore, that if the mean I.Q. of a random sample of third graders from a given school system is 103, then the value 103 is a statistic since it may be used as an estimate of the population mean.

Similarly if the sample SD is 15, this value is a statistic since it estimates σ — the standard deviation of the given population. Also, if the number of pupils in our sample of third graders is 26, the $\sigma_M = \dfrac{15}{\sqrt{26-1}}$ $= 3$ is another statistic: this value, called the standard error the mean, estimates the standard deviation of a distribution of mean I.Q.s of all possible random samples, of size $N=26$, that might be drawn from the hypothetical population of third graders.

Nonparametric or Distribution Free Statistics

It may be recalled from previous discussions of statistics–such as σ_M, the t-ratio and the F-ratio–that certain assumptions regarding the parameters, particularly the form of the distribution, were made in developing the rationale underlying these statistics and their use. In particular, the idea of a normal or near normal distribution of the population measurements is an assumption and the parameters are described accordingly. Nonparametric or distribution free statistics, however, are based upon fewer or even no assumption regarding parameters and the distribution of measurements in the population.

For example, although the chi square statistic is parametric in that tables used to accept or reject the null hypothesis are based upon particular χ^2 distributions and degrees of freedom as mean values of the given distribution, in many of the *applications* of chi square no assumptions are made regarding the type of distribution from which category data has been sampled nor the parameters of the distribution. When a category or a contingency table cell is established, as in the examples of the last chapter, and an expected frequency determined, no assumptions are made that the original distribution was normal nor that the data estimates a mean or standard deviation of the population. All that is assumed is that we are operating in a particular *area* of some sort of distribution. If this is indeed true, then observed frequencies *should* approximate the *expected* frequencies for the given area. If many random samples are taken from such a situation and our original hypothesis holds, then the difference between the observed and expected frequencies will distribute themselves normally around zero or null; thus the null hypothesis. The sums of the ratios $\dfrac{(O_f - E_f)^2}{E}$ of random samples will distribute themselves in one of the chi square distributions depending upon the degree of freedom.

From the discussion above and also the title of this section, the student may conclude that nonparametric and distribution free statistics mean the same thing; indeed the terms are used interchangeably by many authors. Technically, it is not correct to do so. In practice, statistical tests that make no assumptions regarding parameters generally make no assumptions regarding the form of the parent distribution, but using the terms interchangeably may be a bit misleading in that some statistical tests make no assumptions about parameters but do so concerning the distribution and vice versa. Since the term nonparametric is one most often used in the literature, it has, however, been accepted for use in this text for all statistical tests that are considered not to be of the classical parametric type.

The nonparametric tests touched upon in previous chapters include the uses of chi square which were presented and Spearman's coefficient of correlation. The parametric tests included the test for location of a true mean, t-test, F-test, and Pearson's coefficient of correlation.

In the following sections, the binomial test, the sign test for matched pairs, the Wilcoxon Test, the Kruskal-Wallis one-way analysis of variance, and the Kendall Coefficient of Concordance will be discussed briefly.

The Binomial and Sign Tests

In many types of researches in the behavioral sciences, variables studied may be dichotomized in terms of the population from which data is drawn such as male-female, attended college—did not attend college, in school—school dropout, etc.

If P is the *proportion* of the total number of observations that fall into one of two such related classes, and Q is the proportion of the other, then $P + Q = 1$. (Another way of saying this is that P is the *fraction* of cases of one type and Q the *fraction* of cases of the other.)

Since P is the proportion of the total cases of a given population to fall in one of two classes, random samples from the total population will *tend* also to have "P" proportion of their total N in the same category. Due to sampling error, however, one cannot expect P for samples to be necessarily the same as P for the total population.

Also, if R is given as the number of cases from a population that fall into the category for which P is the proportion then $R = PN$. For samples "r" will tend to be equal to R. The r for a given sample may be expressed as $r = p$ (for the sample), n (for the sample), or $r = pn$.

When many representative samples are taken from the distribution which has been described, the mean of r's for the samples will be R or PN.

For small samples the distribution of sample r's is the binomial distribution. To determine the probability of a given r being representative of the a population which has P as the proportion of cases in the category represented by P, one may use the binomial theorm to expand the binomial expression $(P+Q)^N$ to find the probability of r being representative of R. Another method is to use tabled values of difference between r and the predicted R in terms of the sample which may allow null to be rejected at various levels of confidence. These tables are available in terms of P and Q = 1/2; i.e., for the very frequent prediction that there is a 50:50 chance of a given observation being in either the category represented by P or in the other represented by Q.

Small samples will not be considered further in this text. An excellent description of the methods used to make the binomial test of small samples is to be found in Siegel's *Nonparametric Statistics for The Behavioral Sciences.*

When P is predicted as 1/2 and the sample n's are greater than 25, the distribution of r's for samples will tend to be normal with a standard error (deviation) of $\sqrt{nPQ}$. To test, therefore, whether a given r is representative of the predicted R we may use the formula:

$$z = \frac{(r \pm .5) - nP}{\sqrt{nPQ}}$$

Where r is the number in one category of the sample which is represented by P, .5 is a correction factor and nP is the predicted r. (When r < nP, the correction factor .5 is added; and when r > nP, it is subtracted.) If z is greater than 1.96, for example, null may be rejected at the 5% level of confidence; z > 2.58 would allow rejection of null at the 1% level.

At this point the reader may be puzzled by the fact that the normal distribution has entered the picture even though the chapter topic is nonparametric statistics; i.e., statistical tests that do not make assumptions regarding the shape of the distribution from which the samples have been drawn nor the parameters. A careful look at what has been discussed, however, will indicate that no assumptions have been made regarding the population from which the data is to be drawn. All that needs to be known is that the observations are to go into one category or another—nothing else. Once this happens, however, no matter what value P the proportion of cases in one of the categories may have, repeated sampling from the population will tend to give r's (the number in the category represented by P) which will be the same as R. Since the actual value of r's will be a result of chance or random error, then many r's will distribute themselves normally.

The binomial test is best illustrated in its application as the sign test of matched pairs. Suppose, for example, a basketball coach wishes to determine if a beginning basketball player seeing a video tape of his foul shooting accompanied by commentary and suggestions by an expert can improve accuracy.

Further suppose that thirty-six randomly selected beginning players are allowed to attempt twenty foul shots while the performance is video taped. The experiment is concluded as indicated but with a wait of one day to avoid the immediate effect of practice which a pilot study showed wore off after a day. Table 8.1 shows the possible before and after results along with a + or − to indicate improvement or regression.

TABLE 8.1

Student	Before Instruction	After Instruction	Change
1	5	6	+
2	8	7	−
3	6	8	+
4	4	7	+
5	10	9	−
6	11	12	+
7	6	5	−
8	5	4	−
9	3	3	0
10	4	6	+
11	7	10	+
12	8	7	−
13	11	11	0
14	8	9	+
15	7	12	+
16	6	5	−
17	15	14	−
18	12	13	+
19	7	9	+
20	7	10	+
21	4	10	+
22	5	6	+
23	5	6	+
24	4	8	+
25	7	8	+
26	7	6	−
27	6	9	+
28	7	10	+
29	7	8	+
30	8	6	−
31	6	10	+
32	5	7	+
33	12	11	−
34	9	12	+
35	8	10	+
36	7	10	+

Under the experimental hypothesis which we may label H_{exp}, there will be improvement in the group performance; that is, shifts will tend to be +. The null hypothesis which will test Ho is that shifts will just as likely be − as +; or in other words P = 1/2 and Q = 1/2 where P is the proportion of positive shifts and Q is the proportion of negative shifts. Of the thirty-four changes (ties are disregarded) 24 were + and 10 were −. If r is taken to be the number of positive shifts, then

$$z = \frac{(24 - .5) - (34 \cdot 1/2)}{\sqrt{34 \cdot 1/2 \cdot 1/2}} = \frac{23.5 - 17}{\sqrt{8.5}} = \frac{6.5}{2.92} = 2.23$$

This means that Ho (the null hypothesis) can be rejected at better than the 5% level and we conclude that the experimental conditions were effective.

If the t or F tests had been applied to the scores, one would need to assume that the original scores were drawn from a population of scores which were normally distributed. Here no such assumption need be made.

The Wilcoxon Test

The sign test is merely concerned with the direction of difference between matched pairs of scores. The Wilcoxon Test is also concerned with the magnitudes of changes. It will be noted, for example, that student 21 in the example given for the sign test scores 6 more foul shots after instruction while student 25 scored only 1 less. In the sign test, however, the first was scored as (+) and the second (−) without regard to the amount of change.

In the Wilcoxen Test all differences are computed and the *rank* of each difference is assigned from 1 for the lowest. Tied scores are ignored but if the several differences are tied, each of the tied differences is assigned the median rank for the group. The value T is then computed as the absolute value of the sum of all the ranks with the *least* frequent sign (either positive or negative).

For samples larger than 25, T is normally distributed with a mean of $\frac{n(n+1)}{4} = \mu_T$ and a standard deviation $\sigma_T = \sqrt{\frac{n(n+1)(2n+1)}{24}}$. Then $z = \frac{T - \mu_T}{\sigma_T}$.

The same data from Table 8.1 may be used to illustrate the Wilcoxon Test by computing differences as shown in Table 8.2. Note that the difference of 1 occurs 17 times and the median rank would be 9; therefore, 9 is assigned as the rank of all differences which are either $+1$ or -1. Since the less frequently occurring signs are the negatives, the absolute ranks of all negatives are summed as T.

TABLE 8.2

Student	Before	After	d	Rank of d	Rank with less frequent sign
1	5	6	+1	+9	
2	8	7	−1	−9	−9
3	6	8	+2	+20.5	
4	4	7	+3	+27	
5	10	9	−1	−9	−9
6	11	12	+1	+9	
7	6	5	−1	−9	−9
8	5	4	−1	−9	−9
9	3	3	0	0	
10	4	6	+2	+20.5	
11	7	10	+3	+27	
12	8	7	−1	−9	−9
13	11	11	0	0	
14	8	9	+1	+9	
15	7	12	+5	+33	
16	6	5	−1	−9	−9
17	15	14	−1	−9	−9
18	12	13	+1	+9	
19	7	9	+2	+20.5	
20	7	10	+3	+27	
21	4	10	+6	+34	
22	5	6	+1	+9	
23	5	6	+1	+9	
24	4	8	+4	31.5	
25	7	8	+1	+9	
26	7	6	−1	−9	−9
27	6	9	+3	+27	
28	7	10	+3	+27	
29	7	8	+1	+9	
30	8	6	−2	−20.5	−20.5
31	6	10	+4	+31.5	
32	5	7	+2	+20.5	
33	12	11	−1	−9	−9
34	9	12	+3	+27	
35	8	10	+2	+20.5	
36	7	10	+3	+27	

T = 101.5

$$\mu_T = \frac{n\,(n+1)}{4} = \frac{34\,(34+1)}{4} = \frac{1190}{4} = 298.5$$

$$T = \sqrt{\frac{n\,(n+1)\,(2n+1)}{24}} = \sqrt{\frac{34\,(35)\,(69)}{24}} = \sqrt{\frac{82110}{4}}$$

$$= \sqrt{3421} = 58.49$$

$$z = \frac{T - \mu_T}{\sigma_T} = \frac{101.5 - 298.5}{58.5} = \frac{-197}{58.5} = -3.38$$

In comparing the z score obtained from the Wilcoxon Test to that found from the application of the sign test, it will be noted that the Wilcoxon Test leads to a rejection of Ho at better than the 1% level, while the sign test allowed but a 5% level of confidence. The reason for this discrepancy can be seen in Tables 8.1 and 8.2. The Tables show that nine of the ten people who scored lower after the experiment only scored one foul shot lower and the other person was only two foul shots lower. Many of those who improved, on the other hand, made large gains. The magnitude of the gains as compared to losses is taken into account in the Wilcoxon Test and there is a strong indication that a significant shift toward improvement has occurred as a result of the experiment. The sign test is capable only of showing shift of direction and is not sensitive to the magnitude of shifts.

The Kruskal-Wallis One-Way Analysis of Variance by Ranks

The Kruskal-Wallis Test is the nonparametric equivalent of the simple (one way) analysis of variance described in Chapter 6. The purpose is the same: to determine if k independent samples have been drawn from the same population.

In order to make the test, all observations are expressed as ranks in a single series without regard to the k samples in which they are found. The lowest score or measurement is ranked as 1, the next as 2, and the process is continued to the highest which is ranked as N.

The statistic computed to make the test is labeled "H." Since H tends to be distributed in a χ^2 distribution with k-1 degrees of freedom, the χ^2 table is used to interpret the value of H.

The computation of H is as follows:

$$H = \frac{12}{N\,(N+1)} \left[\sum \frac{R^2}{n}\right] - 3\,(N+1)$$

where R^2 = the square of the sum of the ranks (for each of the k samples).

n = the number of cases in each of the k samples.

N = the total number of measurements (or rankings) that were made.

From the equation, it can be seen that the ratios $\frac{R^2}{n}$ are the means of the squares of the sum of ranks for each of the k samples. If the ranks in each of the k samples are distributed in a fairly random manner, the total ranks for each of the k samples will tend to be the same and the mean of the squares will tend to be equal. If, however, some of the k samples get more than their "fair" share of the higher ranks, then the total R's for those samples will be disproportionally large, and when they are squared, the squared values will tend to be exceptionally large and so will their mean values making H larger than anticipated.

Suppose, for example, there were three groups (k=3) and the sum of ranks in each group turned out to be the same at 35. ($R_1 = 35$, $R_2 = 35$, and $R_3 = 35$.) Then $R_1^2 = 1225$, $R_2^2 = 1225$ and $R_3^2 = 1225$. If there were five scores which were ranked in each group, then $\frac{R_1^2}{n_1} = 245$, $\frac{R_2^2}{n_2} = 245$, and $\frac{R_3^2}{n_3} = 245$ and the sum of these ratios is 735. If, on the other hand, $R_1 = 65$, $R_2 = 20$ and $R_3 = 20$, then $R_1^2 = 4225$, $R_2^2 = 400$, and $R_3^2 = 400$. In this case $\frac{R_1^2}{n_1} = 845$, $\frac{R_2^2}{n_2} = 80$ and $\frac{R_3^2}{n_3} = 80$ and the sum of the ratios is 1005 which is considerably larger than 735. In the second case H will turn out to be significantly large while in the first it would not.

The experiment described in Chapter 6, page 170 may be used to illustrate the Kruskal-Wallis test. Recall that the reading improvement of three groups was tested with the results as shown in Table 8.3 below.

TABLE 8.3

Number of Years of Reading Improvement

Group I	Group II	Group III
Years	Years	Years
2.8	2.6	2.3
2.6	1.8	2.4
3.3	2.7	2.1
2.5	2.1	2.5
2.7	2.2	2.6
3.1	2.8	2.2
3.2	2.4	1.6
4.5	3.7	2.0
2.4	1.9	1.5
3.9	2.5	1.4

The results of converting the score gains to a continuous rank order from the lowest to the highest are shown in Table 8.4.

TABLE 8.4

Reading Improvement Scores Shown As Ranks

Group I ranks	Group II ranks	Group III ranks
23.5	19	11
19	4	13
27	21.5	7.5
16	7.5	16
21.5	9.5	19
25	23.5	9.5
26	13	3
30	28	6
13	5	2
29	16	1
$R_1 = 230$	$R_2 = 147$	$R_3 = 88$

From Table 8.4 then $R_1 = 230$, $R_2 = 147$ and $R_3 = 88$. Also $N = 30$ and $n_1 = 10$, $n_2 = 10$, and $n_3 = 10$. Then $H =$

$$\frac{12}{30\ (31)} \left[\frac{221^2}{10} + \frac{147^2}{10} + \frac{88^2}{10} \right] - 3\ (31)$$

$$= .0129\ (8225.3) - 93$$

$$+\ 106 - 93 = 9$$

Since H, in this case, would be distributed as χ^2 with two degrees of freedom (k-1), then the null hypothesis that all three groups could have been selected at random from the same population may be rejected at the 5% level of confidence.

An interesting observation that may be made is that the value 9 is not quite large enough to reject null at the 1% level even though the F ratio, which was computed for the analysis of variance of the original scores in Chapter 6, allowed a 1% level rejection. The Kruskal-Wallis test does not have as much power and efficiency as the F-test, but it is nevertheless most useful. The assumption that must be made for the parametric F-test need not be met for the nonparametric Kruskal-Wallis test.

The Kendall Coefficient of Concordance

The Kendall Coefficient of Concordance provides a method by which research regarding rankings made by independent judges may be analyzed. The coefficient indicates the degree to which judges agree in their assignment of ranks.

Assume, for example, that four supervisors were asked to rank ten teachers in relation to each other. The best teachers are to be ranked 1, the second best 2, up to the poorest of the group ranked as 10. If supervisors agree completely on their rankings of the individuals, the best one will receive $1+1+1+1=4$ for his total of the ranks which may be labeled R_1. The second best will have a total of ranks $R_2 = 2+2+2+2=8$. The poorest teacher's total ranking $R_{10} = 10+10+10 +10=40$. Should the supervisors have no agreement among themselves, then $R_1 = R_2 = R_3 = R_4 = R_5 = R_6 = R_7 = R_8 = R_9 = R_{10}$.

The Kendall Coefficient "W" is based on the deviation of each total ranking (R_1, R_2, R_3, etc.) from the mean RM of these total rankings. If there were no agreement among the judges, $R_1 = R_2 = R_3 = R_4$ $------ = R_M$ and in this case each deviation would be zero and the coefficient W would also be zero. If, however, many of the R's deviate from R_M, W will take on a value larger than O up to $+1$.

$$W = \frac{s}{1/12 \ k^2 \ (n^3 - n)}$$

where s = sums of squares of observed deviations from

$$R_M; \text{ i.e., } s = (R_n - R_M)^2 \text{ where } R_M = \frac{\Sigma R}{n}$$

$$R_M = \frac{R_1 + R_2 + R_3 ------- R_n}{n}$$

n = the number of objects or individuals judged
k = the number of judges
R_1 = sum total of ranks for the first object or individual
R_2 = sum total of ranks for the second object or individual
R_n = sum total of ranks for the nth object or individual
$1/12k^2 \ (n^3 - n)$ = maximum possible sum of the squared deviations
(This is the sum of s which would occur if there were perfect agreement among the k rankings.)

The significance of W may be tested by hypothesizing null; i.e., an observed value of W is assumed to deviate from O due to chance. The statistic $k \ (n-1) \ W$ is used to test the value of W since it tends to be distributed as χ^2 with $n - 1$ df. The value of $k \ (n - 1) \ W$ is taken as χ^2 and if it exceeds the size of χ^2 in Table A.7 of Appendix A for the 5% level, null may be rejected at the 5% level. If $k \ (n-1) \ W = \chi^2$ exceeds the value in Table A.7 for the 1% level, null may be rejected at the 1% level. W is held to be significant at the level at which null is rejected, but this can only be interpreted as meaning that W is not O.

Returning to our hypothetical example involving four supervisors rating ten teachers, suppose that the ratings given were as in Table 8.5. To help simplify things, the order in which the teachers were placed on Table 8.5 is the same as the order in which supervisor A ranked them.

TABLE 8.5

Supervisor	Teacher									
	a	b	c	d	e	f	g	h	i	j
A	1	2	3	4	5	6	7	8	9	10
B	3	5	7	2	1	4	8	10	9	6
C	2	1	4	3	6	5	7	8	10	9
D	4	2	3	5	4	7	6	8	9	10
R totals	$R_1 = 10$	$R_2 = 10$	$R_3 = 17$	$R_4 = 14$	$R_5 = 16$	$R_6 = 22$	$R_7 = 28$	$R_8 = 34$	$R_9 = 37$	$R_{10} = 35$

The computation to find W follows:

$$\Sigma R_n = 10+10+17+14+16+22+28+34+37+35$$

$$R_M = \frac{\Sigma R}{n} = \frac{223}{10} = 22.3$$

$$s = \Sigma (R_n - R_M)^2$$
$$= \Sigma (R_1 - R_M)^2 + (R_2 - R_M)^2 \cdots \cdots (R_{10} - R_M)^2$$
$$= \Sigma (10 - 22.3)^2 + (10 - 22.3)^2 + (17 - 22.3)^2 \cdots + (35 - 22.3)^2$$
$$= \Sigma (-12.3)^2 + (-12.3)^2 + (-5.3)^2 \cdots \cdots + (+12.7)^2$$
$$= 986.10$$

$$W = \frac{s}{1/12k^2(n^3-n)} = \frac{986.1}{1/12\ (16)\ (1000-10)} = \frac{986}{1320} = .747$$

To determine if W is significant we find $\chi^2 = k (n - 1) W = 4$ $(10 - 1) (.747) = 26.89$. Table A.7 indicates what when χ^2 is 26.89 with 9 d. f. null may be rejected a better than the 1% level of confidence.

Selected Exercises

1. A researcher selected fifty students at random from a large school system which had no negro students. He asked the students to check a list of items on an instrument which gives a rough measure of attitudes toward minority races. He then brought young negro college students to the school on each day of the next school week to speak to the group about their plans and ambitions (one student planned to be a medical doctor, another an engineer, etc.). The following week a different form of the same attitude instrument was applied, and the scores indicated that 33 had more positive attitudes toward minorities than before and 17 more negative.
   a. May the researcher claim a significant shift?
   b. Why do researchers say that by using the sign test instead of the original scores "some information is thrown away"?

2. Of the fifty students discussed in question number one above, the sum of differences of positive ranks was 500 and of the negative differences, 200.
   a. Apply the Wilcoxon Test to the data. Is there a significant difference between the T predicted as an average from a random sample and the T value given?
   b. How does your result with the Wilcoxon Test compare to the sign test?

3. A researcher assigned forty students at random to four experimental groups of ten each. Group I students learned to drive an auto on their own time any way they wished; Group II received class instructions; Group III received class instructions and behind the wheel instruction; Group IV received class instruction, behind the wheel instruction, and instruction with an automobile emergency simulator. After one month the students were given a series of tests by a group of state policemen. Each performance was either scored or ranked and a final composite rank was given to each student.
   These data were collected:
   Sum of ranks — Group I, = 65, Group II = 160, Group III = 245, Group IV = 370.
   Is there a significant difference in the performance of the groups?

4. Convert the scores of teachers on the National Teachers Examination, given for question 6 in the selected exercises at the end of Chapter 6, to ranks and perform the Kruskal-Wallis test on the data.

How does the result of the test compare to the F-ratio determined in Chapter 6?

5. Three "critic" teachers were asked to rank five student teachers with the following results:

	Student Teacher				
Supervisor	a	b	c	d	e
A	1	2	3	4	5
B	4	3	1	5	2
C	5	3	2	4	1

a. Are the supervisor's ratings generally in accord?
b. What steps might be taken regarding the situation?

Suggested Activities

Discuss briefly how a researcher might carry out a study in terms of each of the problem statements given below. Include in your discussion the data he would have to collect, and how he might analyze the data.

1. The purpose of the study is to determine if there are sex differences between male and female fraternal twins in their ability to develop skill in the assembly of transistorized electronic equipment.

2. The purpose of the study is to determine if several school guidance counselors tend to agree in regard to the relative emotional disturbance of children who have been referred by the counselors to the school psychiatrist.

3. The purpose of the study is to determine if high school science teachers tend to agree as to the relative evaluation weight which should be placed on quiz grades, final test grades, laboratory work, homework, and class participation.

4. The purpose of the study is to determine if there will be differences in final college class rankings of students who had attended small high schools (up to 1,000 pupils, grades 9-12), medium sized high schools (1,000 to 1,500 pupils in grades 9-12), and large high schools (1,500 or more pupils in grades 9-12).

5. The purpose of the study is to determine if school dropouts are non-dropouts, who are matched in intelligence but differ in self-concept rating as determined by a psychologist.

Selected Readings

1. BLUM, J. R., and N. A. FATTN, "Nonparametric Methods." *Review of Educational Research*, 24:467-487; 1954.
2. BRADLEY, JAMES V., *Distribution—Free Statistical Tests*. Wright-Patterson Air Force Base, Ohio: Wright Air Development Division; 1960.
3. DIXON, W. J. and A. M. MOOD, "The Statistical Sign Test." *Journal of American Statistical Association*, 41:557-566; 1946.
4. KENDALL, M. G., *Rank Correlation Methods*. London: Griffin; 1948.
5. —————, *The Advanced Theory of Statistics*, Vol. 1 (4th Ed.). London: Griffin; 1948.
6. KRUSKAL, W. H., and W. A. WALLIS, "Use of Ranks in One-Criterion Variance Analysis." *Journal of the American Statistical Association*, 47: 583-621; 1952.
7. MANN, H. B. and D. R. WHITNEY, "On a Test of Whether One of Two Random Variables is Stochastically Larger Than the Other," *Annals of Mathematical Statistics*, 18:50-60; 1947.
8. SIEGEL, SIDNEY, *Nonparametric Statistics for the Behavioral Sciences*. New York: Mc-Graw-Hill Book Co., 1956.
9. SNEDECOR, G. W., *Statistical Methods*. Ames, Iowa: Iowa State College Press; 1946.
10. WILCOXON, F., "Individual Comparison by Ranking Methods." *Biometrics Bulletin*, 1:80-83; 1945.

PART III

Application of Theory

Chapter 9

Evaluation and Application of Research

The professional educator, whether he is a researcher or has interest only in the application of research, must become skillful in abstracting and evaluating the research findings of others. A researcher usually finds that his first task is to sift through studies that may have a bearing on his investigation; when doing this, the ability to analyze and digest research reports expeditiously is essential. Similarly, the consumer of educational research, the professional who makes use of the researcher's investigations, needs to develop an ability to abstract and analyze research reports in order to grasp the overall significance of studies that treat the same, or similar, problems.

The Research Report

Before consideration is given to the abstraction or summarization of research reports, it may be helpful to acquaint the reader with the nature and organization of reports of educational research. Whether such reports consist of a few chapters or many, in general four sections compose the body of most of them.

The first section of a research report is concerned with a presentation of the problem; included in the presentation should be the statement of the problem, its scope, and its significance. Generally, the first section of the report begins with an orientation to the nature of the problem area; this is followed by a statement of the specific problem that was investigated. In order to clarify the problem and its significance, the problem statement is followed by a review and analysis of related literature; this is where the researcher's ability to abstract the research of others will contribute to his own study. Also found in the first section will be hypotheses that may have been formulated, assumptions that served as a basis for the investigation, the limitations that were adopted, and the definition of special terms used in the report.

The second, third, and fourth sections of the research report are most critical since the researcher's ability to carry out an original investigation is exposed here. Prior to this point his analytical ability is made evident; from this point on creative, as well as analytical, processes are involved.

The second section of the report describes the procedures and methods used in conducting the research. Here the researcher explains and relates: (1) the rationale he used in designing the study; (2) the selection of tools used to collect data; and (3) the specific steps and procedures used in data analysis.

The third part of a research paper reports the findings of the study. Included in this section should be the data that have been collected as well as an analysis of them.

The fourth and final section of a paper that reports an investigation is concerned with a summary followed by conclusions and implications that have been drawn as a result of the study. Here the researcher develops the solution to the problem if his data indicate a solution, or, if the data do not produce a problem solution, the research may suggest new avenues of approach.

What Is a Summary?

The answer to the question of just what a summary is may seem simple enough, but merely defining a summary as a "brief statement covering the main points," as does the Webster dictionary, is not much help to someone who must summarize a long research paper. An abstract or research summary must do more than briefly cover main points; it must cover the main points of a study without distorting or confusing the concepts involved. Summarizing research is like the preparation of perfume: the secret is to distill the essence from a large quantity of material without destroying or changing the essence.

One way to approach the preparation of a summary that will almost surely distort the meaning and continuity of a research report is what may be called the piecemeal method. Any attempt to summarize a study part-by-part as it is being read, will generally produce poor results. On the other hand, if a report is read in its entirety first, and then summarized in terms of its sections, it is more likely that the summary will reflect the study accurately.

Preparing Formal Abstracts

The researcher, the graduate student in education, and the professional educator in the field are called upon from time to time to prepare formal research abstracts. The researcher needs to summarize his investigation for publication in professional books and journals. Graduate students and active teachers, administrators, and guidance counselors may prepare formal abstracts in order to discuss, evaluate, and apply the knowledge that has been gained by the researcher.

Anyone who sets out to prepare an abstract should keep in mind that it is meant to be a concise document. All too often an abstract develops into a short version of the original study. Although shortened research reports are often found as magazine articles in professional journals, they are not abstracts.

An examination of formal abstracts that have been published will demonstrate that there is no set format in universal use; however, two general styles do prevail. Some writers prepare the abstract in paragraph form without breaking it into the sections found in the full study; others use headings to subdivide the abstract. When the latter method is utilized, it is the normal procedure to incorporate title headings such as:

1. Statement of the Problem
2. Procedure and Data Analysis
3. Findings
4. Summary of Conclusions, Implications and Recommendations

Whatever method is used, the abstract of necessity will tend to become organized in terms of the sections found in the complete report. It therefore probably is wise to use a format which employs headings that correspond to the sections of the research report, or at least to use the headings in the preparation of an outline for the abstract. If the person who is preparing the abstract is interested in conveying his evaluation of the research, an all important "critique" should be added as a fifth part of the formal abstract.

Criteria for Evaluating Research Studies

The elements of research have been stressed throughout this volume in order to acquaint the reader with the concepts which underlie sound research methodology; therefore, the criteria for evaluating educational research are implied in the description and discussions that have preceded. The process of evaluation is expedited, however, if a list of criteria is available. The criteria which follow summarize the ideas concerning research methods that have been presented in previous chapters and sections. Obviously, no such list is accepted as a rigid, absolute, measuring instrument. The purpose in developing criteria is to help the student of research in education establish some basis for evaluating research reports, either his own or those conducted by others. Criteria for evaluating research reports to be discussed in the sections which follow are concerned with:

1. Style used in writing the report and use of language; i.e. grammar, sentence structure, paragraphing, etc.
2. The way in which the research problem is presented.
3. The research design and data analysis.
4. The discussion of findings.
5. Conclusions and implications.

Style of Writing

An important feature of any research report is its ability to communicate. If the report fails as an instrument of communication, the researcher has failed to accomplish a major objective. The production of an understandable report of an investigation should occupy an important place in the researcher's work. Many factors will determine how well a research report conveys the researcher's description of the study he conducted. The following criteria are concerned with a few of the more important aspects of writing style and English usage:

1. Since proper indexing of a study is very important to prospective consumers of educational research, the title should clearly and concisely identify the problem area investigated. A title that is vague, wordy, or worded pretentiously may be misleading to the prospective reader.
2. The format of the report should follow one of the accepted manuals of style, not merely because such manuals standardize the style, but rather because standardization eases the reader's task. Skimming the report for content and important material is expedited.
3. Sentences should be not only grammatically correct, but also structured and worded to convey ideas in clear, concise language.
4. The over-all organization of the sections, subsections, and paragraphs of the paper should allow the reader to follow easily the logic and flow of ideas and concepts. It should not be necessary for the reader to skip back and forth through the paper in order to understand what the author is trying to say.

Presentation of the Problem

The first section of a research report exposes the foundation of the investigation. All that follows, including research methodology, findings, conclusions and implications, is influenced and directed by the way in which the problem or purpose has been identified. In presenting the problem, the researcher, therefore, must demonstrate that he clearly identified a significant problem in education.

After the problem has been introduced and stated, a research report will usually contain a summary and analysis of literature which the researcher feels has a bearing on the study. There are several objectives to be accomplished by the literature review: (1) the review provides the only practical method to determine all that is known about the problem area to be investigated; (2) the significance of the researcher's problem can be determined and demonstrated by a summary of related literature; (3) avenues of approach to the specific problem can be determined and demonstrated by a summary of related literature; (4) avenues of approach to the specific problem can be suggested by previous investigation. (Review Chapter 3 for additional purposes.)

In view of the objectives to be accomplished by the first section of a research report, the following criteria suggest themselves as pertinent to the evaluation of the section:

1. The statement of the problem, proposed hypotheses, and summation of limitations must provide a definite frame of reference within which the investigation was conducted.

2. The researcher must show that the problem is one of significance to education. Generally, the significance of a problem can be established if, from a review of related literature, evidence is presented that a definite need for study existed before the investigation was begun; however, the researcher is also obliged to explain how his study does one of the following:

   a. Presents new data that shed light upon previously unexpected phenomena.

   b. Reorganizes old data — that may have been collected by others — to show relationships not detected previously.

   c. Reinforces tentative findings of other researchers that need verification.

3. In addition to supporting the researcher's presentation of the significance of the study, the literature review should indicate that:

   a. The researcher became thoroughly familiar with the problem through an exhaustive search for related literature.

   b. All material read was carefully analyzed and evaluated.

   c. The researcher has done more than to amass related literature; his summary should show that he has assimilated and integrated the material in order to draw out meaning and relationships not otherwise evident.

4. Assumptions that form a basis for the study must be stated explicitly and shown to be valid, either through reference to previous research or by proving that many authorities accept the assumptions as valid.

5. Hypotheses must be stated so they can be subject to verification. Proposal of hypotheses that prove incapable of being tested would indicate faulty research design that should have been corrected in the early stages of a study.

6. Hypotheses should not conflict with known facts.

7. Hypotheses should offer an explanation of phenomena or provide a better and less complex explanation of phenomena than other possible hypotheses.

8. Important terms that may vary in meaning or terms that may be unfamiliar to the reader must be defined and clarified in the first section of the research paper. Once this is done, it is important that the researcher is consistent in using the terms throughout the paper as he has defined them.

9. In theory oriented research, the hypotheses should relate logically to the original statement of theory.

Research Design and Data

Many factors will affect the design of a study: this complicates the task of the evaluator. There are, however, certain common elements which provide a basis for evaluative criteria that can be applied in judging the design of a piece of educational research. The criteria which follow are drawn from these common elements.

THE GENERAL DESIGN OF THE STUDY

1. The research report should present a detailed explanation of the methodology, tools of research used, and method of data analysis. The report should also give a careful accounting of why the particular methods, tools, and techniques were used.

2. The study design must demonstrate that the proper and most efficient tools and methods were used to gather and analyze data. (The criterion, in turn, is determined by the nature of the problem, hypotheses to be tested, and assumptions adopted.)

3. The research design must further demonstrate that all data required to solve the problem and test hypotheses were collected.

THE DESIGN OF HISTORICAL STUDIES

1. Basic historical research implies that primary sources provide the bulk of data from which conclusions are drawn. Major conclusions and implications should not be based solely upon secondary source data unless: (1) available primary sources are so few that it is not possible to establish concepts of the period studied, and (2) secondary sources present a consistent pattern of concepts that have been derived independently by the authors of the sources.
2. The research report must explain the processes used to subject data to external and internal criticism. In doing this, the researcher must demonstrate that he has exhausted all methods open to him to authenticate and validate his data.

THE DESIGN OF DESCRIPTIVE STUDIES

1. A survey must be wide enough in scope to include all factors that may have an important bearing on the subject of the investigation.
2. Case studies must probe deeply; therefore, a great variety of techniques and tools must be employed to gather data.
3. Comparative studies require the establishment of a definite frame of reference against which comparison can be made.
4. The researcher must demonstrate that he has insured that data collected are reliable and valid. His data collecting instruments must be designed to avoid error and bias.
5. Interviewers or recorders must be qualified and specially trained to do their jobs.
6. If untested instruments such as an original questionnaire are used, the researcher should test, refine, and improve them through a pilot study.
7. Questionnaires or questions used in interviews should show careful preparation and appraisal so that:
   a. Questions are clear and concise.
   b. There are no superfluous questions.
   c. Enough responses are obtained to produce needed data.
   d. Questions are not slanted or loaded to produce a biased result.
   e. Respondents are stimulated to answer.
   f. Directions to respondents are clear.
   g. The data gathering instrument is arranged to permit ease in tabulating and/or scoring data.

8. If the researcher has employed tests or special measuring instruments, he must demonstrate that:

   a. He was thoroughly in control of the techniques needed to administer the instrument(s) and evaluate the data obtained.
   b. The proper instrument(s) were used for the purpose intended.
   c. The instrument(s) have been either previously standardized, or proper procedures were followed to establish the reliability and validity of original instruments.

9. In the application of special statistical methods of analysis, such as chi square or the correlation method, the researcher must demonstrate that:

   a. He has not misused the techniques by violating any of the assumptions upon which they are based.
   b. He has a complete understanding of the methods and their application.
   c. Samplings are adequate in size and representative of the population.
   d. Precautions were taken to prevent sample bias because of inadequate returns or other factors.

THE DESIGN OF EXPERIMENTAL STUDIES

1. The investigator must demonstrate that he has created an experimental condition in which he was able to establish control of the experimental variable.

2. Procedures must be used to expose and to eliminate hidden variables that may influence the experiment. Included in such procedures may be random selection of samples, equation of experimental and control groups through statistical procedures, or careful selection and manipulation such as matched pair selection and group rotation procedures.

3. In the application of statistical analysis, the researcher must demonstrate that he has met the same criteria previously listed in #9 under "The design of descriptive studies."

The Findings

The third section of a research report presents the data that have been collected as well as an analysis of them. Here the investigator's primary concern is to supply the facts that appear within the frame of reference erected by identifying and attacking the problem. The facts will appear as raw data that need interpretation; it is a task of the researcher to arrange the data into meaningful patterns. Some general criteria that can be used to evaluate the way in which researchers present findings follow:

1. Data must be complete, accurate, and applicable to the problem presented.
2. Data should be arranged and analyzed in the light of the problem presented.
3. Whenever applicable, data should be summarized and presented in the form of graphs, tables, diagrams, etc. When these are used, they should be accurate and properly prepared.
4. Footnotes and bibliographies should be supplied whenever the researcher has used published materials as data.
5. Analytical procedures must not stray from the frame of reference erected through the presentation of the problem.
6. The analysis should show that the researcher has command of the technical processes used.
7. The analysis of data must show that the researcher has been able to separate fact from opinions.
8. If data fail to support hypotheses or solve the problem, the researcher should point this out in his analysis.

DATA FROM HISTORICAL STUDIES

1. Since data for historical studies usually cannot be analyzed quantitatively, the researcher must present evidence that the data are as complete as possible and not subject to bias.
2. The researcher must not interpret facts gleaned from historical documents in terms of concepts subsequently developed. Data analysis must be made in terms of the era from which they are taken. Meaning must be determined on the basis of what was understood and accepted at the time an event occurred.
3. The processes of external and internal criticism that the researcher has presented in the design of the study must be carried through in the findings to show the validity of the data.

DATA FROM DESCRIPTIVE STUDIES

1. Since descriptive studies are designed to describe current conditions as outlined in the problem, the findings must present a complete, unbiased picture.
2. Valid standards and criteria for the classification and analysis of data must be described.

DATA FROM EXPERIMENTAL STUDIES

1. Quantitative data and mathematical analysis procedures should be complete enough to allow the reader to follow steps and computations.
2. In analyzing data, care must be taken to observe the limitations of methods and tools being used. For example, the rejection of the null hypothesis when the t-test or F-ratio are computed must be accompanied by the level of significance at which the hypothesis has been rejected.

Conclusions and Implications

A researcher may properly identify and attack a problem, even do an admirable job of presenting and analyzing data, and then fail in his efforts to draw meaningful conclusions. Since all efforts in research are focused toward solving a problem, the presentation of the solution must not confuse or mislead. In evaluating a research report, the reader and the research writer should keep the following factors in mind:

1. The conclusion of a research report should not be excessively wordy or repetitious. Conclusions should be stated in a concise, straightforward manner.
2. Conclusions should fall within the framework of the study and the data presented. The researcher may be tempted to generalize beyond the scope of his study, but this natural impulse must be curbed. Rather than overgeneralize, in drawing implications, the researcher may point out problem areas uncovered by his study that may require further investigation.
3. Evidence must be clear and conclusive, and strongly support conclusions and implications.
4. No new data should be presented with the conclusions.
5. The conclusions must be stated in such a manner that the reader can trace the reasoning back to the supporting evidence.
6. Conclusions must include a summary of the evidence that either confirms or refutes hypotheses.

Applying the Results of Research

No profession worthy of the name can afford to ignore the efforts of researchers who are striving to gain new knowledge at the frontier of a discipline. Some observers feel that as a group, professional educators, teachers, guidance counselors, and especially school administrators have been slow to follow the progress made in educational and related research areas. Part of the difficulty may be an inability of researchers to communicate with the professionals who need to apply the results of research, but it is also likely that professional educators may need to make more effort to understand and apply those results of research that can make a worthwhile contribution. The purpose of the sections that follow in this chapter is to suggest ways in which members of the teaching profession can improve and speed up the metamorphosis necessary for research findings to influence professional practices.

The School Administrator's Role

The leadership position of school administrators imposes a responsibility to insure that a continued effort is made within schools to apply selectively the results of research.

In fulfilling the responsibility to provide leadership, the school administrator must first equip himself with sufficient professional and technical knowledge. It is not necessary for the administrator to be a researcher, rather, his role as school leader requires enough knowledge and leadership ability to:

1. Select, or help select, personnel who have ability to carry out and apply the results of research.
2. Stimulate interest in research and research application among school patrons, school board members, and staff personnel.
3. Provide opportunities for the school staff to grow professionally in the ability to understand and apply educational research.
4. Guide the school board to adopt policies which will encourage research activity and permit research findings to influence educational practice.
5. Organize the administration and teaching staff to facilitate school research projects and the application of research findings in the classroom.

Staff Selection

Probably the most effective means available to the administrator in creating a climate conducive to research activity and application is staff selection. Teachers, guidance counselors and supervisors who have an interest and enthusiasm to try new methods and materials can provide much of what is needed to establish the right climate. Professional personnel who show an interest in research activities can help to insure a dynamic and effective program of instruction.

Even nonprofessional personnel, such as office workers and maintenance people, can do much to stimulate and help carry out school system efforts to improve the instructional program. Recent experiments with windowless school buildings, for example, have been partly a result of the interest shown by superintendents of buildings and grounds in the money such schools can save.

The selection of teachers generally includes some evaluation of professional competence in research application. The administrator may wish to determine answers to the following questions regarding prospective teachers:

1. Is the teacher completely aware of the most recent changes in the subject matter he is to teach? Do the teacher's record and interview indicate that he has made a real effort to keep abreast of new knowledge in the subject he teaches? Has he read studies on the subject? Can he cite literature? Has he attended special institutes dealing with the subject area?

2. Is the teacher knowledgeable with regard to new methods and materials for teaching his subject? Can he cite studies? Does he know the result of recent studies?

3. Is the teacher a graduate of an institution that is noted for its interest and participation in research in education? If the teacher is experienced, does he come from a school system that has built a reputation as one that is in the vanguard of educational research and research application?

4. Does the teacher exhibit knowledge of the literature which can help him keep abreast of research in his subject field(s) and also in the teaching of his subject(s)? Does he subscribe to journals which include literature of this kind?

5. Is the teacher a member of professional organizations that are oriented primarily toward research?

6. Has the teacher participated in research projects in his subject specialty and/or education?

7. Does the teacher exhibit a knowledge of the terminology of educational research?

8. Does the teacher exhibit an understanding of the concepts upon which research in education rests?

Arousing and Maintaining Public Interest in Research

School administrators can do much to stimulate interest in research activities. If the public is approached properly, school administrators generally will find that support for experimentation will be forthcoming.

Many parents, school board members, and other laymen who have an interest in schools realize the need for research activities; the daily lives of these people are touched by the impact of research on many of man's endeavors. What the administration must do is to help people understand the efforts of the school in conducting and applying research.

A most important aspect of any public relations program is to gain confidence and trust. If people get a feeling that a school system engages in poorly planned experiments or useless mass applications of untried methods, they will tend to oppose research activities. The administrator, therefore, should make certain that any research programs are carefully organized and administered. The public should also be kept completely informed regarding aims and purposes of such programs.

The administrator should not overlook the contribution that school patrons can make to school research. Laymen serving on committees can help formulate policy. It is also possible that people who have training and skills in research may wish to become closely involved in school projects. The great emphasis upon research by the government and industries has caused a tremendous increase in technically trained people who have a natural sympathy for, and interest in, endeavors to solve school problems through application of research.

Public interest in school research activities can be maintained by continuing use of mass media of communication. Newspapers, radio, and television stations seldom fail to take an interest in school projects. It merely takes a small amount of effort to make use of these channels of communication with the public. If students are involved in broadcasts and the writing of newspaper columns dealing with research projects, so much the better. If outside consultants or experts are used in establishing projects, it may be desirable to call upon these people to help explain their work to the public.

School administrators hold the key positions in school public relations, and it is the administrator's responsibility to interpret the work of the school. An important part of this responsibility is to carry out a planned program to interpret the school's efforts to conduct and apply educational research.

Staff Professional Growth

School leadership requires the administrator to promote the professional growth of his staff. Since an important aspect of any profession is the ability to apply research findings in professional practice, the school administrator must aid staff members to develop competency in research application.

Many avenues are open to the administrator to encourage professional growth, but the measures that can be taken to help the staff will tend to fall into the following general categories:

1. Establish and maintain the professional library and materials center.
2. Conduct in-service institutes and workshops.
3. Provide professional advice and aid from experts.
4. Release staff members from regular school duties.
5. Provide summer employment to plan or complete research projects.
6. Provide for incentive pay.

The Professional Materials Center

Nothing can be more frustrating to a staff that has an interest in research application than to be handicapped by a lack of needed literature and materials. Every school system should have a conveniently located and up-to-date professional library and materials center. Even if there is a nearby college or university library, graduate student demand for professional books, especially reference volumes, makes it imperative that individual school systems maintain their own library.

Several ways can be utilized to finance the professional library, but the most successful method probably would be one that allows the use of funds from the school budget as well as teacher contributions. Making the professional center a joint staff and school system enterprise should help to maintain the interest of all who have a stake in the school. Teacher contributions can be made through the allocation of a portion of local professional dues, voluntary individual payment, individual contribution of books and materials, or a combination of the methods cited. The school district can provide funds for books and material, or a place for the center, or both.

What should the professional center contain? Certainly there can be no completely correct answer to the question. In terms of the major objective discussed, namely, helping the staff to improve competencies in research and research application, a basic list of books and materials should include most of the following:

1. Professional reference volumes and periodicals such as encyclopedia(s) of education and educational research, the *Educational Index;* the *Review of Educational Research* and a few of the more commonly used journals including journals of research in education and some of the allied fields. (See Chapter 3).

2. Professional books that contain up-to-date ideas, theories, suggestions, and research reviews.
3. Books concerned with tests and measurements, statistical procedures and application, educational research, criteria applicable to the evaluation of all phases of the school program.
4. Samples of all kinds of measuring instruments that are available such as aptitude tests, achievement tests, interest inventories, etc.
5. Duplicating equipment.
6. Calculating machines.

In-Service Institutes and Workshops

Staff members will generally vary widely in their ability to carry out projects in research or research application. If a system is to progress in research endeavors, personnel will need to reach a level of training that many may not possess; perhaps as a result of no previous experience, because their training is a bit out of date, or simply because there is a need for review of half forgotten knowledges and skills. In-service training offers a method by which school personnel can be developed into a working team capable of recognizing needs and applying educationally sound research ideas.

Workshops or institutes can also be used as a means to organize for a project. Before a school system embarks on a study or attempts to apply a new method, each staff member should be prepared for the particular part he will play. Lack of proper staff preparation is surely one way to insure failure of any given project. The administrator who walks into the first faculty meeting of the new school year and announces a radically changed method of teaching, to begin when the children arrive the next day, is asking for trouble. Careful planning and preparation for any new venture requires that those who are to carry out the project must understand their tasks and be capable of carrying them out.

The school administrator's primary role is to organize the required in-service programs for the staff. To a great degree, the success of such programs depends upon the administrator's leadership to establish and help carry them out. Leadership responsibility for the in-service program requires that administrators:

1. Determine the amount of training that the staff will need.
2. Select qualified experts who are to conduct institutes and workshops.
3. Determine when and where institutes and workshops are to be scheduled.

4. Select the participants in programs in terms of their needs and those of the school system.
5. Help select potential key project leaders from the staff.

Professional Advice from Experts

Although the school staff may include people who are very competent in research and its application, it is desirable to bring in outside experts from time to time. New ideas and approaches can result through the interactions of the staff with people from the outside.

It has been suggested that outside experts can serve as instructors for in-service institutes and workshops. It is also good practice, however, to utilize the service of research experts and authorities in various fields as project consultants. Industry and government agencies find the practice of hiring consultants very helpful in carrying out special studies. At the same time the procedure can save money since it avoids the necessity of maintaining a large staff of experts. Whenever a project is to be undertaken, the administrator can bring in the particular consultants who will provide the kind of help needed at the precise time it is needed. Depending on the particular project undertaken by a school system, the administrator may wish to call upon:

1. College professors who are authorities in various disciplines.
2. Teachers, administrators, guidance counselors, and other personnel from other schools who have special preparation or experience.
3. Professional researchers from universities or government staffs.
4. Authorities and researchers from the staffs of professional organizations such as the NEA and state teachers' associations.

Release from Regular School Duties

The school administrator can do much to promote research projects by allowing staff members time during regular school hours to work on the project. Teachers and other school personnel are engaged in a very demanding profession: demanding upon time, physical and emotional effort, and the intellect. If professional practice is to be expanded to include research and efforts to apply research ideas, arrangements should be made to relieve the staff or key personnel on the staff from some of their regular duties.

Release from regular duties need not mean professional duties; for example, some authorities in school administration have proposed various ways to relieve the school staff of clerical tasks. Often teachers and guidance counselors are so overburdened with clerical work that they have a difficult time performing even their basic work. It is the administrator's responsibility to take whatever steps necessary to help his staff members perform in their professional capacities, including work on research projects. The administrators should also see to it that the personnel who are most deeply involved in trying new ideas have time to organize and plan these activities even if it is necessary to curtail some of their other professional duties.

Opportunities should be provided for staff members to make visits and attend conferences which can be helpful in developing background. Research literature may indicate that other school systems are experimenting with a new idea, and observers can be sent to get a firsthand account of the experiment. If it is known that a professional conference is to be focused on a problem which concerns the administrator and his staff, representatives can attend the conference to learn how other school systems are attempting to find a solution.

Summer Employment in Research for Selected Staff Members

School administrators have found it advantageous to utilize the summer months to organize and also to conclude research projects. Since the projects usually require the services of some teachers who ordinarily are not part of the administrative or guidance staff, the summer would find these people not employed by the school. Many teachers spend their summer working in various jobs, often not related to the profession. By employing teachers as key people in a project, the administrator can help insure that the project will be carried out satisfactorily. At the same time, the teachers so employed have an opportunity to further their professional growth.

Incentive Pay

The subject of merit pay for outstanding teachers has received much attention from time to time. Although merit pay is a very controversial issue, of late many school administrations and boards of education have been searching for ways to implement it. Literature on the subject suggests that the methods used fall under two general categories: (1) differential salary schedules, and (2) extra pay for extra duties. Each plan has advantages and disadvantages, but no matter what method is used to provide merit pay, those who administer incentive pay plans are faced with the job of determining criteria to evaluate staff professional effectiveness. If a school system chooses to use incentive pay as a means to stimulate professional growth, criteria related to teacher competency and efforts in the area of research and research application should not be overlooked.

School Board Policies

Obviously the school administrator cannot, on his own authority, put all the measures suggested into effect; many of the steps require authorization by the local school board. It is natural for school board members to look to the school administrative staff for guidance in policy determination; thus, the administrator is in a position to help his board of education develop policies that will encourage school personnel to engage in research application and experimental programs. He can take some or all of the following measures to guide boards of education in adopting policies conducive to research:

1. A committee of school board members on instruction and curriculum can keep in touch with school personnel engaged in studies involving the school program.
2. The administrator can arrange for board members to attend university workshops and institutes dealing with school board responsibilities. Within recent years, many universities throughout the country have organized annual institutes for school board members. Often, sessions in such institutes are devoted to school research activities.
3. The administrator can provide opportunities for school board members to take part in planning school projects in research application.
4. Research consultants can be brought in to inform the board of projects being planned and of progress made in projects under way.
5. The administrator and his staff can draft policy statements concerning research for the board to consider.

Administrative Organization

The administrative organization for school application of research and the conduct of original research will tend to be a function of the size of a school system. Regardless of how large or small a system might be, however, the establishment of machinery for the express purpose of administering programs will help insure that research activities are not relegated to a minor role and that they do not develop haphazardly.

If a school system is large, the chief school officer and his board of education may elect to establish a research bureau with a small staff headed by a research specialist with the rank of assistant or associate superintendent. A school system of moderate size may, on the other hand, appoint a member of the supervising or administrative staff to fill the position of research head as an added duty. Small school systems can use a department head or a member of the teaching staff as chairman of a research committee. The creation of a central research bureau or organization will not, however, necessarily produce results. Each school within a system should have a committee of staff members which will act to help plan and carry out system-wide projects. These committees can serve as liaisons between the central research staff and the local professional staff as well as with staffs of other schools in the system.

Finally, school administrators, by virtue of their positions, have the responsibility for executing any program; they, therefore, should review and examine the plans for research developed by the special committees and central staff and then issue administrative regulations to put plans into action.

The Role of the Classroom Teacher

School administrators, the administrative staff, and the school board can provide a climate conducive to research activities, some of the necessary tools, expert advice and help, but the classroom teacher, as in all phases of the educational program, is the key to success. Nothing can replace the well-trained, enthusiastic professional teacher; the practitioner of the art-science of education. The study, conduct, and application of research should be an integral part of the teacher's professional practice.

If the idea is accepted that all teachers have the foregoing responsibilities, then several corollary responsibilities suggest themselves:

1. Teachers must develop whatever competencies — both knowledges and skills — that will help them to understand and apply research.
2. Teachers must learn to work with each other in research application.
3. Teachers must be willing to make the effort necessary to try new ideas and methods which show promise.

Developing Needed Competencies

Beginning teachers generally have received preparation in the subject or subjects they are to teach and also in educational psychology and methodology; however, undergraduate training in research is often meager or nonexistent. It therefore becomes a matter for the individual teacher and the professional group to insure that he continues to learn and progress in this professional competence throughout his career in education. In this regard, the role of the administrator in promoting professional growth of the teaching staff has been discussed, but as in every profession, the major responsibility for excellence must rest with the practitioners.

An obvious way for the teacher to help himself is to continue his formal education. Of all the professions, teaching provides the greatest opportunity for the individual to stay in touch with academic life, and each year tens of thousands of teachers return to college and university campuses to attend evening and summer school classes. Many of these teachers embark upon graduate programs that lead to advanced degrees. Although graduate courses and programs usually require participants to develop an understanding of research, some teachers fail to see the connection between research and their professional practice; to these people, research is something other than young people and books and learning. Others acknowledge the fact that research in education is important, but they feel that it is not their business to know anything about it since they will not be involved in conducting it; research is for the expert. Teachers who feel that they have no need to understand research fail in an important way to become truly professional.

Continuation of formal course work for individuals is but one method through which teachers can develop competence in research application. Just as important are the measures that teachers can take together as a school staff. The following are examples of such measures:

1. During faculty meetings teachers and administrators can focus their attention upon problems concerning methods of teaching or curriculum arrangements. Discussion and preparation for changes will require the staff to ferret out important research that can help solve the problems.

2. Workshops and institutes have been mentioned as one way that the administration can help school personnel grow professionally. Here again, the success of the measures depends upon teachers' wholehearted participation.

3. Teachers should take active part in professional meetings where they can hear about and discuss recent research.

4. Local professional associations of teachers can devote part of their programs to important educational questions rather than to just social activities or business matters.

What competencies do classroom teachers need to develop in order to carry out professional responsibilities in research application? It would be difficult to answer the question specifically; depending on the circumstances, individual teachers and groups of teachers may need varying amounts of knowledge and degrees of skills. That is why it has been suggested that administrators should provide expert help for their staff as needed. A minimum list of competencies can be derived, however, by contemplating the part that teachers would need to play in any attempt to conduct or apply research. The classroom teacher's role in such projects would require:

1. Understanding of the general principles of research.
2. Understanding of techniques and methods used to conduct various kinds of research.
3. Understanding of the limitations of the various kinds, methods, tools, and analytical procedures of research.
4. Ability to locate helpful literature and information.
5. Ability to summarize and evaluate research quickly.

Working Together

The conduct and application of research in education is so complex that it is all but impossible for an individual to be involved alone in any significant project. The ability to work with others toward the solution of problems therefore is an important aspect of the teacher's professional role. Working together implies that teachers understand not only their own contribution but also how and why the contributions of others are necessary. To bring about a condition in which participants understand each other's roles, a climate of free discussion and flow of ideas must be maintained. Although good leadership will help to establish such a climate, individual responsibility is also important for it takes just one person to "short circuit" lines of communication. It therefore becomes a matter of necessity for team workers — as teachers must be in research activities — to understand thoroughly and be skillful in the application of the principles of good human relations.

Working together also implies that professional participants in school research projects are able to carry out assignments properly, but the term "properly" involves more than possessing the competencies previously discussed. It also means that each individual is able to apply his abilities to the task at hand through performance, timing, and appraisal of results.

The Teacher's Role as a Pathfinder

One of the biggest obstacles to research activities in a school system is inertia. Teachers find it much easier to continue doing things as they have been doing them than to make an effort to bring about changes. The problem is compounded by the fact that many changes generally will involve an entire school system and its staff. The fact that changes invariably cause some confusion when they are first put into effect also contributes to individual and group resistance to change.

What can the individual do to break down resistance to change? Teachers who plan their classwork in terms of a fixed body of subject matter and methods of teaching become prone to entanglement in an unvarying pattern of teaching that will be difficult to change. It is much better practice for the individual classroom teacher to plan each year's work in terms of the nature of the students to be taught. This is not only good practice in terms of staying out of a rut but also is a sound teaching procedure. Flexibility is the key word.

As individuals, teachers can also prevent much of the confusion that results when new ideas are first tried in a school. The surest way to avoid confusion is for each person to make it his business to become aware of his own role in a project. No factor can cause more confusion than the uncertainty of individuals.

Finally, it is the responsibility of each teacher to help the school leadership in the search for new ideas, new ways of doing things. Teachers should be ever alert to research that can improve the process of education. School administrators can devote only a certain amount of time to the task; often they must depend upon the professional staff to suggest improvements and even help lead the way. Workers who are not members of a profession need not worry about why a job is done a particular way or how the job can be better accomplished; as members of a profession, teachers dare not ignore the responsibility without risking their professional status.

The Role of Other School Staff Members

The modern school includes special professional staff members who play vital roles in its program. These specialists can provide leadership and expert knowledge that can insure proper direction and application of research activities. Such staff members include:

1. Guidance counselors
2. Directors of elementary and secondary education
3. Supervisors (of various subjects)

4. Coordinators (of curriculum)
5. Research specialists

Guidance Counselors

School guidance personnel hold important positions in terms of efforts that may be made to conduct research or to implement study findings. Almost without exception, data that are required for or produced by research activities in a school system must be collected and interpreted by personnel who have received the kind of training that guidance counselors have had. Guidance counselors generally are required to have a thorough knowledge of sound evaluation procedures. They must also be expert in the application of the procedures. Since any piece of research or any application of research must be accompanied by continual evaluation, guidance counselors should be able to play a key role in such activities.

Similarly, the administration and interpretation of tests and other measuring instruments are an integral part of the counselor's work. Often the data that constitute many research studies, or that need to be collected to evaluate school projects in the application of research are the result of measurements made with the same or with similar instruments. The statistical procedures applied to interpret research data overlap with the procedures used in the interpretation of test results.

In short, by virtue of their training and position, guidance counselors should be natural leaders and experts in school research activities. As with classroom teachers, however, these staff members can fulfill the role described only if:

1. They have the thorough functional knowledge required — knowledge and skill that are more than mere ability to follow the directions that come with a test package.
2. They have a willingness to apply their knowledge and skill to push forward and improve educational practice.

Directors, Supervisors, Coordinators, and Research Specialists

As members of the school administrative organization, these school personnel can provide the leadership and liaison necessary for the success of school projects. In large school systems it is virtually impossible for principals and superintendents to do all that is necessary to coordinate research activities; often it is a primary responsibility of directors, supervisors, coordinators, and research specialists to carry out the functions.

Much that has been said about the roles of guidance counselors and classroom teachers applies in general to the school administrator's personal staff; however, an examination of the specific functions of the administrative staff specialists reveals the unique contributions that each can make to school research:

1. Directors and coordinators of elementary and secondary education are appointed as curriculum experts. It is the job of these people to provide leadership in development of the program of the school. In this capacity, these members of the administrative staff should pave the way toward developing the best curriculum that can be adopted to meet the needs of the pupils in the school system. It is therefore imperative that directors and coordinators keep abreast of the most recent advances in school curriculum.

2. Supervisors usually are experts in teaching methods and materials; their job is to help classroom teachers improve their day-to-day instruction. The application of promising instructional aids or teaching techniques is within the scope of the responsibilities of supervisors.

3. Obviously, research specialists can provide the know-how necessary to conceive and carry out basic and applied research projects, but the specialist can do more than develop and guide the projects. Equally important functions are: (1) to help the entire school staff understand research activities; (2) to help school staff members develop skill in research application; (3) to aid school administrators in their efforts to bring about a climate of inquiry and experimentation.

Selected Exercises

1. A researcher notices that pupils who come from lower socio-economic families *seem* to have difficulty in school.
   a. State a problem that the investigator might identify from the situation that would require research.
   b. State a hypothesis that the researcher may wish to test.
   c. Explain briefly the methodology that the researcher might employ to solve the problem. How could he test his hypothesis?
   d. What limitations may be imposed?
2. A superintendent of schools is concerned by the fact that only 40 per cent of high school graduates from his system go to college.
   a. Compose a problem statement to help shape research that might provide the superintendent with needed facts regarding his concern.

    b. State a hypothesis that should be tested.

    c. Explain briefly how the research might be conducted and the hypothesis tested.

    d. What limitations should be imposed?

3. Suppose that conclusions drawn from the research for question 2 were that:

    (1) A significantly high percentage of graduates from one of the schools *did* go to college.

    (2) The program of that school and its pupil personnel were remarkably similar to those in other schools.

    (3) The only factor which seemed to differentiate that school from the others was the existence of a College Interest Association which included representatives from the P.T.A., school board, administrative staff, student clubs and groups, and teachers. The express purpose of the organization was to foster interest in higher education and help needy students to go to college.

        a. Explain what steps might be taken by the superintendent and the school board to prepare for an action research project in the school system at large.

        b. Explain what part classroom teachers in the various schools would play in the project.

        c. What should guidance counselors do to carry out the project?

        d. What is the job of the curriculum coordinators and the director of secondary education?

4. A director of elementary instruction attends a regional meeting of school supervisors and hears a talk by a professor of research from a distant university. The professor explains that he and his graduate students have been experimenting with teaching science to elementary school children in the university demonstration school through a strict problem-solving approach. The results are encouraging. The professor mentions that the same kinds of experiments are being tried at several other universities.

    a. What steps should the director of elementary instruction take to study the experiments?

    b. What part should teachers in the director's school system play in the preliminary studies?

    c. Suppose that evidence is not conclusive that the method of problem-solving is working, but that it does look promising. What might the superintendent and his staff do about the idea?

Suggested Activities

1. Select a problem that has been discussed in faculty meetings at your school and determine if the same or similar problems have been researched. (Consult sources listed in Chapter 3.)

2. Compile a bibliography of research summaries and articles that have a bearing on the problem selected for suggested activity 1 or for another problem. (Consult Chapter 3 for suggestions on how to prepare the bibliography.)

3. Make a library search for the material compiled for activities 1 and 2 above and record data and your evaluations of the material on the bibliographic cards.

Selected Readings

1. ADAMS, HAROLD P., AND FRANK G. DICKEY, *Basic Principles of Supervision*. New York: American Book Co., 1953. (Chapters 12 and appendixes A, B, and C)

2. ALEXANDER, CARTER, AND ARVID J. BURKE, *How to Locate Educational Information and Data* (4th Edition, Revised). New York: Bureau of Publications, Teachers College, Columbia University, 1958.

3. American Association of School Administrators, *School Board — Superintendent Relationships*. Washington, D.C.: The Association, 1956.

4. BANGHART, FRANK W. (Editor), *Educational Research*. Bloomington, Indiana: Phi Delta Kappa, Inc., 1960 .

5. BARNES, JOHN B., *Educational Research for Classroom Teachers*. New York: G. P. Pitnam's Sons, 1960. (Appendixes A and B)

6. COCKING, WALTER D., *As I See It*. New York: Macmillan Co., 1955.

7. COREY, STEPHEN M., *Action Research to Improve School Practices*. New York: Bureau of Publications, Teachers College, Columbia University, 1953. (Chapter 5)

8. GOOD, CARTER V., *Introduction to Educational Research*. New York: Appleton-Century-Crofts, 1963. (Chapter 9)

9. GOOD, CARTER V., A. S. BARR, AND DOUGLAS E. SCATES, *The Methodology of Educational Research*. New York: Appleton-Century-Crofts, 1936. (Chapter 14)

10. JACOBSON, PAUL B., WILLIAM C. REAVIS AND JAMES D. LOGSDON, *Duties of School Principals*. New York: Prentice-Hall, Inc., 1953. (Chapters 16, 19 and 22)

11. LEONARD, J. PAUL, *Developing the Secondary School Curriculum* (Revised Edition). New York: Rinehart and Co., Inc., 1953. (Chapter 12)

12. MORT, PAUL R., *Principles of School Administration*. New York: McGraw-Hill Book Co., 1946. (Chapter 16)

13. MOULY, GEORGE, *The Science of Educational Research*. New York: American Book Company, 1963. (Chapters 5, 14 and 15)

14. OLSEN, EDWARD G., and others, *School and Community*. New York: Prentice-Hall, Inc., 1954. (Chapters 16 and 17)

15. The Fund for the Advancement of Education, *Decade of Experiment.* New York: The Fund, 1961.
16. VAN DALEN, DEOBOLD B., *Understanding Educational Research,* 2nd Edition, New York: McGraw-Hill Book Company, 1966. (Chapter 16)
17. YEAGER, WILLIAM A., *School-Community Relations.* New York: Dryden Press, 1951.
18. YOUNG, RAYMOND J., *A Directory of Educational Research Agencies and Studies* (Second Revision) Bloomington, Indiana: Phi Delta Kappa Inc., 1962.

Chapter 10

Typical Research
Studies in Education

The sections that follow include examples of various types of research studies in education. Obviously, it was not possible to present complete research reports; instead digests of the original documents have been selected to:

1. Demonstrate research methodology as applied to current problems in education.
2. Demonstrate the ideas previously discussed concerning the summarization of research reports.
3. Provide the reader with a limited sample of recent studies in education.
4. Give the reader an opportunity to apply what he has learned concerning evaluation of research.

Most of the summaries have been selected from articles that appeared in research journals. Included are examples of historical, descriptive and experimental studies.

The Historical Study

Historical studies often provide a basis for charting the evolution of the social institution we call education. Individual researches in the history of education may be limited to studies of specific school systems, colleges, or restricted to relatively short time periods, but the sum total of such research can give an indication of how and why education developed as it did in a given place and time. In turn, since education has such a profound influence upon other human endeavors, a study of educational evolution can shed much light upon human history in general.

A study carried out in 1957 at the College of William and Mary in Virginia will serve to illustrate how the historical study in education can contribute valuable knowledge. The author examined the relationship between Old World universities during the early Colonial development of America and a New World college, the College of William and Mary, which was founded in 1693. In pursuing the study, the author gathered data both in the United States and in Europe.

The Influence of English and Scottish Universities on the Curriculum of the College of William and Mary

Barbara Wilbur*

The problem was to trace the influence of seventeenth and eighteenth century English and Scottish university education upon the seventeenth and eighteenth century curriculum of the College of William and Mary. Since influence can be traced through men, through ideas, and through customs and practices, the study was not limited to any one of these ways; an attempt was made to explore all three. The broad scope of the problem, however, necessitated a limitation in terms of the universities studied; the English universities investigated were Oxford and Cambridge; the Scottish universities were represented by the University of Edinburgh and St. Andrews. (Early professors at William and Mary had come directly from the universities selected.) The research was also limited in scope in terms of the admissions requirements; requirements for degrees; schools, lectures, and professors; methods of instruction; texts studied; examinations; theses and disputations; and commencements.

Primary sources of data pertaining to the European universities and the College of William and Mary included studies of the Colleges of Oxford; charters and annuals of the colleges; diaries of students and professors of the period; autobiographies and journals by the people of the era; the catalogue of the College of William and Mary; orations of the period; and letters and papers in the collection of the Archives of Colonial Williamsburg, Incorporated. Secondary sources included books and articles pertaining to the British universities and the College of William and Mary; books and articles on education in England in the sixteenth, seventeenth and eighteenth centuries; biographies, and pamphlets and bulletins.

The data were organized and analyzed in accord to the following plan. First an analysis of the courses of study in the English and Scottish universities was made. Next, a summary of trends

---

*Miss Wilbur is an employee of Colonial Williamsburg, Incorporated. The summary of her study has been published in this text with her permission.

in the British universities was determined. Then academic matters at the College of William and Mary were examined. Finally, comparison between the British universities and William and Mary College were drawn.

British Universities — The Seventeenth and Eighteenth Centuries

In 1634 the first copies of the Statutes of Oxford University known as the "new code" were printed. The Statutes reveal that although specific lectures were established by special ordinances, the Regents were still obligated, as of old, to give Ordinary Lectures. Lectures in rhetoric, grammar, logic, and metaphysics were to be elected every two years by students.

The grammar lectures included carefully chosen Latin and Greek authors to be read and criticized. The praelector in rhetoric lectured concerning Aristotle, Cicero, Quintilian, or Hermozes to the same students who were studying grammar twice weekly. The praelectors in dialectic and moral philosophy did not lecture to the first year students but rather to those who had passed the first year but had not taken their degrees.

The "new code" still required lectures in geometry and astronomy. The text for the lectures in natural philosophy was still Aristotle's *Metaphysics.* But the Statutes gave the lecturer in history the freedom to teach historians other than Florus; all Bachelor of Arts and civil law students were required to attend.

Students in their third year or above and Bachelors who were candidates for the degree of Master of Arts were required to attend lectures in Greek. The lectures of the Reguis professors of law and medicine were attended by students of those subjects until they received their Doctors' degrees.

The course of study in Oxford remained fairly constant during the seventeenth and eighteenth century as demonstrated by the journals of several students. Henry Fleming, a squire's son who was at Queen's College, Oxford, in the late 1670's and during various years in the 1680's wrote of his studies as did Anthony Wood who attended in the late 1650's. Wood's diary also gives insight into the life of students of those times as well as some notion of the heightened interest in natural science which was occurring in Britain in the late 1600's.

By the early 1700's lectures in anatomy, oriental studies, and modern languages were being given at Oxford. The classics, logic, and philosophy, however, remained the chief studies at Oxford through the eighteenth century.

The curriculum at both Oxford and Cambridge in the early 1700's was divided into three courses: (1) theological; (2) classical; and (3) philosophical. The philosophy course included both mathematics and science with texts in arithmetics, geometry, trigonometry, astronomy, physics, and chemistry.

Latin and Greek had lost some of their importance in the English universities by the seventeenth and eighteenth centuries, but they still were considered essential. The principal use of Latin in the eighteenth century was for disputations, which were still the order of the day. At Oxford, however, they had degenerated into "doing generals," repeating from memory stock syllogisms whose subject matter was traditional and the significance of which the respondent and opponent often did not comprehend.

The philosophy of Descartes contributed much to the gradual breakdown of the old system of university instruction. The issue which had heretofore been man's relation to God was exchanged for a consideration of the relation of man to Nature. The philosophy of Descartes appealed especially to the young students at Cambridge. By the middle of the eighteenth century nearly twenty chairs, most of which were in scientific and mathematical studies, were established at Oxford and Cambridge.

The old Scottish universities of St. Andrews, Glasgow and Aberdeen were slow to move from the traditional medieval programs. The University of Edinburgh, founded in 1582, was far more liberal. By 1674, a year after James Blair, who was to become the first president of the College of William and Mary in Virginia, had taken his Master of Arts degree at Edinburgh an intellectual revival was dawning. James Gregory, as separate professor of mathematics, was able to devote his genius exclusively to his subject. The department of philosophy had by this time reached its fullest seventeenth century development. Also during the period were sown the seeds of the great medical school of the University of Edinburgh.

The early 1700's saw the Arts faculty at the University of Edinburgh come into existence. It was not long before Aristotelian ethics was abandoned and Newtonian philosophy was taught in its stead. The example was soon followed by the other universities of Scotland including Aberdeen, where in 1755 William Small took his Master of Arts degree. Small was to bring with him to Virginia, where he was to serve as professor of natural philosophy and mathematics at the College of William and Mary, a broad and liberal viewpoint.

As the eighteenth century progressed, the emphasis upon Latin and Greek and the Aristotelian philosophy declined. The influence of Descartes, Locke, and Newton became increasingly evident in the English and Scottish universities.

THE COLLEGE OF WILLIAM AND MARY

Founded in 1693, the College of William and Mary adhered strictly to the Church of England, whereas the New England colleges of Harvard and Yale resulted from and were the expression of nonconformity. All the early professors of the College of William and Mary were English and Scottish university men and, with very few exceptions, were ministers of the Church of England. The primary factor in founding the College was preparation of young men for the ministry.

For twenty years after it was founded, the College of William and Mary was little more than a grammar school for boys from eight to fifteen years of age. The purpose of the college grammar school was to prepare young men for college. It was modeled after the English Latin grammar school. The Statutes of the College indicate that the following subjects were taught in the grammar school: Latin, 1694-1779; mathematics, 1711-1779; natural philosophy (science), 1717-1779.

In a letter of 1780 to Ezra Stiles, president of Yale, James Madison, president of the College from 1777-1812 expressed dissatisfaction with the College organization. In 1780 the College was reorganized into a plan known as the Oxford Curriculum which was copied directly from the English universities. The plan included three schools: the grammar school for classical studies, the philosophical school, and the divinity school.

In 1779 modern languages were introduced into the curriculum and in 1803 a suggestion by an early mathematics professor, Hugh Jones, was put into effect with the establishment of the first chair in history.

Mr. William Small, who taught science at the College from 1758 to 1764, made a great impression on student Thomas Jefferson. Small attempted in his teaching of the natural sciences, to escape the dogmas of the old philosophies. Small is credited with the innovation of the modern lecture system. Small's lectures were punctuated with scientific demonstrations.

The rising importance of science is evidenced by the record, in the Journal of the Faculty, that Benjamin Franklin was awarded an honorary degree of Master of Arts because of his contributions in science. This was the only honorary degree granted by the College prior to the American Revolution. Also indicative of the interest in science is the College's purchase of scientific equipment by Mr. Small. His records show that over three hundred English pounds were invested in what became the finest collection of apparatus of its kind in America.

In the early days, Latin and Greek were taught not as dead but as living languages. Dissertations of the students in the philosophy school were written in good style, and Latin verses were composed by professors and students. By 1771 orations in English had begun to replace the Latin and in 1776 Samuel Herley, professor of moral philosophy, argued that knowledge of physiology, history, mathematics, ethics, or poetry was of greater benefit than a familiarity with the intricacies of style of a dead language.

In 1779 Thomas Jefferson's reorganization of the William and Mary curriculum eliminated the need for professors of Latin or Greek. Jefferson's opposition was not to the classics but to the method of teaching which had prevailed throughout the Colonial period, that of teaching Latin and Greek grammar by memory.

The College government was copied after the English university government, and commencements in the Colonial period were held at the same times as the graduation exercises at Cambridge. From

1729 to 1757 eight of the thirteen masters and presidents at William and Mary had been educated at Oxford. After 1757 fewer faculty members were Oxford graduates and by 1766 the last Oxford man left the College.

CONCLUSIONS

It would appear that the curriculum of the College of William and Mary was a Colonial model scaled to the English pattern of university education. It was a curriculum which, at the outset, allowed for but little deviation. As has been shown, however, at an early date, there were hints of a liberalism which was to become a reality with the Revolution and Thomas Jefferson's subsequent revision of the College curriculum.

With the founding of the Virginia college, the English classical plan for a liberal education was transplanted to England's American colonies. To the time of the break with England, the College remained a "Colonial echo" of the trends voiced in the British universities.

The interest of English universities in philosophy was reflected in the emphasis placed on philosophy at William and Mary. William and Mary philosophy professors taught logic, rhetoric, ethics, physics, and politics, as well as arithmetic, geometry, and astronomy. As Aristotelianism gradually declined in importance in the universities of England and Scotland, the inductive logic of Francis Bacon, recognized after the middle of the century throughout the world, made fertile the Virginia soil for the planting and flourishing of the natural sciences. It was Professor William Small, who had brought with him from Aberdeen the broad and liberal viewpoint of the Newtonian doctrines, that made men such as Jefferson yearn for a freedom which promised much and which finally burst forth in bloom in the American Revolution.

The methods of teaching the classics at William and Mary were very much the same as those of the English universities. As the century wore on, however, the emphasis on Latin and Greek declined in the British universities, and Virginians also became impatient of the bonds imposed by the humanities.

The government of the College was copied after the governmental system of the English universities. The time requirements for degrees were fixed according to English custom. Commencements at the Virginia college were held at the same time as the graduation exercises in the English universities.

Principally, English ideas and methods of higher education were introduced in Virginia through the professors at William and Mary, men who came to the new continent fresh from the influences of the English and Scottish universities. James Blair and Professors Hugh Jones and William Small were to leave the British imprint on the American mind.

The College of William and Mary, founded by the Crown, a college to which was appointed a faculty of English and Scottish university men, a college under the strict supervision of the influential Church of England, throughout the Colonial period remained English in body, even when the spirit began to weaken. The ideas of a liberal education, of the course of study, of the methods of teaching, were all inherited from Britain. William and Mary was the child of the British universities.

Descriptive Research

The term descriptive research includes all studies with purposes aimed primarily to describe conditions as they existed at the time the research was conducted. Since it is desirable to conduct a background investigation in connection with any type of research, descriptive studies often begin with a historical review of literature dealing with the subject to be investigated, but the review should not be confused with historical research. The literature review in descriptive studies is made for the purpose of establishing the relevance of the current investigation and how it fits the pattern set by previous studies. The purpose of the descriptive study also differs from that of an historical study since in the latter the *primary* aim is to determine past conditions. Following are examples of survey, content analysis and comparative investigations.

Surveys

An interesting descriptive survey of teacher views of poverty area children was carried out recently by two researchers in the Southwest United States.

In the study, the authors refer to the *phi coefficient*—a statistic which was not discussed in Part II of the text. A brief explanation of *phi* is that it is an estimate of the coefficient of correlation when each of two variables are expressed as two categories.

Ordinarily the chi square contingency test is employed in such a situation to determine if the hypothesis that there is no relationship may be rejected. If, however, the researcher wishes to go further and determine the *approximate* degree of relationship, the *phi* coefficient may be computed from the data.

Teacher Views of Poverty Area Children

George E. North and O. Lee Buchanan[*]

THERE IS A very major and current concern over the failure of past efforts to impose a traditional or standard kinds of education upon children of different cultural backgrounds and values. The low socioeconomic class or poverty culture is vaguely defined and poorly understood. Teachers have a great deal to do with the general society's acceptance or rejection of this particular different subculture. This state of affairs urges a closer evaluation of teachers' views of children of the poverty culture.

Charters (2) has reviewed the literature on the social background of teaching, and he has approached the central problem of teachers as purveyors and imposers of middle class culture by considering the following questions. First, he asks whether there are value differences in the social classes, and he finds the answer conclusively yes. Second, do teachers internalize middle class values? It seems likely that they do, though research is inconclusive. Third, is there a manifestation of middle class values in the classroom process? Research reports per se are not conclusive, but there is certainly evidence and opinion that this is so. Middle class ways have been shown to be especially rewarded in the classroom; and the school process has been described as inherently middle class.

We believe that a closer examination of teachers' views of poverty children will help in the exploration of how teachers might best approach these children. We have chosen to analyze teachers' views in two ways. We wish to evaluate favorability toward or liking for poverty children as well as the content of their views toward these children. We shall examine several categories of teachers or teacher characteristics as they affect these teacher views. Our independent variables are as follows: First, what differences in attitude and favorability to poverty children are there between teachers who deal closely with them and those who do not? That is, between those who teach a substantial proportion of these children and those who do not? Second, how does a teacher's age relate to these dependent variables? Third, how does a teacher's own childhood economic background affect his disposition toward these children? Fourth, what differences in our dependent variables do we find between those teachers who are rated most successful in teaching poverty children in contrast with those teachers who are not so rated? Fifth, what differences can be found among teachers with Caucasian versus those with Negro backgrounds?

---

[*]The summary of their study appeared in the October, 1967 issue of the *Journal of Educational Research* and has been published in this text with the permission of the *Journal* and the authors.

PROCEDURES

Subjects are all employed elementary school teachers from nine schools in three districts in a southwestern urban area. Schools were selected with the aim of obtaining a sample with a normal range of each of the independent variables. A total of 167 persons responded to the task of describing poverty children.

The views of teachers toward poverty children were assessed with the 300 words of Gough's Adjective Check List (ACL). All 300 adjectives were placed on one page and the subject was directed: "Let us consider families to be in poverty if the family income is below $3,000 (i.e., approximately below $3,300 for a large family, or below $2,700 for a small family). Think of all children in your charge from these poverty families. Scan this whole list of adjectives and then underline the 50 words which best describe these poverty children." We assume that teachers can identify with substantial accuracy those children who are from such poverty families, since the teacher has knowledge of occupations and addresses, as well as "end of the year" acquaintance with each child and family. Subjects were not asked to identify themselves. These ratings were accomplished in the spring of 1965. At this time the Economic Opportunity Act of 1964 and its implementation by community action programs authorized by Title 2 of this Act were under way. Even though there was much increased public attention to poverty children, we assume that the vast majority of teachers were not changed substantially in their views of these children by the public communication media at this point. Information regarding teacher characteristics, our independent variables, was obtained as follows: 1. Regarding the proportion of poverty children in the teacher's present assignment, each S was asked to indicate: 5% or less, about 10%, about 25%, about 50%, about 75%, about 90%, or 95% or more. 2. The teacher was asked to list his or her age. 3. Subjects were asked to rate their own childhood economic circumstances on each of four seven-point scales. These scales are those devised by Werner (3) for determining the Index of Status Characteristics (ISC). An ISC score was then calculated for each subject according to Warner's system. Our score is a self-rated ISC rather than a score derived from outside observers as in the normal Warner procedure. For our fourth and fifth independent variables we have fewer data. For 70 Ss in four schools the curriculum supervisor quietly identified each subject's rating report, usually without the Ss' awareness. This was done by asking the Ss to do their ratings in small groups at grade level meetings. The supervisor could then identify each S after the S had gone. Then the following information was obtained. The supervisor and the principal each made a judgment as to whether or not the teacher should be rated in the upper 20 percent of a population of teachers in terms of his success in teaching poverty area children. The fifth variable is measured simply by an indication of whether the teacher is of Negro or Caucasian background.

In order to compare these independent variables in terms of favorability of views as well as in content of views we have derived a favorability scoring key. A separate sample of 48 teachers was asked to rate each of the 300 words of the ACL in one of four categories as a description of children in general. They were asked to rate whether each adjective was 1) very favorable, 2) slightly favorable, 3) slightly unfavorable, and 4) very unfavorable as a description of children. We then calculated a mean rating for each of the ACL words. This favorability scoring key then allowed us to determine a mean favorability score for each S's 50 word description of poverty area children. Since we were interested in the content of these teacher views as well as the favorability disposition, we also undertook an item analysis of the ACL words in relation to each of the independent variables in order to determine whether the usage of each word was correlated with positions on the independent variables. *Phi* coefficients were obtained in the cases of all words invoked by more than one-fourth of the sample for each independent variable.

RESULTS AND DISCUSSION

Our first grouping of teachers, independent variable 1, presents our sample distributed in accordance with teachers' closeness to poverty children in terms of the proportion of their present class load which is from the poverty subculture. The sample can be divided roughly in half by considering those who teach 10% or fewer poverty children and those who teach more than 10% poverty children. Using the Chi-square statistic, we have compared this dichotomy with the frequency of persons who score above and below a near median score on the dependent variable, the favorability score. The results of this comparison are as shown in Table 10.1 quite negative. There is no apparent association between proportion of poverty children one is presently teaching and our global measure of favorability disposition toward these children. After an item analysis we do, however, find some statistically significant results concerning this grouping of those who teach a substantial proportion of poverty children versus those who do not. Teachers of poverty children described them as loud, rebellious, show-off, stubborn, sulky, and touchy (Table 10.2). Teachers of middle-class children described poverty children as affectionate, changeable, and defensive. Of these nine words which significantly differentiate between the dichotomous grouping of variable 1 at the .05 level of significance, 2.8 could appear simply as a result of random variation. (*Phi* coefficients were determined for those 57 of the 300 adjectives which were used by more than one-fourth of the sample of teachers.) There does seem, however, a real difference in those words used by teachers of poverty children and those used by teachers of middle-class children. One can sense that persons presently teaching poverty children tend to feel a somewhat irritated and frustrated attitude toward these children while those who are not so close to them show a more benign outlook. Thus, while the favorability disposition does not differ between these two groups, one group is perhaps trying harder but is frustrated, while the other is not so frustrated and cares less.

TABLE 10.1   Teacher Characteristics and Favorability
Toward Poverty Children

	Variable 1 Poverty Children Being Taught:		Variable 2 Teacher's Age:	
	10% or less	more than 10%	35 or below	36 or above
Unfavorable	33	40	34	34
Favorable.	39	28	37	35
	n = 140		n = 140	
	chi-square = 1.12		chi-square = .014	

	Variable 3 Teacher's Economic Background		Variable 4 Success with Teaching Poverty Children	
	Better	Poorer	Good	Not Good
Unfavorable	30	38	6	28
Favorable.	36	42	22	14
	N = 146		N = 70	
	Chi-square = .035		Chi-square = 5.91 (significant at .02 level)	

	Variable 5		
		Ethnicity	
		Caucasian	Negro
Unfavorability		14	19
Favorability		15	21
		n = 69	
		Chi-square = .002	

Our second variable, teachers' age, is distributed from age 21 through 63 with a median at 35. There is a moderate skewness with a higher frequency at the younger portion of the distribution. When we consider favorability scoring, above and below a median score, in relation to older and younger teachers as shown in Table 10.1, we find no association. Our item analysis also proved quite negative. The two words shown in Table 10.2 with significant *Phi* coefficients cannot be considered meaningful since one should expect that out of 66 *Phi* coefficients determined, there would be 3.3 significant at the .05 level by reason of random variation.

A variable of much theoretical interest is that of the teachers' childhood economic background. Our measure of this, variable 3, is a self-rated ISC. These scores ranged from 16 to 75, the lower scores reflecting a more affluent background, and the distribution is roughly normal with a modal value of 48. Upon dividing our sample

TABLE 10.2 Correlations of Teacher Characteristics With the Ascription of Words to Poverty Children

Variable 1

Invoked by Teachers with More Than 10% Poverty Children	Invoked by Teachers with 10% or Fewer Poverty Children
loud . . . . phi* = +.21	affectionate . . . phi = -.21
rebellious . . . . +.25	changeable . . . . . -.28
show-off . . . . . +.21	defensive . . . . . . -.21
stubborn . . . . . +.28	
sulky . . . . . . +.20	
touchy . . . . . +.20	

Variable 2

Invoked by Teacher's Age 36 and Above	Invoked by Teacher's Age 35 and Below
unstable phi = +.17	suspicious phi = -.17

Variable 3

Invoked by Teachers with Poor Childhood Economic Background	Invoked by Teachers with Better Childhood Economic Background
	absent-minded . . phi = -.17
	emotional . . . . . -.20
	stubborn . . . . . . -.22
	touchy . . . . . . -.18

Variable 4

Invoked by Teachers Rated Most Successful with Poverty Children	Invoked by Teachers Not Rated Most Successful with Poverty Children
affectionate . . phi = +.34	despondent . . . phi = -.25
friendly . . . . . +.23	indifferent . . . . . -.23
talkative . . . . . +.28	inhibited . . . . . . -.27
	nervous . . . . . . -.26
	slipshod . . . . . . -.32
	sulky . . . . . . -.26
	unstable . . . . . . -.27

Variable 5

Invoked by Caucasian Teachers	Invoked by Negro Teachers
dissatisfied phi = .26	argumentative . . phi = .39
distrustful 28	curious 26
irresponsible 24	evasive 30
prejudiced 47	fussy 59
	indifferent 34
	outspoken 31
	stubborn 47
	talkative 29
	temperamental 30
	withdrawn 32

near the median and considering favorability disposition scores we find no association with this variable either. Our item analysis also shows negative results. The four adjectives with *Phi* coefficients reaching the .05 level cannot be considered meaningful since three of them could occur by chance. Whatever the effect of affluence or poverty in a teacher's background, it does not show in our dependent variables.

Our fourth independent variable, success with teaching poverty area children involves a somewhat smaller sample of 70 teachers. Forty percent of these were rated by both the curriculum supervisor and the principal as falling in the upper 20% of teachers in general, in terms of their success with poverty children. The other 60% were not so rated. Those rated as successful do tend to have favorability scores in a positive direction. (As shown in Table 10.1, the obtained Chi-square is 5.91, significant at the .02 level.) Our item analysis reveals ten words which significantly differentiate the rated successful teachers and the not rated successful teachers, and 3.5 of these words are explainable on the basis of chance variation. There are some apparent differences in those words associated with each end of this "success" distribution. Successful teachers used the words affectionate, friendly, and talkative, and these adjectives carry notes of benevolence and kindness toward these children. Unsuccessful teachers invoked the words despondent, indifferent, inhibited, nervous, slipshod, sulky, and unstable. This grouping seems to carry the notion that there is something wrong, sick, or crippled about poverty children. The writers have informally asked the four principals and three supervisors who made the ratings of teachers' success about their criteria for such ratings. The most common criteria mentioned by these persons was that of whether a teacher seemed to like poverty children. This report certainly fits with our obtained results. Teachers apparently reveal their positive attitudes toward poverty children clearly to administrators as well as in our global measure in this study.

Our variable 5 has 69 teachers dichotomously separated according to racial background. Twenty-nine persons are Caucasian and 40 are Negro. We find no association of this grouping with the favorability-unfavorability grouping. We do, however, find a considerable number of words which significantly differentiate Caucasian from Negro teachers. Of 14 such adjectives, only 3.5 may be expected by reason of random variation. As shown in Table 10.2, Caucasian teachers considered poverty children to be dissatisfied, distrustful, irresponsible, and prejudiced. Negro teachers considered poverty area children to be argumentative, curious, evasive, fussy, indifferent, outspoken, stubborn, talkative, temperamental, and withdrawn. These word groupings do not present an organized picture. To Negro teachers poverty children are somewhat active and autonomous (argumentative, curious, fussy, outspoken, talkative, temperamental) and somewhat resistive (evasive, fussy, indifferent, stubborn, withdrawn). These views may well be related to the reports of the low income Negro subculture as involving rather strict physical and authoritarian discipline (1).

There is a noteworthy observation of our data which we must report. Upon viewing those words which were used most frequently as descriptions of poverty children by our total sample of teachers, those words which represent the general stereotype of poverty children, we were impressed with the negative quality of this stereotype. We find a substantial correlation between frequency of word usage in describing poverty children and the unfavorability values of these words. (The Pearson r is .41, and the *Eta* is .44.) The words most frequently used tend to be unfavorable. The highly negative stereotype is shown further in the following way. When we calculate the mean favorability value for all 800 ACL words we find this to be 2.39, rather close to the completely neutral value of 2.50. When we next look at each Ss mean favorability score, that is, the mean value for each teacher's selected 50 words, and calculate a mean of all of these S means we obtain a value of 2.74. Then, when we look at those 50 words which were most frequently used in describing poverty children, the words which comprise the stereotype, we find the mean favorability score of those to be 2.95, a rather negative value.

References

1. AUSUBEL, D., and AUSUBEL, P., "Ego Development Among Segregated Negro Children," in H. Passow (Ed.) *Education in Depressed Areas* (New York: Teachers College, 1963), pp. 109-141.
2. CHARTERS, W. W., "The Social Background of Teaching," in N. L. Gage (Ed.) *Handbook of research on teaching* (Chicago: Rand McNally Co., 1963).
3. WARNER, W. L., MEEKER, M., and EELLS, K., *Social class in America* (Chicago: Science Research Associates, 1949).

Content Analysis

Content analysis was described in Chapter 2 as a research method used to determine the content of documents. Studies of textbooks, census studies, court case records, minutes of meeting, and records of actions of governing bodies are valuable not only to the historical researcher but also to the student who is interested in present conditions.

The following study is an example of an investigation of the content of newspaper articles concerned with education.

School News in the Local Newspaper

Richard J. Gordon*

A SOUND PUBLIC relations program should be a high priority goal of all administrators. The community must understand the centrality of education in a democracy, and accept and support the school pro-

*The summary of Professor Gordon's study appeared in the June, 1968 issue of the *Journal of Educational Research* and has been published in this text with the permission of the *Journal* and the author.

gram. Public apathy and ignorance probably lie at the root of: poor remuneration for and recruitment of school personnel, outmoded curricula and teaching methods, poorly qualified board members, and the defeat of many school budgets, bond issues, and other referenda.

School news is frequently the most important component of a school-community public relations program. As the American Association of School Administrators notes "The newspaper, because of its space and day-by-day or week-by-week reporting, is the best means of showing the public the complications of its school operations and the integrity . . . of its school heads." (1)

To have a systematic effective school public relations program, with school news in the local newspaper as its hub, it is first necessary to know the type and quantity of school news that American newspapers are publishing which is the purpose of this study.

Only four national studies in this area have been carried out. Two were completed in the 1920's(2,3), the third in 1944(4), and the last in 1966(5). The data presented here are from the last study, although the findings of the four studies show that there have not been significant changes in the forty-four year period.

METHODS AND PROCEDURES

Subscriptions were taken to local newspapers serving twelve school districts in eleven different states. The subscriptions were generally for a three-month period, from which fifty consecutive issues were examined. The subscriptions evenly covered the period from September, 1964, to May, 1965.

The process of "content analysis" was used, whereby all news which could be classified into any of twelve categories of school news (School Buildings; The Value of Education; Pupil Achievement and Progress; Pupil Discipline, Behavior, Attendance; Teachers, Non-Teaching Personnel, Parent-Teachers Association; Methods of Instruction and Student Learning; Business Management and Finance; Administration and the Board of Education; School Sports; Extra-Curricular Activities; Pupil Health; Curriculum) was tabulated to the nearest column inch. A total of 3,588,000 column inches of news were examined in six-hundred issues, of which 62,461 were classifiable under the categories. A separate record of the front page coverage was also kept.

Selection of Newspapers

Social, Ethnic, and Geographical Factors in Selection of Cities. The cities and newspapers used in this study were chosen in order to make the sample as representative as possible of the United States as a whole. The twelve cities whose local newspapers were used encompassed all major ethnic groups and social classes. They are located in eleven different states in all the major geographical regions of the country. Thus Haworth and Guttenberg, New Jersey, and Mt. Vernon, New York, are in the East; Butte, Montana, and Fresno, California, are in the West; Sedalia, Missouri; Massillon, Ohio; Alexandria, Minnesota; and Waukegan, Illinois, are in the Mid-West;

TABLE 10.3   Column Inches Devoted to the Twelve Topics of School News
(Total of 62,456 column inches)

	Sports	Teachers	Administration	Achievement	Extra-Curricular	Methods	Finance	Buildings	Curriculum	Health	Discipline	Value	Totals Column Inches
Park Region Echo	3,062	186	160	237	309	32	24	15	62	45	0	0	4.132
Constitution	568	399	561	189	47	10	402	187	6	47	116	45	2,577
Montana Standard	2,380	351	207	342	494	265	241	29	28	0	0	18	4,355
Bee	1,947	582	822	166	138	336	300	87	185	8	20	34	4,625
Hudson Dispatch	2,515	513	186	172	47	56	65	85	92	34	41	18	3,824
Record	8,403	1,237	891	485	651	1,293	485	336	244	77	64	25	14,191
American Press	3,749	384	381	765	300	130	445	10	20	97	34	31	6,346
Evening Independent	1,528	578	355	660	254	523	144	168	32	137	40	7	4,426
Argus	1,853	660	370	380	266	452	149	119	245	124	35	39	4,692
Democrat	1,173	111	34	182	105	115	95	12	64	29	6	6	1,932
Tri-Cities Daily	2,109	116	36	262	292	268	116	90	78	20	0	24	3,411
News-Sun	3,187	823	1,108	516	1,213	199	465	240	107	45	11	36	7,950
TOTALS	32,474	5,940	5,111	4,356	4,116	3,679	2,931	1,378	1,163	663	367	283	62,461

and Lake Charles, Louisiana; Atlanta, Georgia; and Sheffield, Alabama, are in the South.

Population. The twelve cities in this study ranged in population from 3,800 (Haworth, New Jersey) to 487,455 (Atlanta, Georgia). Cities below three thousand in population often do not have their own school system and/or local newspaper. Those cities above five hundred thousand persons too frequently have newspapers with a national rather than a local orientation, resulting in a paucity of local news coverage, with local school news frequently being particularly neglected.

Economic and Occupational Structure. The twelve cities encompassed many diverse economic enterprises and hence included the majority of the occupational groups in the United States. For example, Guttenberg was made up of a number of small manufacturing concerns and small business enterprises, and Massillon had a large number of foundries and steel mills, in addition to extensive manufacturing. Mt. Vernon and Waukegan had a number of small businesses and manufacturing enterprises, and a large number of professionals; Atlanta was a major industrial city. Sedalia was composed of a large number of farms and quarries and had a television station, and Butte had a large number of mines and was the center of a thriving livestock industry. Lake Charles had oil wells and farms; Sheffield was near a large university and had many farms and mines. Fresno had a great deal of manufacturing, a large number of farms and orchards, and a number of colleges; Alexandria was a resort town with a large number of farms. Haworth was exclusively residential, made up of a large number of businessmen and professionals.

Newspapers. All twelve of the cities in this study had local newspapers. All were dailies, with the exception of Alexandria, whose *Park Region Echo* was published weekly. None of these newspapers was devoted exclusively to news of one particular category (labor news for example), and each was concerned with news of the local area. All the newspapers averaged at least ten pages per issue.

Major Findings
1. School news comprised 1.75 percent of all news. Of a total of 3,588,000 column inches of newspaper print there were 62,461 column inches of school news.
2. Notwithstanding geographic difference there was a marked similarity in the relative coverage of school news; the correlation among the newspapers in relative coverage was + .79. In total coverage, however, there were marked differences. The following total number of column inches of school news was found in the twelve newspapers examined: *Record* (Hackensack, N. J.)— 14,191; *News-Sun* (Waukegan, Ill.)—7,950; *American Press* (Lake Charles, La.)—6,346; *Argus* (Mt. Vernon, N. Y.)—4,692; *Bee*

(Fresno, Calif.)—4,625; *Evening Independent* (Massillon, Ohio)—4,426; *Montana Standard* (Butte, Montana)—4,355; *Park Region Echo* (Alexandria, Minn.)—4,132; *Hudson Dispatch* (Union City, N. J.)—3,824; *Tri-Cities Daily* (Sheffield, Ala.)—3,411; *Constitution* (Atlanta, Ga.)—2,571; and the *Democrat* (Sedalia, Mo.)—1,932. See Table 10.1 for the breakdown by category of school news and newspaper.)

3. There was an average of 5,205 column inches of school news for the fifty issues of each newspaper, or about five columns per issue.

4. School Sports received the most coverage in every newspaper. It received 52 percent of all school news coverage and constituted 42 percent of the total number of articles. (See Table 10.2 for the other percentages.)

5. All school news, less sports news, was equal to 0.84 percent of all news. School news less news of both sports and extra-curricular activities was equal to 0.72 percent of all news.

6. The average school news article was 13.1 column inches in length. The average school news article dealing with sports or extra-curricular activities was 5.4 column inches longer than articles dealing with the other topics.

7. There was an average of slightly more than four column inches of school news per issue on the front page.

8. School news was given proportionately greater coverage on the front page than it was throughout the entire newspaper.

IMPLICATIONS AND CONCLUSIONS

The data of the study show that it is highly doubtful that the citizens were being adequately informed on the activities, programs, and goals of the schools by the local newspaper. School news constituted less than 2 percent of all the news. With the elimination of news of school sports and other extra-curricular activities, the figure was less than three-fourths of one percent! This is equivalent to about five columns per issue including all school news, and a little over two columns per issue with school sports and extra-curricular activities removed.

The local citizens ultimately determine in some measure the nature of their public school system. It is they who in the long run have the opportunity to determine the curricula, the type and quality of the school plant, and the personnel that staff it. Yet for the local citizens to deal intelligently with school problems, they must be adequately informed. They must be made to realize the centrality of education in our contemporary society, and they must be familiar with the major aims of the schools (development of the students' intellectual capacities, the teaching of academic skills, and a major responsibility for the general socialization process of the students, to name a few) and the methods used by the schools to achieve these goals.

The amount of school news that can be printed in the local newspaper is limited, and school news must vie with other news and advertisements for the reader's eye. School administrators must therefore attempt to determine the interests of the people in their district in school news and to provide school news to the local newspaper that will not only satisfy these interests but also educate the public to the programs and activities of the school.

TABLE 10.4   Percentage of Column Inches and Articles
Devoted to the Twelve Topics of School News

Category	Percentage of Total Column Inches	Percentage of All Articles
1. School Sports	51.99	41.93
2. Teachers, Non-Teaching Personnel, Parent-Teachers Association	9.51	13.93
3. Administration and the Board of Education	8.18	9.16
4. Pupil Achievement and Progress	6.97	9.31
5. Extra-Curricular Activities	6.59	6.41
6. Methods of Instruction and Student Learning	5.89	5.21
7. Business Management and Finance	4.69	5.76
8. School Buildings	2.20	2.96
9. Curriculum	1.86	1.95
10. Pupil Health	1.06	2.00
11. Pupil Discipline, Behavior, Attendance	.56	.69
12. The Value of Education	.44	.67

References

1. American Association of School Administrators, *School Board-Superintendent Relationships,* (Washington, D. C.: National Education Association, 1956), p. 122.
2. FARLEY, BELMONT M., *What to Tell the People About the Public Schools,* (New York: Bureau of Publications, Teachers College, Columbia University, 1922).
3. FORD, EDMUND A., "A Study of Educational News in 16 Missouri Daily Newspapers," unpublished doctoral dissertation, University of Missouri, 1953.
4. GORDON, RICHARD J., "School News in the Local Newspaper and Readers' Interests Therein," unpublished doctoral dissertation, New York University, 1966.
5. GRINNELL, JOHN, "Newspaper Publicity for the Public Schools of the State of Minnesota," unpublished master's thesis, University of Minnesota, 1925.
6. MONAHAN, WILLIAM G., "An Analysis of the School Content in Michigan Papers: Comparisons with a Similar Study and Implications for School-Press Relations," unpublished doctoral dissertation, Michigan State University, 1960.
7. REYNOLDS, ROLLO G., *Newspaper Publicity for the Public Schools,* (New York: Columbia University, 1922).
8. THOMAS, WILLIAM J., "A Study of Interest of Readers of Public School Newspaper Publicity," unpublished doctoral dissertation, University of Pittsburgh, 1944.

The Comparative Study

Descriptive studies that make comparisons of phenomena serve a very useful purpose in the determination of relationships. At times comparative studies can show that phenomena have a cause-effect relationship. More often, the first study of a problem area through comparison techniques can only demonstrate associations without being able to establish cause-effect links. Comparative studies that ferret out relationships, however, can provide important clues for researchers who seek to determine causes through experimentation. The study that follows serves to illustrate the point.

The Relationship of Self-Images to Achievement in Junior High School Subjects

Wilbur B. Brookover, Ann Paterson and Shailer Thomas[*]

[*]Dr. Brookover is chairman of the Department of Foundations of Education, School of Education, Michigan State University. Mrs. Paterson is instructor in sociology, Purdue University. Mr. Thomas is assistant instructor of research at Michigan State University. The research survey is published in this text with the permission of the authors.

THE PROBLEM

The twentieth century is increasingly demanding people with high levels of education. In the future the lowest level of education and competence will be above what it is today. Much educational practice in the United States assumes that only a limited proportion of American youth is capable of high level educational attainment. Such an assumption may drastically limit the production of necessary educated personnel.

This study investigates one factor which may limit the learning of many students and thereby prevent them from achieving at higher levels. This factor is the student's self-concept of his ability as a school learner.

Theoretical support for the investigation of self-concept is found in the writings of George Herbert Mead and Arthur Combs and Donald Snygg. Research has indicated that there is a consistent relationship between self-concept and behavior. It is hypothesized that the child performs in the manner that is consistent with his self-concept which is acquired during interaction with significant others who hold expectations of the student as a learner.

In this report we have identified a sample of seventh grade students' self-concepts of themselves as learners; the relationship between self-concept and measured intelligence; and the relationship between self-concept and achievement.

OBJECTIVES

Three hypotheses and several related questions were investigated in this research project. The hypotheses tested may be stated as follows:

1. The self-concepts of high-achievers among junior high school students with similar levels of intelligence as measured by standard tests vary significantly from the self-concepts of low-achievers.
2. Students' self-concepts of ability in specific school subjects vary both from one subject to the other, and from their general self-concepts of ability.
3. The expectations of significant others as perceived by junior high school students are positively correlated with the students' self-concepts as learners.

While our primary focus has been on testing the above hypotheses, we have also raised several questions concerning the relevant variables in the study:

1. How are seventh grade students' self-concepts of ability related to measured intelligence, sex, family socio-economic status?
2. Who are the relevant significant others to whom seventh grade students relate themselves in examining their behavior as learners?
3. Do the significant others of seventh grade students vary by sex, family background, and achievement levels of the students?

4. How are seventh grade students' self-concepts of ability related to other measures of the students' perception of self and ability as a student?

5. What is the relative effectiveness of several measures of self and student ability in predicting school grades.

The questions reflect the exploratory nature of this phase of the study. Although several studies have attempted to relate some measures of self to school achievement, no study has focused on the particular aspect of self which we are seeking to identify — namely, self-concept of ability as a learner in school. We therefore designed a scale, the purpose of which was to assess this aspect of self-concept.

We then investigated the variations in both the students' self-concept of ability and their identification of significant others as these related to measured intelligence, sex, and family socio-economic status. An understanding of the possible variations in students' self-concept of ability and their interaction with their significant others is essential for the second phase of this research.[1] This understanding is necessary before any systematic steps can be taken to enhance school achievement through changes in self-concept.

PROCEDURES

Site of Research: The research was carried out in the four Junior High Schools in a mid-western city.

Sample: The sample consisted of 1,050 white seventh grade students for whom the school system had intelligence test scores and school grades since the fourth grade. For parts of the analysis, sub-samples of over- and under-achieving students were selected. These groups were selected by eliminating one standard error of measurement above and below the mean grade point average and intelligence test scores. This resulted in four categories of students: over- and under-achievers, and high- and low-achievers.

Data were gathered through the group administration of an extended questionnaire. A supplementary hour and a half interview was used to gather additional data from the over- and under-achieving students.

The following data were gathered by questionnaire on the 1,050 students:

Self-Concept of Ability-General, measured by an eight item scale devised for this project
Self-Concept of Ability in specific subjects, measured by items from the above scale
Ten Statements Test, ten responses to the question, "Who Am I?"
Student Role Test, ten responses to the question, "What Does a Student Do?"

[1] U. S. Office of Education, Cooperative Research project #1636 entitled "Improving Academic Achievement through Self-Concept Enhancement," W. B. Brookover, Jean LePere, Don E. Hamachek, and Shailer Thomas, Michigan State University.

General Importance of Grades, measured by a scale devised
for this project

Specific Subject Importance of Grades, measured by items
from the above scale

Ratings of school subjects as "best" and "least" liked

Rank of Importance of Grades in Subject

Model for Self, response to the question, "Who would you
most want to be like?"

Occupational Aspirations and Expectations

Educational Aspirations and Expectations

The following data were gathered from the school records:

4th year California Test of Mental Maturity

6th year California Test of Mental Maturity

California Reading Test

4th through 7th year grades in arithmetic, English, social
studies, and science

Education of Father

Education of Mother

Occupation of Father

Occupation of Mother

Schools attended during the 4th through 6th years

In order to test Hypothesis III concerning the relation of self-concept to the perceived images held by others, and to identify the significant others which were hypothesized to be of importance in the formation of the student's self-concept, one-hundred twelve over- and under-achieving students were interviewed. The topics covered in the interview were as follows:

Filled out by the student:

Identification of general significant others

Identification of academic significant others

Topics on which the subject was interviewed:

Family background

Significant others mentioned in the above identification

Peer group memberships

Daily schedule and activities

General orientation to school, school work, and teachers

Priority of academic role

Perceived images of significant others — ability of interviewee

Perceived images of significant others — attitude toward achievement

Analysis: Product moment, partial and multiple correlations, and
t-tests were the major statistical techniques used.

RESULTS

The major results of this study may be summarized as follows:

1. A self-concept of ability scale was developed in two forms —
general self-concept of ability and self-concept of ability in
specific school subjects.

2. Seventh grade girls have significantly higher mean self-concept of ability scores than seventh-grade boys.

3. Self-concept of ability is significantly related to school achievement of seventh-grade boys and girls. The correlation is .57 for each sex.

4. Self-concept of ability is positively related to school achievement in seventh-grade when measured intelligence is controlled. The correlation, with measured intelligence (partialled) out, is .42 for boys and .39 for girls. High-achieving groups also have a significantly higher mean concept of ability than do low-achieving groups with comparable measured intelligence scores.

5. The correlation between self-concept of ability and measured intelligence is .46 for boys and .48 for girls. However, the low .17 correlation between these variables when grade point average is (partialled) out indicates that self-concept differs from measured intelligence.

6. Self-concept of ability in four specific school subjects are related to seventh-grade achievement in those subjects combined.

7. A student's self-concept of ability in a specific school subject may differ from his self-concept in another subject as well as from his general self-concept of ability. Correlation coefficients between the two scale forms indicate that somewhat different variables are being measured. Mean self-concepts of ability in English and social studies are significantly different from mean general self-concept of ability among the boys. Similar differences are found in mathematic s and social studies among the girls. Specific self-concept of ability is a significantly better predictor of seventh grade boys' grades in mathematics, science, and social studies than general self-concept of ability. Among the girls similar results are found only in social studies. Sex and subject matter variation in these results preclude over-all generalizations concerning differences between a specific subject and general self-concepts of ability.

8. The hypothesis that a student's self-concept of ability is positively related to the image he perceives significant others hold of him is supported when parents, teachers, and peers are identified as significant others.

9. The family socio-economic status is positively related to seventh grade students' self-concept of ability, but it does not materially affect the correlation between self-concept of ability and school achievement or other variables in this study.

10. Parents were named by nearly all students as both "important in their lives" and "concerned about how well they do in school." School personnel, other relatives, and peers were named by many in response to each question, but by smaller proportions and usually after parents were named.

There were few differences in the distribution of persons named by sex, family socio-economic status, or achievement categories. The almost-universal identification of parents as "significant others" was the basis upon which they were selected as the "significant others" whose experimentally induced changes in expectations might affect the self-concepts of ability and subsequently the achievement of low-achieving students. This experiment has been undertaken in the second phase of this study.

11. Self-concept of ability is not highly correlated with other student self-ratings as obtained from the "Ten Statements Test" or the "Student Role Test." All correlations are less than .25.

12. Self-concept of ability is significantly related to "importance of grades," but the latter is not highly correlated with grade point average. Self-concept of ability is independent of importance of grades in predicting grade point average.

13. The mean specific subject self-concept of ability scores were significantly higher for those students who liked a subject best than for those who liked it least. This held for both boys and girls and for all four subjects.

14. Students who aspire or expect to go to college have significantly higher mean self-concepts of ability than students with lower educational aspirations or expectations. Somewhat more over-achieving students had high educational and occupational expectations than under-achievers, but the difference was not significant.

CONCLUSIONS

It is concluded that there is a relationship between self-concept of ability in the school situation and academic achievement. There is also a relationship between self-concept and the evaluations which the student perceives significant others make of him. These conclusions lead to the hypothesis that changes in self-concept will lead to changes in academic performance. The hypothesis that systematic changes in the self-concept of ninth grade low-achievers is associated with changes in school achievement is currently being investigated at Michigan State University.[2] The crucial test of the theory and demonstration of its value in meeting the needs for talented personnel depends upon this further research which will attempt to change self-concept and hence school achievement. The methods being used are: 1) modifying the images and expectations which existing significant others (in this case parents) hold of student's abilities, 2) by way of direct contact with the student introduce a significant other whose high expectations may be communicated to the students, 3) through counseling introduce a new significant other.

---

[2]*Ibid.*

If the hypothesized changes occur in these experiments, it will have been demonstrated that modification of self-concept will result in changes in academic performance. Such results will facilitate the development of talented personnel of our population who have the "innate" ability for successful achievement.

The next study serves to illustrate the use of the correlation method in comparative descriptive research to develop predictive formulae. Through the investigation of various factors, the researcher attempted to determine if it is possible to predict the reading improvement that will be made by children who are given remedial instruction.

Correlates of Reading Improvement
Stanley Krippner*

What differential effect does remedial reading have upon the achievement test scores of poor readers? What are the correlates of this effect? In other words, can reading improvement be predicted to some extent by such measures as mental ability tests, social maturity scales, and other tests of a similar nature?

The etiology of reading difficulties has been studied by several prominent investigators. In addition, the literature contains many valuable suggestions for the remediation of these difficulties. Less has been written, however, concerning the degree of improvement to be expected from a therapeutic program, the correlates of this improvement, and the types of poor readers most likely to benefit from remedial work.

THE PROBLEM

The main purpose of this investigation was to determine whether such variables as intelligence, social competence, vocabulary, mental health, socio-economic status, chronological age, grade placement, and amount of reading retardation were related to the degree of improvement manifested in a remedial program. These findings would be useful, it was thought, in the future selection and grouping of poor readers for their inclusion in therapeutic programs.

A subsidiary aim was to compute the progress made by poor readers categorized as to the major cause of their reading difficulties. It was felt that these results might give information regarding the types of reading problems which would be most responsive to remedial instruction.

All subjects were administered Form W of the California Reading Test on July 24, 1962, the first day of the clinic. The subjects met five days per week for one hour of individual reading instruction

Dr. Krippner is director of the Child Study Center, Kent State University, Kent, Ohio. The summary report of his study has been reprinted from the September, 1963, issue of *Education*. Copyright 1963 by the Bobbs-Merrill Co., Inc., Indianapolis, Indiana.

by 20 graduate students. The graduate students had all completed the sequence of reading specialization courses offered by the Kent State University Child Study Center.

PROCEDURE

The subjects for this study were 26 boys and four girls who received individual reading instruction and one hour of group instruction each day. On August 24, the last day of the clinic, each subject was administered Form X of the CRT. Progress for each subject was computed in years and months of an academic year.

Before the summer reading clinic began, each subject and his parents had been interviewed at the Child Study Center. In addition, each subject had been administered a battery of diagnostic tests. Ten items from these interviews and tests were selected for use in the present investigation. It was decided to correlate the degree of improvement in CRT scores with these ten variables to see which, if any, could have served as predictors of reading success. The variables are listed below:

1. Chronological age. Chronological age was represented in total months for correlation purposes.

2. Grade placement. Because the thirty subjects entered school two weeks after completing their work at the Child Study Center, their grade in school was placed at the beginning of the grade they planned to enter. For example, a child about to enter fourth grade was represented as having a grade placement of 4.0.

3. Degree of retardation. Scores on the initially administered CRT were subtracted from each subject's grade placement to yield his degree of retardation in terms of academic years and months. The Durrell Analysis of Reading Difficulty was administered each client to attain a more thorough understanding of his reading problem.

4. Father's occupational level. The occupations of all subjects' fathers were classified on the basis of the Roe Scale. Roe's classification is based upon the degree of responsibility, capacity, skill, and training demanded by an occupation. A research scientist, for example, is classified at the first, or highest, occupational level; a messenger boy is classified at the sixth, or lowest level. Occupational level is the most widely used single measure of socio-economic status and was included in the investigation for this reason.

5. Vineland Social Quotient. The Vineland Social Maturity Scale is a frequently used measure of social competence. The scale defines social competence in terms of self-sufficiency and utilizes a number of items to arrive at a Social Quotient (SQ). For example, a seven-year-old child is expected to tell time to the quarter hour. An eleven-year-old child should be able to care for himself in his parents' absence, etc. The

scale produces a "Social Age" which is divided by the chronological age and multiplied by 100 to arrive at the SQ.

6. PPVT Vocabulary Quotient. The Peabody Picture Vocabulary Test yields a Vocabulary Quotient (VQ) in much the same way that the Vineland yields an SQ. The test provides a standardized estimate of an individual's listening vocabulary. Since the subject is not required to read, this test is especially useful for work with poor readers. As with the Vineland SQ, a quotient somewhat below 100 indicates below average performance. Scores above 100 are higher than might be expected of the average child at that chronological age.

7. Verbal IQ on the WISC. The Verbal Scale subtests of the Wechsler Intelligence Scale for Children measure the subject's ability to perceive logical relationships and to use verbal and mathematical symbols.

8. Performance IQ on the WISC. The WISC Performance Scale measures the ability to handle practical, concrete, and manipulative situations. These subtests are essentially non-verbal in nature.

9. WISC Full Scale IQ. The WISC Verbal and Performance subtests are combined to yield the Full Scale IQ. This is the single WISC score most frequently utilized in clinical and educational settings.

10. Total Percentile on the Mental Health Analysis. The MHA is a standardized test designed to assess the subject's mental health. The authors of the MHA look upon mental health as the possession of personality assets and the freedom from liabilities to emotional stability. High percentiles, therefore, denote better mental health than lower percentiles.

The appropriate forms[3] of these tests were individually administered to all 30 subjects. The examiner read each question (e.g., "Do you often have bad dreams?") and the subject circled the appropriate response ("Yes" or "No") on his answer sheet. Such projective techniques as the Rorschach, the Thematic Apperception Test, sentence completions, and figure drawings were utilized to a greater extent in the diagnosis of each subject than the MHA but were not adaptable to correlation techniques.

The Pearson product-moment correlation was selected to examine the relationships of the ten variables to reading improvement. It was decided to check for statistical significance at the .05 and the .01

---

[3]Because there are no forms of the MHA below the fourth grade, the Primary Form of the California Test of Personality was used for second and third graders. The two tests are similar, having the same authors and many of the same questions in common.

levels of confidence. The null hypothesis stated that no significant positive relationships would emerge from the ten correlations.

It was also decided to compute the mean improvement scores when the sample was divided into etiological categories. Although reading problems are almost always the result of multiple causation, each subject's clinical interviews and diagnostic tests were used to determine the major underlying factor. An adaptation was made of Rabinovitch's classification system and the subjects were divided into five etiological groups:

1. Primary reading retardation due to brain injury.
2. Primary reading retardation due to a basically disturbed pattern of neurological organization.
3. Primary reading retardation due to visual or auditory impairment.
4. Secondary reading retardation due to emotional disturbance (anxiety, depression, counter-aggression).
5. Secondary reading retardation due to educational frustration and limited school opportunities (inadequate instruction, large classes, unfavorable cultural milieu, etc.).

The amount of improvement on the CRT was averaged for each group. This mean was compared to the mean score of all subjects who did not fall into that etiological category.

RESULTS

Some subjects made an improvement in CRT test-retest scores of considerably above one academic year. On the other hand, two subjects made no improvement. The mean improvement of the sample was .88, or nearly nine months.

All 30 subjects were classified according to the modified Rabinovitch system already described. Four clients were diagnosed as brain-injured, chiefly on the basis of developmental history, neurological records, and high scores on the Memory-for-Designs Test.

Eight poor readers suffered from a basically disturbed pattern of neurological organization. Each was characterized by a considerably higher WISC Performance IQ than Verbal IQ, as well as by symptoms which Rabinovitch has found to typify the neurologically disorganized. These include confused directionality, broad language deficits, body image problems, deficient time and quantity symbolization, and severely retarded spelling ability.

Two clients were visually or aurally impaired. The hearing loss of one client was diagnosed by a pure tone audiometric examination but was not considered serious enough to demand a hearing aid. Glasses had been recommended for the other client, but had not been fitted at the time of the summer clinic.

Seven clients were seen to have emotional problems which were the major factors influencing their reading difficulties. Diagnosis was made on the basis of interviews, projective techniques, and the MHA. In each case the emotional problem was seen to be more the cause than the result of the difficulty.

The largest category of poor readers was the educationally frustrated group. Nine clients were seen to be the victims of inadequate instruction and limited school opportunities.

The t-test was used to check for significance of differences between groups. No significant differences emerged, possibly because of the small numbers involved. However, the group showing the greatest differential effect of the summer program was composed of the educationally frustrated subjects. The mean CRT improvement of this group was 1.34, or one and one-third academic years. The brain-injured group's mean improvement was 1.27, while the neurologically disorganized group made a mean improvement of .70. The groups showing the least improvement were the emotionally disturbed, with a mean score of .44, and the visually or aurally impaired, with a mean of .25.

Table 1 presents the results of correlating ten variables with the degree of improvement noted for each subject. Two measures were found to be significant at the .01 level. These were the MHA percentile ($r = .46$, 28 df) and the WISC Verbal IQ ($r = .44$).

In addition, the WISC Full Scale IQ ($r = .37$) and the subject's grade in school ($r = .36$) were found to be significant at the .05 level. Chronological age ($r = .35$) and PPVT VQ ($r = .31$) approached but did not attain significance at the .05 level. Therefore, the null hypothesis was disproved by four of the correlations attempted.

TABLE I

Correlations of Related Variables to Subjects' Reading Improvement

Variable	Improvement
Age	.35
Grade	.36*
Retardation	−.23
Father's Occupational Level	−.19
Social Quotient	.01
Vocabulary Quotient	.31
WISC Verbal I.Q.	.44*
WISC Performance I.Q.	.05
WISC Full Scale I.Q.	.37*
Mental Health Percentile	.46**

*Significant at the .05 confidence level (28 degrees of freedom).
**Significant at the .01 confidence level.

DISCUSSION

The main purpose of this investigation was to determine whether ten variables were related to the degree of reading improvement manifested in a remedial program. Four of these variables appeared to be related to improvement for the sample studied, and could be considered predictors of success. Two additional variables approached a significant relationship and may, therefore, have some predictive value to the student.

If the purpose of a remedial program were to enroll those boys and girls who could be expected to make the most progress, those in the upper grades with high WISC Verbal and Full Scale IQ's, mental health assets, and extensive listening vocabularies should be selected. Younger subjects with mental health liabilities, lower WISC IQ's, and smaller listening vocabularies would not show as rapid improvement, according to this study.

On the other hand, such variables as the degree of retardation, social maturity, and the father's occupational level had the least predicitve value.

Further studies with larger samples are needed. This investigation, however, indicates that the absence of emotional disturbance and the presence of verbal intelligence can be fairly effective predictors of the progress to be made by poor readers enrolled in an adequately staffed remedial program.

Summary

Thirty subjects were administered Form W of the CRT during the first day of a five-week summer reading clinic. Form X was administered on the final day. The degree of improvement was computed by subtracting CRT W scores from CRT X scores.

Ten additional items were correlated with these scores which represented the differential effect of the remedial program. Those items which attained significance, and which would have the highest predictive efficiency, were the MHA percentile (.01), WISC Verbal IQ (.01), WISC Full Scale IQ (.05), and grade in school (.05).

A mean improvement on the CRT test-retest of nearly nine months was noted, with the educationally frustrated subjects manifesting greater progress than any of the other etiological groups.

Follow-Up

In July, 1963, a follow-up study was inaugurated. On a three-point scale, 16 parents replied that the clinic had been "very helpful"; seven replied that it has "helped somewhat"; no parents replied that the clinic had not helped.

The parents were also asked to record the grade in reading their child had received during the 1961-1962 school year, before attending the summer clinic. They were asked what grade their child had received during the 1962-1963 school year, after attending the summer clinic.

In arriving at a grade point average, no points were given for "F" grades. One point was given for a "D," two points for a "C," three points for a "B," and four points for an "A." Means were computed for the pre-clinic and post-clinic grades.

Before attending the clinic, a mean reading grade of 1.13 ("D") was received. After attending the clinic, a mean reading grade of 2.04 ("C") was received. When pre-clinic and post-clinic grades were compared, almost an entire grade's difference was noted. This is especially remarkable when it is remembered that poor readers often get poorer grades as they progress through school.

The following article by Brown and Galfo describes a causal-comparative study. It cannot be called a true experiment since the two groups compared were not established originally as experimental and control. Instead of this procedure, however, statistical and observational evidence is presented that the two groups were quite likely very similar in significant variables before one of them was exposed to new conditions.

An Evaluation of a Program for Developing the Reading Skills of Culturally Deprived Children

Virginia F. Brown* and Armand J. Galfo

Title I of the 1965 Federal Elementary and Secondary Education Act includes funds for providing programs to meet the needs of educationally deprived children of low-income families.

In February, 1966, the school district encompassing Westmoreland County, Virginia, submitted a project proposal under Title I . . . "designed to develop and improve reading skills of public school pupils . . ." in two schools of the district which have the highest percentages of low-income families. Funds were made available in the spring of 1966 and the project began at that time.

Westmoreland County, Virginia, is in a section of the state that is geographically known as the Northern Neck, the peninsula lying between the Rappahannock and Potomac Rivers. It is a rural county with its chief sources of income being farming, water (oystering, fishing, crabbing), small factories, small businesses, and government (U.S. Naval Weapons Laboratory at Dahlgren, Va.)

It was the purpose of the study, described by this paper, to compare progress in the development of the reading skill of pupils who had taken part in the project to pupils of equal background and ability who had not.

PROCEDURE

The two schools selected for the project in 1966 included about 40 percent of pupils from economically deprived families (as defined by federal regulations). Until recently, (the fall of 1968), the county operated its schools under a "freedom of choice" plan. As a result, the formerly all white schools have been integrated, but all negro schools, including the two target schools, have remained unintegrated.

*Virginia F. Brown is an elementary school librarian in Fredericksburg, Va.

The Title I project, which this study partially evaluated, attempted to create an enriched educational environment for the deprived children in the form of:

1. in-service training for teachers in developmental reading;
2. use of teacher aides in the reading program;
3. field trips designed to broaden cultural background knowledge;
4. increase in literary facilities (including a mobile library);
5. development of multimedia approach to teaching (including the equipping of each classroom with many audio-visual devices and materials).

One of the groups chosen for the study was the 1967-68 fourth grade in the two target schools which had been in the project during the second, third and fourth grades. The comparison group was the fourth grade of 1964-65 which had reached that grade level the year prior to the beginning of the project in the two schools.

A random sample of fifty pupils from each of the fourth grade classes was selected. Sociological variables were judged to be equal: the population of the schools had not changed in any discernible way since the population of the area is relatively static. Integration of the white schools had had but little effect on the target schools. To make sure, however, that the two groups were on a par with each other when they began school, two important variables, school readiness and intelligence, were tested for possible significant differences. This was done with group scores on the Metropolitan Readiness test, which is normally administered to all pupils in the county, during the early months of the first grade. The group I.Q. were also compared in terms of their scores on the Kuhlman-Anderson form (B) given in the second grade, and form (C) given early in third grade. Possible differences in I.Q. at the fourth grade level were also tested by comparing Lorge-Thorndike Intelligence test scores. This test is given in the fall of the fourth grade year.

Achievement at grade level four was measured and compared in terms of the Science Research Associates Achievement series. The areas tested by the series are: reading, language arts, mathematics, science, social studies, and work-study skills. For the purposes of the study, however, only scores on reading comprehension grade equivalent, vocabulary grade equivalent, and the composite grade equivalent scores were compared.

FINDINGS

Table 10.5 shows the results of an analysis of variance test of scores attained by the fifty pupils of the 1967-68 fourth grade and the fifty pupils from the 1964-65 fourth grade.

TABLE 10.5

Test	Grade Taken	F-Ratio
Metropolitan Readiness Test	First	.82
Kuhlman-Anderson (B) I.Q.	Second	1.13
Kuhlman-Anderson (C) I.Q.	Third	.87
Lorge-Thorndike I.Q.	Fourth	
Verbal-Grade Equivalent		4.18*
Total I.Q.		.42
Science Research Associates	Fourth	
Reading Comprehension grade Equivalent		8.64**
Vocabulary Grade Equivalent		6.2 *
Composite Grade Equivalent		1.94

*Significant at 5 per cent (with 1 and 98 df)
**Significant at 1 per cent (with 1 and 98 df)

In all significant comparisons, the 1967-68 class mean scores were higher than those of the 1964-65 group.

SUMMARY AND CONCLUSION

The results of the study indicate that the two groups very likely entered the first grade on an equal footing: most certainly they were equally equipped in terms of the factors measured by the Metropolitan Readiness test and intelligence factors measured by the Kuhlman-Anderson test.

By the time the two groups had reached the fourth grade, however, they could no longer be considered to be random samples of the same population in terms of reading comprehension nor vocabulary, as measured by the Science Research Associate tests. Even in terms of intelligence factors, as measured by the Lorge-Thorndike test, the two groups seem to have diverged when they reached the fourth grade.

Since the 1967-68 fourth grade group scores are higher than those of the 1964-65 fourth grade, it is concluded that the Title I project succeeded in its original goals to improve the reading skills of pupils in the target schools. It is also quite possible that improvement in measured I.Q. was the result of improved vocabulary and reading ability, but of course the study does not demonstrate this directly.

Much has been written lately about the need to provide opportunities for culturally deprived young children which will help them to catch up quickly to their more fortunate peers. It has been emphasized that unless this happens, the frustration of repeated school failure develops into a pattern of defeat that cannot be overcome in later years. The Westmoreland County, Virginia, project provides strong evidence that the school can bring some much needed childhood cultural advantages to the "disadvantaged."

Experimental Research

Experimental studies in education provide a major method to acquire new knowledge concerning the way the teaching-learning process takes place. Although the experimental researcher in the social sciences is faced with a very difficult task in establishing controls, recent developments in statistics have provided ways to design experiments and analyze data to produce meaningful results.

The summary which follows serves to illustrate the sophisticated experimental methodology and data analysis that are possible through the analysis of variance teachnique.

Effects of Rules of Thumb on Transfer of Training

Tracy H. Logan and Kenneth H. Wodtke[*]

A number of previous experiments (Hendrickson & Schroeder, 1941; Hilgard, Irvine, & Whipple, 1953; Judd, 1908; Overing & Travers, 1966) have demonstrated that knowledge of a relevant principle facilitates transfer to problems which involve an application of that principle. Each of the above experiments have in common the fact that the principles taught were applicable to *all* of the transfer problems employed in the experiment. The principle had no exceptions. This situation is somewhat atypical of many instructional situations in which a number of principles of varying generality must be taught. The student's task is complicated by the need to learn exactly when each of several principles is applicable. Such a learning situation would seem to provide many opportunities for *negative* transfer.

A negative transfer situation may arise when rules of thumb for solving problems are taught. In the present discussion a rule of·

[*]This article appeared in the May, 1968 issue of the *Journal of Educational Psychology* and has been republished in this text with the permission of the *Journal* and the authors.

thumb is simply regarded as a principle having only very limited generality. Such rules are often taught in conjunction with a more general principle. They are quite common in subjects such as mathematics, statistics, and science, and are justified as shortcut, time-saving procedures. The great difficulty with most rules of thumb is that they are usually only applicable to a very limited class of problems. Due to its limited generalizability, a rule of thumb can rarely mediate transfer from an original set of problems to a new set of problems. Much more generally applicable principles are needed to facilitate transfer to new problems. In spite of its limited generality, however, a rule of thumb may be invoked in the transfer situation because of the student's tendency to overgeneralize its use, and his failure to recognize its exceptions. Experience in the classroom often testifies to the fact that students appear to have a strong set to "blindly" apply a rule of thumb regardless of its applicability.

Schulz (1960) has suggested that the same principles which govern transfer in verbal learning may apply to some aspects of problem solving. If a general principle and a rule of thumb were both associated with a common class of problems, previous research on transfer would lead to the prediction that each would tend to generalize to similar problems on a transfer task. Any generalization of the limited rule of thumb would lead to incorrect solutions on any transfer problems to which it did not apply. The interference of the rule of thumb with the application of the more general principle would be expected to increase when the transfer problems were highly similar to the training problems, and when students were unable to determine the relevant differences among the problems. This latter expectation is consistent with the finding that inadequate stimulus predifferentiation leads to increased negative transfer (Ellis & Muller, 1964; Gagné & Baker, 1950). Finally, one might also predict from the basic research on transfer that the degree of interference from the rule of thumb would be a function of the degree of original learning of the general principle (Underwood, 1951). If the general principle was overlearned, one might expect less interference from the limited rule of thumb.

The present experiment sought to provide information on two questions related to the above expectations:

1. What is the effect on transfer of including a rule of thumb having only limited generality in an instructional program designed to teach a more general principle?
2. Will additional opportunities to practice using the general principle reduce the amount of negative transfer resulting from the knowledge of the rule of thumb?

Method

Subjects

The subjects (Ss) for the investigation consisted of 79 students from an introductory educational psychology class who volunteered for the experiment, and were given course credit for their participation. The experiment was conducted during the spring term, 1966. Although Ss represented a variety of different majors, a large proportion were enrolled in the teacher education program.

Materials

The topic of instruction chosen for the investigation was the concept of significant figures at the level of high school or introductory college physics. The concept of significant figures was especially suitable for a study of the effects of rules of thumb on transfer, since teachers and textbooks typically employ several rules and principles in teaching the concept.

Instruction was presented to Ss in the form of a self-instructional programmed text. There were three versions of the program corresponding to each of three treatment conditions. Version 1 consisted of 37 main-trunk frames, remedial frames, and several practice problems designed to teach Ss the general principle of significant figures. The Ss were taught the basic reasons for the loss of significance in figures. The Ss were shown that when a measurement is taken, the accuracy of that measurement is restricted by the limits of the scale's graduations. Thus, in a measurement of 9.53 centimeters taken from a typical meter stick, the figure 3 representing 3 hundredths of a centimeter is usually estimated visually since the meter stick is not graduated in hundredths of a centimeter. Since different investigators are likely to vary in their estimates of such figures, the results of calculations involving these estimates will also vary. For example, the following problem illustrates the errors that are likely to be made, and the procedure for arriving at the "significant" figures assuming that the error in the estimated value is $\pm$ .01. The problem is to find the area of a rectangle whose sides are 9.53 and 8.67 centimeters long. One finds the largest and smallest values the length and width could have and from these the largest and smallest values the area could have, for example:

$$9.54 \times 8.68 = 82.8072$$
$$9.53 \times 8.67 = 82.6251$$
$$9.52 \times 8.66 = 82.4432$$

From these values it is seen that the only value that is absolutely certain in the answer is 82. The tenths figure could range from about .4 to .8, but it could not be as little as .2 or as great as .9 so some degree of confidence can be placed in the tenths figure. Since the tenths place was only partially certain, the hundredths place would be completely uncertain and could take any value from 0 to 9. From this reasoning one arrives at $82.\overline{6}$ as the correct number of significant figures with the tenths place marked to indicate only partial certainty in that figure. The above reasoning applies to all calculations involving measurements and therefore has wide generality.

All instruction was provided within the context of multiplication problems. Following the basic instruction on multiplication problems,

Ss' ability to transfer this basic reasoning to addition and trigonometry problems was measured.

Version 2 of the program was exactly like Version 1 except that immediately following the material on the basic principle of significant figures, Ss were given the rule-of-thumb section which included the following frame plus several illustrations of its application:

A Quicker Way For Determining Which Figures In A Calculation Are Significant.

The method you have used is excellent, but a bit slow. Here is a faster way. It is just a rule of thumb, and works only for products and quotients, not for addition.

Rule: When multiplying or dividing, the result has just as many significant figures as the factor with the fewest significant figures.

This version is referred to as the "rule-early" program since the rule of thumb was given immediately following instruction on the basic principle, but prior to a short practice segment.

The third version of the program was exactly like the second version except that the rule of thumb was introduced at the very end of the program following the short practice segment. Version 3 is referred to as the "rule-late" version. The practice segment was designed to provide extra practice using the general principle prior to the introduction to the rule of thumb. Thus, the only difference between Versions 2 and 3 of the program was the placement of the rule of thumb in the instructional sequence; either before or after a short practice segment. Table 10.6 summarizes the instructional sequences in the three experimental treatment conditions, and the associations which the instructional segments had been designed to teach.

The two rule-of-thumb versions of the program also contained several explicit warnings concerning the exceptions to the rule of thumb. Upon introducing the rule of thumb, Ss were told: "It is just a rule of thumb and works only for products and quotients, not for addition." After introducing the rule, Ss were told:

. . . as with many rules, there are occasional exceptions where the rule gives an incorrect answer. Therefore you are strongly advised to check *any* rule result by using the basic reasoning of significant figures until you get a feeling for when the rule works and when it doesn't—say, at least for the next week or so.

Immediately preceding the transfer test Ss were again told: "Although you have not practiced these, you can reason them out. Just trust your brain." In addition to these cues, the rule of thumb itself contains a cue to the limits of its applicability, thus, the rule states, "When *multiplying* or *dividing*, the results has just as many significant figures as the factor with the fewest significant figures." (The italics were not included in the experimental program.)

A pretest and posttest were developed to measure Ss' ability to determine the correct number of significant figures in a calculation. The pretest contained five problems designed to assess Ss' prior knowledge of significant figures. The posttest contained five multiplication problems and eight transfer problems. The eight transfer problems consisted of five addition or subtraction problems, and three trigonometry problems. The transfer problems could not be solved correctly by the simple application of the rule of thumb, but they could be solved by applying the basic principle of significant figures which was taught in Stage 1 of the instructional program. The Kuder-Richardson formula 20 reliability of the total 13-item posttest was .78 for the total sample of 79 Ss. For the sub-samples, the reliabilities for the five-item addition transfer test were .64, .75, and .72 for the no-rule, rule-early, and rule-late groups, respectively. The reliabilities at the three-item trigonometry transfer test were .53, .53, and .64 for the same three treatment groups, respectively. Some of the reliabilities are lower than those usually obtained for mathematics achievement tests. Although the lower reliabilities were in part due to the small number of items making up the subscores, the range of performance was also severely restricted since many Ss achieved perfect scores.

Procedures

A pool of 162 Ss in an introductory educational psychology class were given the significant figures pretest. Twenty-five Ss were uninterested in participating. Of the remaining Ss, only those whose pretest performance indicated minimal knowledge of significant figures (maximum scores of zero or one on addition and never more than two on multiplication with zero on addition) were asked to volunteer for the experiment. Seventy-nine students served as experimental Ss. The Ss were assigned at random to one of the three experimental conditions. Approximately 1 week after the administration of the pretest, Ss reported to a large classroom to complete the instructional program and the posttest. Two groups were tested on two successive evenings. Upon arriving at the experimental room, each S was given the version of the instructional program (either no rule of thumb, rule early, or rule late) depending on the experimental group to which he had been assigned. The seating arrangement in the room was staggered to prevent communication. Following completion of the instructional program each S was given the posttest containing the multiplication and transfer problems. After completing the posttest, the Rokeach Dogmatism Scale was also administered as part of a separate phase of the investigation. Following completion of this scale, Ss were thanked for their participation and dismissed. Approximately 2 weeks later, the nature and purpose of the experiment was explained to Ss.

TABLE 10.6 Experimental Paradigms and Associations Established
During the Different Experimental Stages

Stages of instruction	Condition 1— No rules	Condition 2— Rule early	Condition 3— Rule late
Stage 1—Pretest and basic instruction	Pretest Basic principle of significant figures in multiplication	Pretest Basic principle of significant figures in multiplication	Pretest Basic principle of significant figures in multiplication
Associations established	M→Pr	M→Pr	M→Pr
Stage 2—Introduction to rule of thumb and practice segment	Practice M→Pr	Rule given for multiplication M→Ru Practice M→Pr M→Ru	Practice M→Pr Rule given for multiplication M→Ru
Stage 3—Measure transfer and multiplication posttest	Multiplication posttest Transfer posttest Addition Trigonometry	Multiplication posttest Transfer posttest Addition Trigonometry	Multiplication posttest Transfer posttest Addition Trigonometry

Note.—Abbreviated: M = multiplication problems; Pr = general principle; Ru – rule of thumb.

RESULTS

Results were analyzed by means of one-way classification analysis of variance and Scheffé tests of individual comparisons. As a precaution against the possible effects of violations of assumptions underlying the analysis of variance, a Kruskal-Wallis one-way analysis of variance by ranks (Siegel, 1956) was also employed.

Means and standard deviations for transfer tests under each condition are shown in Table 10.2. Overall F tests were statistically significant for both the addition and trigonometry transfer scores $F = 12$, $df = 2/76$, $p < .001$ and $F = 3.5$, $df = 2/76$, $p < .05$, respectively). The mean of 4.5 achieved by the no-rule group on the addition problems, and the mean of 1.6 achieved by the same group on the trigonometry problems indicates that the instructional program in the basic reasoning of significant figures was successful in producing considerable transfer to problems which were not specifically taught in the program. Eighteen of the 26 Ss in the no-rule group achieved *perfect* scores of five on the addition transfer test. A Scheffé comparison of the mean addition transfer scores of the two rule-of-thumb groups with the no-rule group indicates that the inclusion of the rule of thumb in the instructional program produced a considerable decrement in transfer. The mean addition transfer score of the no-rule group was significantly greater than the means of the rule-early and rule-late groups (p values were less than .05 and .01, respectively). Whereas 18 of 26 Ss in the no-rule group achieved perfect scores on the addition transfer test, only 20 of 53 Ss in the two rule-of-thumb groups achieved perfect scores.

The detrimental effect of the rule of thumb appeared somewhat weaker in the case of the trigonometry subtest. The Scheffé comparisons indicated that the no-rule versus rule-late comparison was the only comparison which approached statistical significance at less than the .10 level, although the other comparisons were consistent in direction with the differences obtained for the addition test. The reduced statistical significance in the analysis of the trigonometry scores as compared to the addition scores may have been due to the smaller number of items and the resultant lower reliability of the trigonometry subtest.

The mean scores on the multiplication posttest (less one item which could not be solved by the rule-of-thumb method) were 2.9, 3.0, and 2.9 for the no-rule, rule-early, and rule-late groups, respectively. Thus, the differences in transfer of the three groups could not be ascribed to differences in achievement on the multiplication problems directly taught in the program.

The second question of interest in the study concerned the effects of the rule-practice sequence on transfer. It was hypothesized that an experimental condition in which a rule was given before a practice segment would have a more detrimental effect on transfer than a condition in which the rule of thumb was given after practice. It was expected that giving the rule of thumb late in the program would provide additional practice with the more general principle, thus reducing the amount of interference from the rule. This hypothesis was not confirmed. In fact, the only difference between the rule-early and rule-late groups which approached significance at less than the .10 level was in the direction opposite to that which was predicted. This unexpected finding may have resulted from the relatively short length of the practice segment (due to a limit on Ss' time only three problems were employed in the practice segment) or from a recency effect of giving the rule of thumb just prior to the transfer test which may have increased its saliency during the test situation.

Since a large number of Ss in the experiment achieved perfect scores on the transfer tests, the distributions of performance were generally negatively skewed. As a precaution against the possible

TABLE 10.7

Descriptive Statistics for the Three
Experimental Groups on the Two Transfer Tests

Transfer test	Condition 1 no-rule		Condition 2 rule-early		Condition 3 rule-late	
	M	SD	M	SD	M	SD
Addition (5 problems)	4.5	.9	3.5	1.6	2.6	1.7
Trigonometry (3 problems)	1.6	.7	1.2	1.0	1.0	1.0

Note.—In Condition 1, N = 26; in Condition 2, N = 27; in Condition 3, N = 27.

effects of violations of the assumptions of normality of distributions, Kruskal-Wallis one-way analyses of variance by ranks were also computed (Siegel, 1956). The results of this analysis were consistent with the results of the parametric analysis of variance (for addition $\chi^2 = 283$, $p < .001$, $df = 2$; for trigonometry $\chi^2 = 292$, $p < .001$, $df = 2$).

Discussion

Although the present findings should be replicated and extended to other subject matters and other rules, the results suggest that teaching a rule of thumb of limited generality in an instructional program designed to facilitate transfer by means of a more general principle may produce considerable interference. Since many subject matters include a number of rules and principles varying in generality, teaching methods may have to provide opportunities to reduce the amount of interference in such situations.

Several tentative explanations may be offered to account for the results obtained. Schulz (1960) and Gagné (1964) have suggested that the same principles which account for simpler forms of associative learning may also occur in more complex forms such as principle learning or problem solving. Following this line of argument, it is interesting to ask whether the transfer paradigm employed in the present experiment in any way resembles the classical negative transfer paradigms employed in experiments on verbal learning? The paradigms of the present investigation are outlined in Table 10.7.

During Stage 1 of the experiment, Ss were taught how to determine the correct number of significant figures in a multiplication problem (M) by resorting to the general principle of significant figures (Pr). During Stage 2, Ss in the two rule-of-thumb groups were taught how to solve the same class of problems (M) by resorting to a much quicker rule of thumb (Ru) and were given practice either before or after the introduction of the rule of thumb. In the no-rule condition, Ss simply received the practice segment. (The practice segments were equated in the three conditions.) During the transfer test or Stage 3, all Ss were exposed to a new set of problems which could be solved by the general principle, but not be the rule of thumb. Although all Ss had instruction in Stage 1 which should have enabled them to solve the addition and trigonometry transfer problems, Ss in the two rule-of-thumb conditions had also acquired the competing response of the rule-of-thumb strategy. If one assumes that the didactic verbal warnings which were provided to warn Ss about the exceptions to the rule were ineffective (an assumption which seems well-founded in the present study), then Ss would be unable to determine the appropriateness of the rule-of-thumb solution during the transfer test. Under such conditions we would expect a high degree of interference in the form of competing responses from the rule-of-thumb solution which had been previously associated with the correct solutions of multiplication problems. Incorrect responses may result from Ss' tendency to overgeneralize the rule of thumb without regard for the distinctions between the multiplication, addition, and trigonometry problems. Since these three classes of problems are by outward appearances quite similar, the tendency of Ss to overgeneralize the use of the rule of thumb would not be surprising. The above interpretation suggests that in teaching rules of limited generality, it will be necessary to provide discrimination training so that the student will be able to make the relatively fine discriminations between the classes of problems to which the rule is applicable and the problems to which the rule is inapplicable.

It is interesting that the present paradigm, although not entirely parallel, bears some resemblance to a retroactive inhibition paradigm in which two competing responses are associated with the same or similar stimuli. One of the authors is conducting follow-up research to determine whether the detrimental effect of the rule of thumb is simply the result of overgeneralization of its use, or whether other factors are involved. A tentative analysis of Ss' errors on the transfer tests suggests that at least part of the effect is attributable to overgeneralizing the rule of thumb or rule misuse.

The effect of the rule of thumb appeared similar to the effect of a strong persistent set which seems to "blind" Ss to alternative solutions as reported in several classical experiments on set by Rees and Israel, (1935) and Luchins (1942). This apparently strong set to use the rule of thumb rather than alternative solution methods may result in part from its simplicity, ease of recall, and ease of application. It is also possible that the typical college student has been strongly preconditioned to use such rules through years of previous instruction which has emphasized rule-of-thumb solutions.

The present results also resemble the results of Wertheimer's (1959) work on teaching children to find the area of a parallelogram, and Katona's (1940) match-stick problems. Both of these investigators found that a condition in which Ss were taught a general principle facilitated transfer when compared to a condition in which a less general principle was taught or where Ss simply practiced problems. In Wertheimer's study, children who were taught to find the area of a parallelogram by a specific solution could not transfer to problems in which the parallelogram was placed in a different position, or to different geometric figures. Furthermore, when the children were presented with the new problems, they would often attempt to blindly apply the old inadequate method. However, there is one important difference in procedure between the Wertheimer and Katona experiments and the present experiment. In these earlier experiments, Ss were taught either by the method utilizing the general principle *or* by the specific solution method. It is not surprising that the methods produced differences in transfer since one group was never taught the relevant general principle. In the present experiment, Ss were taught *both* a method based on a general principle and a method based on the rule of thumb. The fact that the rule of thumb interfered with transfer even when an appropriate alternative solution was available to Ss emphasizes even more strongly the dangers of negative transfer which exist when such rules are available.

It might be argued that the verbal warnings which were given to Ss were simply not strong enough to call their attention to the limitations of the rule. This possibility must be recognized. The writers would agree that other warnings might have been included which might have had the desired effect on Ss' behavior. The warnings used in the present study were selected a priori by the writers, after considerable debate concerning their relative strength. Unfortunately, it was not possible in the present study to determine precisely the effect of the verbal warnings, since a rule-of-thumb group without the warnings was not included. However, it seems likely that didactic statements alone may not be very effective in establishing the discriminations needed to apply different principles to different problems.

Rules and principles may be a great aid in problem solving; however, the present study suggests that teaching rules with only limited generality may actually interfere with transfer. If these findings are replicated in other problem solving situations, one would either recommend that rules of limited generality not be taught where one has the alternative of teaching a more general principle, or that the instruction include opportunities for the student to learn when to use each of the alternative methods. It is possible that the additional instructional time required to teach the student to recognize the exceptions to a rule of thumb will offset the increased problem-solving efficiency in the limited class of problems to which the rule of thumb applies.

References

ELLIS, H. C., AND MULLER, D. G., Transfer in perceptual learning following stimulus predifferentiation training. *Journal of Experimental Psychology,* 1964, 68, 388-395.

GAGNÉ, R. M., Problem solving. In A. W. Melton (Ed.) *Categories of human learning,* New York: Academic Press, 1964. pp. 293-317.

GAGNÉ, R. M., and BAKER, K. W., Stimulus predifferentiation as a factor in transfer of training. *Journal of Experimental Psychology,* 1950, 40, 439-451.

HENDRICKSON, G., and SCHROEDER, W. H., Transfer of training in learning to hit a submerged target. *Journal of Educational Psychology,* 1941, 32, 205-213.

HILGARD, E. R., IRVINE, R. P., and WHIPPLE, J. E., Rote memorization, understanding and transfer: An extension of Katona's card-trick experiments. *Journal of Experimental Psychology,* 1953, 46, 288-292.

JUDD, C. H., The relation of special training to general intelligence. *Educational Review,* 1908, 36, 28-42.

KATONA, G., *Organizing and Memorizing.* New York: Columbia University Press, 1940.

LUCHINS, A. S., Mechanization in problem solving: The effect of Einstellung. *Psychological Monographs* 1942, 54 (6, Whole No. 248).

OVERING, R. L. R., and TRAVERS, R. M. W., Effect upon transfer of variations in training conditions. *Journal of Educational Psychology,* 1966, 57, 179-188.

REES, H. J., and ISRAEL, H. C., An investigation of the establishment and operation of mental sets. *Psychological Monographs,* 1935, 46 (6, Whole No. 210).

SCHULZ, R. W., Problem solving behavior and transfer. *Harvard Educational Review,* 1960, 30, 61-77.

SIEGEL, S., *Nonparametric statistics for the behavioral sciences.* New York: McGraw-Hill, 1956.

UNDERWOOD, B. J., Associative transfer in verbal training as a function of response similarity and degree of first-list learning. *Journal of Experimental Psychology,* 1951, 42, 44-54.

WERTHEIMER, M., *Productive thinking.* New York: Harper's, 1959.

Selected Exercises

1. Prepare abstracts of several of the studies which have been summarized in the chapter. Include in the abstract your own statement of the problem; description of the limitations, working hypothesis and method of research; summary of the findings; summary of the conclusions drawn; and critique of the study.

2. May North and Buchanan conclude from their study that if the teachers of middle-class children exchanged places with teachers of poverty children, the attitudes of both groups would change?

3. What other statistical test could have been used in the study described by Brown and Galfo?

4. Did some of the authors overgeneralize from their studies? If so, give examples and explain why you have selected the examples.

5. Why did Brookover, Paterson and Thomas refrain from concluding that changes in self-concept will lead to changes in academic performance?
6. Could Krippner have used analysis of variance to check for significance of difference between groups? (See his "Results.") Explain your answer.
7. Why did Logan and Wodtke choose to use the analysis of variance method to analyze data?
8. What are some possible reasons why the study described by Brown and Galfo was carried out as a causal-comparative, or ex post facto, research rather than as an experiment?

Suggested Activities

1. Prepare an abstract of the following:
   a. A historical study in education
   b. A survey study in education
   c. A comparative study in education
   d. An experimental study in education

2. For each of the studies abstracted, list the factors that led you to categorize it as historical, survey, comparative, or experimental.
3. In suggested activity number 1 of Chapter 9 you were asked to select a problem that has been discussed in faculty meetings in your school.
   a. State the problem in a clear concise manner.
   b. Prepare a research proposal that may lead to a solution. Include hypotheses to be tested; limitation that may need to be imposed; the method of attack; data to be gathered; and the method by which data would be analyzed.

Selected Readings

1. BARNES, JOHN B., *Educational Research for Classroom Teachers*. New York: G. P. Putnam's Sons, 1960. (Part II Case Studies)
2. COREY, STEPHEN M., *Action Research to Improve School Practices*. New York: Bureau of Publications, Teachers College, Columbia University, 1953. (Chapter 3)
3. GOOD, CARTER V., *Introduction to Educational Research* (Second Edition). New York: Appleton-Century-Crofts, 1963. (Chapter 9)
4. GOOD, CARTER V., A. S. BARR, AND DOUGLAS E. SCATES, *The Methodology of Educational Research*. New York: Appleton-Century-Crofts, Inc., 1941. (Appendices I and II)
5. MOULY, GEORGE J., *The Science of Educational Research*. New York: American Book Co., 1963 (Chapters 14 and 15)
6. VAN DALEN, DEOBOLD B., *Understanding Educational Research*. New York: McGraw-Hill Book Company, Inc., 1962. (Appendices B, C, D, E, F, G and H)

Chapter 11

Typical Applications
of Research

"Action Research"

The term *action research* has been used by Stephen Cory[1] and others. It is meant to distinguish the efforts of practicing school personnel to improve school practices from the endeavors of researchers who are not involved in the everyday business of educating children. Some students of research have become alarmed by the possible implication that action research conducted in schools can differ somehow from what they regard as sound methodology. Trained researchers are also troubled by the possible conflict between research efforts by practitioners and their own investigations. The issue may be clarified if two questions can be answered:

1. Is there conflict between what is implied by "pure" educational research and action research?
2. What should action research entail?

Actually, there should be no more conflict between pure and action research in education than there is between basic investigations in the physical sciences and engineering research or between research in biology and the medical practice. The purpose of basic inquiries in the physical and biological sciences is to gain new knowledge. Engineering and medicine are interested primarily in the application of principles discovered by the theoretical sciences; this is called developmental research.

---

[1]Stephen Cory, *Action Research to Improve School Practices*. New York: Bureau of Publications, Teachers' College, Columbia University 1953.

Then — if an analogy may be drawn in the field of education — basic researchers should discover principles; action researchers should discover how best to apply the principles. Some overlapping of purpose is bound to occur just as it does in the natural sciences, but research application, or developmental research, occupies an important place in education as it does in other fields.

Presented in the sections that follow are a few examples of how school systems have applied ideas that have their foundations in basic research conducted in recent years. The articles have been taken from yearbooks of the Associated Public School Systems. (The Association was established for the purpose of publishing and disseminating the results of studies conducted in schools throughout the country.) The studies were selected because they exemplify "action research" in the sense that it has been defined — as developmental or applied research.

Ungraded Elementary School

The nongraded plan is predicated upon the principle of individual differences in learning. The theory is that since children differ in their ability to learn and since individuals learn different tasks at different rates, lock-step grade promotion is unrealistic.

Sand, Davis, Lammel and Stone,[2] writing in the June, 1960, issue of the *Review of Educational Research*, indicated that ". . . the development of the nongraded elementary school was a significant change in school organization during the period under review . . . . Many of the schools described were reported to have adopted a nongraded structure because of dissatisfaction with promotion policies, reporting practices, and other immediate concerns."

Although the ungraded elementary school has been gaining popularity, the reason for the adoption of the plan caused schools to experiment with similar plans many years ago. The famed Winnetka plan of the 1930's had many characteristics of the modern ungraded school. The characteristics of ungraded schools are as follows:

1. Emphasis on the individual child's development and ability to learn the various things he is required to learn in the elementary school.
2. A flexible organization that allows each child to proceed at his own rate of learning.

---

[2]Ole Sand, Don Davis, Rose Lammel and Thomas Stone, "Components of the Curriculum," *Review of Educational Research*, Chapter III Volume 30, No. 3; June 1960.

Some evidence has accumulated to favor the nongraded elementary school over the graded school. The evidence is not conclusive, however, and it is apparent that more research is needed. Trial of the plan should do much to help educators evaluate the concept. Projects such as the one that follows have resulted from an interest in research into the use of ungraded schools; in turn, the projects themselves can help researchers to develop more studies that may provide answers for emerging questions.

Four Years With the Ungraded Primary Plan
Marlin Baxter*

Historically speaking

Interest in the ungraded plan or organization began in the Moline Schools during the school year of 1956-57. Discussion within several school staff groups on the numerous aspects of such programs then in existence led to a trip by the primary teachers of two schools to visit the schools at Park Forest, Illinois. Their plan had been in operation for a number of years. Following this further orientation was carried out through the Parent Teacher's Association and mother study groups. Letters of information were sent out to parents and others.

By this time teachers and administrators had fairly well developed the plan of organization desired. In the spring of 1957 children in Grant School were not promoted but were merely assigned to a particular group to which they would return in the fall. Grade designations were dropped. The following year Logan and Roosevelt Schools, after considerable discussion and orientation among teachers and parents, decided also to adopt the ungraded or primary plan. Logan had postponed a start a year earlier because of administrative and teacher changes.

At Roosevelt School it was decided to try a somewhat different approach to changing from the graded structure. The first year only the first grade was ungraded, so that orientation principally involved the parents of the kindergarten children. The next year the second grade and in the fall of 1960 the third grade were ungraded and became a part of the primary plan. Present plans call for a fourth school to be involved this coming fall.

We have felt that where proper planning, orientation, and education have been carried out, the result has been significantly improved operation. Another strong factor has been the enthusiasm or desire on the part of the teachers.

Philosophy

Certain fundamental principles as follows are basic to the plan:
1. Growth is continuous, developmental, and multidimensional.

---

*Mr. Baxter is director of curriculum in the Moline, Illinois, public schools. The article has been published in this text with the permission of Mr. Baxter.

2. Each child is unique, having his own rate and pattern of growth. Consequently, each has his own standards of achievement to attain.
3. In the growth structure there may be spurts, plateaus, and even regression in the learning curve.
4. The common developmental tasks faced by all children should be worked at when the appropriate maturity level is reached.

Basic Structure

Replacing the common graded plan of grade one, grade two, and grade three is a series of levels identified as follows:

Level 1 — Readiness Activity
Level 2 — Preprimer
Level 3 — Primer
Level 4 — First Reader
Level 5 — Second Reader, 2/1
Level 6 — Second Reader, 2/2
Level 7 — Third Reader, 3/1
Level 8 — Third Reader, 3/2
Level 9 — Extension of Skills

It can be seen that primary emphasis is given to reading development, however, other academic areas as well as emotional, physical, and social growth needs are given due recognition at all times. We feel that sound and adequate reading skill development in the early school years is most important. Immediately following kindergarten, readiness test data and judgement of the kindergarten teacher are the most significant factors used in the grouping of children. From that point on children are grouped as homogeneously as possible with respect to reading development. Whenever possible class sizes are adjusted so that slow growing children are in smaller groups than others.

Promotion and retention, as commonly defined, have been eliminated for all practical purposes. Each child advances at his own rate, moving to a new level at any time of the year. We feel that each should not leave a particular level until the teacher is satisfied that adequate goals have been reached, thus we are not forcing into the middle grades children who are unprepared for the more difficult tasks there. The child who is mentally low may be an exception. We have found that children tend to move in small groups as a rule, rather than as individuals. Shifting may be carried out within the classroom, or it may mean that the child will go to another classroom. If the latter occurs, the child may be placed in the new situation for a part of the day for several weeks on a trial basis to see how he or she adjusts to the change. Parents are invited for a visit during this period. Children coming in from a "graded" school are placed wherever all of the evidence we can acquire seems to indicate they should be placed. Children leaving the "ungraded" plan are identified by reading level and also as to the grade into which they might best fit. A high degree of flexibility must be maintained over the entire plan.

"Where will the child work best?" and "Where will he accomplish the most?" are important criteria in the shifting or placement of children.

For the most part teachers have a new group of children each year; only rarely does one teacher have a particular child for more than one school year. Different ability groups are rotated among teachers so that one teacher or one classroom does not have the same type of children every year.

Reporting pupil progress

Attempts to measure growth in terms of grades such as A, B, C, etc., and/or other symbols have been eliminated in the plan. Since such symbolization is so largely a matter of competitive evaluation it does not seem to have a place where each child is seeking to attain a goal of his own. Some evaluative terms may be used on daily written work.

Reports to parents are made four times a year in addition to the many informal contacts. An identification of the child's reading level, together with a short letter, goes to the parent at the end of the first nine weeks of school. At midyear a parent-teacher conference program is carried out. At mid-spring and at the end of the year a form, which teachers have developed, is used. The form uses some comparative terms such as seldom, sometimes, competently, carelessly and the like in relation to certain specified academic and social skills. Numerous approaches are used in getting parents to visit in their child's school or classroom. In the initial stages of any primary school plan, parent education is particularly important.

Problems

Orientation of new parents is a continuous responsibility; the kindergarten group brings new parents into the system and new families move in each year. A *Handbook for Parents* provides some help. Parent-teacher contacts bring about the best results.

A second problem arises from those children who may be maturing slowly or developing at a slower rate than others. Frequently parents of these children, and occasionally the teacher too, have a difficult time accepting the point of view that programs need to be "stretched out" for these children. Progress is measured by these people in terms of time only, or in terms of the completion of particular books. The children who mature and learn quite rapidly have problems of an opposite nature; horizontal enrichment seems to be a partial solution. Because of some degree of relationship between mental ability and success in reading, a third problem is tied in with ability grouping. A few parents do not wish to have their children in a slow group regardless of what might be best for the child. A few teachers have not had sufficient skill to deal adequately and in a satisfying manner with children where most of the group tends to be developing slowly. In these situations nonhomogeneous grouping practices have been used, such as placing average and slow or average and high abilities in the same classroom.

Evaluation

Teachers in the plan have said such things as the following:

"We can concentrate on the individual growth patterns of each child rather than on the traditional markings and artificial group standards."

"Ability grouping, which helps to remove the extremes, gives the teacher an opportunity to adapt teaching methods and materials to the individual needs, abilities and interests of each child."

"Even though it is difficult to sell the idea of a lengthened program to some parents of slow-starting children, this child appears to be happier, more secure, and to be making continued progress."

Test scores seem to indicate that high ability children do better under this plan than under a purely hetergeneous grouping arrangement in a graded school. It may be that they have been "freed of the burden" of being so long with slow learning children. Acceleration has not been common; only two children in four years have gone through the three years in less than that amount of time. Approximately ten percent of the children in the three schools have or are spending an additional year in school under the primary ungraded plan. Carefully controlled research experimentation is needed if any reasonably valid conclusions are to be reached on the basis of objective data.

Ability Grouping

Research in ability grouping has been carried out since the 1930's. A superficial examination of the results of studies into the problem indicates that the evidence regarding desirability of grouping is contradictory. Closer scrutiny of the form and substance of the research reveals the reason why the evidence conflicts.

One of the major sources of confusion has been that programs for groups of variable abilities have not always been designed to fit the groups. The problem of selection criteria has also been a difficult one to solve. In earlier studies single or limited criteria such as I.Q. or achievement test scores proved unsatisfactory in differentiating between individual abilities for grouping purposes.

Recent research and critical analysis of studies in grouping indicate that good results tend to occur from ability grouping when the following conditions have been observed:

1. Students are grouped according to ability subject by subject.
2. Many criteria are used in selecting students for groups.
3. Groups are not stable: there is ample opportunity for students to move from one group to another when conditions warrant.
4. An effort is made to bring about understanding on the part of parents and students that the sole purpose of grouping is to facilitate learning.

5. Teaching procedures and courses of study are adopted to fit the abilities of students in the groups.

Two projects conducted in schools that are widely separated geographically will serve to illustrate the use of research findings for the purpose of establishing ability groups.

Grouping by Subject — A Two Pronged Approach
Robert J. Schild*

Introduction

Much has been written and spoken recently on the age-old question of homogeneous grouping, including Dr. Conant's recommendation for grouping by subject. A great many schools are grouping in one fashion or another in the hope that the procedure will bring them somewhat nearer the goal of providing challenges for the different levels of ability. In the secondary schools in Nyack, we believe the goal can be approached by grouping, based on a number of fundamental concepts.

1. Groups remain flexible with regard to movement in and out.
2. Combination of measures is used plus teacher recommendation.
3. Grouping is by subject.
4. The curriculum is significantly modified for the different groups.

How It Works

In social studies and English we have established four basic groups, with an "AD" or honor section for the student with high ability and achievement and a "C" section for those students needing revised approaches to academic material. There are two intermediate groups designated A and B which contain high average youngsters in one and the average and just below average student in the other.

Early in the spring the teacher, guidance counselors and principals make their recommendations for groupings for the following year. This is done individually by the teacher and then conferences are held on the different grade levels, and in the subject concerned, to exchange information and make the decisions on the final grouping designations. Available to teachers and counselors are extensive pupil data sheets produced on the I.B.M. machines and containing all of the ability, aptitude, and achievement test data available for each student. Each teacher, counselor and administrator has copies of these sheets for his particular grade level, with the coded recommendations of teachers for grouping and class grades in the various subjects. Tests included are I.Q., Scholastic Aptitude, School and College Ability Tests, Sequential Tests of Educational Progress, Achievement Tests, Reading Tests and Differential Aptitude Tests.

---

*Mr. Schild is director of research and curriculum in the Nyack, New York, public schools. The article has been published with his permission.

In the grouping process, it is emphasized that there should not be dependence on any one test score or on any individual recommendation. Where there is some doubt as to the proper grouping, conferences are held and the emphasis is placed on giving the student an opportunity to perform at the highest possible level. The student may find himself in a top grouping in English and a somewhat lower grouping in social studies.

Running concurrently with this and based on the same type of selection process, our science and mathematics programs enable the students capable in these subjects to accelerate their program by one year. In mathematics the students complete two years of mathematics in the seventh grade and study biology in the ninth grade; in both cases, they then have additional opportunity for advanced placement work in the senior year.

A careful check is kept at all times on the progress in the Nyack Schools. One of the basic objectives has been to have teachers do a reanalysis of their syllabus with regard to variations for the different groups. Thus, in English for example, a complete new syllabus is just being completed which provides for a different literature, grammar and writing experience for the different groups in English. The AD or Honors group has placed particular emphasis upon a sequential program emphasizing complete works in literature and an expansion of opportunities for written composition. Much of this revision has been done with the help of a university consultant. Similar variations are being made for the other groupings, including differences in both content and methods of instruction for the lower C sections.

Results to date of this program, which has been in operation some three years, have been generally very satisfactory. There has been a very positive reaction on the part of instructors that they are better able to deal with the different general ability levels and the reaction of the students has been one of a general raising of the level of academic achievement and respect for intellectual ability. Everyone agrees that the approach must be constantly evaluated and any problems immediately ironed out and a continuous revision of content and method must be made for the different groups.

Columbus High School's Program for the Academically Talented

John P. Deason°

Introduction

With a student body of whom more than 80 per cent each year go on to college, Columbus High School has traditionally had a curriculum strongly oriented towards college preparatory work. In an effort to strengthen such a curriculum and to offer greater challenge to the superior student, Columbus High moved in the spring of 1960 toward what will

---

°Mr. Deason is the principal of the Columbus High School of Muscognee County, Georgia. The article has been published with Mr. Deason's permission.

be in 1961-62 a three phase program for providing enlarged opportunities for academically talented pupils.

Advanced Placement

In the spring of 1960, six seniors who were chosen on the basis of I.Q. and achievement tests, grades, and recommendations of teachers, were enrolled for one course at Columbus College, a two-year community college, in addition to their normal load at high school. During the 1960-61 school year, seven students have participated in the program. Grades in the college courses have been uniformly high and the pupils' high school work apparently has not suffered from the additional load. Students who have participated have endorsed the program enthusiastically. The evaluation committee, made up of representatives of both the high school and college, has recommended the gradual expansion of the project. It will be continued in 1961-62 for seniors who have been identified as among the academically talented and who choose to participate after personal counseling with professional staff members of the high school.

Enrichment

To provide more practice in writing for pupils in English classes, three lay readers were employed in January, 1960, to work with six English teachers, making it possible for students to have a theme graded and returned each week. The teacher herself grades one set of themes each week, rotating among her classes so that she can keep in touch with the work of individual pupils.

Two social studies teachers experimented in team teaching for one unit in American history in the spring of 1960, making it possible to offer more individualized work for both superior pupils and those less gifted. Other teachers in each department do some grouping within regular classes to offer chances for enrichment to talented pupils.

Enrichment and acceleration opportunities specifically for superior students in 1961-62 will include the following:

1. Being allowed to take a fifth academic course.
2. Special work assigned or developed in regular classes (for example, independent research projects, extensive reporting in classes, entering contests, seminars to make use of community's resource people).
3. Being given the opportunity to help teachers by acting as tutors for those teachers who request this assistance.

Honor Courses

In the fall of 1961, two sections of Algebra I were designated as honor courses. They included pupils from feeder schools who had been given some algebra in eighth grade classes (varying from six weeks to a half a year). It is intended that these classes will cover five years' work in four.

Identifying Talented Students

Under the impetus of membership in the Superior and Talented Student Program (which originated in the North Central Association and has been participated in this year by some half dozen schools in the Southern Association), about 200 pupils have been identified for participation in some phase of the school's program for its most talented students in 1961-62. Each of the pupils, accompanied by at least one parent, has had a personal and/or a group counseling session with guidance and administrative personnel of the school to determine what phase of the program will best suit his needs and challenge his abilities. Only seniors will be eligible for the Columbus College course. Other phases . . . enrollment in honor courses, taking a fifth major subject, doing special work in regular classes, tutoring or acting as teacher assistants . . . will be open to all grade groups.

Talented pupils have been identified using a scale of 20 points and the following criteria:

Intelligence Quotient			*Achievement Test Percentiles*		
79 and below	1	point	19 and below	1	point
80-89	2	points	20-39	2	points
90-110	3	points	40-69	3	points
111-120	4	points	70-89	4	points
121 and above	5	points	90 and above	5	points

Past School Record			*Present School Record*		
Failing (below 70)	1	point	Failing (below 70)	1	point
D average (70-76)	2	points	D average (70-76)	2	points
C average (77-84)	3	points	C average (77-84)	3	points
B average (85-92)	4	points	B average (85-92)	4	points
A average (93-100)	5	points	A average (93-100)	5	points

The composite scores from these four variables are ranged using the scale following. An academically talented pupil must score in the first range of the scale . . .17 to 20.

SCALE

17-20
13-16
8-12
4-7
9-3

In-service Activities

Professional staff members actively engage in attacking cooperatively identified problems through:

1. Reading (The Muscogee County School District not only maintains extensive professional libraries at the Bradley Memorial Library and the central administrative office, but also encourages the development of such collections at each individual building.)
2. Participation at local, state, regional, and national professional conferences and conventions. (Both Dr. J. Lloyd Trump, Associate Secretary of the N.A.S.S.P. and Director of N.A.S.S.P. Staff Utilization Committee, and Dr. J. Ned Bryan, Director of the Project on the Guidance and Motivation of the Superior and Talented Student project, co-sponsored by the North Central Association and the Southern Association of Colleges and Secondary Schools, visited Columbus during the spring of 1961.)
3. Building meetings which include regular general faculty sessions and smaller departmental, grade group and special interest meetings.
4. Supervisory and advisory services from the office of the director of instruction and the State Department of Education.
5. Course work during the summer months in many institutions and regular term work made possible through the efforts of the University of Georgia and Auburn University.
6. A summer workshop in which many staff members have indicated an interest in developing plans and materials at a time when both general and specialized consultative assistance could be made available at Columbus High School.

Major evaluative efforts are being made to measure progress toward stated objectives. These are:

1. To identify academically talented pupils.
2. To plan cooperatively with parents and pupils individual programs for the identified pupils in keeping with their exceptional abilities.
3. To encourage full development of pupil aptitudes and interests through their participation in these planned programs.
4. To utilize staff-talents, abilities and time more effectively.
5. To develop teacher competencies to work with academically talented pupils through varied in-service activities.
6. To use more effectively resources available (local, from foundations, from institutions of higher learning and from the Georgia State Department of Education) in meeting the needs of the Columbus High School pupil population.

Thorough evaluation of this program is developmental in nature in that it must parallel the evolution of the program. Methods to be used are as follows:

1. To undertake a periodic comprehensive study of the pupils' participation in the project in order to appraise the effectiveness of the identifying criteria, to discover possible leads for subsequent counseling interviews with pupils and parents, to determine extent

of participation in projects, and to determine individual growth toward objectives of the project.

2. To hold periodic project committee meetings for the purpose of subjective appraisal of the project to date.

3. To hold periodic meetings with representatives from the project committee, participating teachers, and participating pupils for the purpose of subjective appraisal and feedback (the exchange of ideas, concerns, feelings, or other comments).

4. For each project participant to write a narrative log periodically to record pertinent anecdotes, attitudes, feelings, implications, and ideas.

5. To develop and use a questionnaire type of instrument to aid in determining the extent to which the objectives are being met. A different form will be developed for teachers, pupils, and parents.

6. To institute a comprehensive follow-up study of project pupils which will, among other things, aid in determining the effectiveness of the total program.

Teaching Foreign Languages In the Elementary School

The emergence of the United States from its isolationist position prior to World War II to its present position in the leadership of the free world has stimulated interest in foreign languages at all levels of our society. By 1955 more than one quarter of a million pupils in the elementary grades were involved in foreign language instruction in the elementary school. Since that time many more schools have begun teaching elementary children one or more foreign languages.

Research reports indicate that children are able to make remarkable progress — especially in learning how to speak and understand the spoken word in foreign language learning. For example in an evaluation of pupil progress in French taught in grades 3 and 4 at the University of Chicago Demonstration School, Harold B. Dunkel and Roger A. Pillet[3] found that children's pronunciation was superior to that of adults.

Research shows that the major problems which have cropped up as a result of FLES (Foreign Language in the Elementary School) are:

1. Poor articulation with foreign language instruction in secondary schools.

2. A shortage of teachers qualified to teach in FLES programs.

3. A lack of evaluative devices and criteria for appraisal of FLES programs.

---

[3]Harold B. Dunkel and Roger A. Pillet, "The French Program in the University of Chicago Elementary School." *Elementary School Journal* 57: 17-27; October, 1956.

If schools are to succeed in the initiation of FLES programs, they must take steps to solve the problems. The Collingswood, New Jersey, school system brought foreign language teaching to its elementary schools in 1960 after an extensive study of the research and projects conducted by other school systems.

FLES (Foreign Language in the Elementary School) and the Long Range Language Program in the Collingswood, N. J., Public Schools

Jacqueline Benevento*

Introduction

A great deal has been written in the past few years about the need for increased language study and the importance of teaching the spoken language The traditional two-year high school course, designed to satisfy college entrance requirements, has proved to be very inadequate. Further, the grammar-translation method has produced students who can neither understand the spoken language nor speak it with any degree of confidence.

We recognize that we cannot speak like a native in just a few weeks by buying a set of language records; it is also true that one does not learn to speak a language by the process of translating strange symbols into English, using vocabulary lists and sets of rules and exceptions. Our pupils want to learn to understand and speak as well as to read and write the language they are studying, and in order to train them as hearers and speakers, a much longer sequence than two years is necessary.

Background Study

The decision to start a FLES program in the Collingswood Public Schools was not made hastily. Serious consideration was begun a few years ago. Successful long range programs elsewhere were studied, and in order to learn about the techniques of the audio-lingual method, two members of the department attended NDEA Summer Institute in French and Spanish. We accumulated a large professional library of references pertaining to FLES and longer sequences; attended conferences on the local, state, and regional level; visited schools with language laboratories, and talked with colleagues about the language program in their schools. A very important factor was our community interest in a FLES program.

When the Board of Education and the Superintendent of Schools decided in the Spring of 1960 to introduce the study of a modern language in the grades the following September, we had ample background on which to draw to plan our program.

---

*Miss Benevento is district coordinator of foreign language in the Collingswood, New Jersey, schools. The article has been published with her permission.

Which Language?

We had no large ethnic group in our town to take into consideration, so it was decided to offer either French or Spanish inasmuch as most of the successful programs have been in these languages, and a great percentage of our high school pupils elected them.

The Traveling Teacher

We decided to employ a teacher to move from school to school, since most classroom teachers, however competent, are not prepared to teach foreign languages. Although televised language programs are available in our area, and although TV instruction is better than no instruction or poor instruction, we felt it could not compare with a skilled language teacher in the classroom.

The language to be offered, then, would be determined by the availability of a qualified teacher. We were fortunate to find a teacher who had had two years' experience in working with elementary school children, and who had taught Spanish at the high school level for four and one half years. Although she had no previous experience teaching FLES, she set about enthusiastically to visit schools with FLES programs and to read our accumulated references.

The Time Schedule

Since we would have only one teacher to visit all five elementary schools, we decided to initiate the program in grades 4 and 5, setting up a plan in which she would teach all pupils in these grades three times

	MON.	TUES.	WED.	THURS.	FRI.
9:00-9:20	Garfield 4	Tatem 4a	Tatem 4a	Garfield 4	Garfield 4
9:30-9:50	Garfield 5	Tatem 4b	Tatem 4b	Garfield 5	Garfield 5
10:10-10:30	Zane-North 4	Tatem 5	Tatem 5	Sharp 4a	Zane-North 5a
10:40-11:00	Zane-North 5a	Newbie 4	Zane-North 5a	Sharp 5a	
11:40-12:00				Sharp 4b	
12:00-1:00					
1:00-1:20	Tatem 4a	Sharp 4a	Sharp 4a	Newbie 4	Newbie 4
1:30-1:50	Tatem 4b	Sharp 4b	Sharp 4b	Newbie 5	Newbie 5
2:00-2:20	Tatem 5	Sharp 5a	Sharp 5a	Zane-North 4	Zane-North 4
2:30-2:50		Sharp 5b	Sharp 5b	Zane-North 5b	Zane-North 5b

Note: On Thursday mornings and Wednesday afternoons, the teacher allows less time between classes and schools in order to finish by 11:30 and 2:30, respectively.

weekly in scheduled twenty-minute periods of instruction. Since we also have traveling teachers in music and physical education in the grades, it was necessary to set up a schedule which would not conflict with their classes. The program involved 365 pupils in 14 classrooms, and the actual teaching time varied between 140 and 200 minutes per day.

FLES Offered to All Pupils

We decided to offer Spanish to all pupils, not just those with high I.Q.'s, or those whose parents would give them special permission. The learning of a language from a functional point of view, that is, hearing and speaking, involves mimicry and memorization at this level and does not demand above-average intelligence. Children of average intelligence can do quite well in languages when they start at an age before their linguistic inhibitions set in. Moreover, the child of below-average intelligence often seems to gain confidence in seeing himself on an equal footing with his classmates. The intellectual maturity necessary in other subject areas does not seem to be required for functional language learning at this point.

Immediate Preparation

In the Summer of 1960, our traveling teacher received the MLA Guides in Spanish for Grades 3, 4, and 5[4] and other references which we had ordered for her and began to plan her lessons for the coming year.

Early in the school year of 1960, before she initiated her classes, an overview was sent to all principals and classroom teachers involved, stating that the over-all objectives of language study were the achievement of the skills of understanding, speaking, reading, and writing, an understanding of a culture other than one's own, and personal enrichment. We explained the audio-lingual method and sketched the techniques to be used by the teacher: dialogues based on units of vocabulary concerning familiar daily activities, songs, games, dramatizations, and the use of realia. It also included the goals we expected the pupils to achieve, within the limits of the material taught to them. We explained the importance of cooperation by the classroom teacher in relation to the success of the program. They were not asked to do follow-up instruction but were requested to show their pupils by their attitude that they found the study of Spanish interesting and worthwhile. We suggested that they provide some opportunity during the school day for the use of phrases, games, and songs learned. A bibliography of thirteen references on FLES was added for those interested in additional information.

Our Long Range Program

In addition to good teachers, a long range program is essential to the success of FLES. It is important that one language should be studied long

---

[4]Modern Language Association of America. *MLA Teacher's Guide: Beginning Spanish in Grade 3; Spanish in Grade 4; Spanish in Grade 5*. Darien, Conn., Educational Publishing Corp., 1955.

enough for competence and ease of expression. This means a continuous, well-articulated sequence of several years. The following program was developed by the Assistant to the Superintendent in Charge of Instruction and the Coordinator of Foreign Languages after a great deal of study, conferences, and consultations with language specialists.

Year of Intro-duction	Grade 4	Grade 5	Grade 6	Grade 7	Grade 8	Grade 9	
1960	Spanish	Spanish					
1961	French	Spanish	Spanish				
1962	Spanish	French	Spanish	Spanish			
1963	French	Spanish	French	Spanish	Spanish		
1964	Spanish	French	Spanish	French	Spanish	Spanish	10-11-12
1965	French	Spanish	French	Spanish	French	Spanish	10-11-12
1966	Spanish	French	Spanish	French	Spanish	French	10-11-12
1967	French	Spanish	French	Spanish	French	Spanish	(et seq.)

The district plans to introduce French in the Fall of 1961 in grade 4, while continuing to offer Spanish to the pupils who would then be in grades 5 and 6. French and Spanish will be alternated in grade 4 each year thereafter, so as to maintain a balance between the French and Spanish enrollment at the high school level. Our new senior high school will be ready for occupancy in 1962, and crowded conditions now in existence in both the junior and senior high schools will be eliminated. Our first group of FLES Spanish pupils will reach grade 7 in 1962, so continuity of their language program will be assured.

An Outline of Content and Objectives by Grade Levels

Since our language offerings up to last September comprised only three years of Spanish, French, and German in grades 10, 11, and 12, and three years of Latin in grades 9, 10, and 11, it was imperative that we develop an articulated program. We have been guided in the main by two references: *Modern Foreign Languages and the Academically Talented Student*[5] and Language and Language Learning.[6] It may be necessary as we progress in our program to allocate specific activities to

[5]Starr, W. H., M. P. Thompson and D. D. Walsh. *Modern Foreign Languages and the Academically-Talented Student.* Report of a Conference sponsored jointly by the National Education Association Project on the Academically Talented Student and the Modern Language Association of America, Foreign Language Program. 1960.

[6]Brooks, Nelson. *Language and Language Learning: Theory and Practice.* New York: Harcourt, Brace and Co. 1960.

different grade levels, but at least we have established guidelines to aid us in the planning of our work.

Grades 4, 5, and 6

In grades 4, 5, and 6 language will be offered to all pupils three times a week for twenty-minute periods. Dialogues concerning familiar situations and presenting authentic speech patterns will be introduced by the teacher and then repeated and memorized by the pupils. Dialogue adaptation will be accomplished by means of questions and answers, directed dialogue, and dramatizations. Stories will recombine vocabulary items in narrative form. The objective will not be how much material is covered, but how well it is learned. There will be songs and games, but no grammatical analysis or translation. The skills of reading and writing will be deferred until grade 6, when the skills of hearing and speaking will have been established. The question of whether to give marks to these pupils is still under discussion.

By the end of grade 6, the pupil will be expected to use, without thinking about rules of grammar, most of the syntax patterns of normal conversation. He will have a modest vocabulary, encompassing all the sounds in the target language. He will be able to understand and reply to all material based on the dialogues he has learned, without recourse to English or the printed word. He will not be expected to write what he has not first read, to read what he has not first said, or to say what he has not first heard. He will have a knowledge of some of the culture of the country where the language is spoken.

At the end of grade 6, screening will take place for those pupils who will be continuing the study of language in light of their aptitude and interest. FLES teachers, guidance directors, and parents will cooperate in making this decision. Those who continue will be expected to study the same language.

Grades 7 and 8

Language will be an elective starting in grade 7. In grades 7 and 8, language will be offered three times a week for regular class periods. There will be increased emphasis on reading, with the pupil in grade 8 able to read material which has not been first presented orally. Dialogues and pattern drills will be continued. Writing will take the form of copying of material already read, dictation of known material prepared beforehand, and completion exercises. There still will be no translation. Some recorded materials and filmstrips can be used profitably.

The pupil at the end of grade 8 will be expected to have increased his vocabulary and mastered all the structure patterns. He should be able to read material suitable to his age level and understand without translating.

Grades 9, 10, 11, and 12

In grades 9, 10, 11, and 12 language will be offered five times a week for regular class periods. Reading material of literary merit, consisting of fiction and nonfiction, will be read and discussed with a gradual increase in difficulty. Dictionaries in the foreign language will be used. Writing will include directed compositions, imitations of the style of the author being studied, and résumés. Pattern drills will be completed, and grammatical summaries will be presented. Current magazines and newspapers can now be used to advantage. The language laboratory will play an important part. In grade 12, translation will finally be employed. The Advanced Placement Program can be put into effect in grade 12.

While a person's competence in a foreign language will always fall short of that in his native tongue, we expect the student who has completed the 9-year program to have near-native fluency in understanding, speaking, reading, and writing, and he will be able to express himself confidently and spontaneously. He will have read some works of literary merit, and will have learned to appreciate another culture.

A Two-Track Program

It is in grade 9 that we plan to begin the second track of our program by offering beginning French, Spanish, German, and Latin for those who will have come from sending districts without FLES and for those FLES pupils who are linguistically talented and wish to begin a second language while continuing the first. We do not recommend dropping the FLES language and starting another, since the full benefit of the 9-year sequence will not be realized in that case.

College-bound students should be required to have a 9-year sequence of one language if they have had FLES, a 4-year sequence of one language if they have not. All other pupils should be permitted to discontinue their foreign language studies whenever they show neither interest nor aptitude.

Keeping the Board of Education and the Community Informed

When community support is desired, it is necessary to keep the Board of Education and townspeople informed of progress in all new ventures. The traveling teacher and the Coordinator during this school year have appeared before the Board of Education, the Citizens' Committee on Education, and a Parent Education group, explaining the audio-lingual method, the importance of language study, and the national interest in the teaching of foreign languages. We presented the background of the FLES movement and explained our FLES program: why we are teaching French and Spanish, the traveling teachers' time schedule, why the program is offered to all pupils, and what are the necessary qualifications for FLES teachers. We then outlined our long range program and played a tape of an actual segment of one of our FLES Spanish classes.

At every presentation, the audience reacted to the contagious enthusiasm of our teacher and children as evidenced on the tape — it was most gratifying. Comments from parents assure us that we have embarked upon a worthwhile, vital experience in the education of our boys and girls; one that is continuing the forward motion of our goal of quality instruction to every student.

Science in the Elementary School

Recent emphasis on science teaching in the schools has caused renewed efforts to improve science instructions at the elementary level. George and Jacqueline Mallinson[7] reported in the June, 1961, volume of the *Review of Educational Research* that: "Although the quality of research dealing with elementary school science still leaves much to be desired, there is some evidence that its quality has improved with recent years. More studies now deal with the 'how' of instruction and methods for improving instruction, whereas earlier studies were largely surveys." From the researches they reviewed, Mallinson and Mallinson reported that there are indications that:

1. The elementary science curriculum is generally lacking in continuity and fails to articulate with science instruction in the high school.
2. Two major stumbling blocks to good science instruction are lack of equipment and inadequate teacher preparation.

Some school systems have recognized the validity of the research findings and have solved the problems through reorganization; changes in the curriculum, the staff, and the school plant. This head-on approach is examplified by the Mount Pleasant Special School District of Wilmington, Delaware.

A New Approach to Science in Our Elementary Schools
Mrs. Claude Corty[*]

Fulcrum, protozoa, solute — these are rapidly becoming everyday terms for fourth, fifth, and sixth graders engaged in a new science program at Silverside Elementary School. In addition to gaining scientific knowledge, these pupils are learning to use the scientific method in tackling problems.

This new program was inaugurated because the science subject matter in the upper grades was no longer fully challenging the capabilities of the pupils, nor was it arousing the kind of interest essential in any good science program. Furthermore, there had been too much learning of science by reading in textbooks rather than through active pupil experimentation and discovery.

---

[7]Mallinson, George G., and Jacqueline V. Mallinson, "Science in the Elementary Grades," Chapter I, The Review of Education Research volume 31; No. 3 p. 235-247.
[*]The article was prepared by Mrs. Corty and based upon information supplied to her by J. G. Rockwell, Principal of Silverside Elementary School, and his staff. Mrs. Corty is public relations co-ordinator of the Mount Pleasant Special School District of Wilmington, Delaware. The article was published with her permission.

Organization

Silverside School's new science program for the upper grades involves three basic changes: the subject matter has been revised, the teaching methods have been altered, and the staff has been reorganized.

Three of the upper grade teachers have become science teachers for three class periods each day. These science teachers are relieved from teaching social studies and arithmetic. By the same token, the upper grade teachers of social studies and arithmetic teach only their specialty for these three periods.

Role of Experiments

Experimentation by each pupil working on his own, or in groups of no more than four, is the touchstone of Silverside's new science program. Before carrying out any experiment, pupils, together with the teacher, determine and state the problem they are exploring. They discuss how they could go about investigating the problem. They speculate about what might happen in the experiment. They assemble the equipment and execute the experiment. They then draw their conclusions and, whenever feasible, formulate a generalization. Finally, the students record the experiment step by step in their manuals.

This experimental procedure is followed for all science areas whether they be earth science, plant biology, or chemistry. In former years, the teachers conducted the experiments in front of the entire class or one pupil worked up an experiment and then demonstrated it to the class.

Occasionally, a pupil's experiment does not succeed. This is not considered a failure. The class discusses what could have gone wrong. Were instructions followed? Were the measurements accurate?

The science areas to be covered in the three-year program are wide and varied. They include the following: the universe, matter and energy, conservation, atmosphere, earth science, living things, cells, botany, electricity and magnetism, sound and light, atomic energy, gravitation, human body, and chemical reactions. Currently, materials published by the Living Science Laboratories Inc. and the National Science Foundation are being used by Silverside teachers.

Cost

With only three teachers holding science classes in the upper elementary grades, only three classrooms have had to be supplied with science materials. All the pupils can use the same equipment when their turn for science class comes. As a result, the new science program has not proved to be expensive for the school system.

Tentative Appraisal

The pupils' response to the new program is one of excitement and real interest. Even those with no scientific bent enjoy the individual experimentation and the active participation in the classroom.

For the science classes, the pupils have been grouped according to grade level and their mathematical abilities. This grouping has proved to be very satisfactory.

The teachers are enthusiastic about the new curriculum. They feel that they are really teaching science instead of teaching about science. They find that individual experimentation by the pupil has definitely increased the student's interest in and understanding of science. Since the course of study is new, the three science teachers have to spend much time preparing their daily lessons, but the results are well worthwhile.

The three set periods a day devoted to science, mathematics, and social studies have made the school day somewhat rigid.

Aim Restated

The aim of the new science curriculum at Silverside Elementary School is not to make scientists of all children. It is rather to teach the fundamentals of science in a meaningful way and to develop reasoning skills in all of the pupils. It is hoped that the students will learn from their science courses how to question, how to test, and how to draw their own conclusions. This will be helpful to them whatever they do in later life.

Team Teaching

The term "team teaching" has been used in recent years to describe processes by which pupil instruction becomes a group rather than an individual effort. Unfortunately, although some research has been made on the use of team teaching, there still is not much information available concerning many aspects of the concept. Apparently the team idea has evolved from research into the general area of teacher utilization.

It would seem, therefore, that whatever will be learned about the team concept will need to evolve from a study of experience accumulated by school systems that are willing to experiment with the idea. Two interesting reports on team teaching appeared in the 1963 *Yearbook* of the Associated Public Schools. As with the projects on ability grouping, the two schools reporting are widely separated geographically, but a remarkable similarity in approach can be noted. One of the school systems that reported on team teaching in the 1963 *Yearbook* was Bellevue, Washington, the other was Chatham Borough, New Jersey.

Team Teaching Experiment Draws Enthusiastic Response From Students and Teachers
Jesse M. Hartman*

Introduction

More skillful utilization of teacher talents and flexibility in instructional techniques, possible through a team teaching program, should enable

*Dr. Hartman is the director of community services in the Bellevue, Washington schools. His article was adopted from a report by the Sammamish High School American history and literature teaching team. The article has been published with the permission of Dr. Hartman.

students to acquire a more fundamental and enriched mastery of subject matter and permit them to develop more decisive and functional study skills.

Such, at least, was the premise upon which Bellevue School District's Sammamish High School introduced the team teaching approach to the study of eleventh grade American history, American literature, and composition.

During the 1960-61 school year, a number of teachers at that school investigated the advantages and disadvantages of the team teaching instructional method as it might be applied to several subject areas, either within a single department or as an interdisciplinary approach. As envisioned by the teachers in their initial planning, team teaching could provide opportunities to handle large groups for lectures and films; small groups for discussion, recitation and seminars; and independent study time in which staff members could provide supervisory and instructional assistance to students. It was also felt that the special skills and talents of each teacher could be exercised more efficiently and effectively, thus permitting students to undertake their studies with opportunities for more individual attention than is provided in the additional departmentalized class program.

With administrative approval and encouragement, two teachers from the English department, two from the history department, and the school librarian devised a course in American history and English. With the aid of extended contracts to work a few days prior to the opening of school, the staff members formulated certain objectives to be reached through a team approach with selected classes during the 1961-62 school year.

Objectives

In order to channel its efforts and provide a consistent approach to teaching through the course of the year, the team agreed upon the following objectives:

1. To develop more enriched insights into the development of American literature and its contributions to American culture.
2. To develop more enriched insights into the nature of history, and particularly the development of American history.
3. To enable each student to learn and progress according to his own individual ability.
4. To stimulate and encourage the student to further growth and understanding of human relations.
5. To develop the ability to work independently as well as in various groups.
6. To heighten the students' awareness of the influence of literature upon the nation's development.
7. To show through literature that history is made by people, not events.
8. To enrich the history and English programs through correlation of content and method.

9. To provide flexibility of classroom size which would enable students to participate in various groups and individual activities.
10. To develop a greater responsibility in the student for his own learning.
11. To provide and utilize special teacher talent.

Organization for Learning

Members of the teaching team attempted to use an approach which would avoid segregation of students into artificial ability groupings which might lend themselves to differentiated instructional attitudes. The team tried to provide an opportunity for each student to attain maximum achievement in a learning environment which encouraged competition as well as stimulation for individual self-attainment. The teachers also hoped there would be more opportunity for individualization of instruction through more direct academic counseling by five staff members acting cooperatively.

The experimental program involved ninety-six eleventh grade pupils, and consisted of those students regularly assigned to the participating teachers during the fifth and sixth periods of a seven-period high school day. An effort was made to have heterogeneous grouping, with only those students excluded who were assigned to the special education program. Intelligence quotients ranged from 87 to 141, with accumulative grade point averages ranging from 1.6 to 3.96.

Facilities included the four classrooms normally assigned to the participating teachers. In addition, the choral classroom and choral practice rooms were made available during the two-hour block of time, as were the library classrooms and library conference rooms. With these facilities, learning space was available for large and small group instruction and independent study within the two-hour block of time. The four classrooms were adjacent to one another and located near the choral room, in order that student traffic from one area to another during the two-hour period was made as convenient as possible.

All four teaching members of the team were provided a common planning period for daily consultation and coordination of team efforts. During the course of the program, teachers handled those topics and supervised those activities upon which they had mutually agreed during their daily cooperative planning sessions. Although team members normally alternated their large group lectures, there were opportunities for teachers to prepare in depth for particular topics or themes when the team felt the need for such emphasis.

Coordination of instructional materials was handled by the librarian working with the other four team members and was an integral part of the team approach.

Evaluation

Evaluation of the team teaching program in American History and English at Sammamish High School was limited by a lack of standardized measurements and required a great deal of reliance upon the professional judgments of participating teachers. Sources of evaluation were the student records maintained by teachers and the observations and consultations of the teachers as the program developed and progressed.

The team teaching approach, as employed at Sammamish High School, has proven to be most successful, and though certain aspects of organization and instructional procedure need to be refined, the program merits continuation and expansion.

Faculty members on the team, through a joint daily planning period, were able to plan their activities in such a way as to arrange their major responsibilities in the program considerably in advance of the time that they would have to be carried out, thus enabling better preparation of lectures and more effective organization of material. At the same time, greater confidence in performing various activities was gained as a consequence of better preparation and the sharing of anticipated objectives with other team members. Joint planning for both daily and weekly objectives provided greater sharing of ideas and selection and presentation of materials.

Through a sharing of supervisory activity, each teacher was freed to give more attention to individual students and to various groups of students than could be given in the traditional classroom.

Teachers were able to maximize their strong points and minimize their weak points, particularly with reference to their academic and experience backgrounds. By the very nature of their academic training in the social studies and literary fields, some individuals are more interested in or knowledgeable about special areas than others. By pooling these special areas of interest and skills, the team was able to present to the students a more varied and stimulating program of activities than could one teacher acting alone in a traditional classroom. Team members provided a more valuable use of their time and contributed their talents and skills more ably and effectively than they were able to when acting alone.

Because all members of the teaching team were together at all times during the block period except when students were grouped in classroom sizes with their regular teachers or when members of the team circulated among discussion groups, each teacher became more knowledgeable in the particular topics being discussed by other members of the team. Such close observation and contact among staff members, however, required a teaching team which was in every respect composed of compatible personalities, a factor which cannot be minimized for a successful team program.

The curriculum was strengthened and students were offered more challenges because of the improved instruction and greater variety of activities. In addition, selection of content in the program was evaluated by five persons rather than by one, as would normally occur in the traditional classroom approach.

Facilities were used more effectively in the team approach. For such flexibility of space to be utilized with maximum efficiency, however, flexibility of facility should be incorporated into basic building design. Since existing facilities at Sammamish High School have a rigidity of purpose and a premium for use, less than ideal circumstances existed for team teaching activities. Nevertheless, existing facilities did provide for adequate space and utility to accomplish much more flexibility of space and time than could be achieved in the traditional teaching areas for social studies and language arts.

The most noticeable inadequacy in facilities, other than an appropriate area for large group instruction, was that of library space to handle large groups of students. At no time were all members of a large group able to use the library together; thus independent study activity by individual students was severely limited by the inaccessibility of resource materials, especially since most of the appropriate material was required to be on the reserve list in the library.

Through the coordination and integration of content, instruction, and course organization, students developed better study habits with resulting higher levels of performance than comparable groups in traditional classes taught by members of the teaching team. Especially noticeable was the attitude of the students; those in the team teaching program demonstrated a more independent and aggressive spirit of inquiry and set for themselves higher standards of performance than those in the same subjects in regular classes. Students in the team teaching classes developed much better writing skills, more reflective analysis and evaluation of content, and expressed themselves in both oral and written forms more ably and enthusiastically.

Recommendations

Assuming that the primary purpose of the instructional program is to provide high quality educational opportunities for students of all levels of abilities and academic inclinations, and that this purpose noticeably stands above all other considerations, the following recommendations are presented as outgrowths of the successful team teaching instructional method at Sammamish High School.

1. If the maximum academic potential of all students is to be fully developed — whether the formal education of any particular student is to be terminal or college preparatory at the secondary level — a re-evaluation of the role of the secondary level library should be made. It was demonstrated dramatically through the team teaching approach that existing limitations in the scope and depth of library source material severely restricted the intellectual growth of students, inasmuch as they could not pursue independent inquiry and research as they desired.

2. As careful and as great a consideration should be given to the composition of the personalities of the members of the teaching team as is given to their academic background and professional experience. The compatibility of personalities is essential for the close and harmonious activity and planning necessary to carry through an effective program. While the personalities of the team members must be compatible, they must also be strong in order

to prevent a weakening of the program through submissiveness to unwise or ineffective selection and presentation of such materials.

3. Members of a teaching team should be provided with a joint conference period for coordinating and implementing their daily activities, evaluation of activities already completed or in progress, and future activity planning. This planning period should be exclusive of planning for other classes or responsibilities. Such a joint conference appears to be indispensable for a first attempt at a team approach, especially if team members have had no previous experience with such a demanding endeavor, and if the program involves the tremendous paper work required in the social studies-language arts areas.

4. A teaching team should have assistance for clerical and supervisory activity, and its members should be free to give students more individual attention. The team approach lends itself ideally to the development of the program whereby team members provide a cadre of experienced teachers to supervise and train cadet teachers. Such an arrangement would acquaint future teachers more fully with instructional methods, provide them with a greater variety of activities, familiarize them with more than one academic discipline, and enable them to adapt more readily to teaching by involving them in numerous duties and activities which cannot be realized in a traditional teaching situation. Team members thus would receive valuable assistance and teacher trainees would obtain more valuable training than they could under the supervision of only one teacher.

5. A more direct role should be played by the school librarian in the team teaching program. For this role to be maintained with the necessary thoroughness, the school librarian needs trained adult assistance for clerical and library management duties, thus freeing the librarian to provide additional consultative services for both teachers and students. This is especially necessary if the secondary level school library is to provide educational services for a comprehensive instructional program for students of all ability levels. The role of the school library thus should be considerably expanded to provide materials, space, and services for students to handle the required academic tasks.

6. Physical facilities for team teaching are an integral part of the team program, and areas for this type of instruction should be provided. While the existing facilities at Sammamish High School were adequate, the educational advantages gained by the team method will diminish as that school's student population increases and the premium for housing students removes existing facilities from team use. Incorporation of well-designed physical facilities for both large group and small group instruction should be provided in buildings where they do not now exist.

7. The team approach, where appropriate, should be widened in two directions: to incorporate a wider interdisciplinary approach and

to develop departmental teaching teams within a single academic area. The team approach to history and literature could well be expanded for participation by teachers of art, music, biological sciences, and foreign languages. The educational values and potentials of widening the team approach in this direction appear at this point to be immeasurable. A team effort in this direction would permit greater use of community resource people and visiting experts in particular areas. Expansion of the team teaching approach to departmental teams offers comparable advantages, particularly to the social studies-language arts departments where continuity, scope, and depth can be given to departmental programs by pooling teacher talents and skills.

The Sammamish High School American history and English teaching team believes the foregoing recommendations, stemming from a successful team teaching program, can improve the existing curriculum, develop better staff utilization, provide more fruitful educational development for students of all levels of ability and inclination, and bring closer to actuality that quality of education expected by both the teaching profession and a forward looking and enlightened community.

Summary

The introduction of team teaching into the secondary level as an interdisciplinary approach to teaching and learning has important consequences for utilization of staff members, curriculum development, instructional methods, and facilities design. The primary consideration, of course, is whether or not team teaching results in improved learning skills and greater mastery of existing knowledge by participating students.

The team teaching program in American history and English at Sammamish High School seems to have met satisfactorily most of the basic objectives established when the program was initiated and seems to validate the premise upon which it was based. Constant evaluation of the team teaching method of instruction is necessary, however, to establish higher levels of performance by both teachers and students and to establish that method as an integral part of the instructional program. The one year's experience at Sammamish High School has demonstrated that such an approach is fundamentally sound; however, it has also demonstrated to the participating teachers that it is no panacea for all instructional and learning problems. Much more work and experimentation is necessary to perfect the team teaching method to the point where it, in itself, can become the traditional instructional procedure.

The most pressing problems to be overcome for the most fruitful exploitation of this method at Sammamish High School are those posed by physical facilities and inadequate library materials and space. If participating staff members provide more valuable use of their time and contribute their talents and skills more ably and effectively, if the curriculum structure and organization is strengthened and improved, if modification of instructional methods provide better teaching and greater learning, if facilities are used more efficiently, and if students demonstrate better study skills and greater mastery of ideas and facts, then team teaching merits increased attention of administrators and teachers and parents.

If the participating students exhibit better performance and attain higher achievement in each academic discipline involved in the interdisciplinary team teaching method, then the value of that method will be fully demonstrated. If the team teaching method demonstrates such value, and apparently it has at Sammamish High School, then the curriculum can be structured to provide maximum student achievement through the heterogeneous grouping of students, and staff members can be utilized more wisely.

Team Teaching in the Junior High School
Joseph F. Callahan*

This year (1963) members of the Social Studies Department of the Junior High School are experimenting with a team-teaching program. After two years of exploring the many possible solutions to a curriculum problem which concerned them, the members of the Team are now utilizing the talents of many people to achieve their goal.

This problem was brought into sharp focus in the spring following the launching of Sputnik I. Up until that time, the making of a selection at grade nine between social studies and science presented no serious problem and contributed toward the realization of one of the functions of a junior high school. After that event, however, the tendency away from social studies increased. Thoughts were therefore directed to finding ways of averting a shift of emphasis through panic, restoring the balance which had previously existed between these two subjects, and at the same time preserving the "election and decision making" aspect of the program which we thought was valuable.

The solution eventually decided upon was dissimilar to any we had read or heard about. In addition to utilizing the aspect of the team for planning and producing lessons, a humanities emphasis has been introduced with a hope of encouraging scholarship.

No concrete action beyond the discussion point was taken before the end of the 1962 school year. The opportunity provided by the Board of Education, an eleventh month contract for one of our teachers, furnished just the impetus needed to get the project off the ground. Not much could be done towards the immediate accomplishment of the team concept by one man working in isolation, but that which could only be done in the leisure of the summer was accomplished. For example, the general scheme of operations was decided upon and planned for while the embryonic schedule for 1962-63 was still flexible; the general goals of the experiment

*Dr. Callahan is principal of the Chatham Junior High School, Chatham Borough, New Jersey. The article has been published in this text with the permission of Dr. Callahan.

were sketched out, to serve as guide lines in the selection of topics; outside speakers and materials were contacted far enough in advance to permit scheduling of their time; reports from other school systems, engaged in similar experiments, were sent for to review as aids in setting up our program; background material on team-teaching was researched in preparation for the reconvening of the group to be involved in the project; programs were prepared by at least one of the lecturers who would be involved in the large group meetings. That month of July was a much needed aid in our getting ready for our program of this year.

Our search of the literature revealed little that would be of specific help to us in our project. In concept, our experiment is quite unique. To be sure, our school situation is different from that of most other schools engaged in team teaching. Since the prime motivating force for our original inquiry existed no place else, applicable solutions were not contained in the descriptions of the experiences of others. There were, however, common threads running through all accounts, particularly with reference to goals, which gave us some direction.

Team teaching is a valuable device, we concluded,
- a. Because it economizes teacher time.
- b. Because it enables a school to exploit its best talent.
- c. Because the special talents in particular fields can be utilized as needed.
- d. Because group planning can lighten the burden of the planner.
- e. Because more hands make the job possible.
- f. Because many people are needed for a smooth running presentation in addition to the individuals whose knowledge is desired.

Our team was to be composed of the members of the Social Studies Department. The department chairman, as master teacher, would direct the operations and bear the brunt of the presentation. One teacher, a specialist in government and law; another, a specialist in economics and finance; a third, a specialist in U. S. history and geography; a fourth, a specialist in audio-visual aids, constituted the subject matter committee.

During the summer of 1962 a series of programs which all members of the ninth grade would attend, was planned. At certain times and for certain goals, the large group would be subdivided. No homework assignments were planned in conjunction with these programs and no grades were to be assigned. The main design would be the encouragement of intellectual curiosity, the stimulation of thought and debate upon topics, the provocation to reading and research, the focusing of attention on a fascinating era, topic, personality, to generate student interest into further inquiry.

With the plethora of accumulated knowledge mounting daily in our twentieth century, it has become daily less possible for a student to do more than dip into a few areas of learning. When the pressures of studying for tests, preparing for college, and mastering the elements of a highly selective curriculum are added to the paucity of time allowed by social calendars in our community, little leisure can be found for contemplation, or for research, outside of the required areas. Some topics could be taken completely out of context and presented as interesting things to know. It was not supposed that this knowing would ever help a student to score a higher mark on an examination, nor was it believed that an exposure to any topic would entice him into becoming a student. It was believed, however, that knowing about a topic might occasion a feeling of intellectual satisfaction; it might contribute to the value and depth of future reading by virtue of the broadened background; it might provoke conversation about topics beyond the scope of hot-rods and athletic contests; it might contribute toward a reorientation of opinion concerning the "egg-head," a type not universally admired in adolescent society.

Description of the Program

Two periods per week, one on Monday and the other on Wednesday, were set aside for program activities by adding one period to the school day. Large group meetings were scheduled for the auditorium and small group meetings for various classrooms.

After the first three programs had been well received, it became apparent that the team had to be enlarged. The team group, as composed, was directing its attention primarily toward content — mechanical lapses began to appear. Consequently, a super-team, a Planning Committee, was selected to operate the entire program, to relieve the subject specialists of mechanical details, and to guard the experiment from wholesale encroachments by every good, although extraneous, idea presented. The new committee consisted of the team chairman; the chairman of auditorium operations, stage and mechanical devices; a guidance counselor as a schedule maker and public relations expert who would keep the faculty informed and facilitate movement of students; the chairman of the language arts department, representing the department heads, to keep the team efforts from encroaching upon the regular school program; the school librarian, to provide bibliographies and reading materials for each program where possible; the principal, as chairman and secretary, to administrate the operation.

Goals

The goals for the program were drawn up and circulated as follows:
1. Insure exposures of science students to topics of social nature.
2. Broaden the historical perspective of all 9th grade students.
3. Cultivate an interest in and curiosity about all accumulated knowledge as earmarks of liberally educated people.
4. Touch on topics not generally encompassed by our courses of study in any year.
5. Encourage voluntary reading on eclectic topics.
6. Encourage conversation, debate, speculation, on topics of depth.
7. Illuminate the mind concerning the growth of knowledge and the fallacy that everything great has been done in this generation by one of us.

8. To bring the historical to bear in the examination of the contemporary.

The Planning Committee:

   a. Allocated specific responsibilities to each of its members for each of the programs during the entire year.
   b. Tested the programs planned against the goals, and made changes where scheduled programs were found to be deficient.
   c. Set up weekly times for meeting with the team to insure a smooth performance at the next meeting.
   d. Set up meetings for the Planning Committee to consider the programs listed for the following month.

The problem of evaluation was also considered in great detail. All staff members had been alerted to the importance to the team of student feedback; however, it was felt that in addition to subjective reactions to student questions and conversations, some form of objective criteria should be devised and submitted to students so that their reactions might be charted. A committee was selected to formulate a sample evaluative device and days of evaluation (three per year) were inserted into the schedule.

Incidental evaluation continued to be an ongoing process with the team, the staff, and the planning committee. One small group of students, expressing appreciation and interest in a program, regretted the fact that the "new assemblies" were all of the "learning type" and as a steady diet were not as acceptable as some of our "old assemblies." The comment, casually made, was enough to trigger a reaction in the planning committee, to highlight the necessity for differentiating "team efforts" from "assemblies," to focus on the necessity of tying all team programs deliberately in with the goals and with antecedent team programs. At the general assembly following the comment, the chairman for the day spent several minutes reiterating the difference between the two types of programs, reassured the group that "old-type" assemblies would be forthcoming, and elaborated on the eclectic nature of future team programs. At this meeting the mnemonic name of the program was announced, to avoid any confusion. Team programs would be referred to in the future as WEALTH, projects:

   W — for Wisdom
   E — for Education
   A — for Art
   L — for Literature
   T — for Technology
   H — for History

Apart from the facile reference factor of the name WEALTH, this title was intended to carry a deeper significance. The wealth of the experiment would involve intellectual and spiritual riches, would be the kind that could be possessed by men of modest material means, was within the grasp of any student if he listened attentively, participated actively, read widely, and desired to become a liberally educated person. The subtlety of the concept, it is true, would not be grasped by many students merely by reciting the words of explanation; however, if the thread of its meaning were to be woven into the woof of every program, and if this thread were to be continually tied up with threads that had gone before, it seemed possible that some students would come to realize the significance of the team effort and the experiment would thus be rendered valuable.

Programs of many kinds have been processed through the planning groups. Generally, the nature of the topic dictates the format agreed upon for the presentation.

These topics which are primarily informational are presented in straight lecture form. Such a topic was the program one day entitled, *Origin of the Alphabet.* On that day, the lecturer, after much research and time-consuming preparation, discussed the history of visual communication of thought from the beginnings of recorded time. Using the overhead projector and transparancies which he manufactured, he exposed the students to a very illuminating and interesting historical evolution. A vital item in our daily living, taken completely for granted by every student, was examined in great detail and traced back to its place of origin. When the lecture was completed, there was time for questions from the floor.

Topics which are thought-provoking were presented to smaller groups. *Ancient and Early Man,* the opening program of the series, was introduced to the assembled group via slides and lecture. On the following program day the class was divided into six groups of twenty-five students, each moderated by a member of the team, for the purpose of discussing questions and probabilities about the topic.

One topic was explored in the interesting fashion of pre-Shakespearean morality plays. Each member of the team prepared his facet of the general topic, and then went from room to room with his teaching equipment and aids in an effort to capitalize on the intimacy of the small group to communicate his message.

Some programs in the future will depend upon debates, others on skits, others on student publication accompanying student lectures, to reach their goals.

Some of the already apparent values of Team Teaching are only tangential to the technique but, it appears, are truly vital gains.

Psychologically, a teacher is not disposed to devote endless hours to the preparation of a single lesson. As a matter of fact, the pressures of time and paper grading prohibit meticulous daily planning for a class of twenty-five to a great extent. When, though, a class grows to 150 to 200 students and when fellow teachers are going to be spectators, the incentive to prepare better, to research more intensively, to deliver more dramatically, is markedly increased. Consequently, the chances of producing a better lesson are considerably enhanced.

Such has been our experience to date. Many of the topics explored in group meetings may have found their way into one or another classroom during the year. The classroom presentations would have been much more shallow and more spontaneous than they appeared as presented to the entire group.

At the outset, the subject matter areas for the Team attention revolved around current events and issues of national interest. Gradually the focus shifted to include items of cultural flavor, of historical perspective, or heritage from antiquity. Planning discussion frequently digressed into the vast, fascinating area of anthropology with its ready-made references to preliterate societies in the twentieth century where age old customs still prevail. The finished outline covered the whole gamut from the dawn of civilization to the future life of earthmen on distant planets.

The programs dealing with *Economics,* the *Federal Reserve System,* and *Foreign Ideologies* caused considerable interest. The series creating the most enthusiasm among students, however, was that devoted to *Great Leaders of History.* Winston Churchill was the leader focused upon in the inaugural program of the series. By the use of films, tapes, and lectures, the highlights of his career were sketched in the general meeting. Small groups were then formed, each with a teacher as chairman, to discuss the topic of leadership in general and as exemplified by the leader under discussion. When the small groups reconvened, one student from each was selected as a member of a panel to summarize the discussion of his group and to propose the names of leaders who qualified for the title in their opinion. The most rewarding part of this meeting was the general contribution from the audience in reaction to statements made by the panel. Up until that point in the experiment questions from the floor had not been numerous. The universality of participation reassured the team and the planners that given the right topic the students would respond.

Although the experiment has yet to prove itself a valuable device, some encouraging results are evident. The adults participating in the program, both teachers from within the school and guest lecturers from outside, have expressed delight with the response of the student body. Random samplings of opinion of ninth grade students have been encouraging and illuminating. More important than these clues, however, has been the apparent growth of the student group. There has been a sharp rise in the lending rate of the school library, in addition to a brisk sale of paperbacks in the new book store. The indications are that some of the goals of the program are being achieved and that the WEALTH series should be retained.

Codification of School Board Policies

Authorities have long urged school boards to adopt flexible policy statements that can serve as guides for administrative action. Research into the problem, however, has demonstrated that several difficulties arise when school boards attempt to codify policies. The difficulties can be classified in terms of questions that administrators and school board members ask most frequently when they are engaged in preparing board policy handbooks:[8]

1. What are policies? How can you distinguish between school board policies and administrative regulations?
2. What are the advantages in preparing a handbook of school board policies?
3. How can a handbook that codifies school board policies be organized? What information should it contain? In what order should the information appear?
4. How can a handbook of school board policies be made flexible enough so that outmoded policy statements can be readily changed?

Since the early and middle 1950's many school systems have adopted the findings of research into the problem of school board policy codification. The following report of a project carried out in Chesapeake, Virginia, serves to illustrate how one school system has put the results of research into action.

Policy Adoption in Chesapeake, Virginia
H. I. Willett, Jr.[*]

The formation of the City of Chesapeake, as a result of the merger of Norfolk County and the City of South Norfolk on January 1, 1963, made it necessary to adopt policies in all phases of operation for the schools of the new city. Upon direction by the Norfolk County Board of Supervisors and the South Norfolk City Council, the combined school boards of the two divisions met initially in April of 1962 to prepare for the uniting of the two school systems into one.

An early awareness of the advantages of having written school board policies was exhibited by the combined school board and plans were made to prepare the policies in written form. It was also realized that the combined school board itself did not have the time to cover the details of every policy during its meetings. As a result, at this April meeting the school board appointed committees to study existing policies in both divisions with a view toward recommending policies for the new city. The committees were composed of principals, teachers, and members of the administrative and supervisory staff from each school system.

Meetings were held by the various committees during the spring and summer. The initial step at these meetings was to list the existing policies in the two divisions. Not only were the existing policies studied, but an

---

[8] Galfo, Armand J., *A Guide for Developing Handbooks for Teachers and School Boards*. Buffalo, New York: The Western New York School Study Council, 1956.

[*]Dr. Willett is president of Longwood College, Virginia. The article has been published with the permission of Dr. Willett.

effort was made to examine new trends on both the state and national level. Research studies by the Virginia Education Association showing existing policies throughout the state provided a valuable source of information. Consideration was also given to recommendations presented by the local education association.

At meetings of the combined school board held monthly from September through December of 1962, the recommendations of the committees were presented to the school board. The presentation included a review of existing policies in both divisions, an examination of state and national trends, and the committee's recommendation. Policies were then discussed and adopted by the board.

Although much of the work of policy adoption was completed prior to the effective date of the merger (January 1, 1963), there remained a number of areas of consideration. There was also a feeling on the part of the Chesapeake School Board that policies should be constantly subject to study and review. In order that this might be facilitated, a five-member committee with representation from both former school divisions was appointed as an advisory board on policy development. Committee composition also included various educational levels (elementary and high) as well as varying positions (principal and central office staff member). This committee serves as a research agency for the school board, compiling information as requested by the board. The committee additionally serves as a clearing house for the suggestions and proposals of various school groups. This does not prevent any group from approaching the school board directly in regard to a policy recommendation, but the committee does aid in the coordination and consolidation of recommendations.

After adoption of a policy by the school board, copies are placed in leather bound, loose-leaf notebooks. These policy notebooks are distributed to board members, principals, school libraries, the central office library, and members of the administrative and supervisory staff. This distribution makes copies of existing policies available for examination by all employees of the school system. Having the policies in loose-leaf binders makes it possible to keep copies of the policy book completely up-to-date. In cases where it is necessary to amend a particular policy, only the sheets on which that policy is printed are affected. Each policy carries the date of its adoption or amendment. Policies are placed together under general headings such as personnel, instruction, and finance with a separate section for the bylaws of the school board.

Since policies generally deal with broad areas or topics, it is frequently necessary for the superintendent, department heads, or the staff to establish administrative procedures or regulations to carry out adopted policies. It was decided, therefore, to include administrative regulations within the policy book but to distinguish these administrative regulations from the school board policies. The procedure utilized was to print the administrative regulations on separate pages of a different color but to place these sheets adjacent to the policies which they implemented.

After complete copies of all school board policies and the regulations were placed in each school, it was further felt by the school board that each teacher should have placed in her hands a copy of all policies and regulations applicable to her position. This practice has been recommended by many experts in the field of policy development. Acting on this premise, policy and regulation handbooks will be printed during this coming summer and will be available for distribution to all teachers in September. The ease of reference made possible by having a personal copy of applicable policies and regulations is of great advantage in the day-to-day school operation. At the same time, by eliminating policies not applicable to the teacher, the policy handbook can be made less cumbersome. Provision is being made to keep these handbooks up-to-date through the use of plastic binders which allow pages to be inserted and removed.

In addition to including applicable adopted school board policies and administrative regulations, the handbook will contain information on a number of topics of interest and concern to teachers. Among the areas to be covered will be certification, income tax information for teachers, social security, the Virginia Supplemental Retirement System, professional ethics and organizations, and voting eligibility requirements and procedures.

Although the placing of written policies and regulations in each school and in the hands of the individual teachers aids in the dissemination of this information among the total school staff, need for further publicizing of these policies was considered to be essential. As a result of these considerations, articles describing policies of interest to patrons and the general public were prepared for release to the local newspapers. Further publicity was given through the school division's own newspaper which circulates to both school staff and the community. Representatives of the central office staff appeared at faculty and PTA meetings to explain policies, solicit suggestions, and clarify and answer questions concerning them.

Since many requests are received for the school system's policy or regulation on a particular subject or topic, a file of several hundred copies of each policy and regulation is kept on hand for immediate distribution and mailing. A local group may request information in regard to the community use of school buildings while a neighboring school division may desire to know your promotion policy or requirements for graduation.

In 1960, a joint committee of the National School Boards Association and the National Education Association established a set of nine recommendations for good school board policies. The nine recommendations are quoted following:

1. WRITTEN SCHOOL BOARD POLICIES SHOULD BE KEYED TO THE NEEDS OF THE LOCAL SCHOOL DISTRICT AND BE THE PRODUCT OF LOCAL EFFORT.
2. WRITTEN POLICIES SHOULD BE DEVELOPED AND PERIODICALLY REVISED BY COOPERATIVE ACTION REFLECTING THE EFFORTS AND POINTS OF VIEW OF THE SCHOOL BOARD, THE SCHOOL ADMINISTRATION, THE SCHOOL STAFF, AND THE PUBLIC.
3. WRITTEN POLICIES SHOULD BE CONVENIENTLY AND EFFICIENTLY ARRANGED IN A MANUAL OR HANDBOOK IN SUCH A WAY AS TO MAKE THEM EASY TO LOCATE AND USE.

4. WRITTEN POLICIES SHOULD BE COMPREHENSIVE, COV-
   ERING ALL MAJOR AREAS WITH WHICH SCHOOL BOARDS
   ARE CONCERNED.
5. SCHOOL BOARD ORGANIZATION AND OPERATION AND
   THE ORGANIZATIONAL STRUCTURE OF THE SCHOOL
   SHOULD BE EXPLAINED CLEARLY IN BYLAWS AND
   POLICIES WHICH ARE PLACED NEAR THE FRONT OF
   THE POLICY MANUAL.
6. WRITTEN POLICIES AND RULES AND REGULATIONS
   SHOULD BE DEVELOPED SEPARATELY BY THE BOARD
   AND SUPERINTENDENT.
7. THE FORMAT OF THE POLICY MANUAL SHOULD BE
   CAREFULLY PLANNED.
8. ABRIDGED POLICY MANUALS SHOULD BE UTILIZED TO
   SUPPLEMENT THE COMPREHENSIVE POLICY MANUAL IN
   MEETING THE INFORMATIONAL NEEDS OF INTERESTED
   GROUPS SUCH AS PARENTS, TEACHERS, AND PUPILS.
9. COPIES OF POLICY MANUALS SHOULD BE STRATEGI-
   CALLY DISTRIBUTED.

Procedures of policy adoption in Chesapeake attest to the belief by the
Chesapeake School Board in these nine principles of sound policy development.

Selected Exercises

1. In Chapter 9, the roles of school administrators in research activities and application were discussed in detail. From the studies
   presented in the text of Chapter 11, select an example and cite
   evidence of:

   a. A study that shows that staff personnel have been employed
      because they have ability to carry out and apply research.
   b. A study in which an attempt was made to stimulate lay in-
      terest in research activities of the school.
   c. A study that indicates opportunities for the school staff to
      grow professionally.

2. Select studies from Chapter 11 that give evidence of:

   a. Classroom teacher attempts to develop needed competencies
      in order to carry out research application projects.
   b. Classroom teacher approaches to projects as cooperative ven-
      tures.

3. What evidence can you find that special staff members such as
   guidance counselors, supervisors, etc., have taken active parts
   in the studies cited?

4. Give evidence from the studies in Chapter 11 that would indicate that they should be categorized under "action research" as defined in the chapter.
5. In evaluating the experience of Moline, Illinois, public schools with the ungraded plan, Baxter concludes that carefully controlled experimentation is needed in order to reach valid conclusions. Outline such an experiment in terms of the problem, hypotheses, method of attack, and analytical procedures to be used.
6. Compare and contrast the two studies of ability grouping described by Schild and by Deason. How do the results of the two studies compare to the general results of research on the topic?
7. What evidence can you find that studies cited in Chapter 11 were preceded by a search of the literature?

Suggested Activities

1. Select a school problem and locate a study in the literature that can be categorized as research on the problem. Locate another study on the same problem that is more nearly "action," or application of, research. Explain your selections.
2. Obtain a copy of a *Yearbook* of the Associated Public School Systems and abstract one of the studies that pertains to a problem that interests you or your school system.
3. School agencies in many regions of the country have established "School Study Councils." These councils help school systems to conduct research projects. Obtain the name of the nearest council and request a list of publications. Do the studies described seem to be "pure" or "action" research?

Selected Readings

1. Associated Public School Systems, *1961 APSS Yearbook.* New York 27, New York: The Association, 1961.
2. Associated Public School Systems, *1962 APSS Yearbook.* New York 27, New York: The Association, 1962.
3. Associated Public School Systems, *1963 APSS Yearbook,* New York 27, New York: The Association, 1963.

Appendix A

Table of Squares and Square Roots of the Numbers From 1 to 1000

NUMBER	SQUARE	SQUARE ROOT	NUMBER	SQUARE	SQUARE ROOT
1	1	1.000	41	16 81	6.403
2	4	1.414	42	17 64	6.481
3	9	1.732	43	18 49	6.557
4	16	2.000	44	19 36	6.633
5	25	2.236	45	20 25	6.708
6	36	2.449	46	21 16	6.782
7	49	2.646	47	22 09	6.856
8	64	2.828	48	23 04	6.928
9	81	3.000	49	24 01	7.000
10	1 00	3.162	50	25 00	7.071
11	1 21	3.317	51	26 01	7.141
12	1 44	3.464	52	27 04	7.211
13	1 69	3.606	53	28 09	7.280
14	1 96	3.742	54	29 16	7.348
15	2 25	3.873	55	30 25	7.416
16	2 56	4.000	56	31 36	7.483
17	2 89	4.123	57	32 49	7.550
18	3 24	4.243	58	33 64	7.616
19	3 61	4.359	59	34 81	7.681
20	4 00	4.472	60	36 00	7.746
21	4 41	4.583	61	37 21	7.810
22	4 84	4.690	62	38 44	7.874
23	5 29	4.796	63	39 69	7.937
24	5 76	4.899	64	40 96	8.000
25	6 25	5.000	65	42 25	8.062
26	6 76	5.099	66	43 56	8.124
27	7 29	5.196	67	44 89	8.185
28	7 84	5.292	68	46 24	8.246
29	8 41	5.385	69	47 61	8.307
30	9 00	5.477	70	49 00	8.367
31	9 61	5.568	71	50 41	8.426
32	10 24	5.657	72	51 84	8.485
33	10 89	5.745	73	53 29	8.544
34	11 56	5.831	74	54 76	8.602
35	12 25	5.916	75	56 25	8.660
36	12 96	6.000	76	57 76	8.718
37	13 69	6.083	77	59 29	8.775
38	14 44	6.164	78	60 84	8.832
39	15 21	6.245	79	62 41	8.888
40	16 00	6.325	80	64 00	8.944

*Table A.1 is reprinted from Table II of Lindquist, E. L. *A First Course in Statistics* (revised edition), published by Houghton Mifflin Company, by permission of the publishers.

Table of Squares and Square Roots—*Continued*

NUMBER	SQUARE	SQUARE ROOT	NUMBER	SQUARE	SQUARE ROOT
81	65 61	9.000	126	1 58 76	11.225
82	67 24	9.055	127	1 61 29	11.269
83	68 89	9.110	128	1 63 84	11.314
84	70 56	9.165	129	1 66 41	11.358
85	72 25	9.220	130	1 69 00	11.402
86	73 96	9.274	131	1 71 61	11.446
87	75 69	9.327	132	1 74 24	11.489
88	77 44	9.381	133	1 76 89	11.533
89	79 21	9.434	134	1 79 56	11.576
90	81 00	9.487	135	1 82 25	11.619
91	82 81	9.539	136	1 84 96	11.662
92	84 64	9.592	137	1 87 69	11.705
93	86 49	9.644	138	1 90 44	11.747
94	88 36	9.695	139	1 93 21	11.790
95	90 25	9.747	140	1 96 00	11.832
96	92 16	9.798	141	1 98 81	11.874
97	94 09	9.849	142	2 01 64	11.916
98	96 04	9.899	143	2 04 49	11.958
99	98 01	9.950	144	2 07 36	12.000
100	1 00 00	10.000	145	2 10 25	12.042
101	1 02 01	10.050	146	2 13 16	12.083
102	1 04 04	10.100	147	2 16 09	12.124
103	1 06 09	10.149	148	2 19 04	12.166
104	1 08 16	10.198	149	2 22 01	12.207
105	1 10 25	10.247	150	2 25 00	12.247
106	1 12 36	10.296	151	2 28 01	12.288
107	1 14 49	10.344	152	2 31 04	12.329
108	1 16 64	10.392	153	2 34 09	12.369
109	1 18 81	10.440	154	2 37 16	12.410
110	1 21 00	10.488	155	2 40 25	12.450
111	1 23 21	10.536	156	2 43 36	12.490
112	1 25 44	10.583	157	2 46 49	12.530
113	1 27 69	10.630	158	2 49 64	12.570
114	1 29 96	10.677	159	2 52 81	12.610
115	1 32 25	10.724	160	2 56 00	12.649
116	1 34 56	10.770	161	2 59 21	12.689
117	1 36 89	10.817	162	2 62 44	12.728
118	1 39 24	10.863	163	2 65 69	12.767
119	1 41 61	10.909	164	2 68 96	12.806
120	1 44 00	10.954	165	2 72 25	12.845
121	1 46 41	11.000	166	2 75 56	12.884
122	1 48 84	11.045	167	2 78 89	12.923
123	1 51 29	11.091	168	2 82 24	12.961
124	1 53 76	11.136	169	2 85 61	13.000
125	1 56 25	11.180	170	2 89 00	13.038

Table of Squares and Square Roots—*Continued*

NUMBER	SQUARE	SQUARE ROOT	NUMBER	SQUARE	SQUARE ROOT
171	2 92 41	13.077	216	4 66 56	14.697
172	2 95 84	13.115	217	4 70 89	14.731
173	2 99 29	13.153	218	4 75 24	14.765
174	3 02 76	13.191	219	4 79 61	14.799
175	3 06 25	13.229	220	4 84 00	14.832
176	3 09 76	13.266	221	4 88 41	14.866
177	3 13 29	13.304	222	4 92 84	14.900
178	3 16 84	13.342	223	4 97 29	14.933
179	3 20 41	13.379	224	5 01 76	14.967
180	3 24 00	13.416	225	5 06 25	15.000
181	3 27 61	13.454	226	5 10 76	15.033
182	3 31 24	13.491	227	5 15 29	15.067
183	3 34 89	13.528	228	5 19 84	15.100
184	3 38 56	13.565	229	5 24 41	15.133
185	3 42 25	13.601	230	5 29 00	15.166
186	3 45 96	13.638	231	5 33 61	15.199
187	3 49 69	13.675	232	5 38 24	15.232
188	3 53 44	13.711	233	5 42 89	15.264
189	3 57 21	13.748	234	5 47 56	15.297
190	3 61 00	13.784	235	5 52 25	15.330
191	3 64 81	13.820	236	5 56 96	15.362
192	3 68 64	13.856	237	5 61 69	15.395
193	3 72 49	13.892	238	5 66 44	15.427
194	3 76 36	13.928	239	5 71 21	15.460
195	3 80 25	13.964	240	5 76 00	15.492
196	3 84 16	14.000	241	5 80 81	15.524
197	3 88 09	14.036	242	5 85 64	15.556
198	3 92 04	14.071	243	5 90 49	15.588
199	3 96 01	14.107	244	5 95 36	15.620
200	4 00 00	14.142	245	6 00 25	15.652
201	4 04 01	14.177	246	6 05 16	15.684
202	4 08 04	14.213	247	6 10 09	15.716
203	4 12 09	14.248	248	6 15 04	15.748
204	4 16 16	14.283	249	6 20 01	15.780
205	4 20 25	14.318	250	6 25 00	15.811
206	4 24 36	14.353	251	6 30 01	15.843
207	4 28 49	14.387	252	6 35 04	15.875
208	4 32 64	14.422	253	6 40 09	15.906
209	4 36 81	14.457	254	6 45 16	15.937
210	4 41 00	14.491	255	6 50 25	15.969
211	4 45 21	14.526	256	6 55 36	16.000
212	4 49 44	14.560	257	6 60 49	16.031
213	4 53 69	14.595	258	6 65 64	16.062
214	4 57 96	14.629	259	6 70 81	16.093
215	4 62 25	14.663	260	6 76 00	16.125

Table of Squares and Square Roots—*Continued*

NUMBER	SQUARE	SQUARE ROOT	NUMBER	SQUARE	SQUARE ROOT
261	6 81 21	16.155	306	9 36 36	17.493
262	6 86 44	16.186	307	9 42 49	17.521
263	6 91 69	16.217	308	9 48 64	17.550
264	6 96 96	16.248	309	9 54 81	17.578
265	7 02 25	16.279	310	9 61 00	17.607
266	7 07 56	16.310	311	9 67 21	17.635
267	7 12 89	16.340	312	9 73 44	17.664
268	7 18 24	16.371	313	9 79 69	17.692
269	7 23 61	16.401	314	9 85 96	17.720
270	7 29 00	16.432	315	9 92 25	17.748
271	7 34 41	16.462	316	9 98 56	17.776
272	7 39 84	16.492	317	10 04 89	17.804
273	7 45 29	16.523	318	10 11 24	17.833
274	7 50 76	16.553	319	10 17 61	17.861
275	7 56 25	16.583	320	10 24 00	17.889
276	7 61 76	16.613	321	10 30 41	17.916
277	7 67 29	16.643	322	10 36 84	17.944
278	7 72 84	16.673	323	10 43 29	17.972
279	7 78 41	16.703	324	10 49 76	18.000
280	7 84 00	16.733	325	10 56 25	18.028
281	7 89 61	16.763	326	10 62 76	18.055
282	7 95 24	16.793	327	10 69 29	18.083
283	8 00 89	16.823	328	10 75 84	18.111
284	8 06 56	16.852	329	10 82 41	18.138
285	8 12 25	16.882	330	10 89 00	18.166
286	8 17 96	16.912	331	10 95 61	18.193
287	8 23 69	16.941	332	11 02 24	18.221
288	8 29 44	16.971	333	11 08 89	18.248
289	8 35 21	17.000	334	11 15 56	18.276
290	8 41 00	17.029	335	11 22 25	18.303
291	8 46 81	17.059	336	11 28 96	18.330
292	8 52 64	17.088	337	11 35 69	18.358
293	8 58 49	17.117	338	11 42 44	18.385
294	8 64 36	17.146	339	11 49 21	18.412
295	8 70 25	17.176	340	11 56 00	18.439
296	8 76 16	17.205	341	11 62 81	18.466
297	8 82 09	17.234	342	11 69 64	18.493
298	8 88 04	17.263	343	11 76 49	18.520
299	8 94 01	17.292	344	11 83 36	18.547
300	9 00 00	17.321	345	11 90 25	18.574
301	9 06 01	17.349	346	11 97 16	18.601
302	9 12 04	17.378	347	12 04 09	18.628
303	9 18 09	17.407	348	12 11 04	18.655
304	9 24 16	17.436	349	12 18 01	18.682
305	9 30 25	17.464	350	12 25 00	18.708

Table of Squares and Square Roots—*Continued*

NUMBER	SQUARE	SQUARE ROOT	NUMBER	SQUARE	SQUARE ROOT
351	12 32 01	18.735	396	15 68 16	19.900
352	12 39 04	18.762	397	15 76 09	19.925
353	12 46 09	18.788	398	15 84 04	19.950
354	12 53 16	18.815	399	15 92 01	19.975
355	12 60 25	18.841	400	16 00 00	20.000
356	12 67 36	18.868	401	16 08 01	20.025
357	12 74 49	18.894	402	16 16 04	20.050
358	12 81 64	18.921	403	16 24 09	20.075
359	12 88 81	18.947	404	16 32 16	20.100
360	12 96 00	18.974	405	16 40 25	20.125
361	13 03 21	19.000	406	16 48 36	20.149
362	13 10 44	19.026	407	16 56 49	20.174
363	13 17 69	19.053	408	16 64 64	20.199
364	13 24 96	19.079	409	16 72 81	20.224
365	13 32 25	19.105	410	16 81 00	20.248
366	13 39 56	19.131	411	16 89 21	20.273
367	13 46 89	19.157	412	16 97 44	20.298
368	13 54 24	19.183	413	17 05 69	20.322
369	13 61 61	19.209	414	17 13 96	20.347
370	13 69 00	19.235	415	17 22 25	20.372
371	13 76 41	19.261	416	17 30 56	20.396
372	13 83 84	19.287	417	17 38 89	20.421
373	13 91 29	19.313	418	17 47 24	20.445
374	13 98 76	19.339	419	17 55 61	20.469
375	14 06 25	19.363	420	17 64 00	20.494
376	14 13 76	19.391	421	17 72 41	20.518
377	14 21 29	19.416	422	17 80 84	20.543
378	14 28 84	19.442	423	17 89 29	20.567
379	14 36 41	19.468	424	17 97 76	20.591
380	14 44 00	19.494	425	18 06 25	20.616
381	14 51 61	19.519	426	18 14 76	20.640
382	14 59 24	19.545	427	18 23 29	20.664
383	14 66 89	19.570	428	18 31 84	20.688
384	14 74 56	19.596	429	18 40 41	20.712
385	14 82 25	19.621	430	18 49 00	20.736
386	14 89 96	19.647	431	18 57 61	20.761
387	14 97 69	19.672	432	18 66 24	20.785
388	15 05 44	19.698	433	18 74 89	20.809
389	15 13 21	19.723	434	18 83 56	20.833
390	15 21 00	19.748	435	18 92 25	20.857
391	15 28 81	19.774	436	19 00 96	20.881
392	15 36 64	19.799	437	19 09 69	20.905
393	15 44 49	19.824	438	19 18 44	20.928
394	15 52 36	19.849	439	19 27 21	20.952
395	15 60 25	19.875	440	19 36 00	20.976

Table of Squares and Square Roots—*Continued*

NUMBER	SQUARE	SQUARE ROOT	NUMBER	SQUARE	SQUARE ROOT
441	19 44 81	21.000	486	23 61 96	22.045
442	19 53 64	21.024	487	23 71 69	22.068
443	19 62 49	21.048	488	23 81 44	22.091
444	19 71 36	21.071	489	23 91 21	22.113
445	19 80 25	21.095	490	24 01 00	22.136
446	19 89 16	21.119	491	24 10 81	22.159
447	19 98 09	21.142	492	24 20 64	22.181
448	20 07 04	21.166	493	24 30 49	22.204
449	20 16 01	21.190	494	24 40 36	22.226
450	20 25 00	21.213	495	24 50 25	22.249
451	20 34 01	21.237	496	24 60 16	22.271
452	20 43 04	21.260	497	24 70 09	22.293
453	20 52 09	21.284	498	24 80 04	22.316
454	20 61 16	21.307	499	24 90 01	22.338
455	20 70 25	21.331	500	25 00 00	22.361
456	20 79 36	21.354	501	25 10 01	22.383
457	20 88 49	21.378	502	25 20 04	22.405
458	20 97 64	21.401	503	25 30 09	22.428
459	21 06 81	21.424	504	25 40 16	22.450
460	21 16 00	21.448	505	25 50 25	22.472
461	21 25 21	21.471	506	25 60 36	22.494
462	21 34 44	21.494	507	25 70 49	22.517
463	21 43 69	21.517	508	25 80 64	22.539
464	21 52 96	21.541	509	25 90 81	22.561
465	21 62 25	21.564	510	26 01 00	22.583
466	21 71 56	21.587	511	26 11 21	22.605
467	21 80 89	21.610	512	26 21 44	22.627
468	21 90 24	21.633	513	26 31 69	22.650
469	21 99 61	21.656	514	26 41 96	22.672
470	22 09 00	21.679	515	26 52 25	22.694
471	22 18 41	21.703	516	26 62 56	22.716
472	22 27 84	21.726	517	26 72 89	22.738
473	22 37 29	21.749	518	26 83 24	22.760
474	22 46 76	21.772	519	26 93 61	22.782
475	22 56 25	21.794	520	27 04 00	22.804
476	22 65 76	21.817	521	27 14 41	22.825
477	22 75 29	21.840	522	27 24 84	22.847
478	22 84 84	21.863	523	27 35 29	22.869
479	22 94 41	21.886	524	27 45 76	22.891
480	23 04 00	21.909	525	27 56 25	22.913
481	23 13 61	21.932	526	27 66 76	22.935
482	23 23 24	21.954	527	27 77 29	22.956
483	23 32 89	21.977	528	27 87 84	22.978
484	23 42 56	22.000	529	27 98 41	23.000
485	23 52 25	22.023	530	28 09 00	23.022

Table of Squares and Square Roots—*Continued*

NUMBER	SQUARE	SQUARE ROOT	NUMBER	SQUARE	SQUARE ROOT
531	28 19 61	23.043	576	33 17 76	24.000
532	28 30 24	23.065	577	33 29 29	24.021
533	28 40 89	23.087	578	33 40 84	24.042
534	28 51 56	23.108	579	33 52 41	24.062
535	28 62 25	23.130	580	33 64 00	24.083
536	28 72 96	23.152	581	33 75 61	24.104
537	28 83 69	23.173	582	33 87 24	24.125
538	28 94 44	23.195	583	33 98 89	24.145
539	29 05 21	23.216	584	34 10 56	24.166
540	29 16 00	23.238	585	34 22 25	24.187
541	29 26 81	23.259	586	34 33 96	24.207
542	29 37 64	23.281	587	34 45 69	24.228
543	29 48 49	23.302	588	34 57 44	24.249
544	29 59 36	23.324	589	34 69 21	24.269
545	29 70 25	23.345	590	34 81 00	24.290
546	29 81 16	23.367	591	34 92 81	24.310
547	29 92 09	23.388	592	35 04 64	24.331
548	30 03 04	23.409	593	35 16 49	24.352
549	30 14 01	23.431	594	35 28 36	24.372
550	30 25 00	23.452	595	35 40 25	24.393
551	30 36 01	23.473	596	35 52 16	24.413
552	30 47 04	23.495	597	35 64 09	24.434
553	30 58 09	23.516	598	35 76 04	24.454
554	30 69 16	23.537	599	35 88 01	24.474
555	30 80 25	23.558	600	36 00 00	24.495
556	30 91 36	23.580	601	36 12 01	24.515
557	31 02 49	23.601	602	36 24 04	24.536
558	31 13 64	23.622	603	36 36 09	24.556
559	31 24 81	23.643	604	36 48 16	24.576
560	31 36 00	23.664	605	36 60 25	24.597
561	31 47 21	23.685	606	36 72 36	24.617
562	31 58 44	23.707	607	36 84 49	24.637
563	31 69 69	23.728	608	36 96 64	24.658
564	31 80 96	23.749	609	37 08 81	24.678
565	31 92 25	23.770	610	37 21 00	24.698
566	32 03 56	23.791	611	37 33 21	24.718
567	32 14 89	23.812	612	37 45 44	24.739
568	32 26 24	23.833	613	37 57 69	24.759
569	32 37 61	23.854	614	37 69 96	24.779
570	32 49 00	23.875	615	37 82 25	24.799
571	32 60 41	23.896	616	37 94 56	24.819
572	32 71 84	23.917	617	38 06 89	24.839
573	32 83 29	23.937	618	38 19 24	24.860
574	32 94 76	23.958	619	38 31 61	24.880
575	33 06 25	23.979	620	38 44 00	24.900

Table of Squares and Square Roots—*Continued*

NUMBER	SQUARE	SQUARE ROOT	NUMBER	SQUARE	SQUARE ROOT
621	38 56 41	24.920	666	44 35 56	25.807
622	38 68 84	24.940	667	44 48 89	25.826
623	38 81 29	24.960	668	44 62 24	25.846
624	38 93 76	24.980	669	44 75 61	25.865
625	39 06 25	25.000	670	44 89 00	25.884
626	39 18 76	25.020	671	45 02 41	25.904
627	39 31 29	25.040	672	45 15 84	25.923
628	39 43 84	25.060	673	45 29 29	25.942
629	39 56 41	25.080	674	45 42 76	25.962
630	39 69 00	25.100	675	45 56 25	25.981
631	39 81 61	25.120	676	45 69 76	26.000
632	39 94 24	25.140	677	45 83 29	26.019
633	40 06 89	25.159	678	45 96 84	26.038
634	40 19 56	25.179	679	46 10 41	26.058
635	40 32 25	25.199	680	46 24 00	26.077
636	40 44 96	25.219	681	46 37 61	26.096
637	40 57 69	25.239	682	46 51 24	26.115
638	40 70 44	25.259	683	46 64 89	26.134
639	40 83 21	25.278	684	46 78 56	26.153
640	40 96 00	25.298	685	46 92 25	26.173
641	41 08 81	25.318	686	47 05 96	26.192
642	41 21 64	25.338	687	47 19 69	26.211
643	41 34 49	25.357	688	47 33 44	26.230
644	41 47 36	25.377	689	47 47 21	26.249
645	41 60 25	25.397	690	47 61 00	26.268
646	41 73 16	25.417	691	47 74 81	26.287
647	41 86 09	25.436	692	47 88 64	26.306
648	41 99 04	25.456	693	48 02 49	26.325
649	42 12 01	25.475	694	48 16 36	26.344
650	42 25 00	25.495	695	48 30 25	26.363
651	42 38 01	25.515	696	48 44 16	26.382
652	42 51 04	25.534	697	48 58 09	26.401
653	42 64 09	25.554	698.	48 72 04	26.420
654	42 77 16	25.573	699	48 86 01	26.439
655	42 90 25	25.593	700	49 00 00	26.458
656	43 03 36	25.612	701	49 14 01	26.476
657	43 16 49	25.632	702	49 28 04	26.495
658	43 29 64	25.652	703	49 42 09	26.514
659	43 42 81	25.671	704	49 56 16	26.533
660	43 56 00	25.690	705	49 70 25	26.552
661	43 69 21	25.710	706	49 84 36	26.571
662	43 82 44	25.729	707	49 98 49	26.589
663	43 95 69	25.749	708	50 12 64	26.608
664	44 08 96	25.768	709	50 26 81	26.627
665	44 22 25	25.788	710	50 41 00	26.646

Table of Squares and Square Roots—*Continued*

NUMBER	SQUARE	SQUARE ROOT	NUMBER	SQUARE	SQUARE ROOT
711	50 55 21	26.665	756	57 15 36	27.495
712	50 69 44	26.683	757	57 30 49	27.514
713	50 83 69	26.702	758	57 45 64	27.532
714	50 97 96	26.721	759	57 60 81	27.550
715	51 12 25	26.739	760	57 76 00	27.568
716	51 26 56	26.758	761	57 91 21	27.586
717	51 40 89	26.777	762	58 06 44	27.604
718	51 55 24	26.796	763	58 21 69	27.622
719	51 69 61	26.814	764	58 36 96	27.641
720	51 84 00	26.833	765	58 52 25	27.659
721	51 98 41	26.851	766	58 67 56	27.677
722	52 12 84	26.870	767	58 82 89	27.695
723	52 27 29	26.889	768	58 98 24	27.713
724	52 41 76	26.907	769	59 13 61	27.731
725	52 56 25	26.926	770	59 29 00	27.749
726	52 70 76	26.944	771	59 44 41	27.767
727	52 85 29	26.963	772	59 59 84	27.785
728	52 99 84	26.981	773	59 75 29	27.803
729	53 14 41	27.000	774	59 90 76	27.821
730	53 29 00	27.019	775	60 06 25	27.839
731	53 43 61	27.037	776	60 21 76	27.857
732	53 58 24	27.055	777	60 37 29	27.875
733	53 72 89	27.074	778	60 52 84	27.893
734	53 87 56	27.092	779	60 68 41	27.911
735	54 02 25	27.111	780	60 84 00	27.928
736	54 16 96	27.129	781	60 99 61	27.946
737	54 31 69	27.148	782	61 15 24	27.964
738	54 46 44	27.166	783	61 30 89	27.982
739	54 61 21	27.185	784	61 46 56	28.000
740	54 76 00	27.203	785	61 62 25	28.018
741	54 90 81	27.221	786	61 77 96	28.036
742	55 05 64	27.240	787	61 93 69	28.054
743	55 20 49	27.258	788	62 09 44	28.071
744	55 35 36	27.276	789	62 25 21	28.089
745	55 50 25	27.295	790	62 41 00	28.107
746	55 65 16	27.313	791	62 56 81	28.125
747	55 80 09	27.331	792	62 72 64	28.142
748	55 95 04	27.350	793	62 88 49	28.160
749	56 10 01	27.368	794	63 04 36	28.178
750	56 25 00	27.386	795	63 20 25	28.196
751	56 40 01	27.404	796	63 36 16	28.213
752	56 55 04	27.423	797	63 52 09	28.231
753	56 70 09	27.441	798	63 68 04	28.249
754	56 85 16	27.459	799	63 84 01	28.267
755	57 00 25	27.477	800	64 00 00	28.284

Table of Squares and Square Roots—*Continued*

NUMBER	SQUARE	SQUARE ROOT	NUMBER	SQUARE	SQUARE ROOT
801	64 16 01	28.302	846	71 57 16	29.086
802	64 32 04	28.320	847	71 74 09	29.103
803	64 48 09	28.337	848	71 91 04	29.120
804	64 64 16	28.355	849	72 08 01	29.138
805	64 80 25	28.373	850	72 25 00	29.155
806	64 96 36	28.390	851	72 42 01	29.172
807	65 12 49	28.408	852	72 59 04	29.189
808	65 28 64	28.425	853	72 76 09	29.206
809	65 44 81	28.443	854	72 93 16	29.223
810	65 61 00	28.460	855	73 10 25	29.240
811	65 77 21	28.478	856	73 27 36	29.257
812	65 93 44	28.496	857	73 44 49	29.275
813	66 09 69	28.513	858	73 61 64	29.292
814	66 25 96	28.531	859	73 78 81	29.309
815	66 42 25	28.548	860	73 96 00	29.326
816	66 58 56	28.566	861	74 13 21	29.343
817	66 74 89	28.583	862	74 30 44	29.360
818	66 91 24	28.601	863	74 47 69	29.377
819	67 07 61	28.618	864	74 64 96	29.394
820	67 24 00	28.636	865	74 82 25	29.411
821	67 40 41	28.653	866	74 99 56	29.428
822	67 56 84	28.671	867	75 16 89	29.445
823	67 73 29	28.688	868	75 34 24	29.462
824	67 89 76	28.705	869	75 51 61	29.479
825	68 06 25	28.723	870	75 69 00	29.496
826	68 22 76	28.740	871	75 86 41	29.513
827	68 39 29	28.758	872	76 03 84	29.530
828	68 55 84	28.775	873	76 21 29	29.547
829	68 72 41	28.792	874	76 38 76	29.563
830	68 89 00	28.810	875	76 56 25	29.580
831	69 05 61	28.827	876	76 73 76	29.597
832	69 22 24	28.844	877	76 91 29	29.614
833	69 38 89	28.862	878	77 08 84	29.631
834	69 55 56	28.879	879	77 26 41	29.648
835	69 72 25	28.896	880	77 44 00	29.665
836	69 88 96	28.914	881	77 61 61	29.682
837	70 05 69	28.931	882	77 79 24	29.698
838	70 22 44	28.948	883	77 96 89	29.715
839	70 39 21	28.965	884	78 14 56	29.732
840	70 56 00	28.983	885	78 32 25	29.749
841	70 72 81	29.000	886	78 49 96	29.766
842	70 89 64	29.017	887	78 67 69	29.783
843	71 06 49	29.034	888	78 85 44	29.799
844	71 23 36	29.052	889	79 03 21	29.816
845	71 40 25	29.069	890	79 21 00	29.833

Table of Squares and Square Roots—*Continued*

NUMBER	SQUARE	SQUARE ROOT	NUMBER	SQUARE	SQUARE ROOT
891	79 38 81	29.850	936	87 60 96	30.594
892	79 56 64	29.866	937	87 79 69	30.610
893	79 74 49	29.883	938	87 98 44	30.627
894	79 92 36	29.900	939	88 17 21	30.643
895	80 10 25	29.916	940	88 36 00	30.659
896	80 28 16	29.933	941	88 54 81	30.676
897	80 46 09	29.950	942	88 73 64	30.692
898	80 64 04	29.967	943	88 92 49	30.708
899	80 82 01	29.983	944	89 11 36	30.725
900	81 00 00	30.000	945	89 30 25	30.741
901	81 18 01	30.017	946	89 49 16	30.757
902	81 36 04	30.033	947	89 68 09	30.773
903	81 54 09	30.050	948	89 87 04	30.790
904	81 72 16	30.067	949	90 06 01	30.806
905	81 90 25	30.083	950	90 25 00	30.822
906	82 08 36	30.100	951	90 44 01	30.838
907	82 26 49	30.116	952	90 63 04	30.854
908	82 44 64	30.133	953	90 82 09	30.871
909	82 62 81	30.150	954	91 01 16	30.887
910	82 81 00	30.166	955	91 20 25	30.903
911	82 99 21	30.183	956	91 39 36	30.919
912	83 17 44	30.199	957	91 58 49	30.935
913	83 35 69	30.216	958	91 77 64	30.952
914	83 53 96	30.232	959	91 96 81	30.968
915	83 72 25	30.249	960	92 16 00	30.984
916	83 90 56	30.265	961	92 35 21	31.000
917	84 08 89	30.282	962	92 54 44	31.016
918	84 27 24	30.299	963	92 73 69	31.032
919	84 45 61	30.315	964	92 92 96	31.048
920	84 64 00	30.332	965	93 12 25	31.064
921	84 82 41	30.348	966	93 31 56	31.081
922	85 00 84	30.364	967	93 50 89	31.097
923	85 19 29	30.381	968	93 70 24	31.113
924	85 37 76	30.397	969	93 89 61	31.129
925	85 56 25	30.414	970	94 09 00	31.145
926	85 74 76	30.430	971	94 28 41	31.161
927	85 93 29	30.447	972	94 47 84	31.177
928	86 11 84	30.463	973	94 67 29	31.193
929	86 30 41	30.480	974	94 86 76	31.209
930	86 49 00	30.496	975	95 06 25	31.225
931	86 67 61	30.512	976	95 25 76	31.241
932	86 86 24	30.529	977	95 45 29	31.257
933	87 04 89	30.545	978	95 64 84	31.273
934	87 23 56	30.561	979	95 84 41	31.289
935	87 42 25	30.578	980	96 04 00	31.305

Table of Squares and Square Roots—*Continued*

NUMBER	SQUARE	SQUARE ROOT	NUMBER	SQUARE	SQUARE ROOT
981	96 23 61	31.321	991	98 20 81	31.480
982	96 43 24	31.337	992	98 40 64	31.496
983	96 62 89	31.353	993	98 60 49	31.512
984	96 82 56	31.369	994	98 80 36	31.528
985	97 02 25	31.385	995	99 00 25	31.544
986	97 21 96	31.401	996	99 20 16	31.559
987	97 41 69	31.417	997	99 40 09	31.575
988	97 61 44	31.432	998	99 60 04	31.591
989	97 81 21	31.448	999	99 80 01	31.607
990	98 01 00	31.464	1000	100 00 00	31.623

TABLE A.2*

Per Cent of the Total Area Under the Normal Distribution Curve between the Mean and another ordinate at any given distance from the mean (expressed in sigma or z score units).

z	.00	.01	.02	.03	.04	.05	.06	.07	.08	.09
0.0	00.00	00.40	00.80	01.20	01.60	01.99	02.39	02.79	03.19	03.59
0.1	03.98	04.38	04.78	05.17	05.57	05.96	06.36	06.75	07.14	07.53
0.2	07.93	08.32	08.71	09.10	09.48	09.87	10.26	10.64	11.03	11.41
0.3	11.79	12.17	12.55	12.93	13.31	13.68	14.06	14.43	14.80	15.17
0.4	15.54	15.91	16.28	16.64	17.00	17.36	17.72	18.08	18.44	18.79
0.5	19.15	19.50	19.85	20.19	20.54	20.88	21.23	21.57	21.90	22.24
0.6	22.57	22.91	23.24	23.57	23.89	24.22	24.54	24.86	25.17	25.49
0.7	25.80	26.11	26.42	26.73	27.04	27.34	27.64	27.94	28.23	28.52
0.8	28.81	29.10	29.39	29.67	29.95	30.23	30.51	30.78	31.06	31.33
0.9	31.59	31.86	32.12	32.38	32.64	32.90	33.15	33.40	33.65	33.89
1.0	34.13	34.38	34.61	34.85	35.08	35.31	35.54	35.77	35.99	36.21
1.1	36.43	36.65	36.86	37.08	37.29	37.49	37.70	37.90	38.10	38.30
1.2	38.49	38.69	38.88	39.07	39.25	39.44	39.62	39.80	39.97	40.15
1.3	40.32	40.49	40.66	40.82	40.99	41.15	41.31	41.47	41.62	41.77
1.4	41.92	42.07	42.22	42.36	42.51	42.65	42.79	42.92	43.06	43.19
1.5	43.32	43.45	43.57	43.70	43.83	43.94	44.06	44.18	44.29	44.41
1.6	44.52	44.63	44.74	44.84	44.95	45.05	45.15	45.25	45.35	45.45
1.7	45.54	45.64	45.73	45.82	45.91	45.99	46.08	46.16	46.25	46.33
1.8	46.41	46.49	46.56	46.64	46.71	46.78	46.86	46.93	46.99	47.06
1.9	47.13	47.19	47.26	47.32	47.38	47.44	47.50	47.56	47.61	47.67
2.0	47.72	47.78	47.83	47.88	47.93	47.98	48.03	48.08	48.12	48.17
2.1	48.21	48.26	48.30	48.34	48.38	48.42	48.46	48.50	48.54	48.57
2.2	48.61	48.64	48.68	48.71	48.75	48.78	48.81	48.84	48.87	48.90
2.3	48.93	48.96	48.98	49.01	49.04	49.06	49.09	49.11	49.13	49.16
2.4	49.18	49.20	49.22	49.25	49.27	49.29	49.31	49.32	49.34	49.36
2.5	49.38	49.40	49.41	49.43	49.45	49.46	49.48	49.49	49.51	49.52
2.6	49.53	49.55	49.56	49.57	49.59	49.60	49.61	49.62	49.63	49.64
2.7	49.65	49.66	49.67	49.68	49.69	49.70	49.71	49.72	49.73	49.74
2.8	49.74	49.75	49.76	49.77	49.77	49.78	49.79	49.79	49.80	49.81
2.9	49.81	49.82	49.82	49.83	49.84	49.84	49.85	49.85	49.86	49.86
3.0	49.87									
3.5	49.98									
4.0	49.997									
5.0	49.99997									

*Original data for Table A.2 was published in *Tables for Statisticians and Biometricians,* edited by Karl Pearson and published by Cambridge University Press. An adaptation of these data was taken from Lindquist, E. L., *A First Course in Statistics* (revised edition), published by Houghton Mifflin Company. The table is used here with the permission of the publishers.

TABLE A.3*

Values of t at the 5% and 1% Levels of Significance

DEGREES OF FREEDOM (df)	5%	1%
1	12.706	63.657
2	4.303	9.925
3	3.182	5.841
4	2.776	4.604
5	2.571	4.032
6	2.447	3.707
7	2.365	3.499
8	2.306	3.355
9	2.262	3.250
10	2.228	3.169
11	2.201	3.106
12	2.179	3.055
13	2.160	3.012
14	2.145	2.977
15	2.131	2.947
16	2.120	2.921
17	2.110	2.898
18	2.101	2.878
19	2.093	2.861
20	2.086	2.845
21	2.080	2.831
22	2.074	2.819
23	2.069	2.807
24	2.064	2.797
25	2.060	2.787
26	2.056	2.779
27	2.052	2.771
28	2.048	2.763
29	2.045	2.756
30	2.042	2.750

*Table A.3 was abridged from Table III of Fisher and Yates: *Statistical Tables For Biological, Agricultural and Medical Research,* 4th edition 1953, published by Oliver and Boyd, Limited, Edinburgh. The abridged table appeared in *Elementary Statistics,* by Underwood et al, published by Appleton-Century-Crofts. Permission to use the table has been obtained from the authors, Fisher and Yates, and the publishers, Oliver and Boyd, Limited and Appleton-Century-Crofts.

TABLE A.4*

Values of F at the 5% and 1% Significance Levels

(df ASSOCIATED WITH THE DENOMINATOR)		(df ASSOCIATED WITH THE NUMERATOR)								
		1	2	3	4	5	6	7	8	9
1	5%	161	200	216	225	230	234	237	239	241
	1%	4052	5000	5403	5625	5764	5859	5928	5982	6022
2	5%	18.5	19.0	19.2	19.2	19.3	19.3	19.4	19.4	19.4
	1%	98.5	99.0	99.2	99.2	99.3	99.3	99.4	99.4	99.4
3	5%	10.1	9.55	9.28	9.12	9.01	8.94	8.89	8.85	8.81
	1%	34.1	30.8	29.5	28.7	28.2	27.9	27.7	27.5	27.3
4	5%	7.71	6.94	6.59	6.39	6.26	6.16	6.09	6.04	6.00
	1%	21.2	18.0	16.7	16.0	15.5	15.2	15.0	14.8	14.7
5	5%	6.61	5.79	5.41	5.19	5.05	4.95	4.88	4.82	4.77
	1%	16.3	13.3	12.1	11.4	11.0	10.7	10.5	10.3	10.2
6	5%	5.99	5.14	4.76	4.53	4.39	4.28	4.21	4.15	4.10
	1%	13.7	10.9	9.78	9.15	8.75	8.47	8.26	8.10	7.98
7	5%	5.59	4.74	4.35	4.12	3.97	3.87	3.79	3.73	3.68
	1%	12.2	9.55	8.45	7.85	7.46	7.19	6.99	6.84	6.72
8	5%	5.32	4.46	4.07	3.84	3.69	3.58	3.50	3.44	3.39
	1%	11.3	8.65	7.59	7.01	6.63	6.37	6.18	6.03	5.91
9	5%	5.12	4.26	3.86	3.63	3.48	3.37	3.29	3.23	3.18
	1%	10.6	8.02	6.99	6.42	6.06	5.80	5.61	5.47	5.35
10	5%	4.96	4.10	3.71	3.48	3.33	3.22	3.14	3.07	3.02
	1%	10.0	7.56	6.55	5.99	5.64	5.39	3.20	5.06	4.94
11	5%	4.84	3.98	3.59	3.36	3.20	3.09	3.01	2.95	2.90
	1%	9.65	7.21	6.22	5.67	5.32	5.07	4.89	4.74	4.63
12	5%	4.75	3.89	3.49	3.26	3.11	3.00	2.91	2.85	2.80
	1%	9.33	6.93	5.95	5.41	5.06	4.82	4.64	4.50	4.39
13	5%	4.67	3.81	3.41	3.18	3.03	2.92	2.83	2.77	2.71
	1%	9.07	6.70	5.74	5.21	4.86	4.62	4.44	4.30	4.19
14	5%	4.60	3.74	3.34	3.11	2.96	2.85	2.76	2.70	2.65
	1%	8.86	6.51	5.56	5.04	4.70	4.46	4.28	4.14	4.03
15	5%	4.54	3.68	3.29	3.06	2.90	2.79	2.71	2.64	2.59
	1%	8.68	6.36	5.42	4.89	4.56	4.32	4.14	4.00	3.89
16	5%	4.49	3.63	3.24	3.01	2.85	2.74	2.66	2.59	2.54
	1%	8.53	6.23	5.29	4.77	4.44	4.20	4.03	3.89	3.78
17	5%	4.45	3.59	3.20	2.96	2.81	2.70	2.61	2.55	2.49
	1%	8.40	6.11	5.18	4.67	4.34	4.10	3.93	3.79	3.68
18	5%	4.41	3.55	3.16	2.93	2.77	2.66	2.58	2.51	2.46
	1%	8.29	6.01	5.09	4.58	4.25	4.01	3.84	3.71	3.60

*Merrington, M., and Thompson, C. M. Tables of percentage points of the inverted beta (F) distribution, *Biometrika*, 1943, 33, 73-88, by permission of the editor.

Table A.4 (**Continued**)

(df ASSOCIATED WITH THE DENOMINATOR)		(df ASSOCIATED WITH THE NUMERATOR)								
		1	2	3	4	5	6	7	8	9
19	5%	4.38	3.52	3.13	2.90	2.74	2.63	2.54	2.48	2.42
	1%	8.18	5.93	5.01	4.50	4.17	3.94	3.77	3.63	3.52
20	5%	4.35	3.49	3.10	2.87	2.71	2.60	2.51	2.45	2.39
	1%	8.10	5.85	4.94	4.43	4.10	3.87	3.70	3.56	3.46
21	5%	4.32	3.47	3.07	2.84	2.68	2.57	2.49	2.42	2.37
	1%	8.02	5.78	4.87	4.37	4.04	3.81	3.64	3.51	3.40
22	5%	4.30	3.44	3.05	2.82	2.66	2.55	2.46	2.40	2.34
	1%	7.95	5.72	4.82	4.31	3.99	3.76	3.59	3.45	3.35
23	5%	4.28	3.42	3.03	2.80	2.64	2.53	2.44	2.37	2.32
	1%	7.88	5.66	4.76	4.26	3.94	3.71	3.54	3.41	3.30
24	5%	4.26	3.40	3.01	2.78	2.62	2.51	2.42	2.36	2.30
	1%	7.82	5.61	4.72	4.22	3.90	3.67	3.50	3.36	3.26
25	5%	4.24	3.39	2.99	2.76	2.60	2.49	2.40	2.34	2.28
	1%	7.77	5.57	4.68	4.18	3.86	3.63	3.46	3.32	3.22
26	5%	4.23	3.37	2.98	2.74	2.59	2.47	2.39	2.32	2.27
	1%	7.72	5.53	4.64	4.14	3.82	3.59	3.42	3.29	3.18
27	5%	4.21	3.35	2.96	2.73	2.57	2.46	2.37	2.31	2.25
	1%	7.68	5.49	4.60	4.11	3.78	3.56	3.39	3.26	3.15
28	5%	4.20	3.34	2.95	2.71	2.56	2.45	2.36	2.29	2.24
	1%	7.64	5.45	4.57	4.07	3.75	3.53	3.36	3.23	3.12
29	5%	4.18	3.33	2.93	2.70	2.55	2.43	2.35	2.28	2.22
	1%	7.60	5.42	4.54	4.04	3.73	3.50	3.33	3.20	3.09
30	5%	4.17	3.32	2.92	2.69	2.53	2.42	2.33	2.27	2.21
	1%	7.56	5.39	4.51	4.02	3.70	3.47	3.30	3.17	3.07
40	5%	4.08	3.23	2.84	2.61	2.45	2.34	2.25	2.18	2.12
	1%	7.31	5.18	4.31	3.83	3.51	3.29	3.12	2.99	2.89
60	5%	4.00	3.15	2.76	2.53	2.37	2.25	2.17	2.10	2.04
	1%	7.08	4.98	4.13	3.65	3.34	3.12	2.95	2.82	2.72
120	5%	3.92	3.07	2.68	2.45	2.29	2.18	2.09	2.02	1.96
	1%	6.85	4.79	3.95	3.48	3.17	2.96	2.79	2.66	2.56

TABLE A.5*

Values of r at the 5% and 1% Levels of Significance

DEGREES OF FREEDOM (df)	5%	1%	DEGREES OF FREEDOM (df)	5%	1%
1	.997	1.000	24	.388	.496
2	.950	.990	25	.381	.487
3	.878	.959	26	.374	.478
4	.811	.917	27	.367	.470
5	.754	.874	28	.361	.463
6	.707	.834	29	.355	.456
7	.666	.798	30	.349	.449
8	.632	.765	35	.325	.418
9	.602	.735	40	.304	.393
10	.576	.708	45	.288	.372
11	.553	.684	50	.273	.354
12	.532	.661	60	.250	.325
13	.514	.641	70	.232	.302
14	.497	.623	80	.217	.283
15	.482	.606	90	.205	.267
16	.468	.590	100	.195	.254
17	.456	.575	125	.174	.228
18	.444	.561	150	.159	.208
19	.433	.549	200	.138	.181
20	.423	.537	300	.113	.148
21	.413	.526	400	.098	.128
22	.404	.515	500	.088	.115
23	.396	.505	1000	.062	.081

*A portion of Table A.5 was abridged from Table VI of Fisher and Yates: *Statistical tables for biological agricultural, and medical research,* 4th edition 1953, published by Oliver and Boyd, Limited, Edinburgh, by permission of the authors and publishers. The remainder of the table was from Snedecor, *Statistical methods,* by permission of the publisher, The Iowa State College Press, and the author. The above table is taken from *Elementary Statistics,* Underwood et al, published by Appleton-Century-Crofts, by permission of the publisher.

TABLE A.6*

Values of ρ (rank-order correlation coefficient) at the 5% and 1%
Levels of Significance

N	5%	1%
5	1.000	—
6	.886	1.000
7	.786	.929
8	.738	.881
9	.683	.833
10	.648	.794
12	.591	.777
14	.544	.715
16	.506	.665
18	.475	.625
20	.450	.591
22	.428	.562
24	.409	.537
26	.392	.515
28	.377	.496
30	.364	.478

*Computed from Olds, E. G., Distribution of the sum of squares of rank differences for small numbers of individuals, *Ann. Math. Statist.*, 1938, 9, 133-148, and, the 5% significance levels for sums of squares of rank differences and a correction, Ann. *Math. Statist.*, 1949, 20, 117-118, by permission of the author and the Institute of Mathematical Statistics. Table A.6 is taken from *Elementary Statistics*, Underwood et al, by permission of the publisher, Appleton-Century-Crofts.

TABLE A.7*

Values of Chi-square (χ^2) at the 5% and 1% Levels of Significance

DEGREES OF FREEDOM (df)	5%	1%
1	3.84	6.64
2	5.99	9.21
3	7.82	11.34
4	9.49	13.28
5	11.07	15.09
6	12.59	16.81
7	14.07	18.48
8	15.51	20.09
9	16.92	21.67
10	18.31	23.21
11	19.68	24.72
12	21.03	26.22
13	22.36	27.69
14	23.68	29.14
15	25.00	30.58
16	26.30	32.00
17	27.59	33.41
18	28.87	34.80
19	30.14	36.19
20	31.41	37.57
21	32.67	38.93
22	33.92	40.29
23	35.17	41.64
24	36.42	42.98
25	37.65	44.31
26	38.88	45.64
27	40.11	46.96
28	41.34	48.28
29	42.56	49.59
30	43.77	50.89

*Table A.7 was abridged from Table IV of Fisher and Yates: *Statistical tables for biological, agricultural, and medical research,* 4th edition 1953, published by Oliver and Boyd, Limited, Edinburgh, by permission of the authors and publishers. The abridged table is taken from *Elementary Statistics,* Underwood et al, by permission of the publisher, Appleton-Century-Crofts.

Appendix B

THE GALFO STATISTICS PACKAGE (GSP)

Programmed by Mr. J. R. Dawson,* College of William and Mary Computer Center.

The laborious computational chores which accompany many statistical analyses of data are often discouraging to students of research. Machine calculators can be most helpful; but even with such machines, solving problems may take much time.

For this reason alone, it is natural that some colleges are beginning to allow students the use of computers in work which requires long computations.

The computer can offer added advantages as an instructional tool in research courses, however. Its use can help students to become familiar with computor capabilities and limitations. Preparation of data and acquaintance with how the data is processed by the computer can add new dimensions to the student's developing concepts of statistical tests.

I. *Computer Requirements for the Package*
   The Galfo Statistics Package is written in IBM Basic Fortran IV compiler language. It is intended for use on an IBM System/360 digital computer with 60k background storage supplied with an IBM Fortran IV compiler and an IBM Scientific Subroutine Package.

II. *Purpose*
   The purpose of the GSP is to provide a convenient method for solving common statistical problems on a digital computer without the necessity for the user to acquire experience in programming. The GSP allows the students to solve at one time single or multiple problems of the same type or of all types which are included in the package. Once the master deck of program cards (or magnetic storage) has been prepared in a computer center using the program outlined in this appendix, students need only to prepare control and data information in appropriate form to call the proper program(s) that process the data.

III. *List of Statistical Problems That May Be Solved by the GSP*
   (For further information about many of these problems see IBM Document H20-0205-F)

---

*The authors are indebted to Mr. Dawson for developing the package and to Mr. Peter Hoyle, of the College of William and Mary Computer Center, for his invaluable advice and assistance in the project. The authors are also grateful to the International Business Machines Company for permission to reprint their several subroutine programs which were incorporated in the package.

Problem Type Number	Statistical Problem Name	Data Input (not including control and Title information)	Statistical Output
1	Means $\bar{X}$	N # of X's (N $\leq$ 3000)	$\bar{X} = \Sigma X/N$
2	*Variance* using the definition formula	N # of X's (N $\leq$ 3000)	$\underline{\text{VAR}}$ Def. $= \Sigma\ (X - \bar{X})^2/N$
3	*Variance* using the efficient formula (VAR eff.)	N # of X's (N $\leq$ 3000)	$\underline{\text{VAR}}$ eff. $= (\Sigma X^2/N) - \bar{X}^2$
4	Unbiased est. of the Variance $(V\hat{A}R)$	N # of X's (N $\leq$ 3000)	$\underline{V\hat{A}R} = \Sigma\ (X - \bar{X})^2/(N - 1)$
5	*Standard Deviation* (SD)	N # of X's (N $\leq$ 3000)	$\text{SD} = \sqrt{\text{VAR}_{eff}}$
6	Unbiased est. of the Standard Deviation (SD)	N # of X's (N $\leq$ 3000)	$\text{SD} = \sqrt{V\hat{A}R}$
7	t-test with population Means (U) Given (+)	N # of X's (N $\leq$ 3000)	$t = (\bar{X} - U)/(^{SD}/\sqrt{N-1})$
8	t-test for Sample Means Difference Assuming $U_x - U_y$ and $VAR_x = VAR_y^{(+)}$	N # of X's (N $\leq$ 300) M # of Y's (M $\leq$ 300)	$t = \dfrac{\bar{X} - \bar{Y}}{\sqrt{\dfrac{SD_x^2}{N - 1} + \dfrac{(SD_y)^2}{N - 1}}}$ (See IBM Doc. #20-0205 p. 22)
9	Total Correlation Coefficient: Pearson's r (R)	N # of X's (N $\leq$ 300) N # of Y's	$R = \dfrac{\dfrac{XY}{N} - \bar{X}\ \bar{Y}}{(SD_x)\ (SD_y)}$
10	Analysis of Variance	List of Values for each level in each factor (# of factors $\leq$ 6 and the total # of values in the list should be $\leq$ 3000)	A table of (a) Variations (sums of squares) (b) Degrees of Freedom (c) and Variances (Mean Squares for each factor) (See IBM Doc. H20-0205-F, p. 303-305 for detailed information)
11	Chi Square χ^2	On N x M Frequency Table (N $\leq$ 120 and M $\leq$ 10)	$\chi^2 = \Sigma\ (F_o - F_e)/F_e$ with a special formula for a 2x2 table. (See IBM doc. H20-0205-1, p. 47)
12	Mann-Whitney U-Test (U)	N # of X's and M # of Y's (Data may be ranked or unranked N or M $\leq$ 300)	(a) U-value (b) Z-value (See IBM doc. H20-0205-1, pg. 48)

Problem Type Number	Statistical Problem Name	Data Input (not including control and Title information)	Statistical Output
13	Friedman two-way Analysis of Variance (χ^2_r)	N x M table of values where N = # of groups and M = # of cases per group. (Data may be ranked or unranked and N x M ≤ 900)	$\chi^2_r = \left(\sum_{j=1}^{M} R_j^2 \right) \left[12/(NM)(M+1) \right] - 3N(M+1)$ (See IBM doc. H20-0205-1, pg. 40)
14	Spearman Rank Correlation coefficient (r_s)	N # of X's and N # of Y's (Data may be ranked or unranked and N ≤ 300)	(a) $r_s = 1 - \Sigma (X - Y)/(N^3 - N)$ where a special formula is used in case of ties (b) $t = r_s \sqrt{(N - 2)/(1 - r_s^2)}$
15	Kendall rank correlation coefficient (Tau)	N # of X's and N # of Y's (Data may be ranked or unranked and N ≤ 300)	(a) $Tau = S/\frac{1}{2}[N(N - 1)]$ where a special formula is used in case of ties (b) $SD = \sqrt{2(2N + 5)/9N(N - 1)}$ (c) $Z = Tau/SD$ (See IBM doc. H20-0205-1, pg. 51)
16	Kendall coefficient of concordance (w)	An N x M table of values where N = # of variables and M = # of cases per variable (Data may be ranked or unranked and N x M ≤ 900)	$W = S/[1/12N^2(M^3 - M) - NT]$ $\chi^2 = N(M - 1)W$ (See IBM doc. H20-0205-F, p. 52)

In addition to the output indicated above the ranks of each input data value are listed with the data print out.

IV. *Preparation of the GSP*

Figure B.1 shows the configuration of the entire job deck for the GSP. The program which follows may be used to prepare the program deck which   marked Galfo Statistical Package in Figure B.1. Preparation of control and data cards is described in the next section (Section V) of this Appendix.

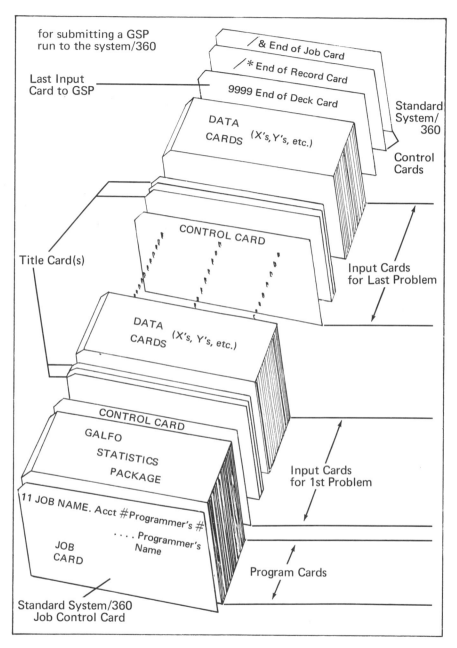

Figure B.1. Job Deck Configuration

```
// EXEC FORTRAN                                                                            GSP000
C                                                                                          GSP001
C                                                                                          GSP002
C       THE GALFO STATISTICS PACKAGE:  A PROGRAM FOR SOLVING                               GSP003
C                                      STATISTICAL PROBLEMS                                GSP004
C       °      °      °      °      °      °      °      °                                  GSP005
C       °      °      °      °      °      °      °      °                                  GSP006
C       DEVELOPED BY J. ROBERT DAWSON, JR. AT THE WILLIAM AND MARY COLLEGE                 GSP007
C       COMPUTER CENTER AT THE REQUEST OF DR. ARMAND J. GALFO OF THE                       GSP008
C       WILLIAM AND MARY COLLEGE SCHOOL OF EDUCATION. ACKNOWLEDGEMENTS                     GSP009
C       ARE GIVEN TO MR. PETE HOYLE FOR HIS INVALUABLE ADVICE.                             GSP010
C                                                                                          GSP011
C            .      .      .      .      .      .      .                                    GSP012
C       I. COMPUTER REQUIREMENTS                                                           GSP013
C       -      -      -      -      -      -      -                                         GSP014
C            THE GALFO STATISTICS PACKAGE IS WRITTEN IN IBM BASIC FORTRAN                  GSP015
C            IV COMPUTER LANGUAGE. IT IS INTENDED FOR USE ON AN IBM                        GSP016
C            SYSTEM/360 DIGITAL COMPUTER WITH 60K BACKGROUND STORAGE                       GSP017
C            SUPPLIED WITH AN IBM FORTRAN IV COMPILER AND AN IBM                           GSP018
C            SCIENTIFIC SUBROUTINE PACKAGE.                                                GSP019
C                                                                                          GSP020
C       -      -      -      -      -      -      -                                         GSP021
C       II. SUBROUTINE REQUIREMENTS                                                        GSP022
C       -      -      -      -      -      -      -                                         GSP023
C                                                                                          GSP024
C            IN ADDITION TO USING ORIGINALLY DEVELOPED SUBROUTINES (SEE                    GSP025
C            LISTINGS OF THESE SUBROUTINES AFTER THE MAIN PROGRAM LIST),                   GSP026
C            THE GALFO STATISTICS PACKAGE USES STATISTICS SUBROUTINES FROM                 GSP027
C            THE IBM SCIENTIFIC SUBROUTINE PACKAGE AS DESCRIBED IN IBM DOC                 GSP028
C            H 20-0205-1, 1966. ALSO THE ANALYSIS OF VARIANCE MAIN PROGRAM                 GSP029
C            DESCRIBED ON PAGES 303-305 OF THE ABOVE DOCUMENT HAS BEEN                     GSP030
C            CONVERTED TO SUBROUTINE: ANOVA . . . WHICH WITH MINOR CHANGES IS              GSP031
C            USED BY THE GALFO STATISTICS PACKAGE.                                         GSP032
C                                                                                          GSP033
C                                                                                          GSP034
C            THE FOLLOWING IS A LIST OF THE SUBROUTINES REQUIRED BY THE                    GSP035
C            GALFO STATISTICS PACKAGE:                                                     GSP036
C       -      -      -      -      -      -      -                                         GSP037
C       (A) ORIGINAL SUBROUTINES (THOSE PRODUCED SPECIALLY FOR THIS                        GSP038
C           PACKAGE)                                                                       GSP039
C                                                                                          GSP040
C                (1)  PTITLE                                                               GSP041
C                (2)  SREAD                                                                GSP042
C                (3)  FREAD                                                                GSP043
C                (4)  SPRINT                                                               GSP044
C                (5)  CAL1                                                                 GSP045
C                (6)  CAL2                                                                 GSP046
C                (7)  CAL3                                                                 GSP047
C                                                                                          GSP048
C       -      -      -      -      -      -      -                                         GSP049
C       (B) IBM SCIENTIFIC PACKAGE SUBROUINTES (PER IBM DOC. H 20-0205-1)                  GSP049
C                                                                                          GSP050
C                (1)  AVCAL                                                                GSP051
C                (2)  AVDAT                                                                GSP052
C                (3)  CHISQ                                                                GSP053
C                (4)  KRANK                                                                GSP054
C                (5)  MEANQ                                                                GSP055
C                (6)  RANK                                                                 GSP056
C                (7)  SRANK                                                                GSP057
C                (8)  TIE                                                                  GSP058
C                (9)  TTEST                                                                GSP059
C                (10) TWOAV                                                                GSP060
C                (11) UTEST                                                                GSP061
C                (12) WTEST                                                                GSP062
C                                                                                          GSP063
C       -      -      -      -      -      -      -                                         GSP064
C       (C) STANDARD FORTRAN FUNCTIONS (PER IBM DOC. C28-6629-0)                           GSP065
C                                                                                          GSP066
C                (1)  MAXO                                                                 GSP067
C                (2)  MINO                                                                 GSP068
C                (3)  SQRI                                                                 GSP069
C       -      -      -      -      -      -      -                                         GSP070
C       (D) CONVERTED SUBROUTINES                                                          GSP071
C                                                                                          GSP072
C                (1)  ANOVA . . . . CONVERTED FROM THE IBM                                 GSP073
C            ANALYSIS OF VARIANCE MAIN PROGRAM                                             GSP074
C            (PER IBM DOC. H 20-0205-1, 1966, PAGES 303-305).                             GSP075
C                                                                                          GSP076
C
```

```
C      III.  GENERAL  FORMAT  FOR  DATA  CARD  INPUT                      GSP077
C               (1)  CONTROL  CARD:  (SEE  GALFO  STATISTICS  PACKAGE  DOCUMENTATION)  GSP078
C               (2)  TITLE  CARD(S)                                       GSP079
C                       COL.  1:  CONTINUATION  CODE;  IF=0,  THEN  NO  MORE  TITLE  CARDS;  GSP080
C                                IF=1,  TITLE  CARDS  CONTINUE.           GSP081
C                       COLS.  2-80:  CHARACTER  INFORMATION  TO  BE  PRINTED  AS  THE  GSP082
C                                TITLE  OF  THE  CURRENT  STATISTICS  PROBLEM.  GSP083
C               (3)  DATA  CARDS                                          GSP084
C                       DATA  ARRANGED  IN  AGREEMENT  WITH  THE  CONTROL  CARD;  GSP085
C                       NO  DATA  IS  REQUIRED  IF  NRR  FLAG  SET = 1  (DATA  CURRENTLY  GSP086
C                       IN  STORAGE  IS  USED  RATHER  THAN  THAT  READ  IN)  GSP087
C               (4)  END  OF  JOB  CARD                                   GSP088
C                       9999  IS  PUNCHED  IN  COLS.  1-4                 GSP089
C                       (THIS  CARD  IS  USED  ONLY  AT  THE  VERY  END  OF  THE  DATA  DECK)  GSP090
C                                                                         GSP091
       COMMON  X(300,10),  NP,NRR,NWR,NDF,NC1,NC2,NC3,NC4,NC5,NC6,NC7,NC8,NC  GSP092
      :9,NC10,11,12,J1,J2                                                 GSP093
       DIMENSION  NCC(1)                                                  GSP094
         EQUIVALENCE  (NC1,  NCC(1))                                      GSP095
       INTEGER  DF                                                        GSP096
C                                                                         GSP097
C      °    °    °    °    °    °    °    °                               GSP098
C      MAIN  CONTROL                                                      GSP099
C      °    °    °    °    °    °    °    °                               GSP100
C                                                                         GSP101
C      °    °    °    °    °    °    °    °                               GSP102
C      READ  IN  A  CONTROL  CARD                                         GSP103
C      °    °    °    °    °    °    °    °                               GSP104
C                                                                         GSP105
    1      READ(1,9100)          NP,NRR,NWR,NDF,NC1,NC2,NC3,NC4,NC5       GSP106
 9100  FORMAT(2014)                                                      GSP107
       IF(NP-9999)3,2,3                                                  GSP108
    2      STOP                                                          GSP109
    3      NPL9=NP-9                                                     GSP110
       GO  TO  (1000,4,9,4,9,9,4),NPL9                                   GSP111
       GO  TO  9                                                         GSP112
    4      11=NC1                                                        GSP113
       12=NC2                                                            GSP114
       NC1=11°12                                                         GSP115
       NC2=0                                                             GSP116
C                                                                         GSP117
C      °    °    °    °    °    °    °    °                               GSP118
       READ  AND  PRINT  TITLE  CARD(S)                                   GSP119
C      °    °    °    °    °    °    °    °                               GSP120
C                                                                         GSP121
    9      CALL  PTITLE                                                   GSP122
C                                                                         GSP123
C      °    °    °    °    °    °    °    °                               GSP124
C      THIS  SECTION  READS  THE  DATA  IF  REQUESTED  BY  A  NON-ZERO  IN  NRR  GSP125
C      °    °    °    °    °    °                                         GSP126
C                                                                         GSP127
       DU  10  NJ=L,  11                                                  GSP128
       IF(NCC(NJ))  10,11,10                                             GSP129
   10      CONTINUE                                                      GSP130
   11      NJ=NJ-1                                                       GSP131
       CALL  SREAD(NDF,X,NJ)                                             GSP132
       NPL11=NP-11                                                       GSP133
       GO  TO  (1200,  1300,  1400,  1500,  1600),  NPL11               GSP134
C                                                                         GSP135
C      °    °    °    °    °    °    °    °                               GSP136
C      THIS  SECTION  PRINTS  THE  DATA  IF  REQUESTED  BY  A  NON-ZERO  NWR  GSP137
C      °    °    °    °    °    °    °    °                               GSP138
C                                                                         GSP139
   12      CALL  SPRINT  (NDF,X,NCC,NJ)                                   GSP140
C                                                                         GSP141
C      °    °    °    °    .    °    °    °                               GSP142
C      SWITCH  TO  THE  APPROPRIATE  SECTION  FOR  COMPUTING  THE  STATISTICS  PRO  GSP143
C      °    °    °    °    °    °    °    °                               GSP144
C                                                                         GSP145
       GO  TO  (100,  200,  300,  400,  500,  600,  700,  800,  900,  1000,  1100,  1210,  1310,  GSP146
      :1410,  1510,  1610),  NP                                          GSP147
       WRITE  (3,  40)  NP                                               GSP148
   40      FORMAT  (1HO,  'NO  STATISTICAL  CALCULATION  ASSOCIATED  WITH  THE  FOLLOWI  GSP149
      :NG  GIVEN  CODE:',  14)                                           GSP150
       GO  TO  1                                                         GSP151
C                                                                         GSP152
C      °    °    °    °    °    °    °    °                               GSP153
```

```
C      PROBLEM 1      MEAN CALCULATION                                  GSP154
C      °      °      °      °      °      °      °      °               GSP155
C                                                                      GSP156
  100  CALL CAL1 (1, NC1, X, XBAR)                                     GSP157
       WRITE (3, 101) XBAR                                             GSP158
  101  FORMAT (1HO, //, 1H, 11X, 'XBAR (FROM THE FORMULA, XBAR = (SUM OF  GSP159
      :X(1))/N)', //, F16.4)                                          GSP160
       GO TO 1                                                        GSP161
C                                                                      GSP162
C      °      °      °      °      °      °      °      °               GSP163
C      PROBLEM 2      VARIANCE CALCULATION FROM THE DEFINITION FORMULA  GSP164
C      °      °      °      °      °      °      °      °               GSP165
C                                                                      GSP166
  200  CALL CAL2(1,NC1,X(1,1),XVAR)                                    GSP167
       XVAR=XVAR/FLOAT(NC1)                                           GSP168
       WRITE (3,201) XVAR                                             GSP169
  201  FORMAT (1HO,//,8X, 'VARIANCE      USING THE DEFINITION FORMULA, VAR. =  GSP170
      (SUM OF (X(I)-XBAR) SQUARED,) /N )',//, F16.4)                  GSP171
       GO TO 1                                                        GSP172
C                                                                      GSP173
C      °      °      °      °      °      °      °      °               GSP174
C      PROBLEM 3      VARIANCE CALCULATION FROM THE EFFICIENT FORMULA   GSP175
C      °      °      °      °      °      °      °      °               GSP176
C                                                                      GSP177
  300  CALL CAL2 (2, NCL, X, XVAR)                                     GSP178
       WRITE (3, 301) XVAR                                            GSP179
  301  FORMAT (1HO,//,8X, 'VARIANCE      (FROM THE EFFICIENT FORMULA, VAR. =  GSP180
      :          ,' (SUM OF (X(I)SQUARED))/N-(XBAR)SQUARED)',//,F16.4)  GSP181
       GO TO 1                                                        GSP182
C                                                                      GSP183
C      °      °      °      °      °      °      °      °               GSP184
C      PROBLEM 4      UNBIASED ESTIMATE OF THE VARIANCE                 GSP185
C      °      °      °      °      °      °      °      °               GSP186
C                                                                      GSP187
  400  CALL CAL2 (2, NC1, X, XVAR)                                     GSP188
       XVAR=(FLOAT (NC1)/(FLOAT (NC1-1)))°XVAR                        GSP189
       WRITE (3,401) XVAR                                             GSP190
  401  FORMAT (1HO,//,3X,'UNBIASED EST.',/,' OF THE VARIANCE   (FROM THE  GSP191
      FORMULA, UNBIAS. EST. = N/(N-1) TIMES THE BIASED ESTIMATE,'     GSP192
      ,/,20X,' WHERE THE BIASED EST. =                                GSP193
      :          ,' (SUM OF (X(I)SQUARED)/N - (XBAR) SQUARED), //, F16.4)  GSP194
       GO TO 1                                                        GSP195
C                                                                      GSP196
C      °      °      °      °      °      °      °      °               GSP197
C      PROBLEM 5      STANDARD DEVIATION                               GSP198
C      °      °      °      °      °      °      °      °               GSP199
C                                                                      GSP200
  500  CALL CAL2 (3,NC1,X,SD)                                          GSP201
       WRITE (3,501)SD                                                GSP202
  501  FORMAT (1HO,//,5X, 'STAND. DEV.      FROM THE FORMULA, S.D. = SQ. ROOT  GSP203
      OF THE VARIANCE'/20X,' WHERE THE VARIANCE = '                   GSP204
      :          ,' (SUM OF (X(I) SQUARED))/N -(XBAR) SQUARED)',//,F16.4)  GSP205
       GO TO 1                                                        GSP206
C                                                                      GSP207
C      °      °      °      °      °      °      °      °               GSP208
C      PROBLEM 6      UNBIASED ESTIMATE OF THE STANDARD DEVIATION       GSP209
C      °      °      °      °      °      °      °      °               GSP210
C                                                                      GSP211
  600  CALL CAL2 (2, NC1, X, XVAR)                                     GSP212
       SD=SQRT (FLOAT (NC1)/(FLOAT (NC1-1)°XVAR)                      GSP213
       WRITE (3,601) SD                                               GSP214
  601  FORMAT (1HO,//,3X,'UNBIASED EST.',/ OF THE ST. DEV.      (FROM THE SQ  GSP215
      ROOT OF THE UNBIASED VARIANCE'/20X, 'WHERE THE UNBIASED VAR. =   GSP216
      (N/(N-1) TIMES '                                                GSP217
      :               (SUM OF (X(I) SQUARED))/N - (XBAR) SQUARED)',//, F16.4)  GSP218
       GO TO 1                                                        GSP219
C                                                                      GSP220
C      °      °      °      °      °      °      °      °               GSP221
C      PROBLEM 7      T-TEST ASSUMING THAT MU(POP. MEANS) IS GIVEN      GSP222
C      °      °      °      °      °      °      °      °               GSP223
C                                                                      GSP224
  700  N=NC1-1                                                        GSP225
       CALL TTEST (X(1,1),1,X(2,1),N, 1,DF,T)                         GSP226
       WRITE (3,701)T                                                 GSP227
  701  FORMAT (1HO,//,9X,                                             GSP228
      :               'T-VALUE      ASSUMING THAT THE POPULATION MEANS (MU)  GSP229
      IS GIVEN',/,20X, '(WHERE T = (XBAR-MU)/(S.D./SQ. ROOT(N-1))     GSP230
```

```
          F16.4)                                                         GSP231
          GO TO 1                                                        GSP232
C                                                                        GSP233
C        °    °    °    °    °    °    °    °                             GSP234
C        PROBLEM 8       T-TEST FOR SAMPLE MEANS DIFFERENCE DISTRIBUTION ASUM   GSP235
C                        MU(1) = MU(2) AND VAR(1) NOT = VAR(2)           GSP236
C        °    °    °    °    °    °    °    °                             GSP237
C                                                                        GSP238
  800   CALL T-TEST(X,NC1,X(1,2),NC2, 3,DF,T)                            GSP239
        WRITE (3,801)T                                                   GSP240
  801   FORMAT (1HO,//,8X,                                               GSP241
        :           'T-VALUE   FOR SAMPLE MEANS DIFFERENCE DISTRIBUTION  GSP242
        ASSUMING THAT MU(1) = MU(2) AND VAR(1) NOT = VAR(2)',//,F16.4)   GSP243
        GO TO 1                                                          GSP244
C                                                                        GSP245
C        °    °    °    °    °    °    °    °                             GSP246
C        PROBLEM 9      PERARSON'S R: TOTAL CORRELATION COEFFICIENT      GSP247
C        °    °    °    °    °    °    °                                  GSP248
C                                                                        GSP249
  900   CALL CAL3 (1,NC1,X(1,1),X(1,2),1,2,R)                            GSP250
        WRITE (3,901)R                                                   GSP251
  901   FORMAT (1HO,//,4X, 'CORRELATION',/,3X, 'COEFFICIENT R     (FROM THE FOR   GSP252
        MULA, R = SUM OF  (X(I)°Y(I))/NP − XBAR°YBAR',/,43X,' ALL DIVEDED BY   GSP253
        ',            'S.D.(X)°S.D.(Y);      WHERE NP = # OF X, Y PAIRS    )'   GSP254
        ,/,F16.4)                                                        GSP255
        GO TO 1                                                          GSP256
C                                                                        GSP257
C        °    °    °    °    °    °    °                                  GSP258
C        PROBLEM 10     ANALYSIS OF VARIANCE                             GSP259
C        °    °    °    °    °    °    °                                  GSP260
C                                                                        GSP261
 1000   CALL ANOVA(NRR)                                                  GSP262
        GO TO 1                                                          GSP263
C                                                                        GSP264
C        °    °    °    °    °    °    °                                  GSP265
C        PROBLEM 11 CHI-SQUARE                                           GSP266
C        °    °    °    °    °    °    °                                  GSP267
C                                                                        GSP268
 1100   CALL CHISQ (X, 11, 12, CS, DF, IERR, X(1,4), X(1,5)             GSP269
        IERR=IERR+1                                                      GSP270
        GO TO (1120, 1111), IERR                                         GSP271
        WRITE (3, 1101)                                                  GSP272
 1101   FORMATION (1HO, 'ERROR . . . DEGRESS OF FREEDOM = 0 . . . CHI-SQ. SET = 0')   GSP273
        GO TO 1120                                                       GSP274
 1111   WRITE (3, 1112)                                                  GSP275
 1112   FORMAT (1HO, 'EXPECTED VALUE < ONE IN ONE OR MORE CELLS.')       GSP276
 1120   WRITE (3, 1121) CS                                               GSP277
 1121   FORMAT (1HO,//,6X,'CIII-SQUARE     (FROM THE FORMULA, CHI-SQ. = SUM OF   GSP278
        :((F-OBS (I, J)-F-EXP (I,J))/F-EXP (I.J))',/,20X,' . . . .',     GSP279
        :                         EXCEPT FOR A 2 × 2',                   GSP280
        :'TABLE WHER',                                                   GSP281
        :E CHI-SQ. = N°(IF-OBS (1,1)°F-OBS (2,2)-F-OBS (1,2)°F-OBS (2, 1) | − N/   GSP282
        :2)SQUARED'   ,/,F16.4,4X                                        GSP283
        :             ,'ALL DIVIDED BY (F-OBS(1,1)+F-OBS(1,2)° . . . . .   GSP284
        :°(F-OBS(1,2)+F-OBS(2,2))'/,20X,       'WHERE N = GRAND TOTAL)'  GSP285
        :)                                                               GSP286
        GO TO 1                                                          GSP287
C                                                                        GSP288
C        °    °    °    °    °    °    °    °                             GSP289
        PROBLEM 12     MANN-WHITNEY U-TEST                               GSP290
C        °    °    °    °    °    °    °                                  GSP291
C                                                                        GSP292
 1200   J1=1                                                             GSP293
        J2=2                                                             GSP294
        11=MINO (NC1, NC2)                                               GSP295
        12=MAXO (NC1, NC2)                                               GSP296
        IF (NC1-NC2) 1206, 1206, 1201                                    GSP297
 1201   J1=2                                                             GSP298
        J2=1                                                             GSP299
 1206   DO 1207 I=1, 12                                                  GSP300
        J=11+I                                                           GSP301
 1207   X (J, J1) = X (I, J2)                                            GSP302
        NC10 = NC1 + NC2                                                 GSP303
        CALL UTEST (X (1, J1), X (1, 6) I1, I2, U, Z)                    GSP304
        GO TO 12                                                         GSP305
 1210   WRITE (3, 1211) U, Z                                             GSP306
 1211   FORMAT (1HO,//, 9X, 'U-VALUE    (FROM THE FORMULA, U=N1°N2 − U-PRIME'   GSP307
```

```
          :,/,20X, 'WHERE U-PRIME = N1°N2 + (N2°(N2 + 1))/2 – R2 AND WHERE N1 =      GSP308
          :# OF SMALLER GROUP CASES AND N2 = # OF LARGER GROUP CASES',/,F16.4,'        GSP309
          :    AND WHERE R2 = SUM OF RANKS OF THE LARGER GROUP . . . . . . NOTE THA    GSP310
          :T IF U-PRIME < U THEN U IS SET = U-PRIME)',//,9X, Z-VALUE     (FRO          GSP311
          :M THE FORMULA, Z = (U-XBAR)/S WHERE XBAR = (N1°N2)/2',/, 20X,' AND WH        GSP312
          :ERE S = THE SQ. ROOT OF (N1°N2 (N1 + N2 + 1))/12 IF THERE ARE NO TIES,'      GSP313
          :/,F16.4, 4X, 'OR WHERE IF THERE ARE TIES, S = SQ. ROOT OF ((N1°N2)/          GSP314
          :N° (N – 1)) TIMES ((N(CUBED) – N)/12 –T)'                                    GSP315
          WRITE (3, 1212)                                                              GSP316
     1212 FORMAT                              20X, 'WHERE HERE N = N1 +                 GSP317
          :N2 AND T = THE SUM OF (LITTLE-T) CUBED – LITTLE-T)/12',/,20X,                GSP318
          :WHERE LITTLE-T = # OF MEASURES TIED FOR A GIVEN RANK)')                      GSP319
          GO TO 1                                                                      GSP320
C                                                                                      GSP321
C          °     °    °     °     °     °     °                                         GSP322
C          PROBLEM 13      FRIEDMAN TWO-WAY ANALYSIS OF VARIANCE                        GSP323
C          °     °    °     °     °     °     °                                         GSP324
C                                                                                      GSP325
     1300 CALL TWOAV (X, X (1,6), 11, 12, X (1, 9), XR, DF, O)                          GSP326
          GO TO 12                                                                     GSP327
     1310 WRITE (3, 1311) XR                                                           GSP328
     1311 FORMAT (1HO,//,2X, 'FRIEDMAN 2-WAY',/,3X, 'ANAL. OF VAR.'/7X, 'STATIST        GSP329
          :IC    (FROM THE FORMULA, FRIEDMAN STAT. = 12/(N°N° (M + 1)) TIMES THE S      GSP330
          :UM (FROM J = 1, M) OF (R(J) SQUARED) ALL MINUS 3N(M + 1)',20X, 'WHERE R      GSP331
          :(J) = ',                                                                    GSP332
          :THE SUM OF THE RANKS OF N NUMBER OF GROUPS FOR THE J TH CASE',               GSP333
          :/,F16.4,'    AND WHERE N = # OF GROUPS AND M = # OF CASES PER GROU           GSP334
          :P)'                                                                         GSP335
          GO TO 1                                                                      GSP336
C                                                                                      GSP337
C          °     °    °     °     °     °     °                                         GSP338
C          PROBLEM 14      SPEARMAN RANK CORRELATION COEFFICIENT                        GSP339
C          °     °    °     °     °     °     °                                         GSP340
C                                                                                      GSP341
     1400 DO 1401 I = 1, 2                                                             GSP342
     1401 CALL RANK (X(1, I), X(1, I + 5), NC1)                                        GSP343
          GO TO 12                                                                     GSP344
     1410 CALL SRANK (X, X (1, 2), X (1, 6), NC1, RS, T, DF, O)                        GSP345
          WRITE (3, 1411) RS, T                                                        GSP346
     1411 FORMAT (1HO,//,3X, 'SPEARMAN RANK',/, 2X, 'CORREL. COEFF.     (FROM THE       GSP347
          :FOLLOWING FORMULAS: ',/,20X, 'CASE-1 (NO TIES OF RANKS): SPEARMAN R          GSP348
          :K CORREL. COEFF. (RS) = 1 – 6D/(N(CUBED) – N)' ,/,F16.4, '     CASE-2 (      GSP349
          :AT LEAST ONE TIE): RS = (A+B–D)/(2°SQ. ROOT A°B))',/,20X, 'WHERE D           GSP350
          : = SUM OF (X(I) – Y(I)) SQUARED FROM I = 1 TO N AND N = THE # OF RANK        GSP351
          :S PER VARIABLE',/,20X,                                                      GSP352
          :                     'AND WHERE A = (N(CUBED) – N)/12 – TX AND WHERE         GSP353
          :B = (N(CUBED) – N)/12 – TY',/,20X,                                          GSP354
          :                     'AND WHERE TX = SUM OF (LITTLE-T (CUBED) – LI           GSP355
          :TTLE-T)/12 OVER X AND TY IS SIMULARLY CALCUL. OVER Y'                        GSP356
          :                          ////,9X, 'T-VALUE    (FROM THE FORMULA,           GSP357
          :T = RS°SQ. ROOT OF ((N – 2)/(1 – RS(SQUARED))  ',//,F16.4)                   GSP358
          GO TO 1                                                                      GSP359
C                                                                                      GSP360
C          °     °    °     °     °     °     °                                         GSP361
C          PROBLEM 15      KENDALL RANK CORRELATION COEFFICIENT                         GSP362
C          °     °    °     °     °     °     °                                         GSP363
C                                                                                      GSP364
     1500 DO 1501 I = 1, 2                                                             GSP365
     1501 CALL RANK (X (1, I), X (1, I + 5), NC1)                                      GSP366
          GO TO 12                                                                     GSP367
     1510 CALL KRANK (X, X (1, 2), X (1, 6), NC1, TAU, SD, Z, O)                       GSP368
          DO 1520 I = 1, NC1                                                           GSP369
          J = NC1 + 1 – I                                                              GSP370
          X(I, 3) = X(J, 1)                                                            GSP371
     1520 X(1, 4) = X(J, 2)                                                            GSP372
          CALL KRANK (X(1, 3), X(1, 4), X(1,6), NC1, TAU1, SD, Z, O)                   GSP373
          TAU = (TAU1 + TAU)/2.                                                        GSP374
          WRITE (3, 1511) TAU                                                          GSP375
          WRITE (3, 1512) SD, Z                                                        GSP376
     1511 FORMAT (1HO,//,4X, 'KENDALL RANK' ,/,2X, 'CORREL. COEFF.     (FROM THE F      GSP377
          :OLLOWING FORMULAS:',/,20X,                                                  GSP378
          :'CASE-1 (NO TIES OF RANKS): KENDALL RK CORREL. COEFF. (TAU) = S/M            GSP379
          :',/,F16.4,'    CASE-2 (AT LEAST ONE TIE):  TAU = S/(SQ. ROOT OF ((          GSP380
          :M – TX)°(M – TY))',/,20X, 'WHERE M = (1/2)°N°(N – 1)'                        GSP381
          :,'AND WHERE TX = SUM OF (LITTLE-T (SQUARED) – LITTLE-T)/2 OVER THE VA        GSP382
          :RIABLE X',/,20X, 'WHERE TY IS CALCUL. SIMILARLY FOR Y ,           'AND       GSP383
          :WHERE S = TOTAL SCORE CALCULATED FOR RANKS IN VARIABLE Y',/,20X,            GSP384
```

```
          :'BY SELECTING EACH RANK IN TURN,   ',                              GSP385
          :                           'ADDING +1 FOR EACH LARGER RANK TO IT   GSP386
          :S RIGHT,')                                                         GSP387
     1512 FORMAT (20X,                                                        GSP388
          :'AND ADDING −1 FOR EACH SMALLER RANK;  HOWEVER, THOSE RANKS WHICH  GSP389
          : HAVE TIES IN EITHER VARIABLE ARE NOT COMPARED WITH EACH OTHER;',  GSP390
          :/,20X, 'N = THE NUMBER OF RANKS PER VARIABLE' ,/,20X,              GSP391
          :'(NOTE:  RANKS OF Y HAVE BEEN SORTED IN SEQUENCE WITH RANKS OF X)  GSP392
          :)',////,3X, 'STANDA',                                              GSP393
          :RD DEV.    (FROM THE FORMULA, SD = SQ. ROOT OF (2(2N + 5)/(9N(N − 1))  GSP394
          :   ) ' ,//,F16.4,///,9X, 'Z-VALUE    (FROM THE FORMULA, Z = TAU/SD)',  GSP395
          ://,F16.4)                                                          GSP396
          GO TO 1                                                             GSP397
    C                                                                         GSP398
    C    °    °    °    °    °    °    °    °                                  GSP399
    C    PROBLEM 16    KENDALL COEFFICIENT OF CONCORDANCE                     GSP400
    C    °    °    °    °    °    °    °    °                                  GSP401
    C                                                                         GSP402
     1600 CALL WTEST (X, X(1, 6), I1, I2, X (1, 9), W, CS, DF, O)             GSP403
          GO TO 12                                                            GSP404
     1610 WRITE (3, 1611)W                                                    GSP405
          WRITE (3, 1612)CS                                                   GSP406
     1611 FORMAT (1HO,//,2X, 'KENDALL COEFF.',/,2X, 'OF CONCORDANCE    (FROM THE  GSP407
          : FORMULA, KENDALL COEFF. OF CONCORD. (W) = S/((1/12)°N(SQUARED)°(M  GSP408
          :(CUBED) − M) −N°7)',/,F16.4,'    WHERE S = SUM OF (Y(J) −RBAR)SQUA  GSP409
          :RED FROM J = 1 TO M',/,20X, 'AND WHERE Y(J) = SUM OF R(I, J) FROM I = 1  GSP410
          :TO N WHERE R(I, J) = TO THE',                                      GSP411
          :RANK OF THE J TH CASE OF THE I TH VARIABLE',/,20X, 'AND WHERE RBAR  GSP412
          : = SUM OF Y(J) FROM J = 1 TO M ALL DIVIDED BY N',/,20X, 'AND WHERE T =  GSP413
          : SUM OF ((LITTLE-T) CUBED − LITTLE-T)/12 FROM I = 1 TO N',/,20X, 'AND  GSP414
          :FINALLY WHERE N = THE # OF VARIABLES AND M = THE # OF CASES PER VA  GSP415
          :RIABLE)')                                                          GSP416
     1612 FORMAT (////,6X, 'CHI-SQUARE    (WHERE CHI-SQ. = N(M − 1)°W)',       GSP417
          ://,F16.4)                                                          GSP418
          GO TO 1                                                             GSP419
          END                                                                 GSP420


    // EXEC FORTRAN
          SUBROUTINE PTITLE                                                   PTITLE00
          DIMENSION TITLE (20)                                                PTITLE01
     3    WRITE (3, 9101)                                                     PTITLE02
     9101 FORMAT (1H1)                                                        PTITLE03
     4    READ (1, 9102) J, (TITLE (I), I = 1, 20)                            PTITLE04
     9102 FORMAT (11, 19A4, A3)                                               PTITLE05
          WRITE (3, 9103) TITLE                                               PTITLE06
     9103 FORMAT (1H, 20A4)                                                   PTITLE07
          GO TO (4), J                                                        PTITLE08
          RETURN                                                              PTITLE09
          END                                                                 PTITLE10


    // EXEC FORTRAN
          SUBROUTINE SREAD (NF, X, NJ)                                        SREAD000
          DIMENSION X(300, 10), NCC (1)                                       SREAD001
          COMMON Y(300, 10),NP,NRR,NWR,NDF,NC1,NC2,NC3,NC4,NC5,NC6,NC7,NC8,NC  SREAD002
          :9, NC10, 11, 12                                                    SREAD003
          EQUIVALENCE (NC1, NCC (1))                                          SREAD004
          CALL FREAD (−1, X)                                                  SREAD005
          IF (NRR) 99, 100, 99                                               SREAD006
     99   GO TO (20), NF                                                      SREAD007
          DO 1 J = 1, NJ                                                      SREAD008
     1    CALL FREAD (NCC (J), X (1, J))                                      SREAD009
     100  CONTINUE                                                            SREAD010
          RETURN                                                              SREAD011
     20   DO 21 I = 1, NC1                                                    SREAD012
          DO 21 J = 1, NJ                                                     SREAD013
     21   CALL FREAD (1, X (I, J))                                            SREAD014
          GO TO 100                                                           SREAD015
     50   FORMAT (16F5.0)                                                     SREAD016
          END                                                                 SREAD017


    // EXEC FORTRAN
          SUBROUTINE FREAD (N, A)                                             FREAD000
          DIMENSION N(1), A(1), NCARD(80)                                     FREAD001
```

```
      DOUBLE PRECISION    NUMB, NUMBA                          FREAD002
      EQUIVALENCE (R, NA)                                      FREAD003
C                                                              FREAD004
C      o    o    o    o    o    o    o    o                    FREAD005
C                                                              FREAD006
C     INITIALIZATIONS                                          FREAD007
C      o    o    o    o    o    o    o                         FREAD008
C                                                              FREAD009
      NF = 0                                                   FREAD010
      NPERF = 0                                                FREAD011
      NDEC = 0                                                 FREAD012
      NEF = 0                                                  FREAD013
      NE = 0                                                   FREAD014
      NTF = 0                                                  FREAD015
      NQF = 0                                                  FREAD016
      NUMBA = 0                                                FREAD017
      NUMB = 0                                                 FREAD018
      INTF = 0                                                 FREAD019
      ISIGN = 1                                                FREAD020
      KSIGN = 1                                                FREAD021
      I = 1                                                    FREAD022
      NN = N(1)                                                FREAD023
C                                                              FREAD024
C      o    o    o    o    o    o    o    o                    FREAD025
C                                                              FREAD026
C     START                                                    FREAD027
C      o    o    o    o    o    o    o                         FREAD028
C                                                              FREAD029
      IF (NN) 1, 2, 5                                          FREAD030
    1 IC = 80                                                  FREAD031
      NTEST = 7835192                                          FREAD032
      IF (NN) 100, 7, 7                                        FREAD033
    2 NN = -1                                                  FREAD034
    5 IF (NTEST - 7835192) 200, 6, 200                         FREAD035
    6 IF (IC - 80) 9, 7, 9                                     FREAD036
    7 IC = 1                                                   FREAD037
C                                                              FREAD038
C      o    o    o    o    o    o    o    o                    FREAD039
C                                                              FREAD040
C     READ IN A NEW CARD                                       FREAD041
C      o    o    o    o    o    o    o    o                    FREAD042
C                                                              FREAD043
      READ (1, 8) (NCARD(II), II = 1,80)                       FREAD044
    8 FORMAT (80A1)                                            FREAD045
      GO TO 10                                                 FREAD046
    9 IC = IC + 1                                              FREAD047
   10 CONTINUE                                                 FREAD048
   14 IF (NQF) 20, 11, 20                                      FREAD049
   11 NCHAR = NCARD (IC)                                       FREAD050
      IF (NCHAR) 13, 15, 15                                    FREAD051
   13 NCHAR = (2147483647 + NCHAR) + 1                         FREAD052
   15 NCHAR = NCHAR/16777216                                   FREAD053
      IF (NCARD(1C)) 40, 23, 23                                FREAD054
   23 IF (NCHAR - 64) 27, 24, 27                               FREAD055
   24 IF (NF) 80, 25, 80                                       FREAD056
   25 NOF = 0                                                  FREAD057
      GO TO 99                                                 FREAD058
   27 IF (NCHAR-75) 29, 28, 29                                 FREAD059
   28 NPERF = 1                                                FREAD060
      GO TO 6                                                  FREAD061
   29 IF (NCHAR - 78) 31, 30, 31                               FREAD062
   30 JSIGN = 1                                                FREAD063
      GO TO 35                                                 FREAD064
   31 IF (NCHAR - 96) 33, 32, 33                               FREAD065
   32 JSIGN = -1                                               FREAD066
      GO TO 35                                                 FREAD067
   33 IF (NCHAR - 123) 210, 34, 210                            FREAD068
   34 NTF = 1                                                  FREAD069
      IF (N(1)) 210, 39, 210                                   FREAD070
   39 N (1) = I                                                FREAD071
      IF (NF) 80, 38, 80                                       FREAD072
   20 IF (NCARD (10) - 1077952576) 6, 25, 6                    FREAD073
   35 IF (NEF) 37, 36, 37                                      FREAD074
   36 ISIGN = JSIGN                                            FREAD075
      GO TO 6                                                  FREAD076
   37 KSIGN = JSIGN                                            FREAD077
      GO TO 6                                                  FREAD078
   38 N(1) = I - 1
      GO TO 100
   40 IF (NCHAR/16 - 7) 41, 45, 41
```

```
41    IF (NCHAR − 69) 43, 42, 43                                    FREAD079
42    NEF = 1                                                       FREAD080
      NPERF = 0                                                     FREAD081
      GO TO 6                                                       FREAD082
43    IF (NCHAR − 73) 210, 44, 210                                  FREAD083
44    INTF = 1                                                      FREAD084
      GO TO 6                                                       FREAD085
45    NF = 1                                                        FREAD086
      IF (NPERF) 46, 48, 46                                         FREAD087
46    IF (NEF) 220, 47, 220                                         FREAD088
47    NDEC = NDEC + 1                                               FREAD089
      GO TO 60                                                      FREAD090
48    IF (NEF) 49, 60, 49                                           FREAD091
49    NE = NE*10 + (NCHAR − 112)                                    FREAD092
      GO TO 65                                                      FREAD093
60    NUMBA = NUMBA*10.DO + DFLOAT (NCHAR − 112)                    FREAD094
65    CALL OVERFL (II)                                              FREAD095
      GO TO (79), II                                                FREAD096
      NUMB = NUMBA                                                  FREAD097
      GO TO 6                                                       FREAD098
79    NQF = 1                                                       FREAD099
80    NUMB = FLOAT (ISIGN)*NUMB                                     FREAD100
      NDEC = KSIGN*NE − NDEC                                        FREAD101
      NUMB = NUMB* (10.DO**NDEC)                                    FREAD102
88    CALL OVERFL (II)                                              FREAD103
      GO TO (240, 90, 230), II                                      FREAD104
90    GO TO (91), INTF                                              FREAD105
      A(I) = NUMB                                                   FREAD106
93    IF (I − NN) 92, 100, 92                                       FREAD107
91    NA = NUMB + SIGN (.5, NUMB)                                   FREAD108
      CALL OVERFL (II)                                              FREAD109
      GO TO (240, 94, 240), II                                      FREAD110
94    A(I) = R                                                      FREAD111
      GO TO 93                                                      FREAD112
92    I = I + 1                                                     FREAD113
      GO TO (100), NTF                                              FREAD114
99    NF = 0                                                        FREAD115
      NE = 0                                                        FREAD116
      NUMBA = 0                                                     FREAD117
      NUMB = 0                                                      FREAD118
      NPERF = 0                                                     FREAD119
      NDEC = 0                                                      FREAD120
      NEF = 0                                                       FREAD121
      NE = 0                                                        FREAD122
      ISIGN = 1                                                     FREAD123
      KSIGN = 1                                                     FREAD124
      INTF = 0                                                      FREAD125
      GO TO 6                                                       FREAD126
100   RETURN                                                        FREAD127
200   WRITE (3, 201)                                                FREAD128
201   FORMAT (  '0 FREAD ERR . . . NO INITIALIZATION OF THIS ROUTINE . . . AUTO FREAD129
     :MATICALLY DONE THIS TIME')                                    FREAD130
      GO TO 1                                                       FREAD131
210   WRITE (3, 211) NCARD (IC), NCARD                              FREAD132
211   FORMAT (1HO, 'FREAD ERR . . . THE ILLEGAL CHARACTER " ',A1,' " WAS READ FR FREAD133
     :OM THE FOLLOWING CARD:',                                      FREAD134
     :               //,1X' " ' , 80A1, ' " ')                     FREAD135
      GO TO 6                                                       FREAD136
220   WRITE (3, 221)                                                FREAD137
221   FORMAT (1HO, 'FREAD ERR . . . . DEC. POINT FOUND IN EXPONENT NUMBER . . . FREAD138
     :IGNORED')                                                     FREAD139
      GO TO 6                                                       FREAD140
230   CONTINUE                                                      FREAD141
240   WRITE (3,231)                                                 FREAD142
231   FORMAT (1HO, 'FREAD ERR . . . NUMBER TOO LARGE OR TOO SMALL TO READ . . . FREAD143
      SET = 0')                                                     FREAD144
      NUMB = 0                                                      FREAD145
      GO TO 90                                                      FREAD146
      END                                                           FREAD147


// EXEC FORTRAN
      SUBROUTINE SPRINT (NF, X, N, NJ)                              SPRINT00
      DIMENSION X(300, 10), N(1)                                    SPRINT01
      COMMON Y(300, 10), NP, NRR, NWR, NDF, NC1, NC2, NC3, NC4, NC5, NC6, NC7,  SPRINT02
     :NC8, NC9, NC10, 11, 12, J1, J2                                SPRINT03
      IF (NWR)1, 100, 1                                             SPRINT04
```

```
1       WRITE (3, 2)                                                    SPRINT05
        WRITE (3, 3)                                                    SPRINT06
2       FORMAT (1HO, // ,' DATA PRINTOUT')                             SPRINT07
3       FORMAT (1H+,13('−'))                                           SPRINT08
        I = NP − 10                                                     SPRINT09
        GO TO (40, 60, 70, 80, 70), I                                  SPRINT10
        GO TO (20), NF                                                 SPRINT11
10      DO 11 J = 1, NJ                                                 SPRINT12
        NI = N(J)                                                       SPRINT13
11      WRITE (3, 50) (X(I,J), I = 1, NI)                              SPRINT14
100     CONTINUE                                                       SPRINT15
        WRITE (3, 31)                                                  SPRINT16
        WRITE (3, 32)                                                  SPRINT17
31      FORMAT (1HO, 'OUTPUT STATISTIC')                              SPRINT18
50      FORMAT (///,(1X,8F12.4,/))                                     SPRINT19
32      FORMAT (1H+, 16 ('−'))                                         SPRINT20
        RETURN                                                         SPRINT21
20      NI = N(1)                                                      SPRINT22
        WRITE (3, 50) ((X(I, J), J = 1, NJ), I = 1, NI)               SPRINT23
        GO TO 100                                                     SPRINT24
40      WRITE (3, 41)                                                  SPRINT25
41      FORMAT (1H+, 15X, '(IN CONTINGENCY TABLE FORM)')              SPRINT26
        DO 42 I = 1, I1                                                SPRINT27
42      WRITE (3, 43) (X(J, 1), J = I, NC1, I1)                       SPRINT28
43      FORMAT (///, 1X, 10F12.4)                                      SPRINT29
        GO TO 100                                                     SPRINT30
60      WRITE (3, 61)                                                  SPRINT31
61      FORMAT (1H+, 15X, '(WITH RANKS OF EACH MEASURE ... TIED MEASURES HAVE  SPRINT32
        :BEEN ASSIGNED THE AVERAGE OF THE TIED RANKS)')               SPRINT33
        I1 = 1                                                        SPRINT34
63      I2 = MINO (NC10, 8) + I1 − 1                                  SPRINT35
        WRITE (3, 62) (X(I, J1), I = I1, I2)                          SPRINT36
        WRITE (3, 64) (X(I, 6), I = I1, I2)                           SPRINT37
        NC10 = NC10 − B                                               SPRINT38
        I1 = I2 + 1                                                   SPRINT39
        IF (NC10) 100, 100, 63                                        SPRINT40
62      FORMAT (///, 'MEASURED VALUE', 8F12.4)                        SPRINT41
64      FORMAT (1H,/, 'RANK', 11X, 8F12.4)                            SPRINT42
70      WRITE (3, 71)                                                  SPRINT43
71      FORMAT (1H+, 15 X, '(BY GROUPS OR VARIABLES WITH RANKS OF EACH MEAS  SPRINT44
        :URE; TIED MEASURES HAVE BEEN ASSIGNED THE AVERAGE OF THE TIED  SPRINT45
        :RANKS)'                                                       SPRINT46
        DO 75 I = 1, I1                                                SPRINT47
75      WRITE (3, 73) I, (X(J, 1), X (J, 6), J = I, NC1, I1)          SPRINT48
73      FORMAT (1HO, //, 'GROUP OR VARIABLE NUMBER', 12, //    4('MEASURED VA  SPRINT49
        :LUE   RANK'),(/4(1X, F15.4, F7.2))                           SPRINT50
        GO TO 100                                                     SPRINT51
80      WRITE (3, 71)                                                  SPRINT52
        DO 81 J = 1, 2                                                 SPRINT53
81      WRITE (3, 73) J, (X(I, J), X (I, J+5), I = 1, NC1)            SPRINT54
        GO TO 100                                                     SPRINT55
        END                                                          SPRINT56
```

```
// EXEC FORTRAN
        SUBROUTINE CAL1 (NC, N, X, A)                                 CAL10000
        COMMON Y(300, 10), NP, NRR, NWR, NDF, NC1, NC2, NC3, NC4, NC5, NC6, NC7,  CAL10001
        :NC8, NC9, NC10, 11, 12                                       CAL10002
        DIMENSION X(300, 10)                                          CAL10003
        GO TO (10, 20, 30), NC                                        CAL10004
1       RETURN                                                       CAL10005
10      A = 0                                                        CAL10006
        DO 11 I = 1, N                                                CAL10007
11      A = A + X (I, 1)                                              CAL10008
        A = A/FLOAT(N)                                                CAL10009
        GO TO 1                                                      CAL10010
20      A = 0                                                        CAL10011
        DO 21 I = 1, N                                                CAL10012
21      A = Y(I, I1)°Y(I, I2) +A                                      CAL10013
        GO TO 1                                                      CAL10014
30      A = 0                                                        CAL10015
        DO 31 I = 1, N                                                CAL10016
        XX = X(I, 1)                                                  CAL10017
31      A = A + XX°XX                                                 CAL10018
        GO TO 1                                                      CAL10019
        END                                                         CAL10020
```

```
// EXEC FORTRAN
      SUBROUTINE  CAL2 (NC, N, X, A)                                        CAL20000
      COMMON Y(300, 10), NP, NRR, NWR, NDF, NC1, NC2, NC3, NC4, NC5, NC6, NC7,  CAL20001
     :NC8, NC9, NC10, I1, I2                                              CAL20002
      DIMENSION X(300, 10)                                                CAL20003
      GO TO (10, 20, 30), NC                                             CAL20004
1     RETURN                                                            CAL20005
10    A = 0                                                              CAL20006
      CALL CAL 1 (1, N, X, XB)                                           CAL20007
      DO 11 I = 1, N                                                     CAL20008
      XC = X(I, 1) — XB                                                  CAL20009
11    A = A + XC°XC                                                      CAL20010
      GO TO 1                                                            CAL20011
20    NDR2 = 1                                                           CAL20012
21    CALL CAL 1 (1, N, X, XB)                                           CAL20013
      CALL CAL 1 (3, N, X, SX2)                                          CAL20014
      A = SX2/FLOAT(N) — XB°XB                                           CAL20015
      GO TO (1, 31), NDR2                                                CAL20016
30    NDR2 = 2                                                           CAL20017
      GO TO 21                                                           CAL20018
31    A = SQRT(A)                                                        CAL20019
      GO TO 1                                                            CAL20020
      END                                                                CAL20021


// EXEC FORTRAN
      SUBROUTINE CAL3 (NC, N, X1, X2, J1, J2, A)                         CAL30000
      DIMENSION X1(1), X2(1)                                             CAL30001
      COMMON Y(300, 10), NP, NRR, NWR, NDF, NC1, NC2, NC3, NC4, NC5, NC6, NC7,  CAL30002
     :NC8, NC9, NC10, I1, I2                                             CAL30003
      GO TO (10, 20), NC                                                CAL30004
1     RETURN                                                            CAL30005
10    I1 = J1                                                            CAL30006
      I2 = J2                                                            CAL30007
      CALL CAL1 (2, N, O, CXP)                                           CAL30008
      CALL CAL1 (1, N, X1, X1B)                                          CAL30009
      CALL CAL1 (1, N, X2, X2B)                                          CAL30010
      A = (CXP/FLOAT(N)) — X1B°X2B                                       CAL30011
      CALL CAL2 (3, N, X1, SD1)                                          CAL30012
      CALL CAL2 (3, N, X2, SD2)                                          CAL30013
      A = A/(SD1°SD2)                                                    CAL30014
      GO TO 1                                                            CAL30015
20    GO TO 1                                                            CAL30016
      END                                                                CAL30017


// EXEC FORTRAN
C                                                                        ANOVA000
C     .   .   .   .   .   .   .   .   .   .   .   .   .                   ANOVA001
C                                                                        ANOVA002
C     SUBROUTINE ANALYSIS OF VARIANCE (ANOVA)                            ANOVA003
C                                                                        ANOVA004
      SUBROUTINE ANOVA (NRR)                                             ANOVA005
      COMMON X(1)                                                        ANOVA006
C                                                                        ANOVA007
C     SUBROUTINES AND FUNCTION SUBPROGRAMS REQUIRED                      ANOVA008
C         AVDAT                                                          ANOVA009
C         AVCAL                                                          ANOVA010
C         MEANQ                                                          ANOVA011
C                                                                        ANOVA012
C         METHOD                                                         ANOVA013
C         THE METHOD IS BASED ON THE TECHNIQUE DISCUSSED BY H. O.        ANOVA014
C         HARTLEY IN 'MATHEMATICAL METHODS FOR DIGITAL COMPUTERS',       ANOVA015
C         EDITED BY A. RALSTON AND H. WILF, JOHN WILEY AND SONS,         ANOVA016
C         1962, CHAPTER 20.                                              ANOVA017
C                                                                        ANOVA018
C     .   .   .   .   .   .   .   .   .   .   .   .   .                   ANOVA019
C                                                                        ANOVA020
C     THE FOLLOWING DIMENSION MUST BE GREATER THAN OR EQUAL TO THE       ANOVA021
C     CUMULATIVE PRODUCT OF EACH FACTOR LEVEL PLUS ONE (LEVEL(I)+1)      ANOVA022
C     FOR I = 1 TO K, WHERE K IS THE NUMBER OF FACTORS.                  ANOVA023
C                                                                        ANOVA024
C                                                                        ANOVA025
C     THE FOLLOWING DIMENSIONS MUST BE GREATER THAN OR EQUAL TO THE      ANOVA026
C     NUMBER OF FACTORS.                                                 ANOVA027
C                                                                        ANOVA028
```

```
          DIMENSION HEAD(6), LEVEL(6), ISTEP(6), KOUNT(6), LASTS(6)              ANOVA029
C                                                                               ANOVA030
C     THE FOLLOWING DIMENSIONS MUST BE GREATER THAN OR EQUAL TO 2 TO            ANOVA031
C     THE K-TH POWER MINUS 1, ((2**K) − 1).                                     ANOVA032
C                                                                               ANOVA033
          DIMENSION SUMSQ(63), NDF(63), SMEAN(63)                               ANOVA034
C                                                                               ANOVA035
C     THE FOLLOWING DIMENSION IS USED TO PRINT FACTOR LABELS IN ANALYSIS        ANOVA036
C     OF VARIANCE TABLE AND IS FIXED.                                           ANOVA037
C                                                                               ANOVA038
          DIMENSION FMT(15)                                                     ANOVA039
C     .   .   .   .   .   .   .   .   .   .   .                                  ANOVA040
C                                                                               ANOVA041
        1 FORMAT (A4, A2, I2, A4, 3X, 11 (A1, I4)/(A1, I4, A1, I4, A1, I4, A1, I4, A1, I4))  ANOVA042
        2 FORMAT (26HO ANALYSIS OF VARIANCE . . . . A4, A2//)                   ANOVA043
        3 FORMAT (18HO LEVELS OF FACTORS/(3X, A1, 7X, I4))                      ANOVA044
        4 FORMAT (1HO//11H GRAND MEAN F20.5//)                                  ANOVA045
        5 FORMAT (10HO SOURCE OF 18X, 7HSUMS OF 10X, 10H DEGREES OF 9X, 4HMEAN/ ANOVA046
          10H VARIATION 18X, 7H SQUARES 11X, 7H FREEDOM 10X, 7H SQUARES/)       ANOVA047
        6 FORMAT (1H 15A1, F20.5, 10X, 16, F20.5)                               ANOVA048
        7 FORMAT (6H TOTAL 10X, F20.5, 10X, 16)                                 ANOVA049
        8 FORMAT (16F5.0)                                                       ANOVA050
C                                                                               ANOVA051
C     .   .   .   .   .   .   .   .   .   .   .                                  ANOVA052
C                                                                               ANOVA053
C     READ PROBLEM PARAMETER CARD                                              ANOVA054
C                                                                               ANOVA055
      100 READ (1, 1)    PR, PR1, K, BLANK, (HEAD(I), LEVEL (I), I = 1, K)       ANOVA056
          IF(K) 51, 50, 51                                                      ANOVA057
       51 CALL PTITLE                                                           ANOVA058
C         PR . . . . .PROBLEM NUMBER (MAY BE ALPHAMERIC)                        ANOVA059
C         PR1 . . . .PROBLEM NUMBER (CONTINUED)                                 ANOVA060
C         K . . . . .NUMBER OF FACTORS                                          ANOVA061
C         BLANK . .BLANK FIELD                                                  ANOVA062
C         HEAD . . .FACTOR LABELS                                              ANOVA063
C         LEVEL . .LEVELS OF FACTORS                                           ANOVA064
C                                                                               ANOVA065
C     PRINT PROBLEM NUMBER AND LEVELS OF FACTORS                               ANOVA066
C                                                                               ANOVA067
C                                                                               ANOVA068
C     CALCULATE TOTAL NUMBER OF DATA                                           ANOVA069
C                                                                               ANOVA070
          N = LEVEL(1)                                                          ANOVA071
          DO 102 I = 2, K                                                       ANOVA072
      102 N = N*LEVEL(I)                                                        ANOVA073
          IF(NRR) 103, 104, 103                                                 ANOVA074
C                                                                               ANOVA075
C     READ ALL INPUT DATA                                                      ANOVA076
C                                                                               ANOVA077
      103 CALL FREAD (−1, X)                                                    ANOVA078
          CALL FREAD (N, X)                                                     ANOVA079
C                                                                               ANOVA080
      104 CALL SPRINT (O, X, N, 1)                                              ANOVA081
          WRITE (3, 2) PR, PR1                                                  ANOVA082
          WRITE (3, 3) (HEAD(I), LEVEL(I), I = 1, K)                            ANOVA083
          CALL AVDAT (K, LEVEL, N, X, L, ISTEP, KOUNT)                          ANOVA084
          CALL AVCAL (K, LEVEL, X, L, 1 STEP, LASTS)                            ANOVA085
          CALL MEANQ (K,LEVEL,X,GMEAN,SUMSQ,NDF,SMEAN,ISTEP,KOUNT,LASTS)        ANOVA086
C                                                                               ANOVA087
C     PRINT GRAND MEAN                                                         ANOVA088
C                                                                               ANOVA089
          WRITE (3, 4) GMEAN                                                    ANOVA090
C                                                                               ANOVA091
C     PRINT ANALYSIS OF VARIANCE TABLE                                         ANOVA092
C                                                                               ANOVA093
          WRITE (3, 5)                                                          ANOVA094
          LL = (2**K) − 1                                                       ANOVA095
          ISTEP(1) = 1                                                          ANOVA096
          DO 105 I = 2, K                                                       ANOVA097
      105 ISTEP(I) = 0                                                          ANOVA098
          DO 110 I = 1, 15                                                      ANOVA099
      110 FMT(I) = BLANK                                                        ANOVA100
          NN = 0                                                                ANOVA101
          SUM = 0.0                                                             ANOVA102
      120 NN = NN + 1                                                           ANOVA103
          L = 0                                                                 ANOVA104
          DO 140 I = 1, K                                                       ANOVA105
```

```
       FMI(I) = BLANK                                              ANOVA106
       IF(ISTEP(I)) 130, 140, 130                                 ANOVA107
130    L = L + 1                                                  ANOVA108
       FMT(L) = HEAD(I)                                           ANOVA109
140    CONTINUE                                                   ANOVA110
       WRITE (3, 6) (FMT(I), I = 1, 15) SUMSQ(NN), NDF(NN), SMEAN(NN)  ANOVA111
       SUM = SUM + SUMSQ(NN)                                      ANOVA112
       IF(NN - LL) 145, 170, 170                                  ANOVA113
145    DO 160 I = 1, K                                            ANOVA114
       IF(ISTEP(I)) 147, 150, 147                                 ANOVA115
147    ISTEP(I) = 0                                               ANOVA116
       GO TO 160                                                  ANOVA117
150    ISTEP(I) = 1                                               ANOVA118
       GO TO 120                                                  ANOVA119
160    CONTINUE                                                   ANOVA120
170    N = 1 - 1                                                  ANOVA121
       WRITE (3, 7) SUM, N                                        ANOVA122
50     RETURN                                                     ANOVA123
       END                                                        ANOVA124
```

V. *Input Requirements* (Preparation of Control and Data Cards)

  A. General Requirements

   1. Control Card(s)—Each statistical test in the package requires one control card *except* the analysis of variance which requires two.

   2. Title Card(s)—A single title card follows the control card(s) unless the title must take up more space than the 80 columns which make up a standard IBM card.

   3. Data Card(s) follow the title card(s).

     The entire packet of control card(s), title card(s), and data card(s) is placed in the deck between the Execute card (last card in the program package) and an end of deck card (which is punched with a 9999). See Figure B.1.

  B. Preparation of control card(s)

   1. Columns 1-4 are used to specify which statistical test is to be made. The tests are coded as follows:

Code	Statistic
1	mean
2	variance (from the definition formula)
3	variance (from a more efficient formula)
4	unbiased estimate of the variance from a single random sample
5	standard deviation (square root of the variance)
6	unbiased estimate of SD (square root of statistic number four)
7	t-test for an assumed or hypothetical mean
8	t-test for the difference of means of two samples
9	Pearson's product-moment of linear correlation
10	analysis of variance
11	chi-square
12	Mann-Whitney U-test
13	Friedman two-way analysis of variance
14	Spearman rank order correlation
15	Kendall rank order correlation
16	Kendall coefficient of concordance

   2. Columns 5-8: only column 8 is used to either request that the data is to be "read in" by the computer or that the data has already been read in previously and a new test is to be performed on it. If data is to be read in, a numeral 1 is punched in column 8. If the data was read in previously

and another test is to be performed on it, a numeral 0 is punched in column 8.

3. Columns 9-12: only column 12 is used to either request that the data be printed out with the solution or not. Again a 1 is punched if a print out is requested and an 0 if a print out is not requested.

4. Columns 13-16 are left blank.

5. Columns 17-20 are used to specify the number of X values which will be placed on the data cards.

6. Columns 21-24 are used to specify the number of Y values (if there are any) which will be on the data cards.

7. Columns 25-28: the number of Z values . . . etc.

Table B.1 shows how control cards are prepared for the various types of statistical problems.

C. Preparation of Title Card(s)

The title card(s) follow the control cards. The title is printed on the card(s). The only precaution that must be taken is that the particular title card which concludes the title must have a blank column 1. If anything is printed in column 1, the computer will treat the next card which follows as another title card. When column 1 is blank, the computer is signaled that the particular card is the *last* title card. For example, if only one card is to be used for the title, *column one must be left blank*. If two cards are to be used for a title, the first one should have a numeral one punched in the first column and the second card is to have column one blank; etc.

D. Preparation of the Data Card(s)

The program for the GSP includes an ability for the computer to "free field" read data. This particular program, which Mr. Dawson and Mr. Hoyle developed for the package, makes it easy for the student to prepare data cards since he need not concern himself as to which particular places on the cards he punches data. The only precaution he must take is to put *at least* one blank space *between* each bit of data; i.e., if three scores such as 101.5, 10 and 26.78 constitute three pieces of data that follow one another, the first is punched, then the second, and then the third, with one or more spaces between each score. Even if the end of a card is reached in the middle of a score, it is merely continued on the next card.

TABLE B.1 Control Card Preparation for the Various Types of Problems

Problem Name and Code Number	Col. 1-4	Col. 5-8	Col. 9-12	Col. 13-16	-Col. 17-20	Col. 21-24	etc.
	1 2 3 4	5 6 7 8	9 10 11 12				
#1 Mean	1	0 or 1 in col. 8 (1 is read - 0 is not)	0 no print 1 is print (in col.12)	blank	# of X's		
#2 Variance	2	same as above	same as above	same as above	same as above		
#3 Variance	3	same	same	same	same		
#4 Unbiased est. of Var.	4	same	same	same	same		
#5 Stand. Dev.	5	same	same	same	same		
#6 Unbiased est. of SD	6	same	same	same	same		
#7 t-test for given mean	7	same	same	same	1 plus the number of X's (put given mean on first data card as first number)		
#8 t-test for diff. of means	8	same	same	same	# of X's	# of Y's	
#9 Coef. of Corrl.	9	same	same	same	# of X's	# of Y's	
#10 Analysis of Var. a.	10	same	same	same	blank	blank	

(two control cards) b.	Col. 1-6 1 2 3 4 5 6 A N O V A	7-8 7 8 number of factors	9-15 blank	16 Label 1st factor	17-20 no. of levels for 1st factor	21 Label second factor	22-25 no. of levels of second factor etc.
#11 Chi-Square	11	same	same	same	the no. of rows in the contingency table	the no. of cols. in the contingency table	
#12 Mann. Whitney U-test	12	same	same	same	no. of X vaules	no. of Y vaules	
#13 Friedman two way analysis of Variance	13	same	same	same	no. of rows in the input table	no. of cols. in the input table	
#14 Spearman Rank order Correlation	14	same	aame	same	no. of X values	no. of Y values	
#15 Kendall rank order correlation	15	same	same	same	no. of X values	no. of Y values	
#16 Kendall coeff. of concordance	16	same	same	same	no. of rows in the input table	no. of cols. in the input table	

TABLE B.2 shows how data cards are to be prepared for the various statistical tests.

Problem Type and Number	Data Card
1. Mean	Each X value is punched
2. Variance	Each X value is punched
3. Variance	Each X value is punched
4. Unbiased Estimate of Variance	Each X value is punched
5. Standard Deviation	Each X value is punched
6. unbiased Estimate of SD	Each X value is punched
7. t-test (given M)	The hypothetical true mean is made the first piece of data and the X values follow.
8. t-test (diff. between sample means)	The X values are placed on the data card(s) first, immediately followed by the Y values.
9. Pearson's coefficient of correlation	X values are placed on the data card(s) first, followed immediately by the corresponding Y values in the same order.
10. Analysis of variance	(See Table B.3 for an illustration of how to prepare the second control card and data cards for a three way classification of data.)
11. Chi-Square	Values from a contingency table are placed on cards in column order (first column, followed by the next one, etc.)
12. Mann Whitney U-Test	X values followed by Y values
13. Friedman two way analysis of variance	Same as chi-square
14. Spearman rank order correlation	Same as Pearson's coefficient of correlation. For the Spearman test, either scores or ranks may be used as data. (The program will rank the data that is given.)
15. Kendall rank order correlation	Same as Spearman and Pearson's correlation.
16. Kendall coefficient of concordance	Same as chi-square

TABLE B.3　Illustration of the Preparation of the Second (ANOVA) Card in Analysis of Variance

Scholastic Groups (factor A)	Grade Levels (factor C)						Sex (factor B)
	Grade 3		Grade 4		Grade 5		
	Boys	Girls	Boys	Girls	Boys	Girls	
Good	81	88	83	89	94	98	
	80	85	80	92	91	94	
	72	90	80	78	80	93	
Average	70	79	73	78	79	88	
	73	76	75	76	84	87	
	69	71	78	80	82	89	
Poor	60	58	63	69	71	73	
	63	68	54	74	58	78	
	50	67	69	73	57	74	

Although there are but three factors, the replications are labeled R as a fourth factor on the second control card.

Suppose the control card had been made up as follows:

```
                                                                                          ↓ no. of 4th factor
                                                                    ↓ no. of 3rd factor
                                                                    ↓ Label of 4th factor
                                              ↓ no. of 2nd factor
                                              ↓ Label of 3rd factor
                        ↓ no. of 1st factor
                        ↓ Label of second factor
        ↓ no. of factors (4)
        ↓ Label of 1st factor
        (replications)

name of second
control card
  / 1 2 3 4 5 6 7 8 9 10 11 12 13 14 15 16 17 18 19 20 21 22 23 24 25 26 27 28 29 30 31 32 33 34 35 36
 / A N O V A    4                 R           3 A         3 B           2 C               3
```

In preparing data cards, data would be punched so that the first group of R (replication) scores are exhausted first; the first group of scores of scholastic factor A next; the first group of scores of the sex factor B scores next; and the first group of scores of the grade level factor C last. In terms of Table B.3 this means that the values would be placed on the data cards in the order of the first column followed by the next, etc.; that is, 81, 80, 72, 70, 73, 69, 60, 63, 50, 88, 85, etc.

Glossary

Abstract — a formal short summary of a research study.

Analysis of variance (simple) — a statistical method utilizing the F test which compares the variability within samples to the variability among two or more samples to determine the probability that the variability among samples is due to chance and not due to sampling from populations having different means.

Average deviation (AD) — the average sum of the absolute values of the deviations of each score from the mean of scores. $AD = \frac{\Sigma |x|}{N}$. N equals the number of scores and x equals the difference between each score and the mean or $x = X - M$. The algebraic sign of x is disregarded when these values are summed as if all deviations were positive.

Bias — the researcher's conscious or subconscious influence during the process of collecting, analyzing and/or interpreting data which can distort the results of a study.

Case studies — a type of research investigation utilizing an intensive study of phenomena. The subject of case studies is not usually a representative sample. The purpose is to identify significant factors without any attempt to generalize to a larger population.

chi-square (χ^2) — a mathematical distribution presented in table form that can be used to determine whether a set of observed frequencies differs sufficiently from a set of hypothesized **expected** frequencies that the conclusion can be made that the difference is not due to chance or random selection of the sample being studied. One form of the equation is $\chi^2 = \Sigma \frac{(O_f - E_f)^2}{E_f}$ where O_f is the observed frequency and E_f is the frequency expected for the given hypothesis.

Comparative studies — descriptive research studies in which an attempt is made to determine common factors or relationships among phenomena.

Conclusions — generalizations made as a result of research.

383

Confidence interval — a range of values in a mathematical distribution used to make statistical inferences (such as acceptance or rejection of hypotheses); generally, confidence intervals are established to reject or fail to reject the null hypothesis which states that differences found between samples are zero, or null, or that any differences could well be a result of random or chance factors.

Content analysis — a research method used to extract data from documents and other written materials in a systematic way.

Correlation coefficient (r or ρ) — a mathematical measure of the degree of relatedness between two common sets of measurements. Values range from -1 (an inverse relationship) to 0 (no relationship) to $+1$ (a perfect direct relationship). Pearson's formula is $r = \dfrac{\Sigma xy}{N\,\sigma_x\,\sigma_y}$, xy is the product of deviations of x measurements and y measurements from the mean of x and the mean of y respectively. N is the number of pairs of measurements and $\sigma_x\,\sigma_y$ are the standard deviations of the group x and y scores. If scores are in ordinal form, Spearman's formula is used. $\rho = 1 - \dfrac{6\Sigma d^2}{N(N^2 - 1)}$ The X and Y scores are ranked 1, 2, 3 . . . . N. The value d is the difference in ranks between corresponding X and Y measurements and N equals the number of pairs of measurements. The value of ρ is interpreted in the same manner as r.

Data (sing. or pl.) or datum (sing.) — a fact or statistic.

Descriptive research — research dealing with a description of current conditions.

Deviation (or x) — the amount by which a particular score or measurement in a distribution deviates from the mean of the distribution; $x = X-M$ where x is the deviation of a score, X is the score, and M is the mean of the distribution.

Experimental research — research in which the investigator seeks to determine what can happen under a given set of circumstances. It is characterized by rigid control of the conditions in which the independent variable and dependent variable function.

F-ratio — a mathematical comparison of the variability found between two or more groups of measurements with the variability expected to be found within the population(s) from which the groups were selected; the F-ratio provides a method by which measured differences between groups may be attributed to those expected as a result of chance if the groups were selected at random from the same population, or if the differences are unlikely to result from chance and thus may be attributed to the fact that the groups were selected from different populations; $F = \dfrac{M_{S_{bg}}}{M_{S_{wg}}}$ where $M_{S_{bg}}$ is the mean square between groups and $M_{S_{wg}}$ is the mean square within groups.

Frequency distribution — an arrangement (from the highest to the lowest) of all possible measurements within a given range along with an indication of how frequently each measurement was actually found to occur.

A grouped *frequency distribution* is similar except that frequencies of measurements are grouped into *intervals* of measurements; i.e., an interval of 90-94 indicates that all measurements between 89.5 to 94.5 would be counted to be included in the single interval 90-94.

Historical research — research which represents a critical description and analysis of past conditions.

Hypotheses — tentative propositions which are subject to verification through subsequent investigation.

Inductive-deductive method — a combination of the inductive and deductive methods of logical analysis. A general statement of theory is developed. More specific hypotheses are formulated from the general statement by the deductive reasoning process. The more specific hypotheses refer to observable phenomena and indicate that type of investigation necessary to confirm or to reject the hypothesis through a process of inductive reasoning. Verification of the hypotheses strengthens the general statement while refutation weakens or results in a modification of the general theoretical statement.

Inductive reasoning — a form of logical analysis that moves from specific observations to a generalization that expresses a relationship among the specifics observed.

Interview — a method of seeking research data that utilizes two-way verbal communication with the respondent.

Mean (abbr. M) — a measure of central tendency in a distribution of measures; found by dividing the sum of all measurements by the number of measurements.

Median (abbr. Mdn.) — the 50th percentile; the score, measurement, or point in a rank order distribution below which and above which would be found one-half or 50% of all measurements in the distribution; one of the measures of central tendency.

Mode (abbr. Mo) — the measurement in a group of measurements that has occurred most often; one of the measures of central tendency.

Normal distribution — a mathematical distribution which tends to approximate the measurements found in nature; graphically the normal distribution curve tends to be similar to the bell shaped probability curve of chance happenings.

Null hypothesis — a statement which asserts that differences between samples are close enough to zero that the differences are attributable to random selection of the samples from the same population; rejection of null at a given level of confidence means that the differences are large enough to suspect that they are not due to chance selection; rejection of null at the 5% level of confidence indicates that differences as large as those measured would tend to come about as a result of chance in 5 cases or less out of 100; rejection of null at the 1% level indicates that such a difference would tend to be a result of chance only 1 time or less out of 100 samples from the same population.

Observation — a research method utilizing direct contact between the researcher and the phenomena under study. The researcher usually avoids interfering with or influencing the subject(s) of study. The method is also useful when working with subjects such as infants or mentally ill persons who cannot verbally communicate with the researcher.

Operation definition — a definition expressed in terms of the operations or methods used to measure or determine the quantity in question, i.e., "Intelligence is a characteristic measured by an intelligence test" or more broadly "Intelligence is a measure of an organism's ability to adjust, abstract and learn. In this study, a child is of superior intelligence if and only if his score exceeds 131 as measured by form LM of the Stanford Binet."

Parsimony, Law of — explanations of behavior should be made as simple as possible and consistent with observations. (Complex explanations are to be avoided unless evidence clearly dictates the need for them.)

Percentile (or centile) — when a group of measurements is arranged in *rank order* from the highest to the lowest, the per cent of measurements that rank at or below a given measurement in the distribution is called the percentile rank of the given measurement.

Population — a statistical term referring to the larger group from which a sample is selected for study. The sample is studied and generalizations are made concerning the population from which the sample was taken through the process of statistical inference. The population is also referred to as the universe.

Questionnaire — an instrument used to gather data from subjects who are not contacted on a face-to-face basis.

Random selections — selections made without any preconceived pattern; selections that occur purely as a result of chance so that the probability that one element of the population will be selected is the same as the probability that any other element will be selected.

Regression line — when points are placed on a graph to represent two kinds of measurements X and Y, the straight line that comes closest to the points, if they are considered as a group, is called a regression line or line of best fit; the slope of the regression line closest to the points in terms of vertical distances gives an indication of the correlation between the two kinds of measurements.

Reliability — the property of an instrument to measure the same conditions consistently with unvarying results.

Research — *systematic* study of phenomena.

Scales — a means used to quantify data. *Interval scales* denote equal intervals among measurements at all ranges of the distribution of measurements. *Ordinal scales* signify rank or order such as first, second, third, etc. and may not signify equal intervals. *Nominal scales* are used to classify data in categories such as male, female; employed, unemployed; yes or no.

Schedule — an instrument that is completed by the respondent in the presence of the researcher.

Significant difference — differences that are unlikely to be due to chance or random selections of samples.

Standard deviation (SD or σ) — the square root of the mean of squared deviations; $\sigma = \sqrt{\dfrac{\Sigma x^2}{N}}$ where x is the deviation of each measurement in distribution from the mean; N is the number of measurements (therefore, $\frac{\Sigma x^2}{N}$ is the mean of the squared deviations); in a normal distribution of measurements, $\pm 1 \sigma$ occurs at the points of inflection of the graph of the curve and encompasses about 68% of all measurements in the distribution; a measure of variability.

Standard error of the difference (σ_{diff}) − an estimate, from a single pair of samples, of the standard deviation that would result in a distribution if the differences of means of many pairs of random samples were selected from a given population; $\sigma_{diff} = \sqrt{\sigma_{M1}^2 + \sigma_{M2}^2}$ where σ_{M1} is the standard error of the mean determined from one of the samples and σ_{M2} is the standard error of the mean determined from the other sample.

Standard error of the mean (σ_M) − an estimate, from a single sample, of the standard deviation of a distribution of means that would result from many random samples from the same population; $\sigma_M = \frac{SD}{\sqrt{N-1}}$ where SD is the standard deviation of the sample and N is the size of the sample.

Statistical inference − a process of indirect measurement. Measurements are made of a sample from a larger population. From these measurements (statistics) inferences about the larger population are formulated. If the sample is representative of the larger population, the probability of the accuracy of the estimates can be determined.

Theory − a formal tentative statement of relationships among a class of phenomena. A theory is elevated to the status of a *law* when repeated observations confirm its predictive value. A formal theory is usually stated in three parts: (a) the *postulates* and *constructs* that represent a conceptualization of phenomena which cannot be directly observed or measured and the relations among these phenomena, (b) the *paradigm* or *model* which presents the relation among constructs in schematic form and, (c) the specific hypotheses which are deduced from the theory and express expected relationships among observed phenomena.

t-test (or ratio) — the ratio of the variability between two groups of measurements, as expressed by the difference of means, to the variability expected within the population(s) from which the groups were selected. The t ratio provides a method by which measured differences between groups may be compared to those expected as a result of chance. If the difference is sufficiently large, the conclusion can be made that it is unlikely that the two samples were selected from the same population. $t = \frac{M_2 - M_1}{\sigma_{diff}}$ where M_1 is the mean of one group of measurements, M_2 is the mean of the second group and σ_{diff} is the standard error of the difference.

Validity − the property of an instrument to measure that for which it is designed.

Variability − property of a distribution of measurements to vary or deviate from the average of the distribution. Measures of variability include average deviation, standard deviation and variance.

Variance (σ^2) − the square of the standard deviation. The quantity is used in place of the standard deviation because of the mathematical properties which permit it to be summed or broken down into component parts.

Index

Answers to Problems
in the Selected Exercises

Chapter 5, pages __137__ to __140__

2. a. SD = 1.73 and M = 5.
   b. 6 is high average; 3 is poor; 8 is above average.
7. a. M_I is approximately 97; M_{II} is approximately 97.
   b. No, Group II is more homogeneous than Group I but the mean gives no indication of this.
   c. The most typical measurement in Group I and Group II is 97. Group II is more homogeneous than Group I. Comparison of the means is precise to the extent that it is a quantitative expression of measurements which were made. Saying that Group II is more homogeneous than Group I lacks precision in that there is no indication of *how much* less variability is to be found in Group I as compared to Group II.
8. 13 seconds is the mean; a better indicator of typical time is the mode, 14 seconds.
9. a. Sd of Group I = 10.35 and SD of Group II = 8.45 therefore the range of typical scores for Group I is from about 97± 10; i.e., 87 to 107; and for Group II from about 97± 8; i.e., 89 to 105.
   b. The most typical score for both groups is 97 but typical variations from the mean in Group II are three points less than those of Group I.
10. a. about 26
    b. about 25
    c. about 84

11. a. Using the distribution for Group I, $17+12+8+4+2 = 43$, scored 100 or more and in Group II, 39 scored 100 or more. Using the z-score for 100, $z_I = \dfrac{100\text{-}97}{10} = .3$ and $z_{II} = \dfrac{100\text{-}97}{8}$ $= .38$. The area under the normal curve beyond $z = .35$ about 38%, and 38% of 109 = about 41. The area beyond $z = .38$ is about 39%, and 39% of 104 = about 40.

    b. about 51

    c. 84% for Group I, 89% for Group II.

12. a. about 1 out of 10 for Group I and 1 out of 20 for Group II.

    b. about 24 to 1.

Chapter 6 pages __172__ to __175__

1. a. Since $\sigma_M = 1$ and $\dfrac{M_s - M_{hypot}}{\sigma_M} = \dfrac{72 - 65}{1} = 7$, it is very improbable that 65 could be the average grade on the test for the eleventh grade pupils in the school system.

    b. $72\pm$ (1.96) (1) or approximately from 70 to 74 for the 5% interval and $72\pm$ (2.58) (1) or approximately from 69 to 75 for the 1% interval.

2. a. $t = \dfrac{76 - 72}{\sqrt{1^2 + 3^2}} = \dfrac{4}{3.16} = 1.27$; this indicates that there is no significant difference (the researcher was wrong).

3. a. The administrator is incorrect. $t = \dfrac{9.8}{\sqrt{.007 + .03}} = \dfrac{1}{\sqrt{.04}} = \dfrac{1}{.2}$ $= 5$; with a "t" of 5, null may be rejected at better than the 1% level.

    b. σ diff is about .2, then $O\pm$ (1.96) (.2) or beyond about $+.4$ or $-.4$ would allow 5% level rejection of null, and $O\pm$ (2.58) (.2) or differences beyond about $+.5$ or $-.5$ would allow a 1% level rejection.

4. b. $t = \dfrac{150 - 140}{\sqrt{6^2 + 7^2}} = \dfrac{10}{9.2}$ or about 1; accept null.

    c. $t = \dfrac{150 - 140}{\sqrt{1.44^2 + 1.68^2}} = \dfrac{10}{2.2} = 4.54$; reject null at better than the 1% level.

5. b. $F = 1.69$ with 2 and 45 df; accept null (there are no significant differences among the performances of the groups).

6. b. $F = 7.35$ with 2 and 27 d.f.; reject null at better than the 1% level. Group differences are significant.

7. b. $F = 12.7$ with 3 and 46 d.f.; significant at better than the 1% level.

Chapter 7 pages __206__ to __210__

1. a. r math-physics $= +.45$ or about $+.5$
   b. r physics-latin $= -.32$ or about $-.3$
   c. r latin-biology $= -.04$ or about 0
2. a. $M_{IQ} = 106.2$, $M_{AG} = 84.5$
   b. $r = +.75$
   c. $p = +.74$
3. a. $r = +.80$
   e. $r = +.20$, accept null
   f. $R = .22$ in.
4. a. $p = +.53$, null may be rejected at the 5% level, but the cor-relation between the supervisor's ratings is not likely to be very high.
5. b. $\chi^2 = 4.46$ with 1df, reject null at the 5% level of confidence (there is a difference between elementary and secondary teachers in their attitudes toward the question of pupil retention).
6. $\chi^2 = 18.91$; there has been a significant shift.
7. $\chi^2 = 50.04$ with 12 df, reject null ($p < .01$).
8. $M = 73$, $SD = 11.4$; $\chi^2 =$ about 39 with 9 df, reject null ($p < .01$); this means that either the sample may not be considered a random sample or that the population from which is drawn is not normally distributed.

Chapter 8, pages __225__ and __226__

1. a. $z = 2.11$, reject null ($p < .05$)
2. a. $z = 4.22$, reject null ($p < .01$)
3. $\chi^2 = 35.73$ with 3 df; reject null ($p < .01$), same result as analysis of variance test.
4. $\chi^2 = 12.6$ with 2 df; reject null ($p < .01$)
5. $\chi^2 = 5.28$ with 4 df.